THE ANIME IS ON THE AIR!

Rikuo and Tsurara are in action!!
Yes, when I really think about it, it's
an amazing thing! Music and voices
get added, color is added and
Nura: Rise of the Yokai Clan is right
there on television...
This really only happened because
of everyone's support! At the "Nura
Festival" premiere event, it was also
great to meet all you guys. (I was
secretly watching from the corner.)

—HIROSHI SHIIBASHI,
2010

HIROSHI SHIIBASHI debuted in BUSINESS JUMP
magazine with *Aratama*. NURA: RISE OF THE YOKAI CLAN
is his breakout hit. He was an assistant to manga artist Hirohiko Araki,
the creator of *Jojo's Bizarre Adventure*. *Steel Ball Run* by Araki is one of
his favorite manga.

NURA: RISE OF THE YOKAI CLAN
VOLUME 12
SHONEN JUMP Manga Edition

Story and Art by HIROSHI SHIIBASHI

Translation — Yumi Okamoto
Adaptation — Mark Giambruno
Touch-up Art and Lettering — Vanessa Satone
Graphics and Cover Design — Fawn Lau
Editor — Joel Enos

NURARIHYON NO MAGO © 2008 by Hiroshi Shiibashi. All rights reserved. First published in Japan in 2008 by SHUEISHA Inc., Tokyo. English translation rights arranged by SHUEISHA Inc.

Printed in the U.S.A.

Published by VIZ Media, LLC
P.O. Box 77010
San Francisco, CA 94107

10 9 8 7 6 5 4 3 2 1
First printing, December 2012

www.viz.com   www.shonenjump.com

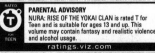

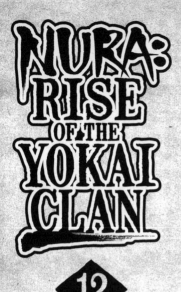

NURA: RISE OF THE YOKAI CLAN

◆12◆

DEVIL'S DRUM

STORY AND ART BY
HIROSHI SHIIBASHI

CHARACTERS

NURARIHYON

Rikuo's grandfather and the Lord of Pandemonium. He intends to pass leadership of the Nura clan—leaders of the yokai world—to Rikuo. He's mischievous and likes to dine and ditch.

RIKUO NURA

Though he appears to be a human boy, he's actually the grandson of Nurarihyon, a yokai. His grandfather's blood makes him one-quarter yokai, and he transforms into a yokai at times.

KIYOTSUGU

Rikuo's classmate. He has adored yokai ever since Rikuo saved him in his yokai form, leading him to form the Kiyojuji Paranormal Patrol.

KANA IENAGA

Rikuo's classmate and a childhood friend. Even though she hates scary things, she's a member of the Kiyojuji Paranormal Patrol for some reason.

YUKI-ONNA

A yokai of the Nura clan who is in charge of looking after Rikuo. She disguises herself as a human and attends the same school as Rikuo to protect him from danger. When in human form, she goes by the name Tsurara Oikawa.

YURA KEIKAIN

Rikuo's classmate and a descendant of the Keikain family of onmyoji. She transferred into Ukiyoe Middle School to do field training in yokai exorcism. She has the power to control her shikigami and uses them to destroy yokai.

HIDEMOTO

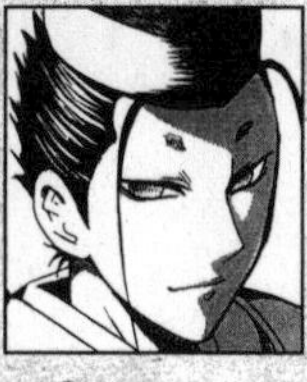

The 13th Master of the Keikain family. A genius onmyoji who created Nenekirimaru and the eight seals of the capital. Through Yura's Hagun, he has been brought into the present as a shikigami.

GYUKI

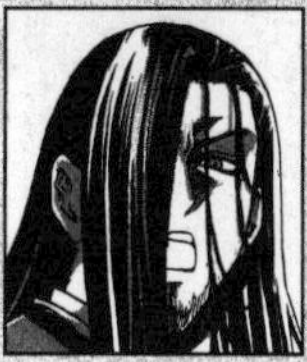

The leader of the Nura clan subgroup, the Gyuki clan. His headquarters are located at the top of Mt. Nejireme, in the westernmost region of Nura clan territory. He has a personality that is scholarly, calm and collected.

TSUCHIGUMO

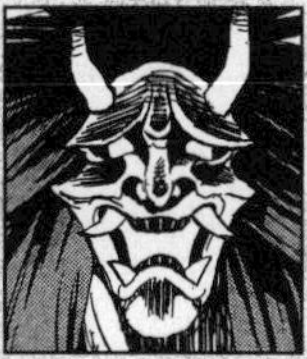

He is one of the Kyoto yokai, but he does not bow to Hagoromo-Gitsune and takes action on his own. He's so strong that he's called the ayakashi to avoid.

HAGOROMO-GITSUNE

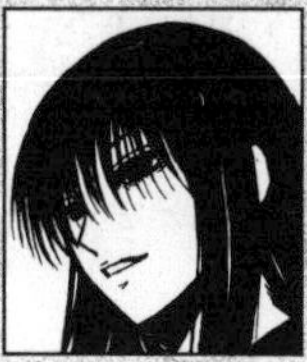

A great Kyoto yokai who has a fateful connection to Nurarihyon and the Keikain family. She possesses humans and forces them to do evil things. She was revived after 400 years.

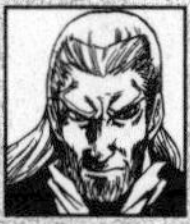

KIDOMARU

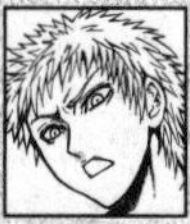

ZEN

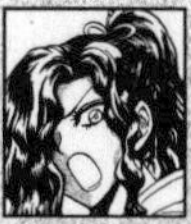

KEJORO

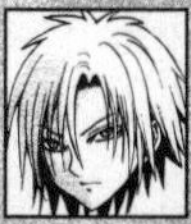

KUBINASHI

STORY SO FAR

At a glance, Rikuo Nura appears to be just another average, normal boy, just a seventh-grader at Ukiyoe Middle School. But he's actually the grandson of the yokai Overlord Nurarihyon. And he's now the Underboss of the Nura clan, the most powerful collection of yokai in the Tokyo region. He is expected to become a great Overlord like his grandfather, but in the meantime lives his days as a human being.

Having cut through the fear of the capital's gate guard, Hakuzozu, Rikuo and the Nura clan forces have landed in Kyoto and head to the Fushime Inari Shrine, the location of the first spiral seal of Hidemoto. After touching the Heavy Light Stone, Awashima becomes trapped along with a young child within the realm of the guardian ayakashi of the torii, the 27 Faced Senju-Mukade. Things look bad, but realizing that the child's fear is making the enemy stronger, Awashima figures out a way to destroy the ayakashi.

Rikuo then comes face-to-face with Hidemoto, who asks Rikuo to repair the seals that have been broken and defeat Hagoromo-Gitsune before she gives birth. But he only has seven days to stop her, and Rikuo and his comrades have just been brutally attacked by the ayakashi to avoid, Tsuchigumo!

TABLE OF CONTENTS

NURA: RISE OF THE YOKAI CLAN

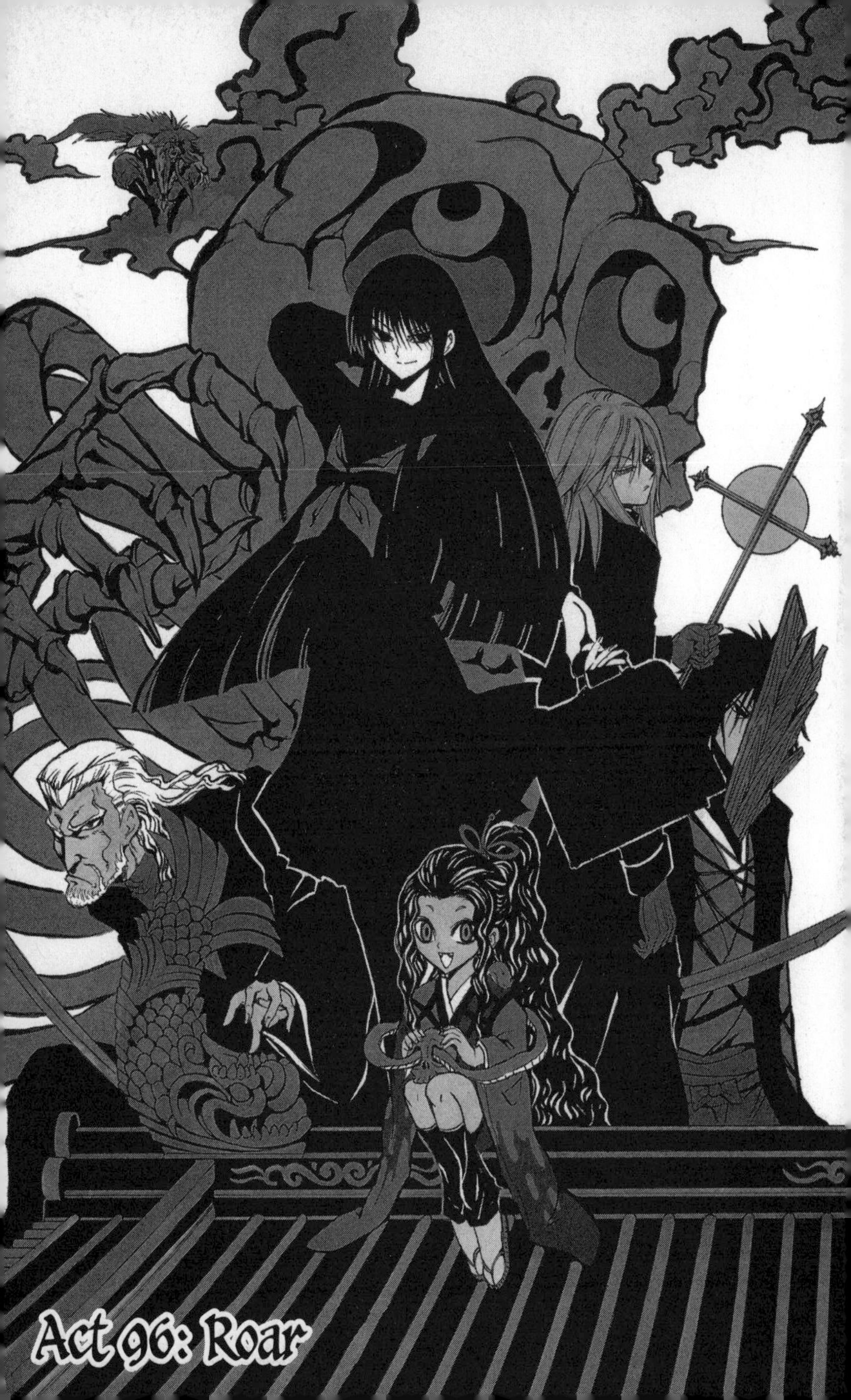

Act 96: Roar

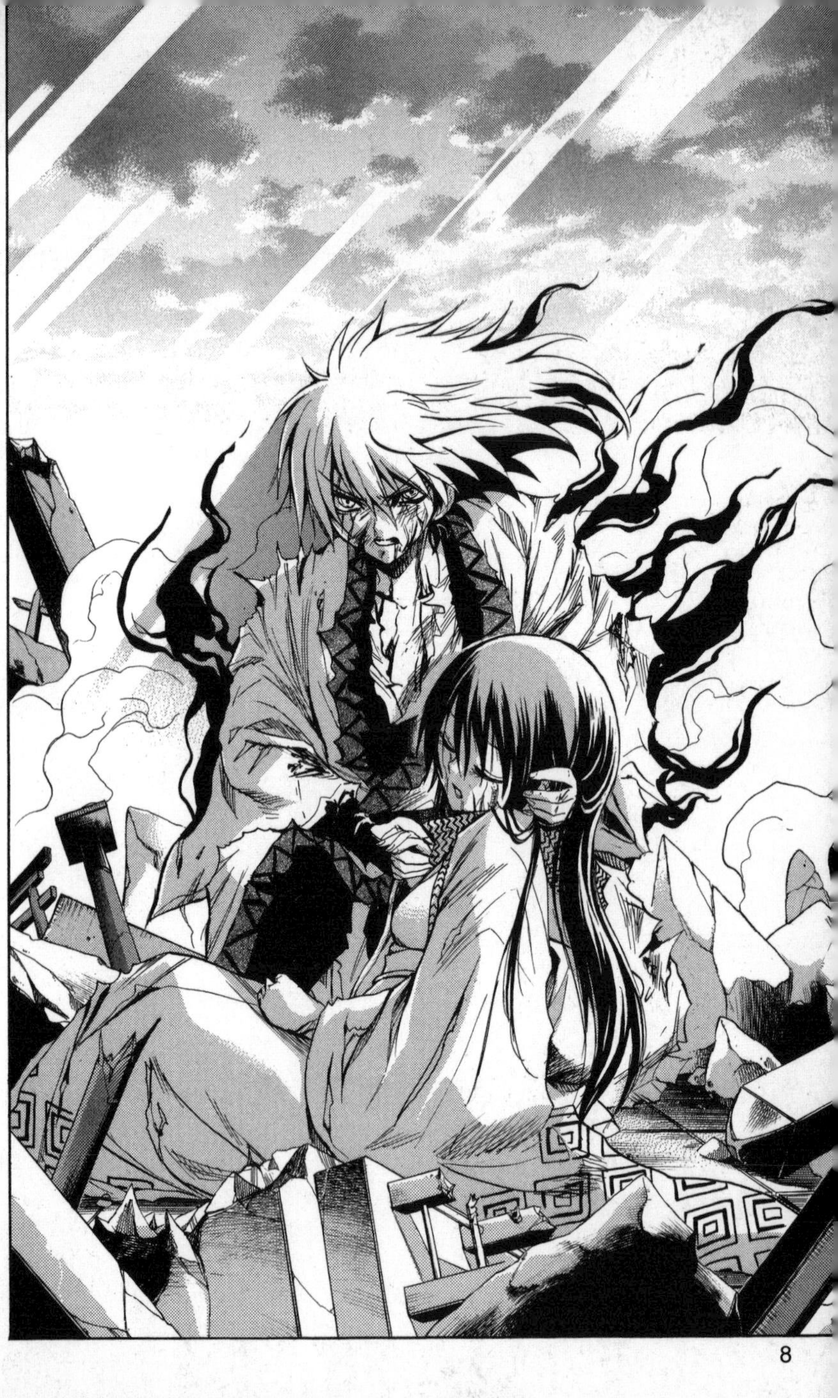

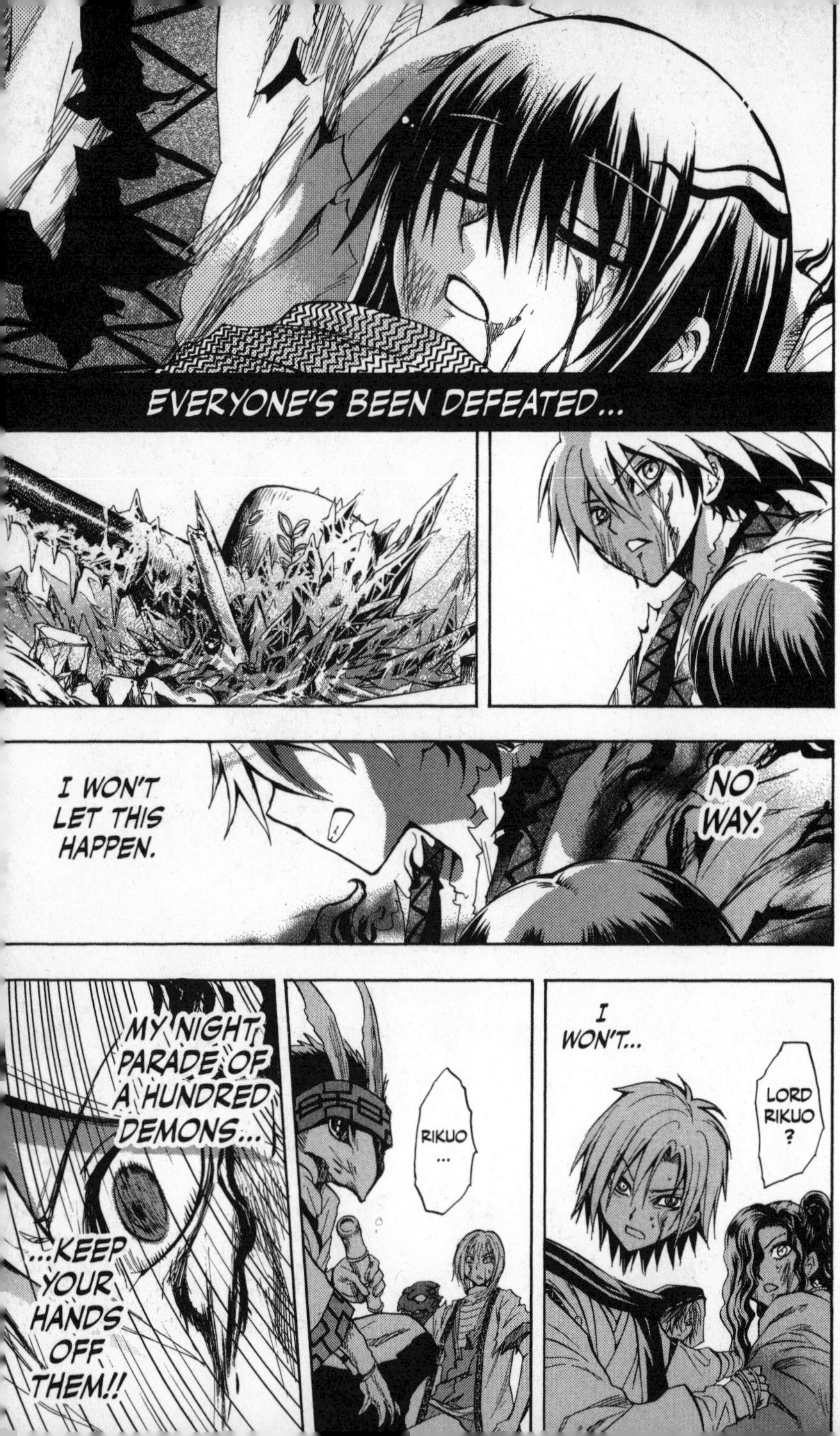
EVERYONE'S BEEN DEFEATED...
NO WAY.
I WON'T LET THIS HAPPEN.
I WON'T...
LORD RIKUO?
RIKUO...
MY NIGHT PARADE OF A HUNDRED DEMONS...
...KEEP YOUR HANDS OFF THEM!!

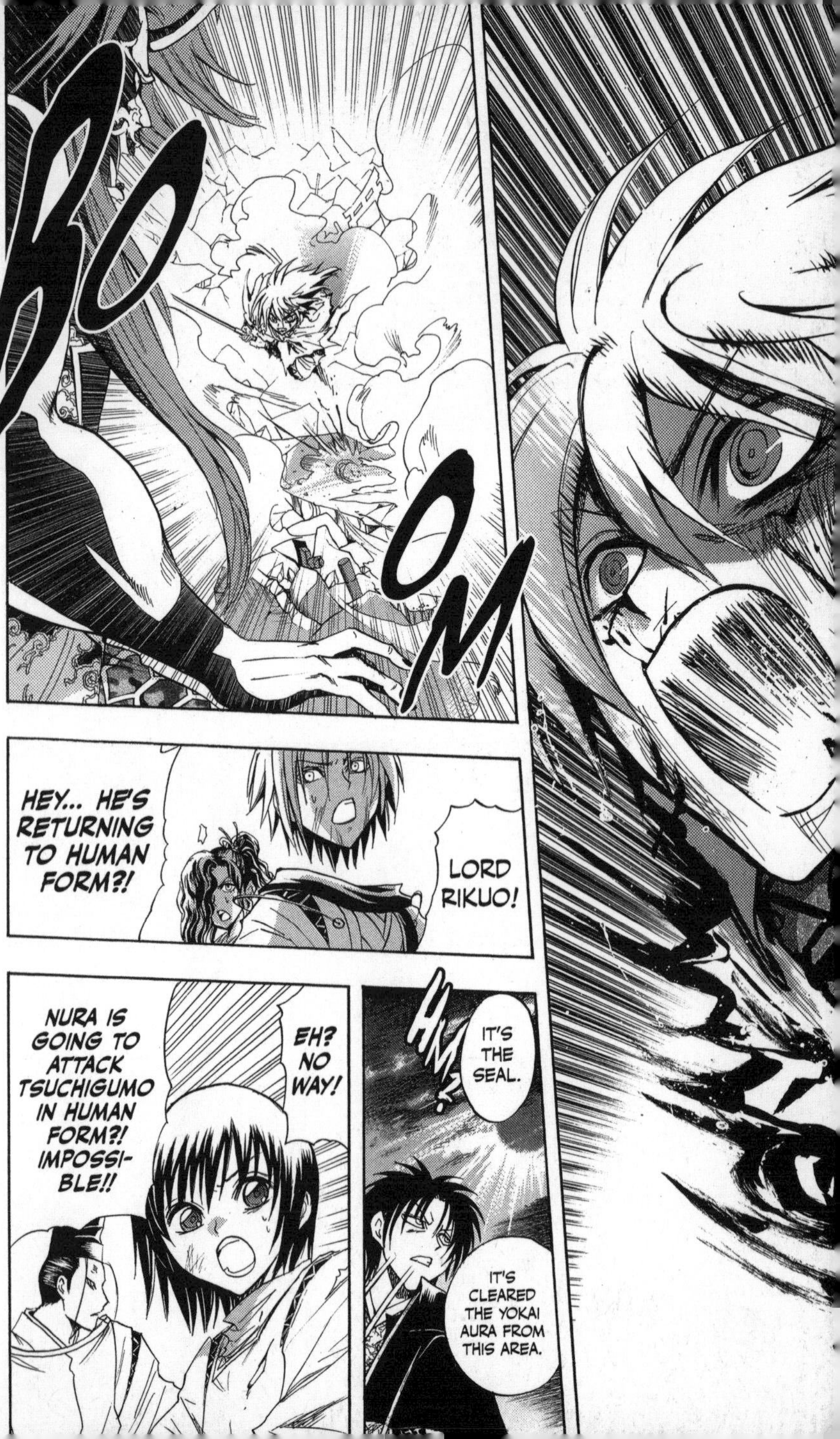
BOOM
LORD RIKUO!
HEY... HE'S RETURNING TO HUMAN FORM?!
HM?!
IT'S THE SEAL.
IT'S CLEARED THE YOKAI AURA FROM THIS AREA.
EH? NO WAY!
NURA IS GOING TO ATTACK TSUCHIGUMO IN HUMAN FORM?! IMPOSSIBLE!!

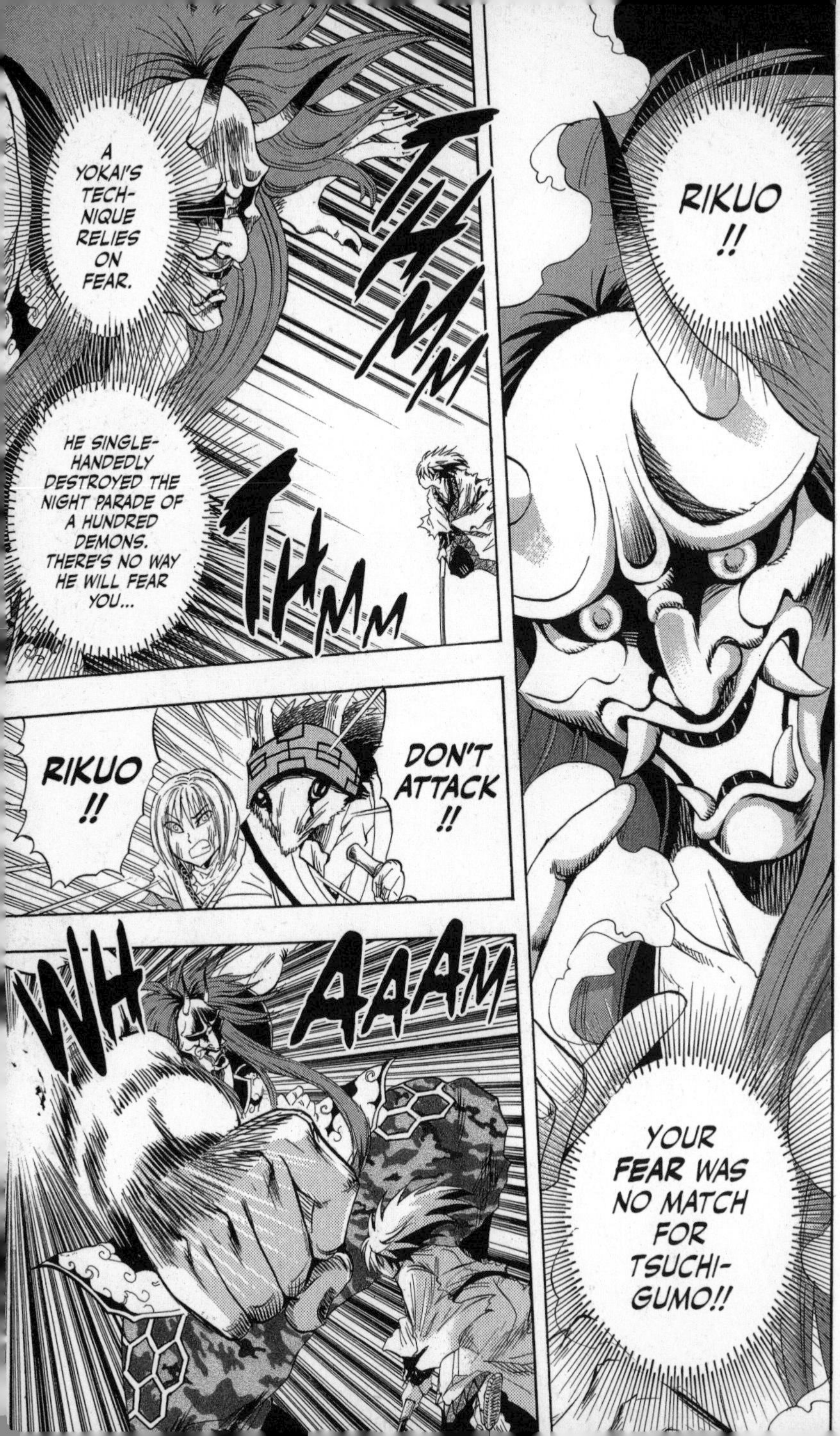

RIKUO !!
YOUR FEAR WAS NO MATCH FOR TSUCHI-GUMO!!
THMMM
A YOKAI'S TECH-NIQUE RELIES ON FEAR.
HE SINGLE-HANDEDLY DESTROYED THE NIGHT PARADE OF A HUNDRED DEMONS. THERE'S NO WAY HE WILL FEAR YOU...
THMM
DON'T ATTACK !!
RIKUO !!
WH AAAM

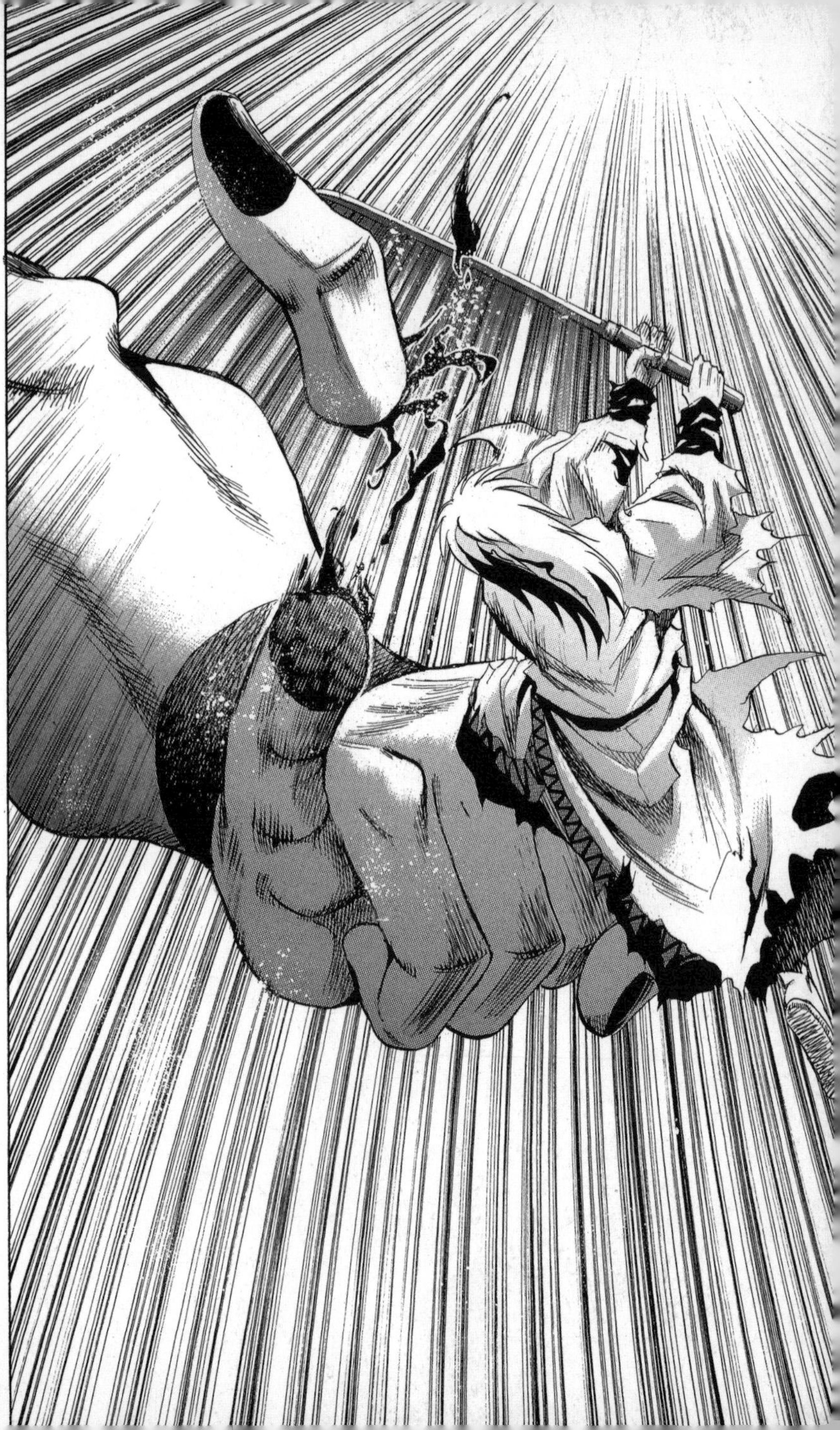

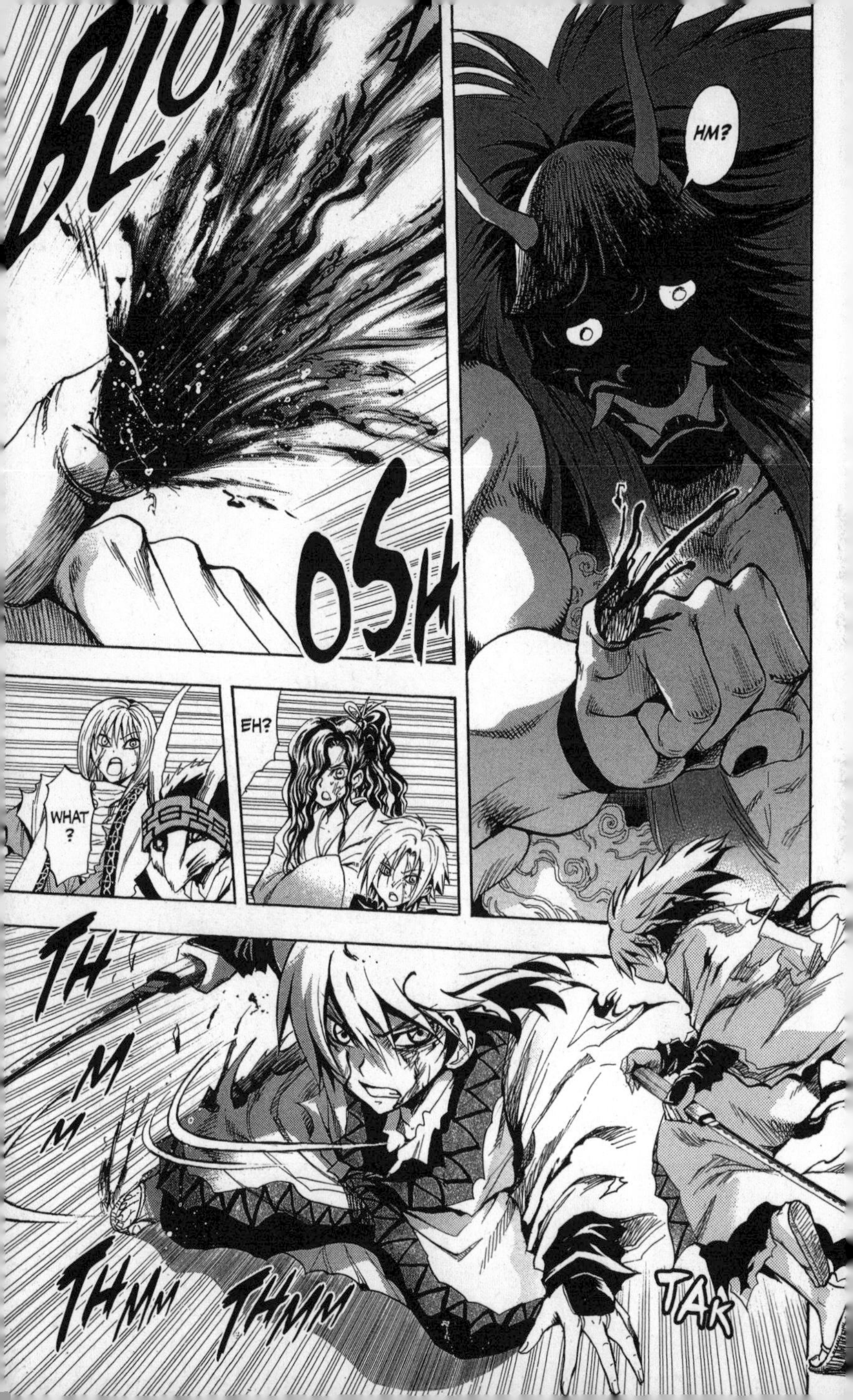

HM?
BLO
OSH
EH?
WHAT?
THMMM
THMM
THMM
TAK

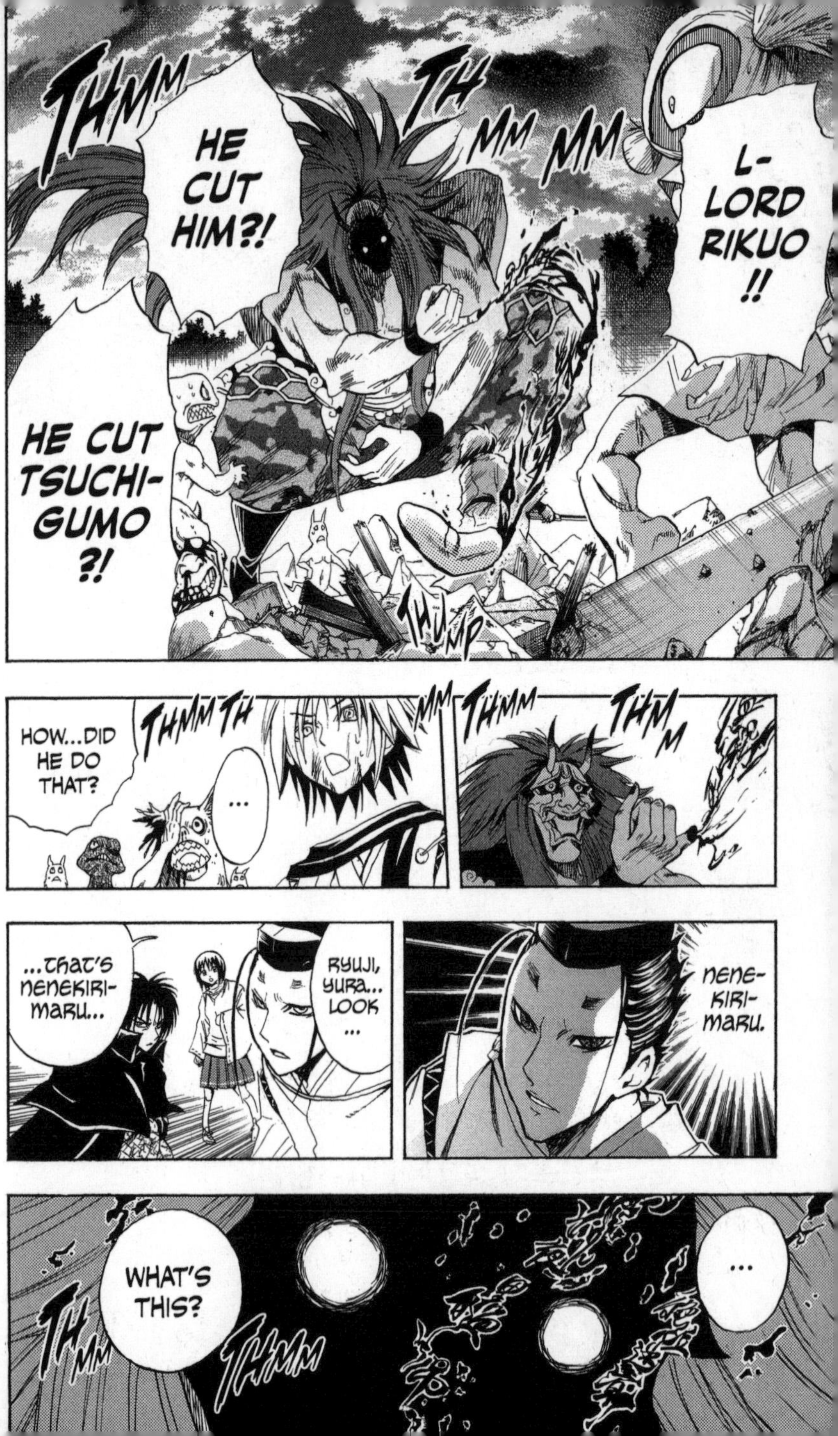
L-LORD RIKUO!!
THMMMM
HE CUT HIM?!
THMM
HE CUT TSUCHIGUMO?!
THUMP
THMM THMM
THMMTHMM
...
HOW...DID HE DO THAT?
NENE-KIRI-MARU.
RYUJI, YURA... LOOK...
...THAT'S NENEKIRI-MARU...
...
THMM
WHAT'S THIS?
THMM

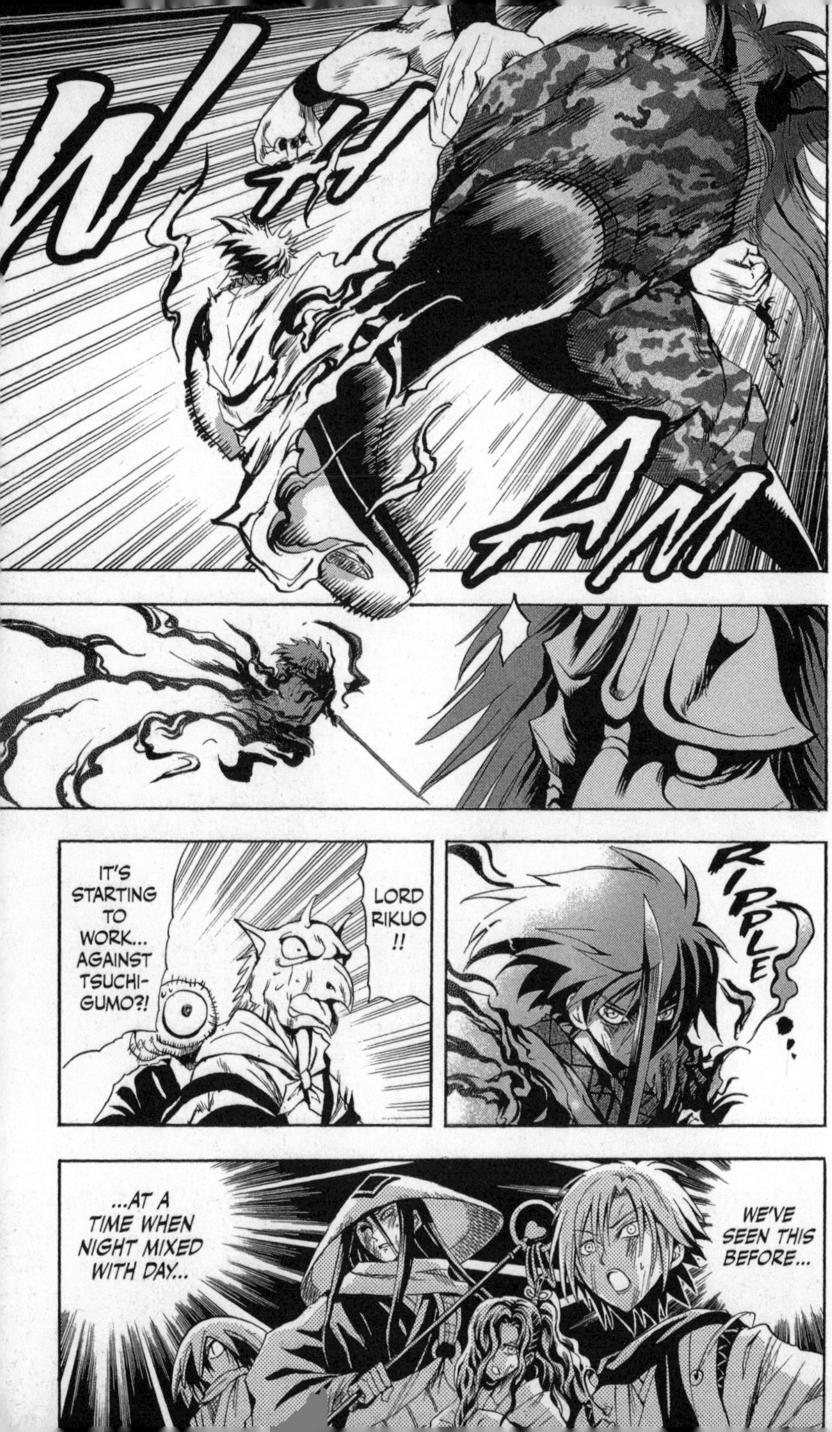
WHAM
RIPPLE
LORD RIKUO!!
IT'S STARTING TO WORK... AGAINST TSUCHI-GUMO?!
WE'VE SEEN THIS BEFORE...
...AT A TIME WHEN NIGHT MIXED WITH DAY...

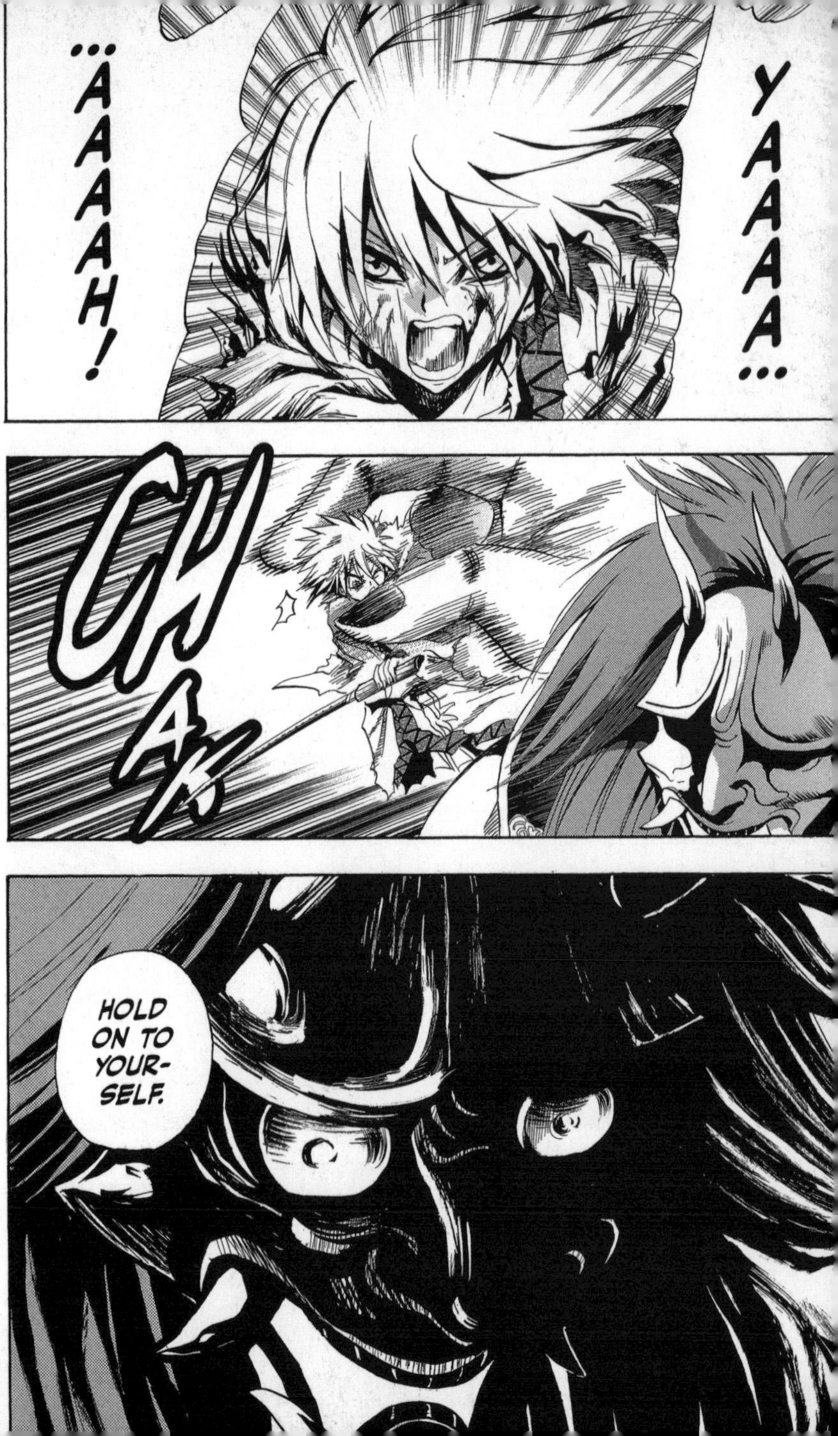
YAAAA...
...AAAAH!
CHAK
HOLD ON TO YOURSELF.

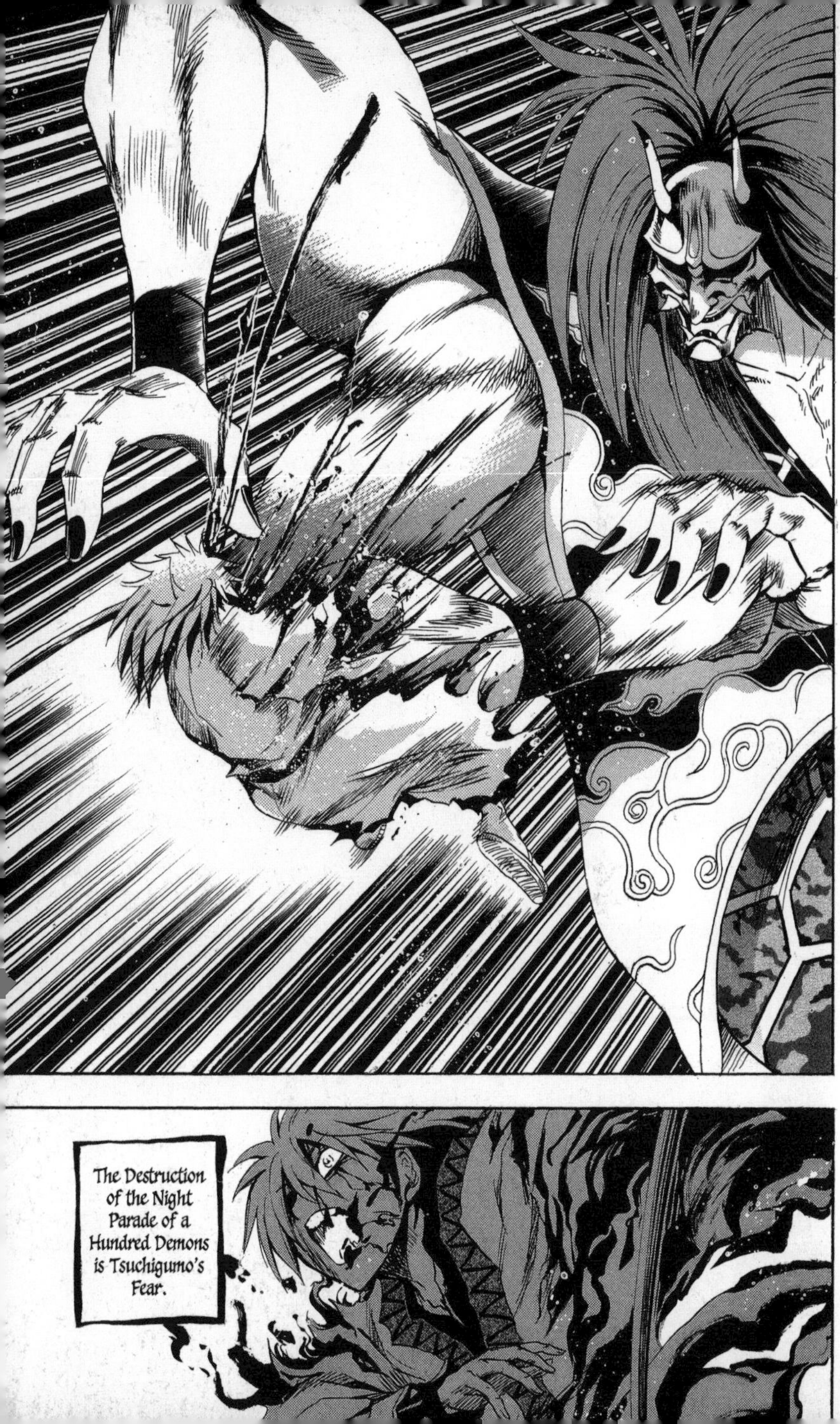
The Destruction of the Night Parade of a Hundred Demons is Tsuchigumo's Fear.

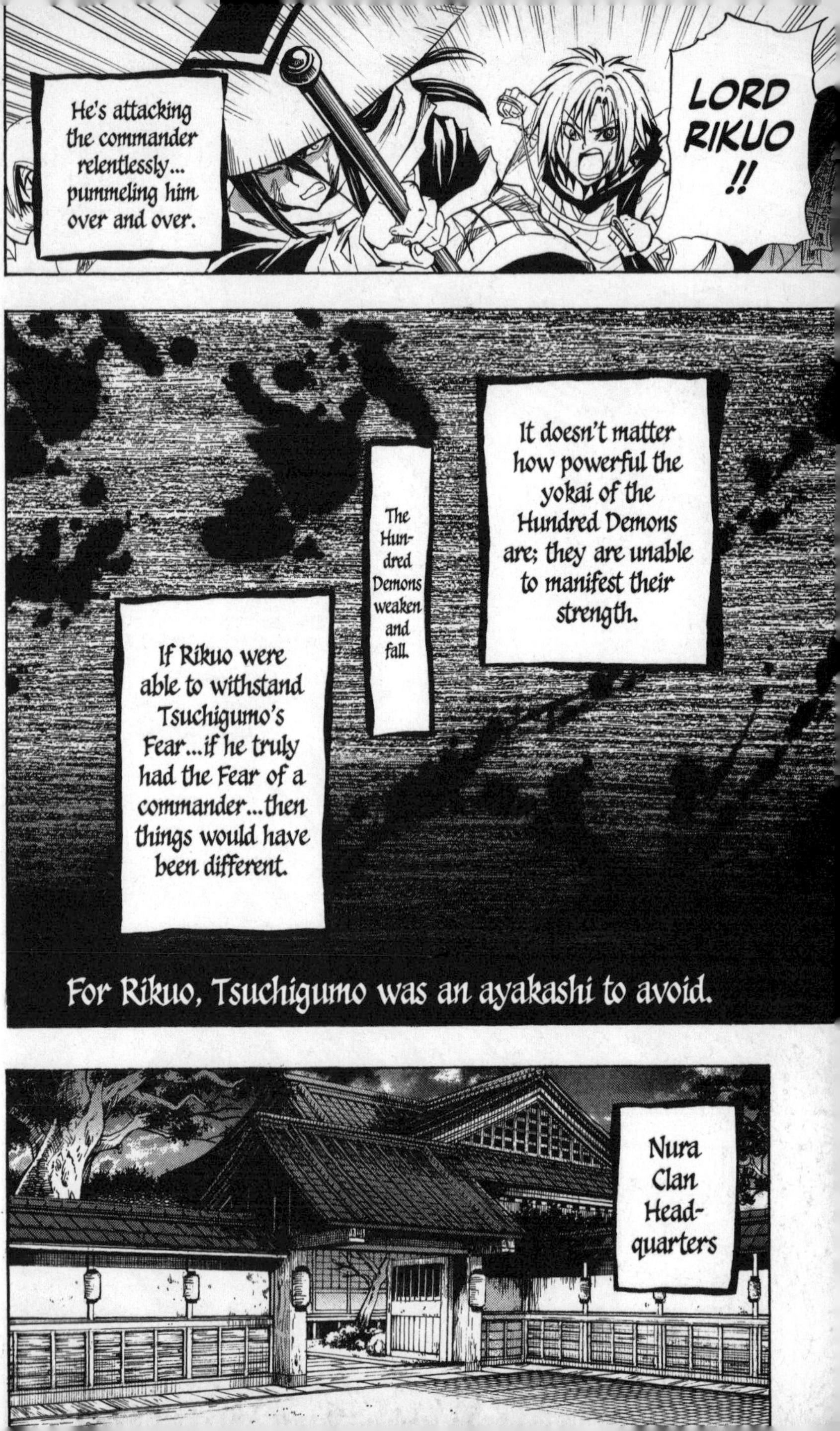
LORD RIKUO !!
He's attacking the commander relentlessly... pummeling him over and over.
It doesn't matter how powerful the yokai of the Hundred Demons are; they are unable to manifest their strength.
The Hun-dred Demons weaken and fall.
If Rikuo were able to withstand Tsuchigumo's Fear...if he truly had the Fear of a commander...then things would have been different.
For Rikuo, Tsuchigumo was an ayakashi to avoid.
Nura Clan Head-quarters

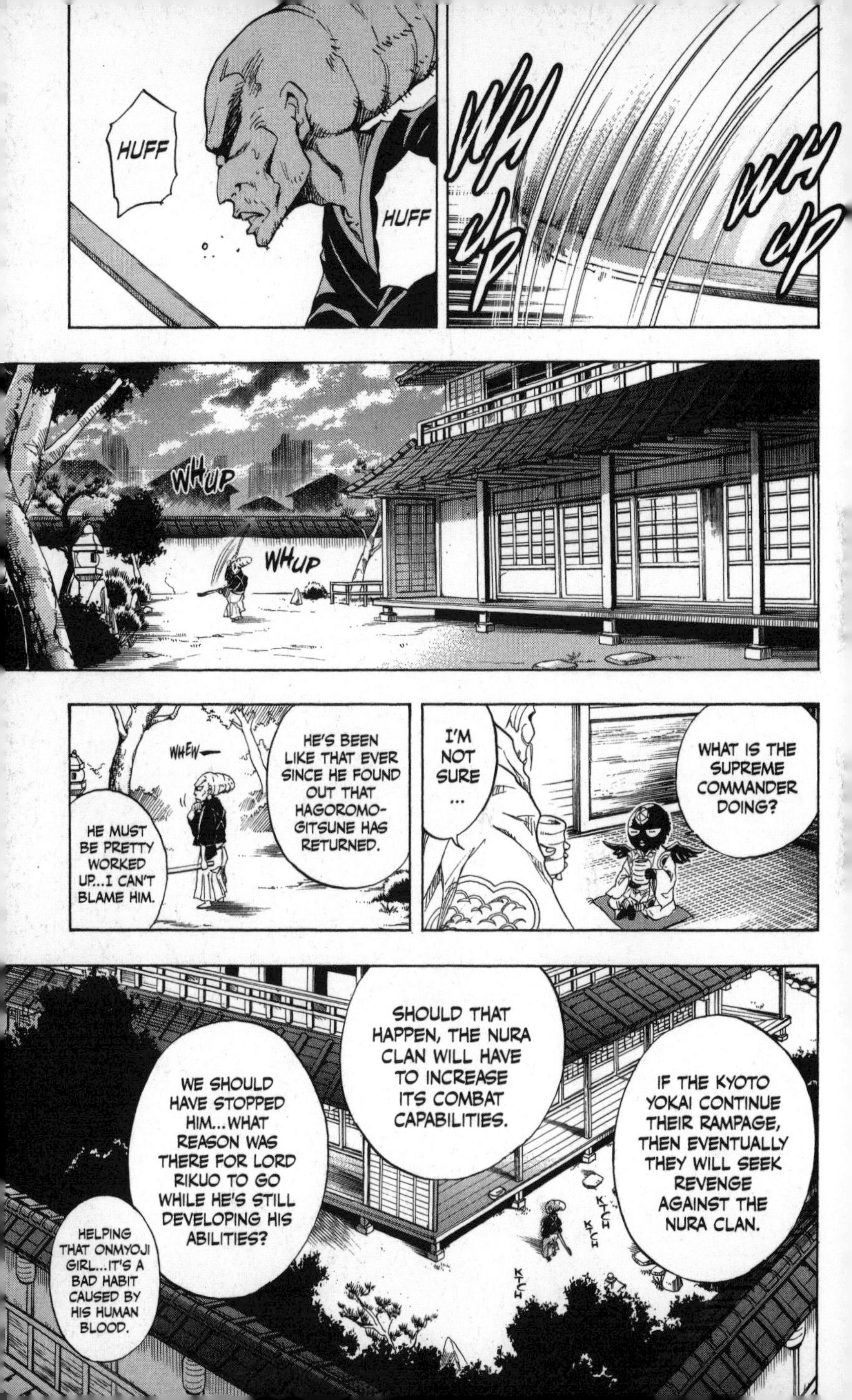
WHUP
WHUP
HUFF
HUFF
WHUP
WHUP
WHAT IS THE SUPREME COMMANDER DOING?
I'M NOT SURE...
HE'S BEEN LIKE THAT EVER SINCE HE FOUND OUT THAT HAGOROMO-GITSUNE HAS RETURNED.
WHEW
HE MUST BE PRETTY WORKED UP...I CAN'T BLAME HIM.
IF THE KYOTO YOKAI CONTINUE THEIR RAMPAGE, THEN EVENTUALLY THEY WILL SEEK REVENGE AGAINST THE NURA CLAN.
SHOULD THAT HAPPEN, THE NURA CLAN WILL HAVE TO INCREASE ITS COMBAT CAPABILITIES.
KTCH
KTCH
WE SHOULD HAVE STOPPED HIM...WHAT REASON WAS THERE FOR LORD RIKUO TO GO WHILE HE'S STILL DEVELOPING HIS ABILITIES?
HELPING THAT ONMYOJI GIRL...IT'S A BAD HABIT CAUSED BY HIS HUMAN BLOOD.
KTCH

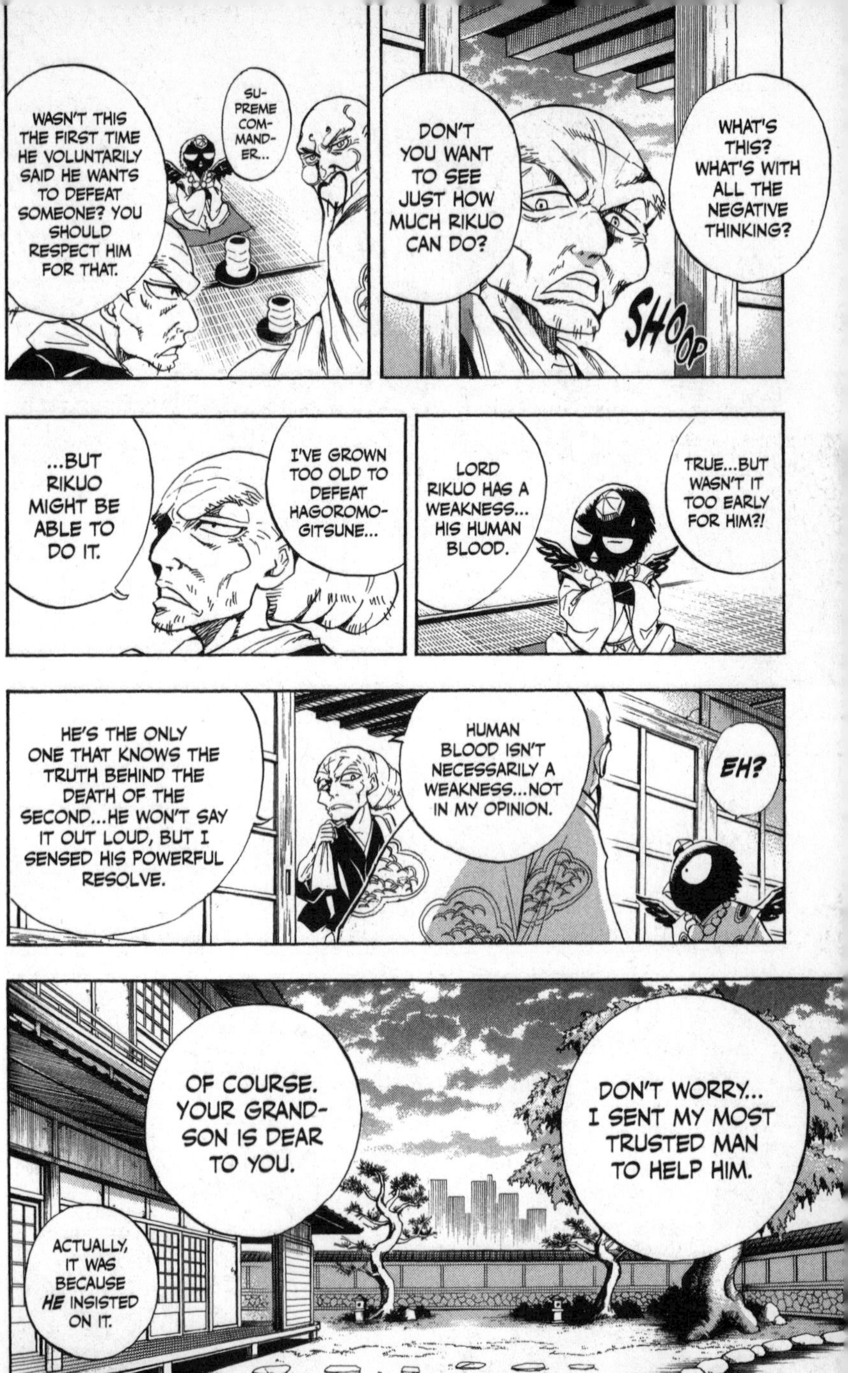
WHAT'S THIS? WHAT'S WITH ALL THE NEGATIVE THINKING?
DON'T YOU WANT TO SEE JUST HOW MUCH RIKUO CAN DO?
SHOOP
SU-PREME COM-MANDER...
WASN'T THIS THE FIRST TIME HE VOLUNTARILY SAID HE WANTS TO DEFEAT SOMEONE? YOU SHOULD RESPECT HIM FOR THAT.
TRUE...BUT WASN'T IT TOO EARLY FOR HIM?!
LORD RIKUO HAS A WEAKNESS... HIS HUMAN BLOOD.
I'VE GROWN TOO OLD TO DEFEAT HAGOROMO-GITSUNE...
...BUT RIKUO MIGHT BE ABLE TO DO IT.
EH?
HUMAN BLOOD ISN'T NECESSARILY A WEAKNESS...NOT IN MY OPINION.
HE'S THE ONLY ONE THAT KNOWS THE TRUTH BEHIND THE DEATH OF THE SECOND...HE WON'T SAY IT OUT LOUD, BUT I SENSED HIS POWERFUL RESOLVE.
DON'T WORRY... I SENT MY MOST TRUSTED MAN TO HELP HIM.
OF COURSE. YOUR GRAND-SON IS DEAR TO YOU.
ACTUALLY, IT WAS BECAUSE *HE* INSISTED ON IT.

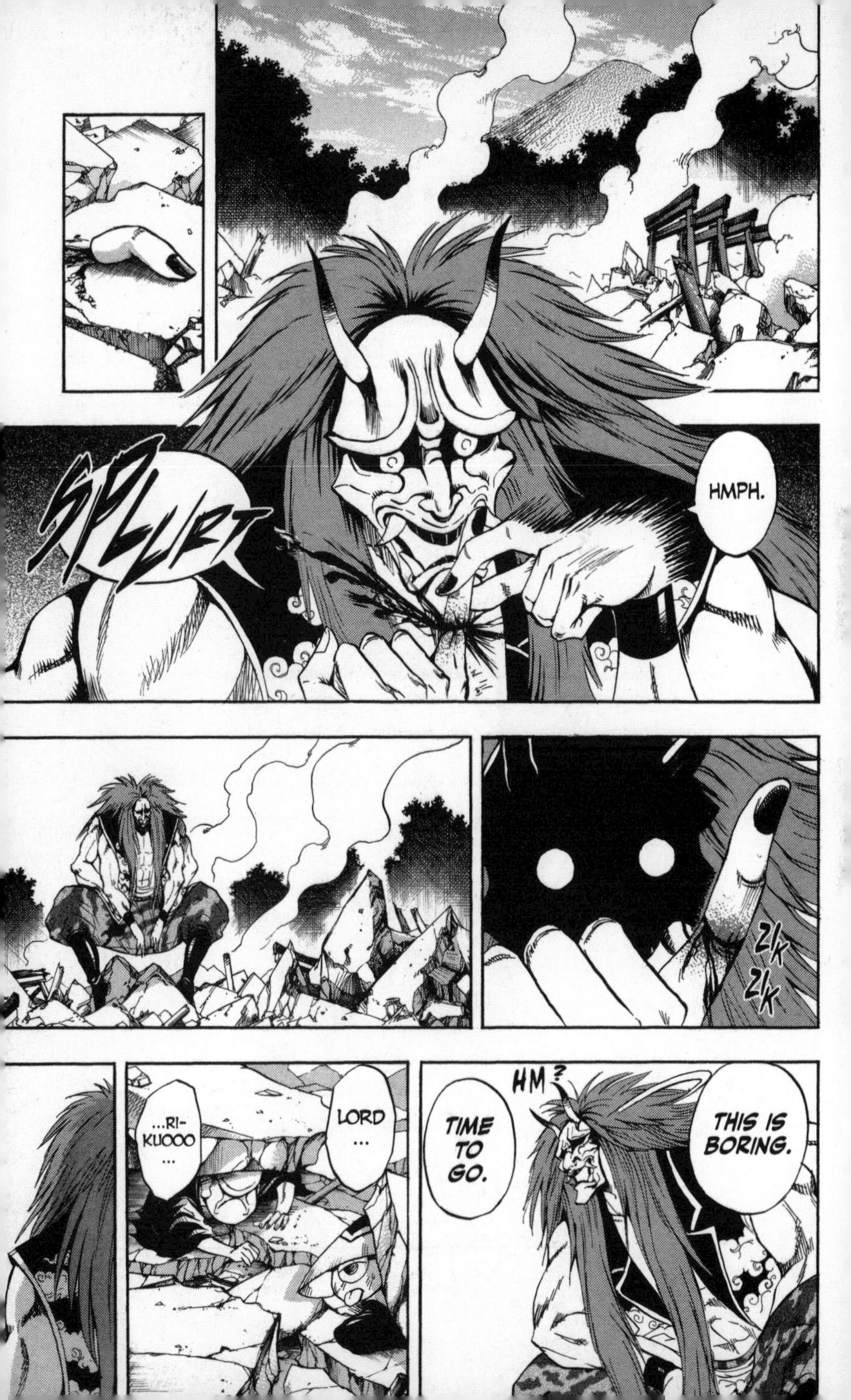
HMPH.
SPLURT
ZIK ZIK
HM?
THIS IS BORING.
TIME TO GO.
LORD ...
...RI-KUOOO ...

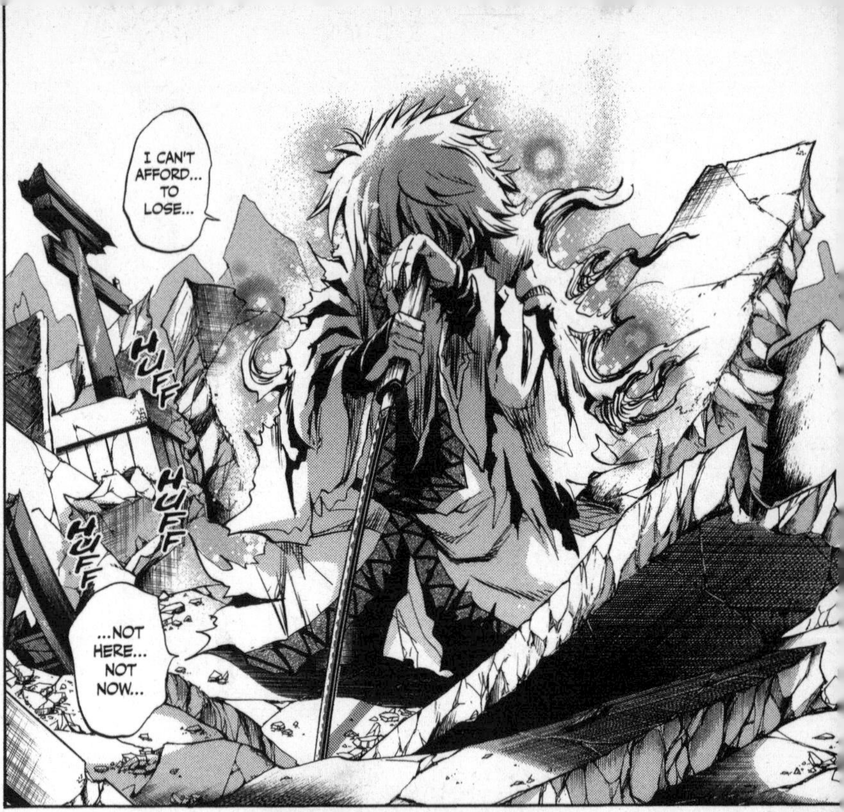
I CAN'T AFFORD... TO LOSE...
HUFF
HUFF
HUFF
...NOT HERE... NOT NOW...
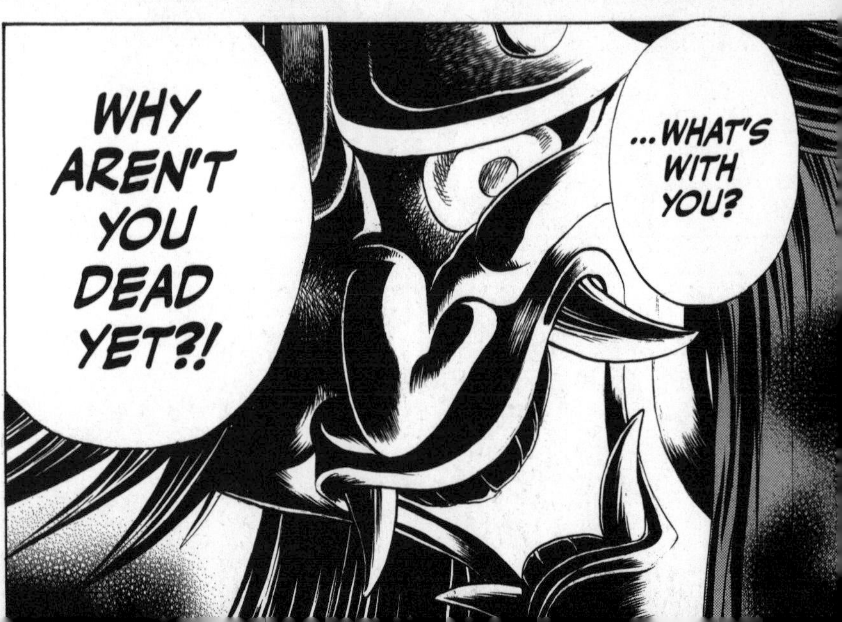
...WHAT'S WITH YOU?
WHY AREN'T YOU DEAD YET?!

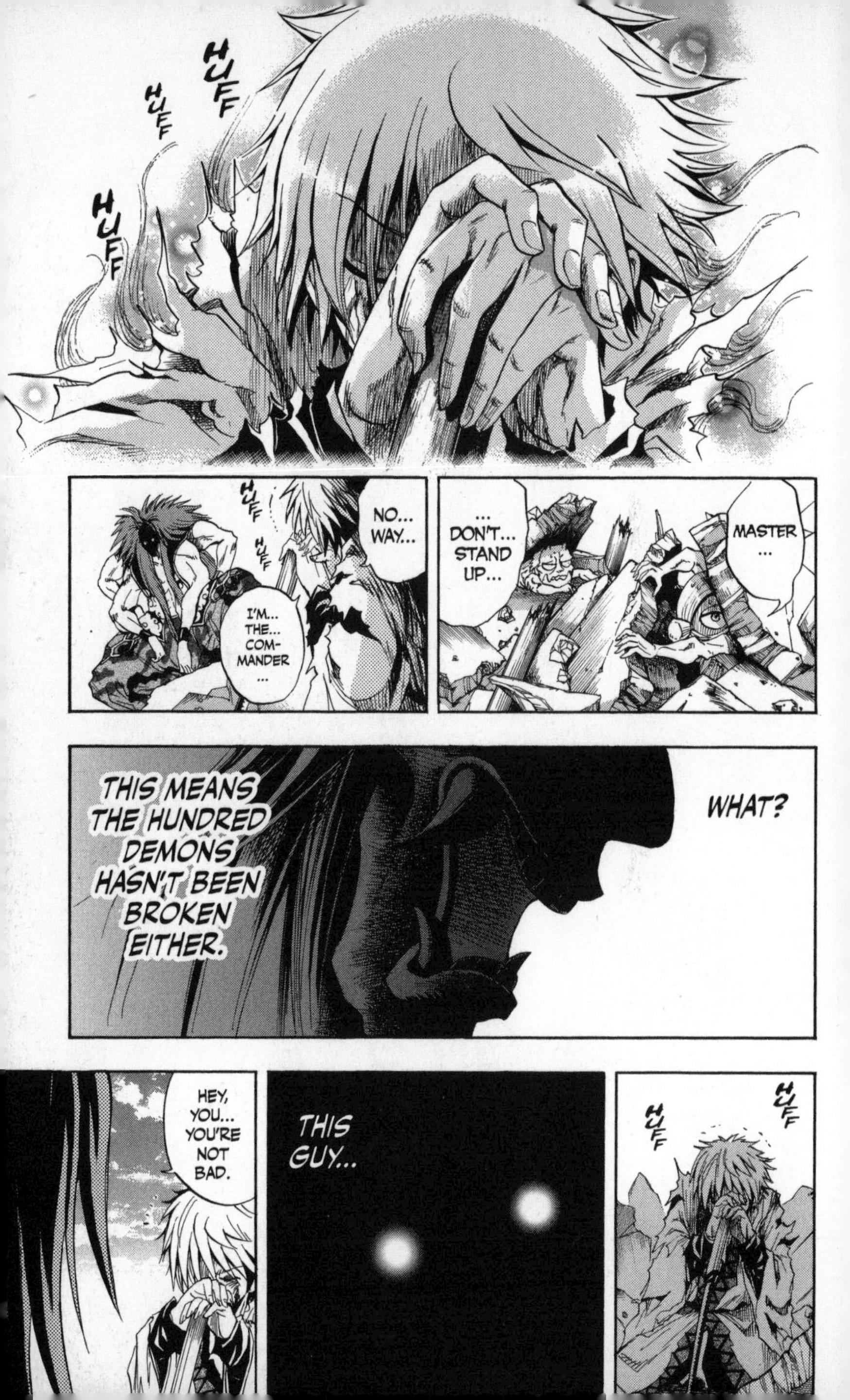
HUFF
HUFF
HUFF
HUFF
MASTER ...
... DON'T... STAND UP...
NO... WAY...
HUFF
HUFF
I'M... THE... COM-MANDER ...
WHAT?
THIS MEANS THE HUNDRED DEMONS HASN'T BEEN BROKEN EITHER.
HUFF
HUFF
THIS GUY...
HEY, YOU... YOU'RE NOT BAD.

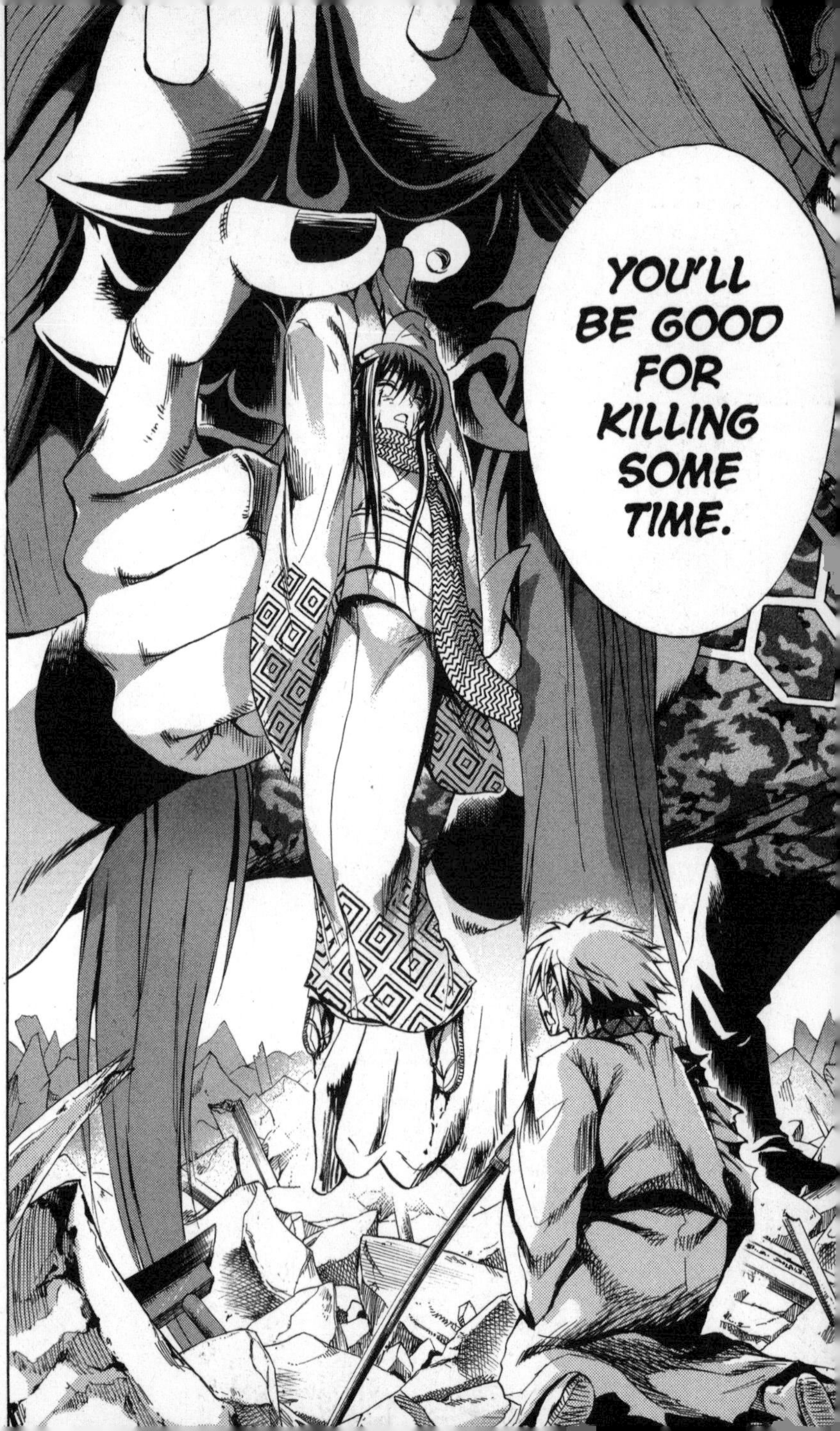
YOU'LL BE GOOD FOR KILLING SOME TIME.

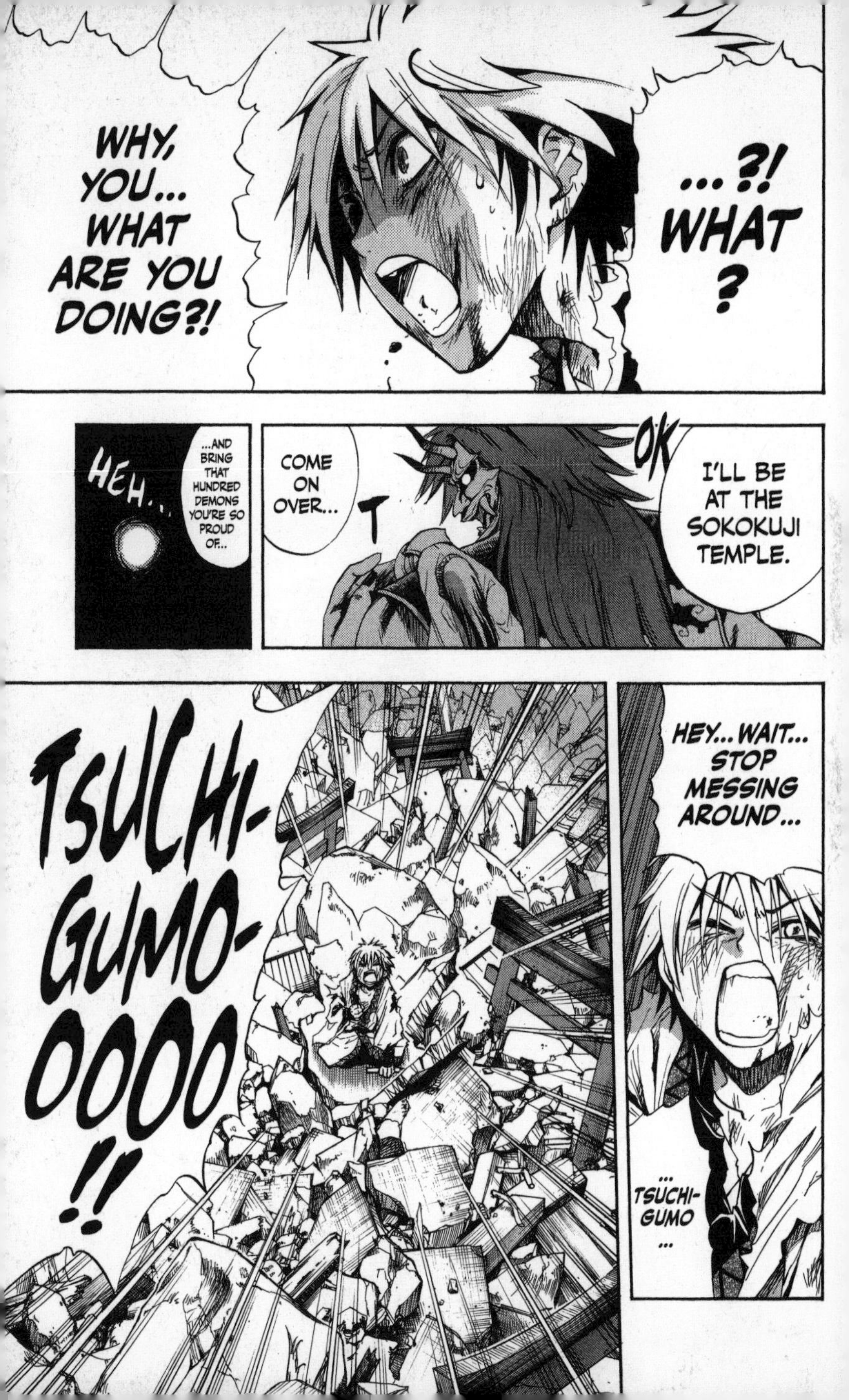
...?! WHAT?
WHY, YOU... WHAT ARE YOU DOING?!
OK
I'LL BE AT THE SOKOKUJI TEMPLE.
COME ON OVER...
T
...AND BRING THAT HUNDRED DEMONS YOU'RE SO PROUD OF...
HEH...
HEY...WAIT... STOP MESSING AROUND...
...TSUCHI-GUMO...
TSUCHI-GUMO-OOOO!!

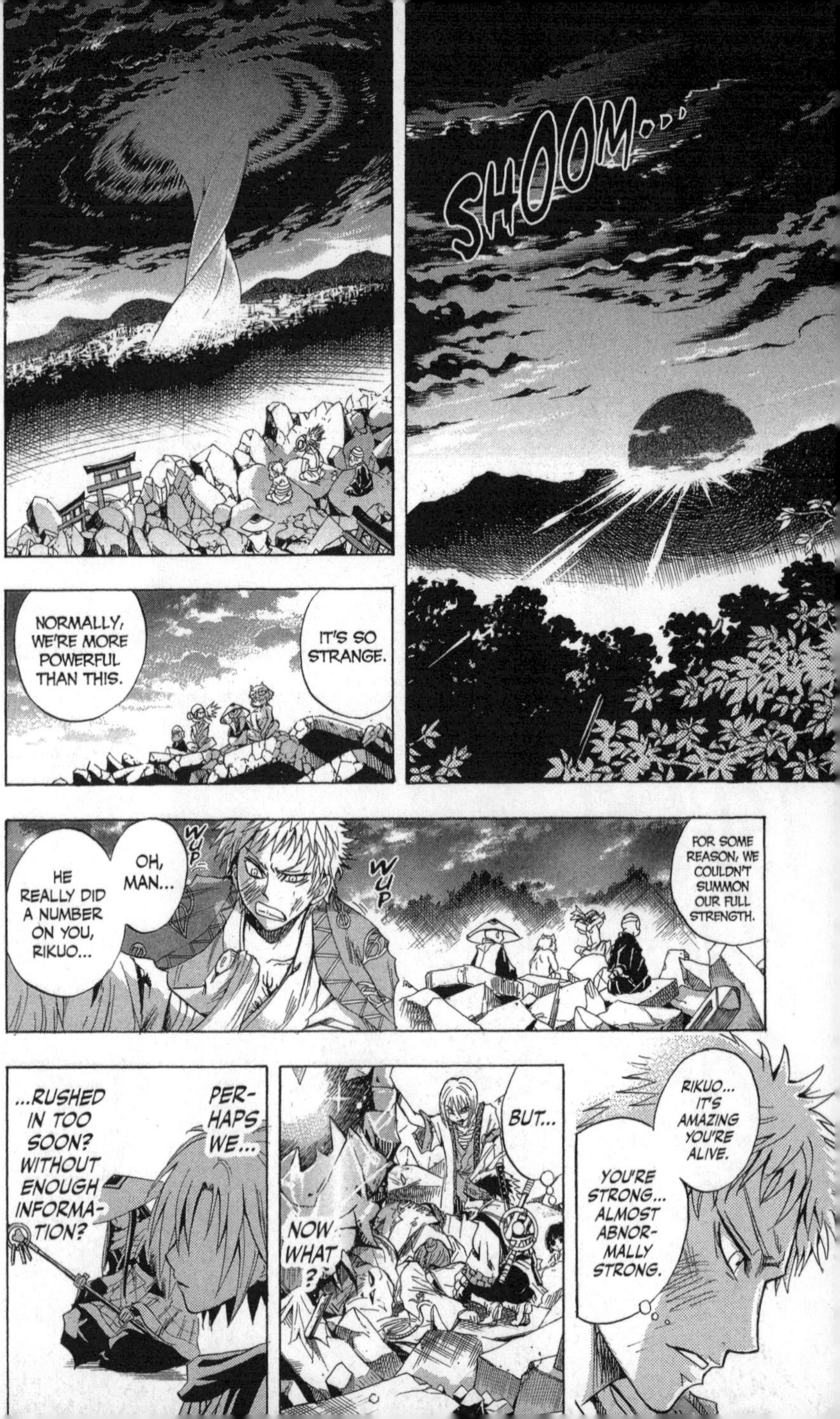
SHOOM...
IT'S SO STRANGE.
NORMALLY, WE'RE MORE POWERFUL THAN THIS.
FOR SOME REASON, WE COULDN'T SUMMON OUR FULL STRENGTH.
WUP
WUP
OH, MAN...
HE REALLY DID A NUMBER ON YOU, RIKUO...
RIKUO... IT'S AMAZING YOU'RE ALIVE.
YOU'RE STRONG... ALMOST ABNORMALLY STRONG.
BUT...
NOW WHAT?
PERHAPS WE...
...RUSHED IN TOO SOON? WITHOUT ENOUGH INFORMATION?

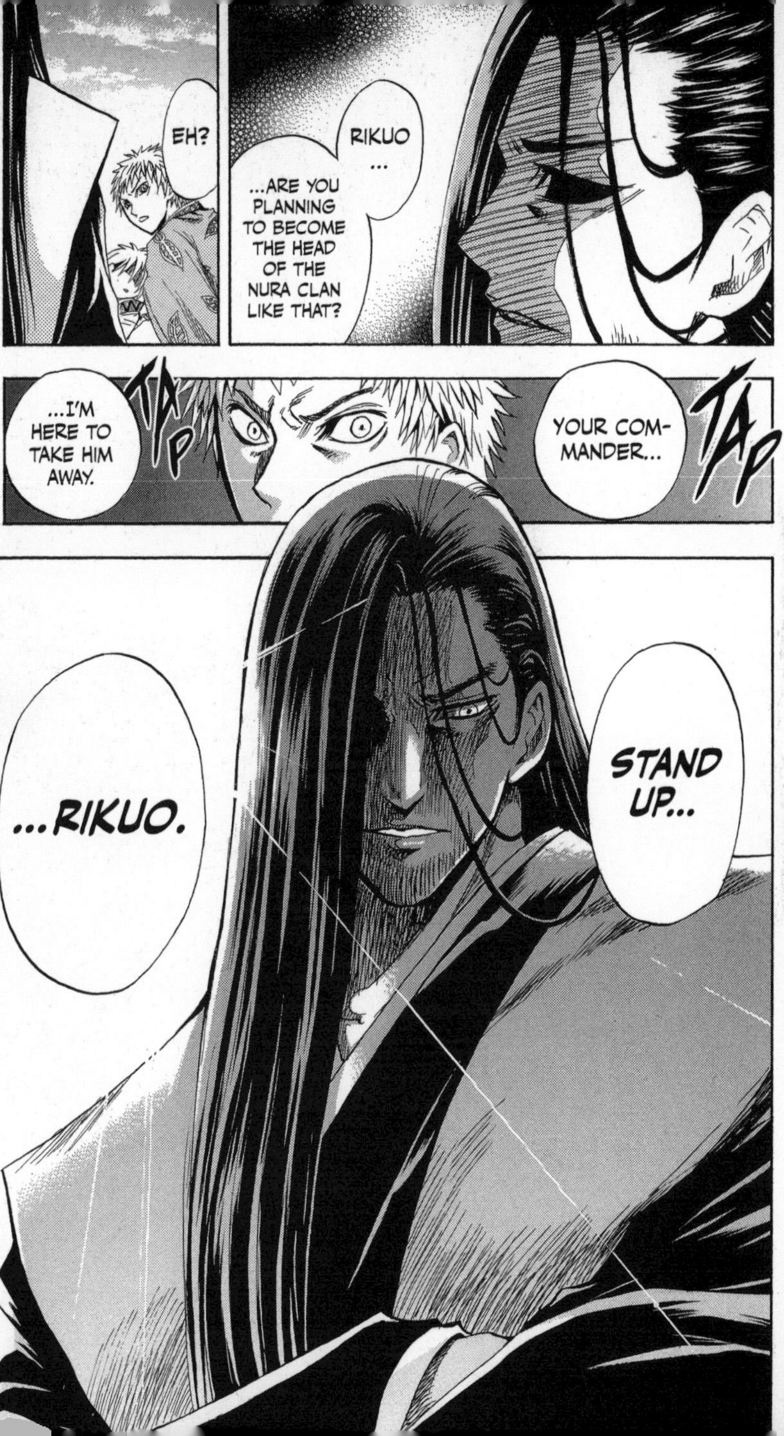

RIKUO ...
...ARE YOU PLANNING TO BECOME THE HEAD OF THE NURA CLAN LIKE THAT?
EH?
TAP
YOUR COMMANDER...
TAP
...I'M HERE TO TAKE HIM AWAY.
STAND UP...
...RIKUO.

NURA: RISE OF THE YOKAI CLAN

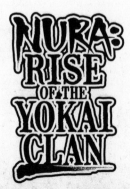

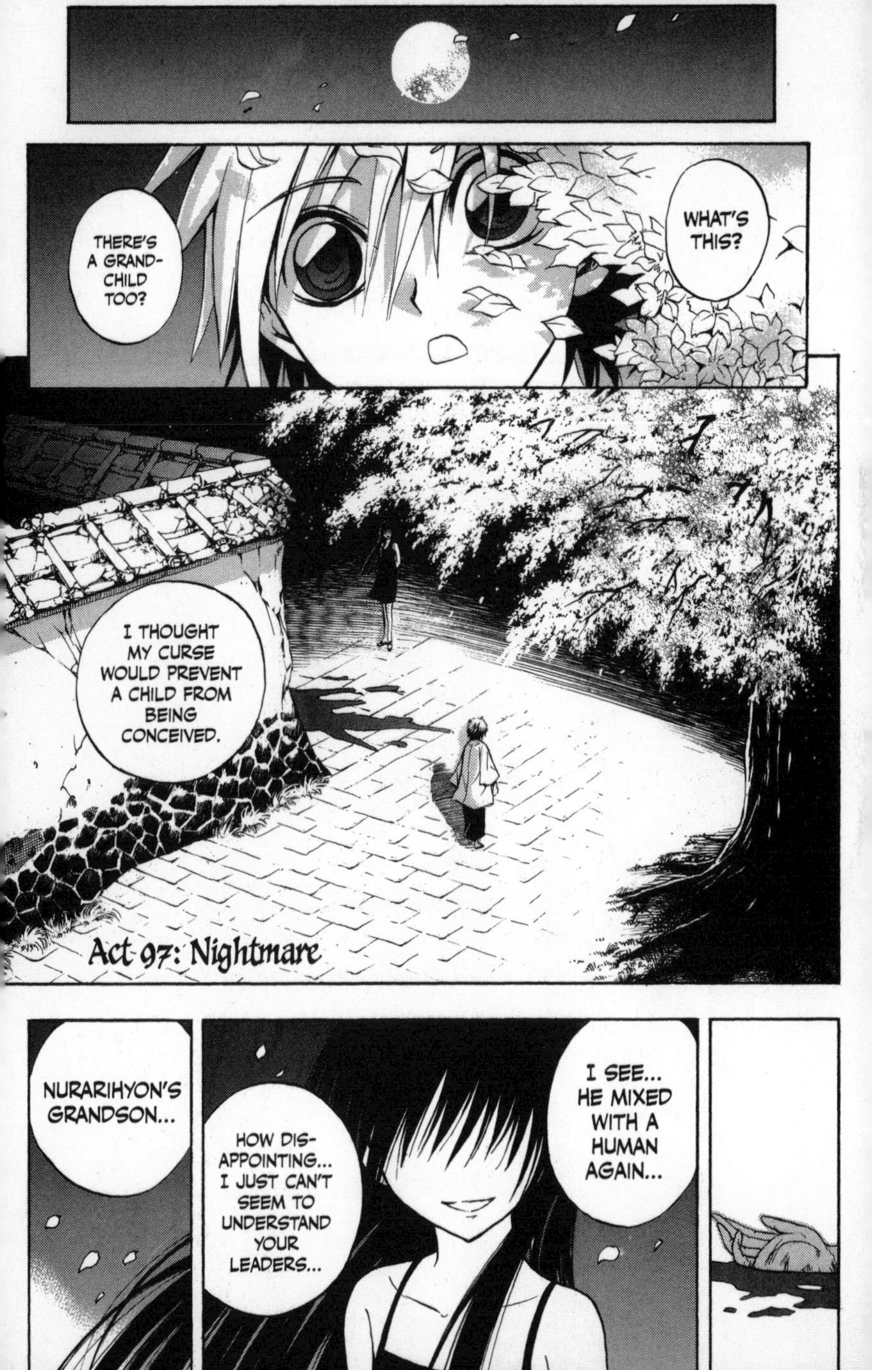
WHAT'S THIS?
THERE'S A GRAND-CHILD TOO?
I THOUGHT MY CURSE WOULD PREVENT A CHILD FROM BEING CONCEIVED.
Act 97: Nightmare
I SEE... HE MIXED WITH A HUMAN AGAIN...
HOW DIS-APPOINTING... I JUST CAN'T SEEM TO UNDERSTAND YOUR LEADERS...
NURARIHYON'S GRANDSON...

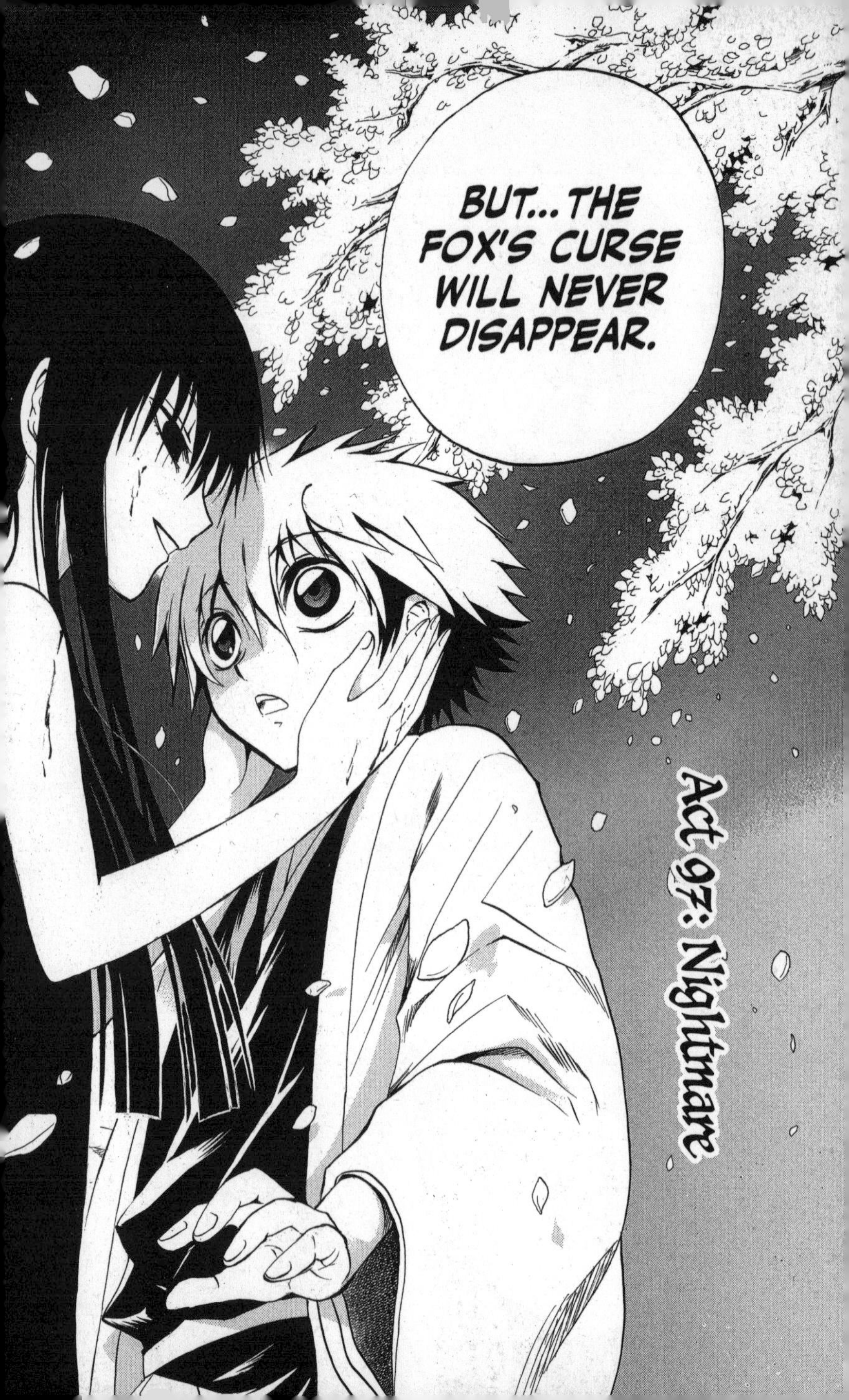
BUT... THE FOX'S CURSE WILL NEVER DISAPPEAR.
Act 97: Nightmare

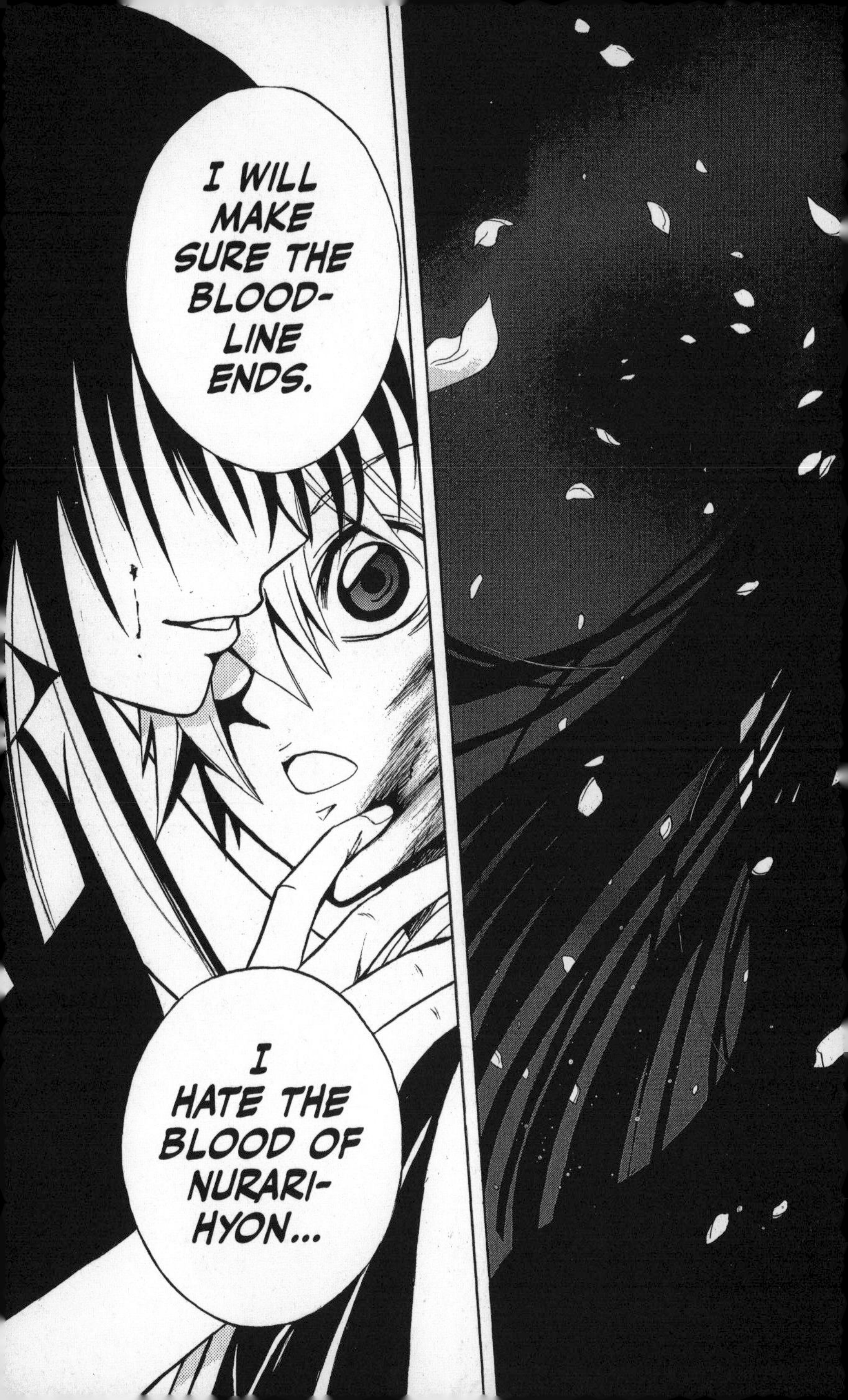
I WILL MAKE SURE THE BLOOD-LINE ENDS.
I HATE THE BLOOD OF NURARI-HYON...

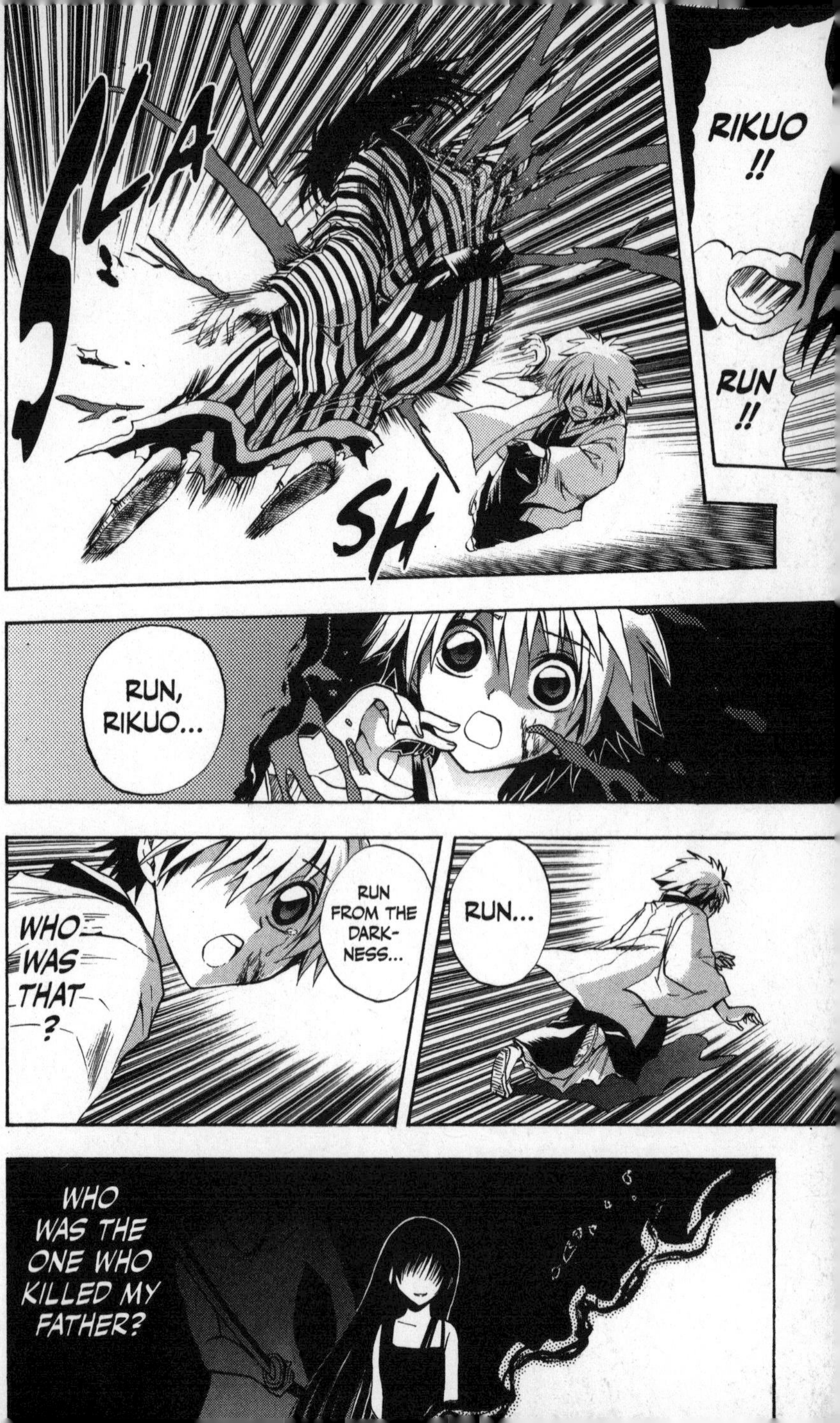
RIKUO !!
RUN !!
SH
RUN, RIKUO...
RUN...
RUN FROM THE DARK- NESS...
WHO WAS THAT?
WHO WAS THE ONE WHO KILLED MY FATHER?

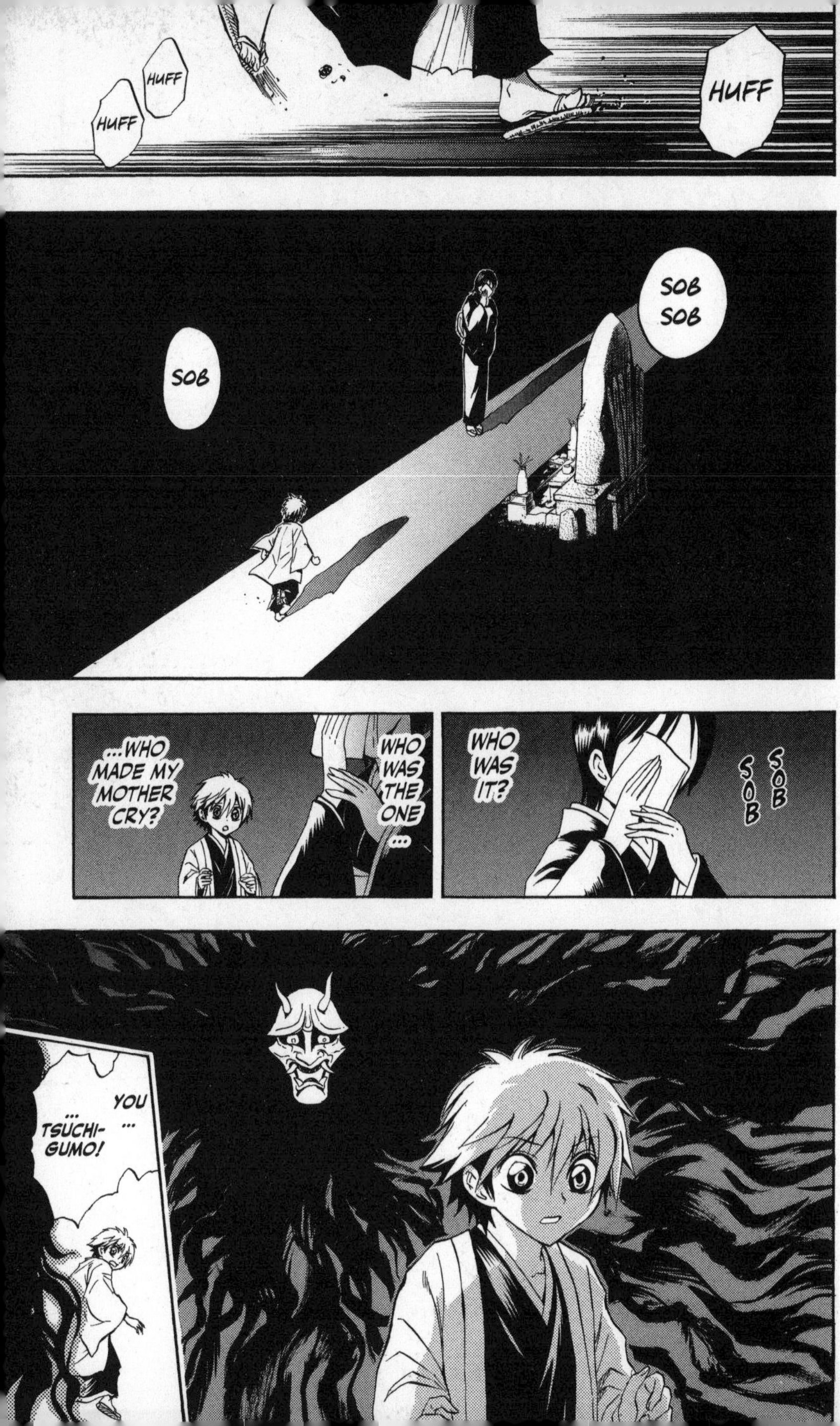
HUFF
HUFF
HUFF
SOB SOB
SOB
SOB SOB
WHO WAS IT?
WHO WAS THE ONE...
...WHO MADE MY MOTHER CRY?
YOU...
...TSUCHI-GUMO!

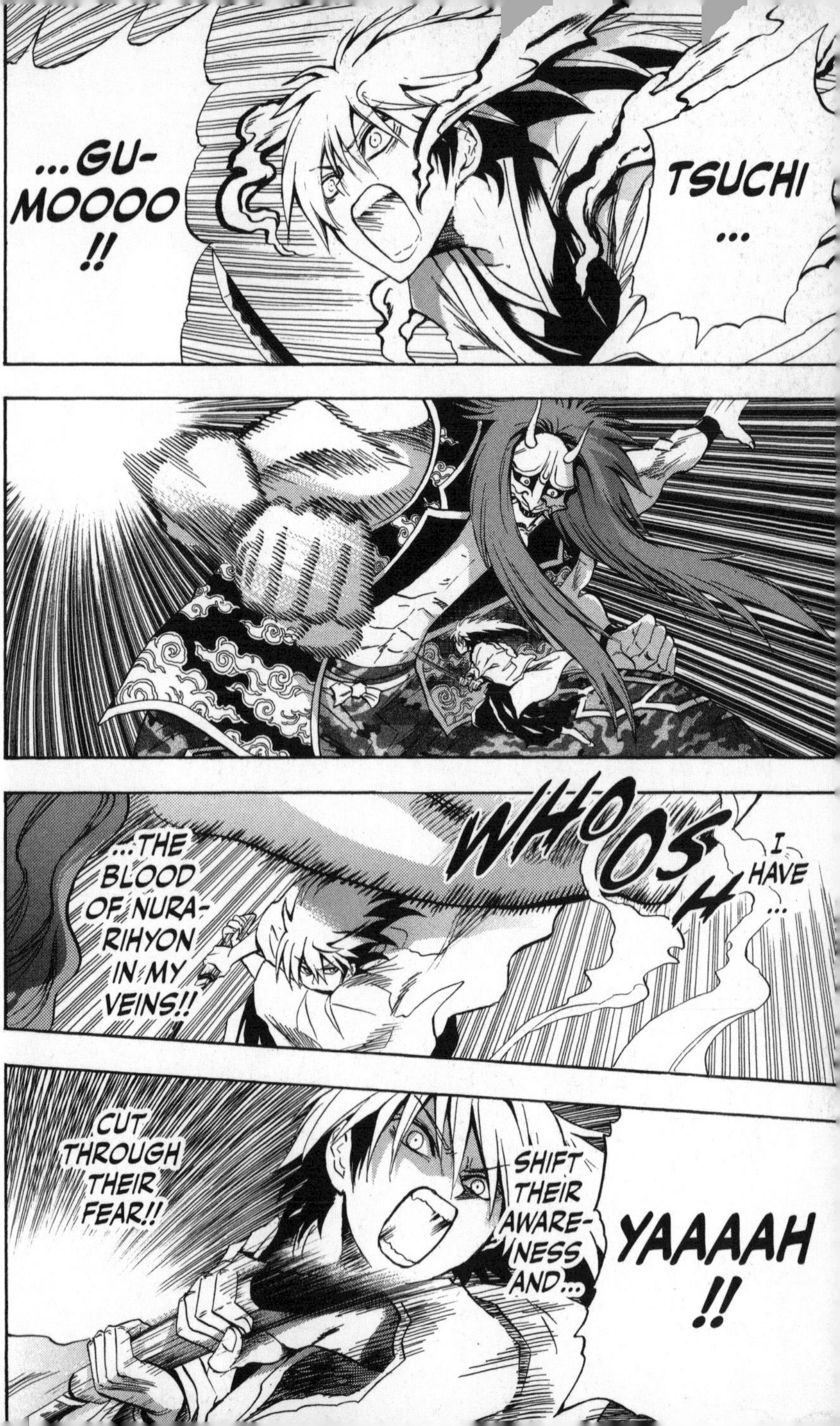
TSUCHI...
...GU-MOOOO!!
I HAVE...
WHOOSH
...THE BLOOD OF NURA-RIHYON IN MY VEINS!!
SHIFT THEIR AWARENESS AND...
CUT THROUGH THEIR FEAR!!
YAAAAH!!

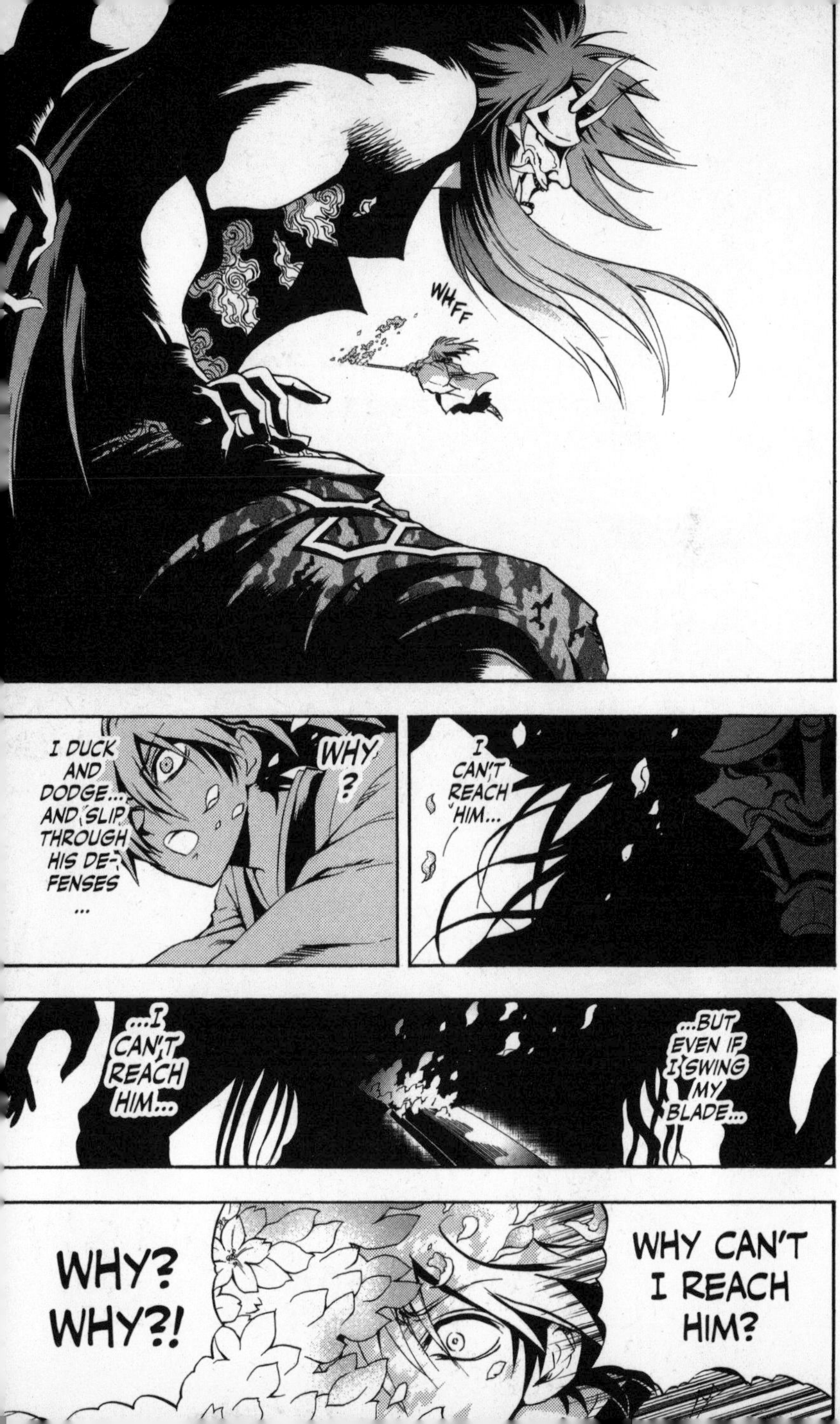
WHFF
I CAN'T REACH HIM...
WHY?
I DUCK AND DODGE... AND SLIP THROUGH HIS DEFENSES...
...BUT EVEN IF I SWING MY BLADE...
...I CAN'T REACH HIM...
WHY CAN'T I REACH HIM?
WHY? WHY?!

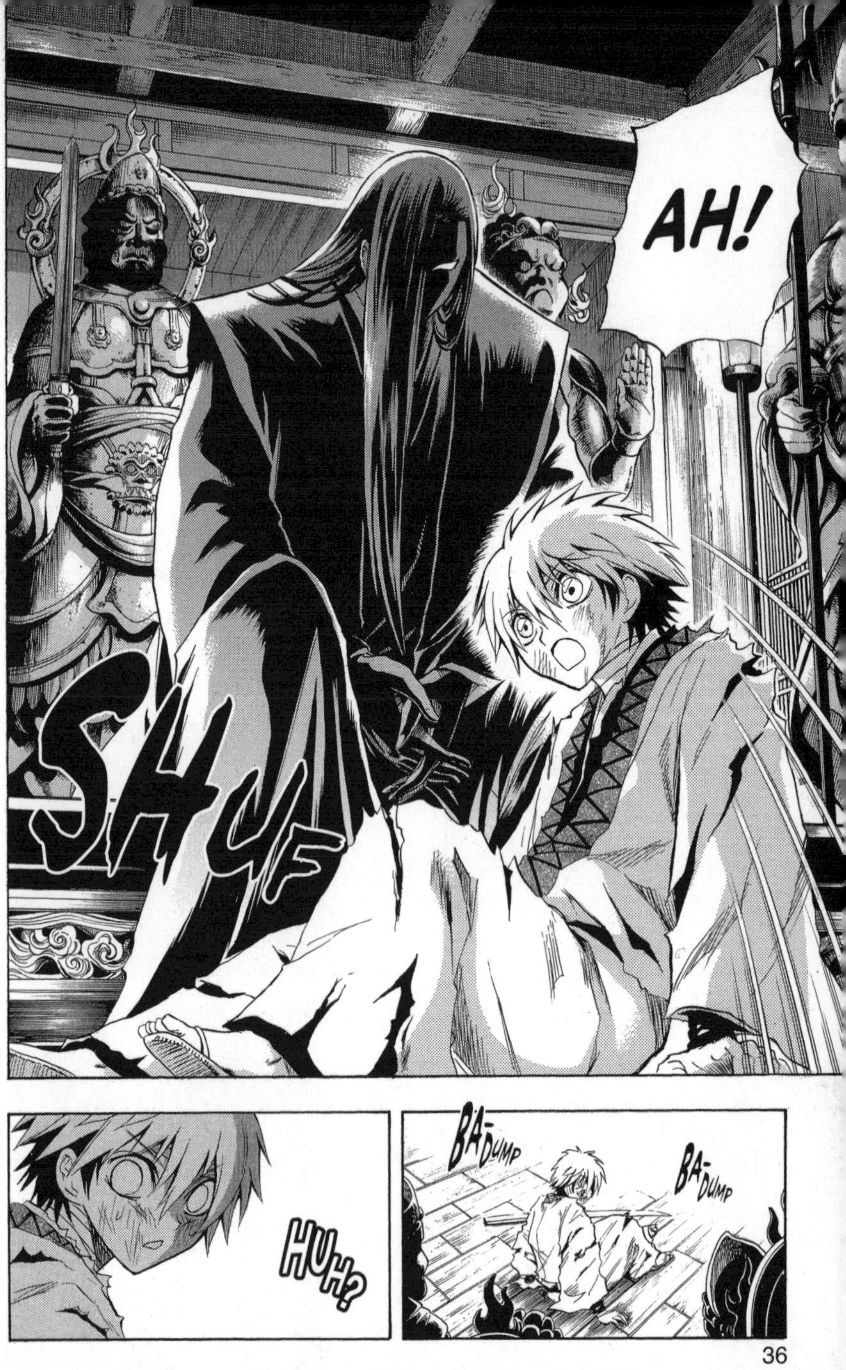
AH!
SHUF
BA-DUMP
BA-DUMP
HUH?

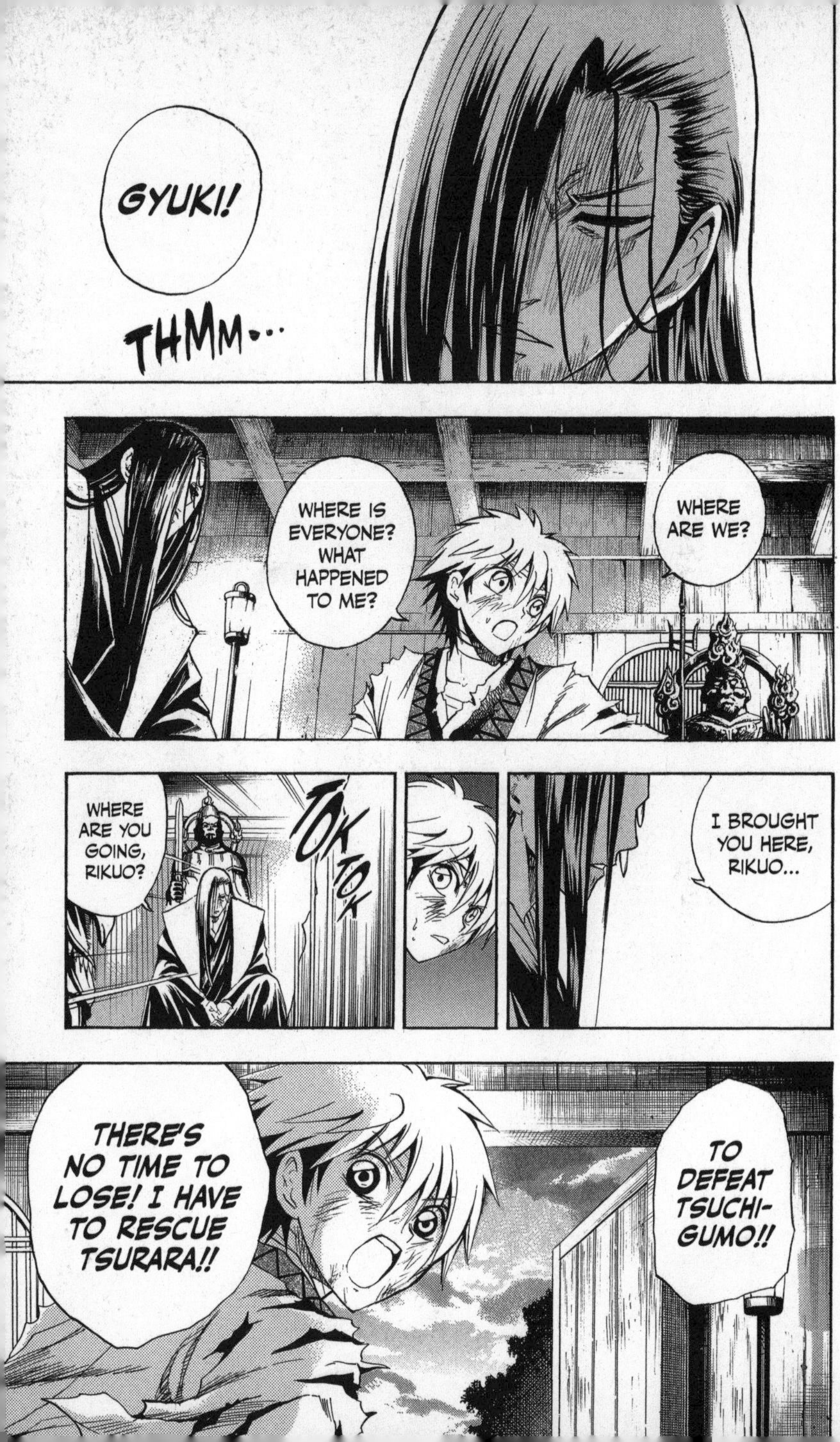
GYUKI!
THMM...
WHERE ARE WE?
WHERE IS EVERYONE? WHAT HAPPENED TO ME?
I BROUGHT YOU HERE, RIKUO...
TOK TOK
WHERE ARE YOU GOING, RIKUO?
TO DEFEAT TSUCHI-GUMO!!
THERE'S NO TIME TO LOSE! I HAVE TO RESCUE TSURARA!!

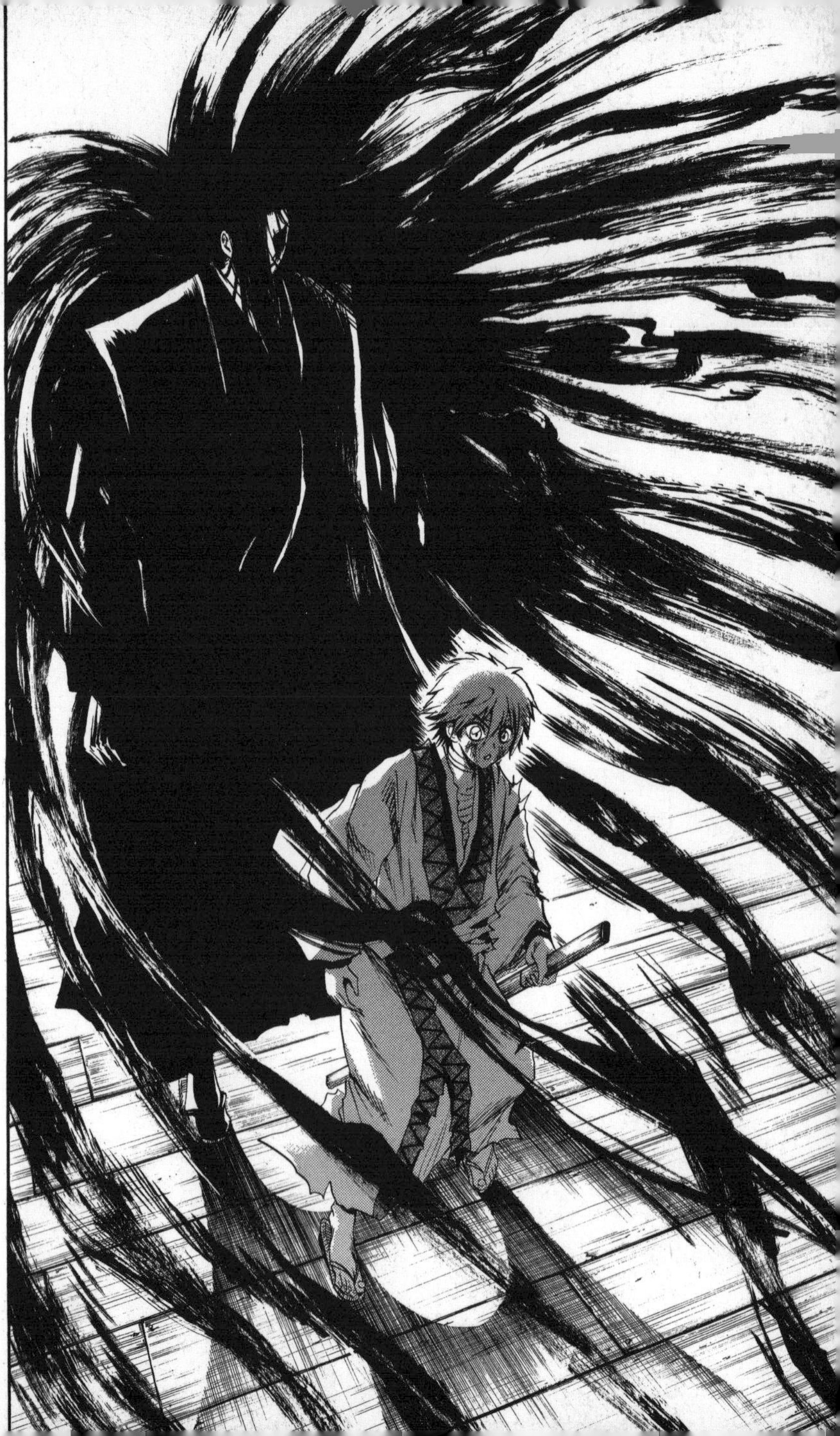

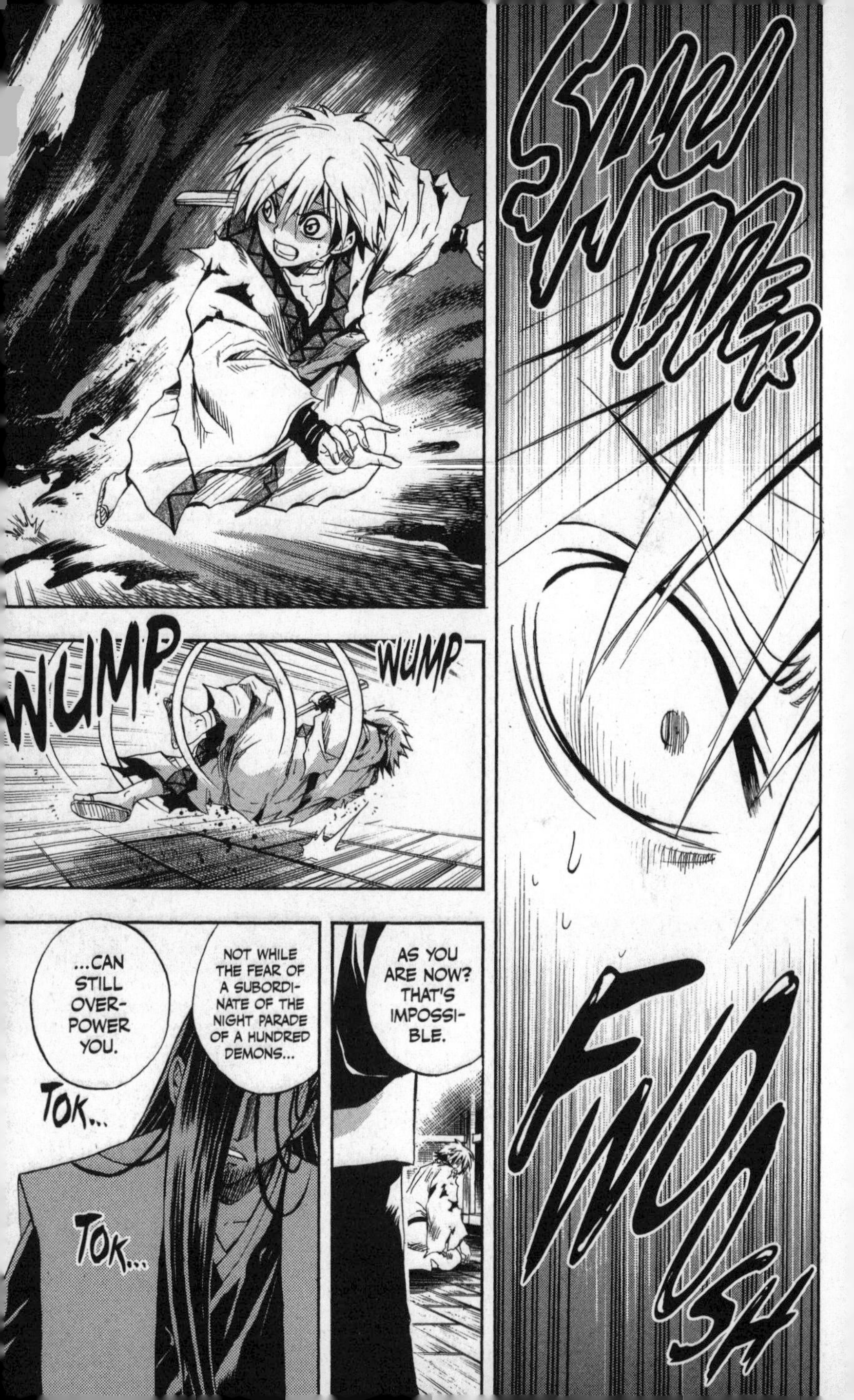
FWUSH
WUMP
WUMP
AS YOU ARE NOW? THAT'S IMPOSSIBLE.
NOT WHILE THE FEAR OF A SUBORDINATE OF THE NIGHT PARADE OF A HUNDRED DEMONS...
...CAN STILL OVERPOWER YOU.
TOK...
TOK...

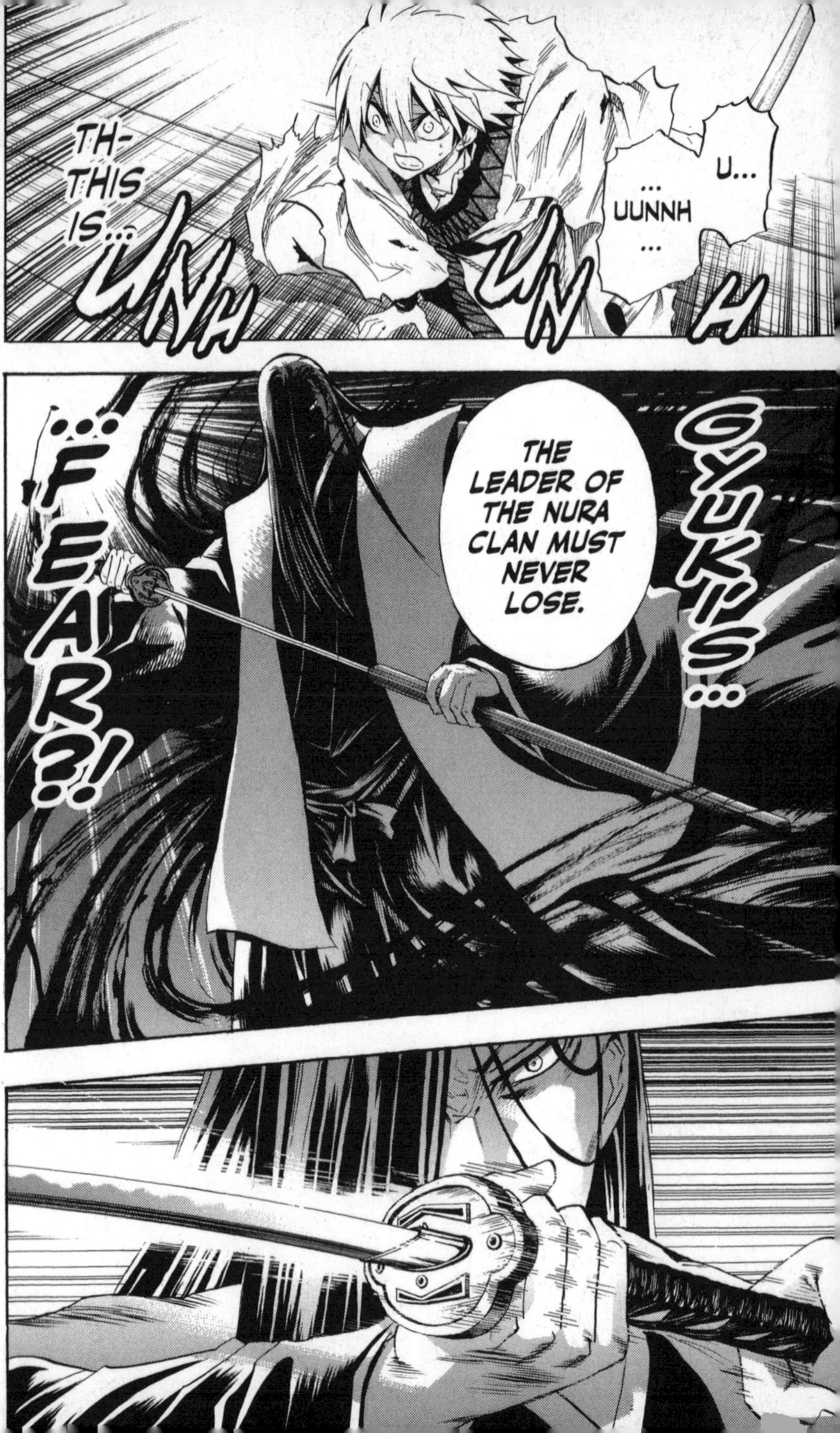
U...
... UUNNH ...
TH- THIS IS...
UNH UN H
GYUKI'S...
THE LEADER OF THE NURA CLAN MUST NEVER LOSE.
...FEAR?!

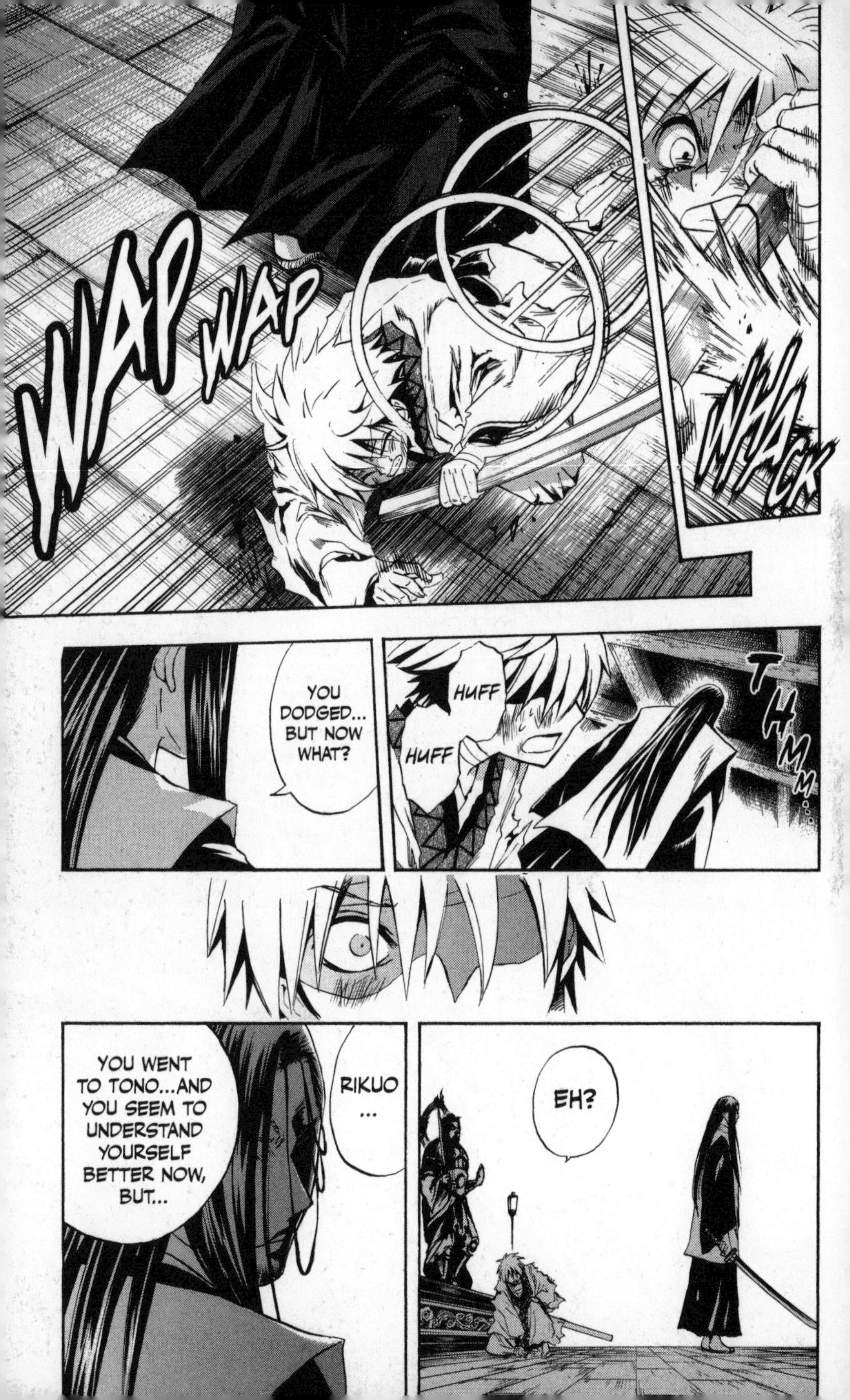
WHACK
WAP WAP
THMM...
HUFF
HUFF
YOU DODGED... BUT NOW WHAT?
EH?
RIKUO ...
YOU WENT TO TONO...AND YOU SEEM TO UNDERSTAND YOURSELF BETTER NOW, BUT...

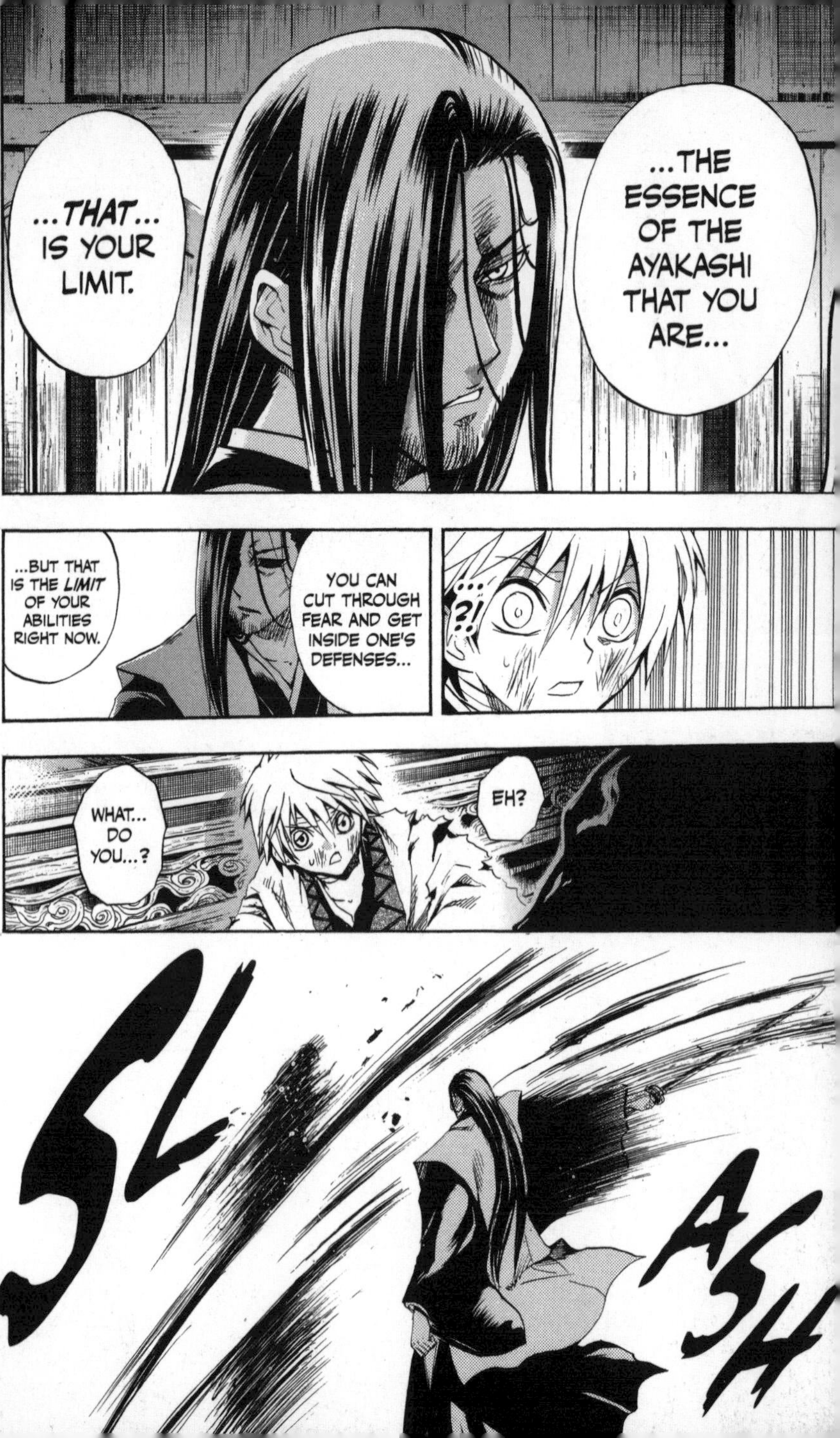
...THE ESSENCE OF THE AYAKASHI THAT YOU ARE...
...*THAT*... IS YOUR LIMIT.
...?!...
YOU CAN CUT THROUGH FEAR AND GET INSIDE ONE'S DEFENSES...
...BUT THAT IS THE *LIMIT* OF YOUR ABILITIES RIGHT NOW.
EH?
WHAT... DO YOU...?
SLASH

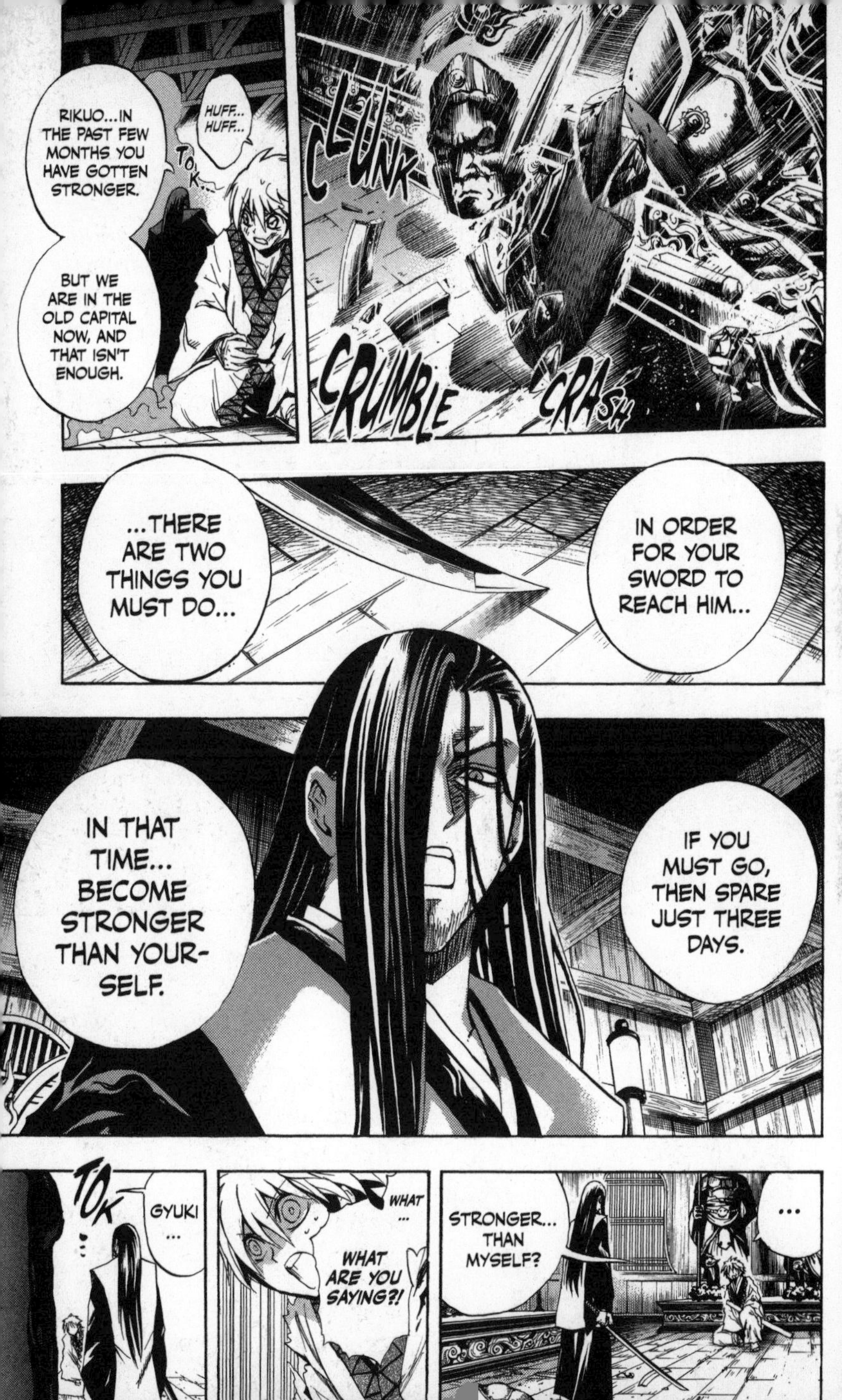
CLUNK
CRUMBLE
CRASH
HUFF... HUFF...
TOK...
RIKUO...IN THE PAST FEW MONTHS YOU HAVE GOTTEN STRONGER.
BUT WE ARE IN THE OLD CAPITAL NOW, AND THAT ISN'T ENOUGH.
IN ORDER FOR YOUR SWORD TO REACH HIM...
...THERE ARE TWO THINGS YOU MUST DO...
IF YOU MUST GO, THEN SPARE JUST THREE DAYS.
IN THAT TIME... BECOME STRONGER THAN YOUR-SELF.
...
STRONGER... THAN MYSELF?
WHAT ...
WHAT ARE YOU SAYING?!
GYUKI ...
TOK

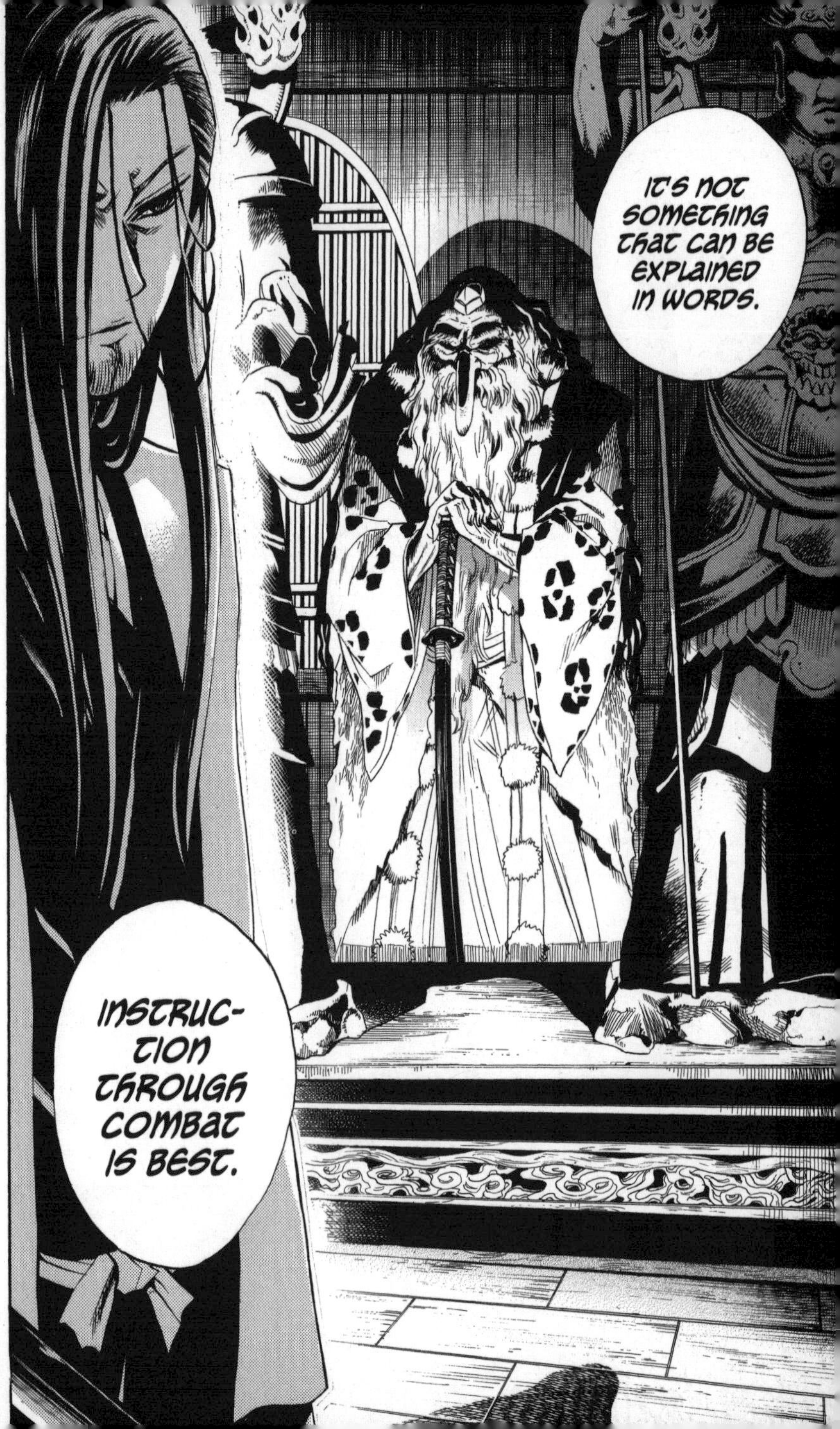
IT'S NOT SOMETHING THAT CAN BE EXPLAINED IN WORDS.
INSTRUCTION THROUGH COMBAT IS BEST.

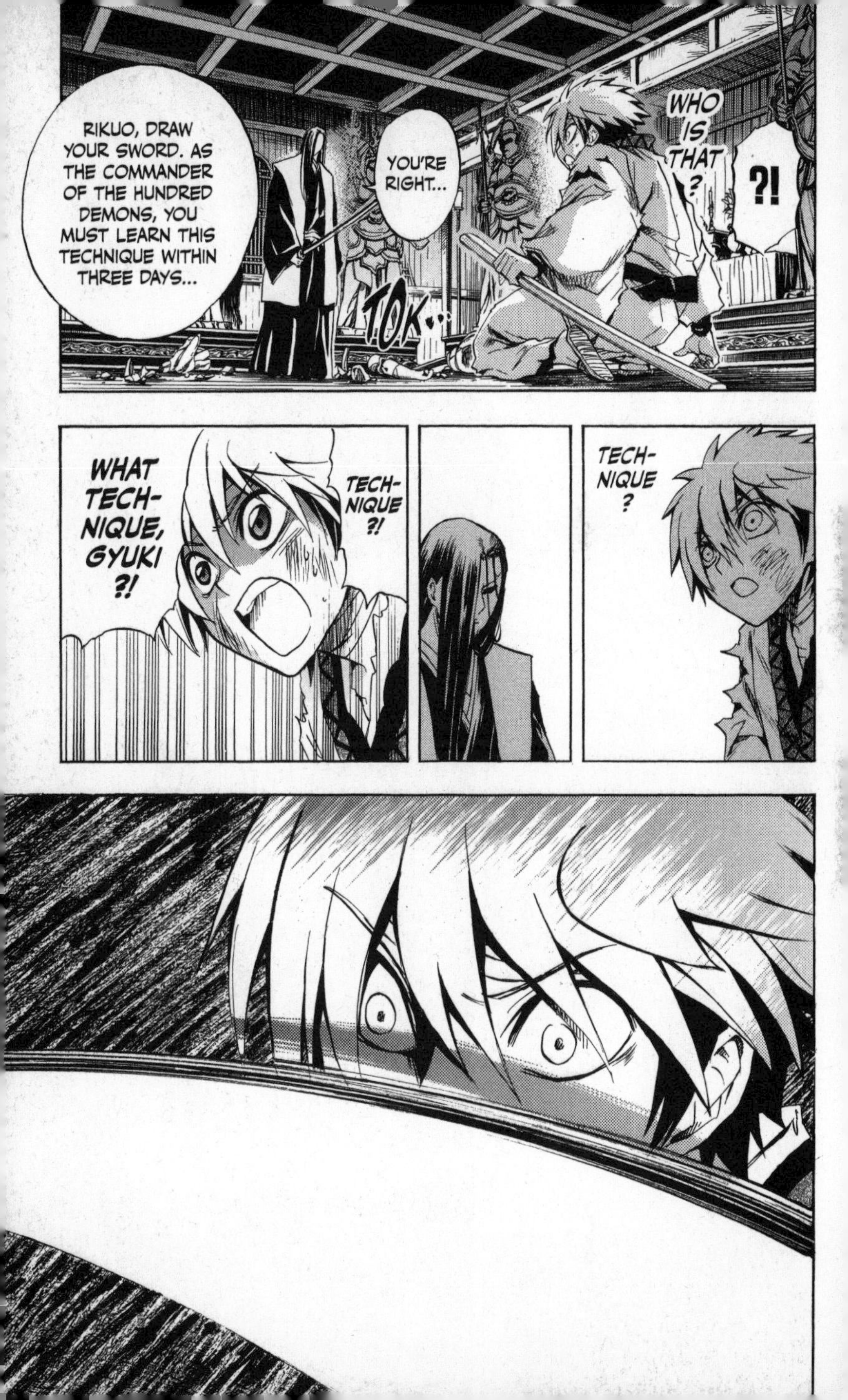
WHO IS THAT?
?!
YOU'RE RIGHT...
TOK...
RIKUO, DRAW YOUR SWORD. AS THE COMMANDER OF THE HUNDRED DEMONS, YOU MUST LEARN THIS TECHNIQUE WITHIN THREE DAYS...
TECH-NIQUE?
TECH-NIQUE?!
WHAT TECH-NIQUE, GYUKI?!

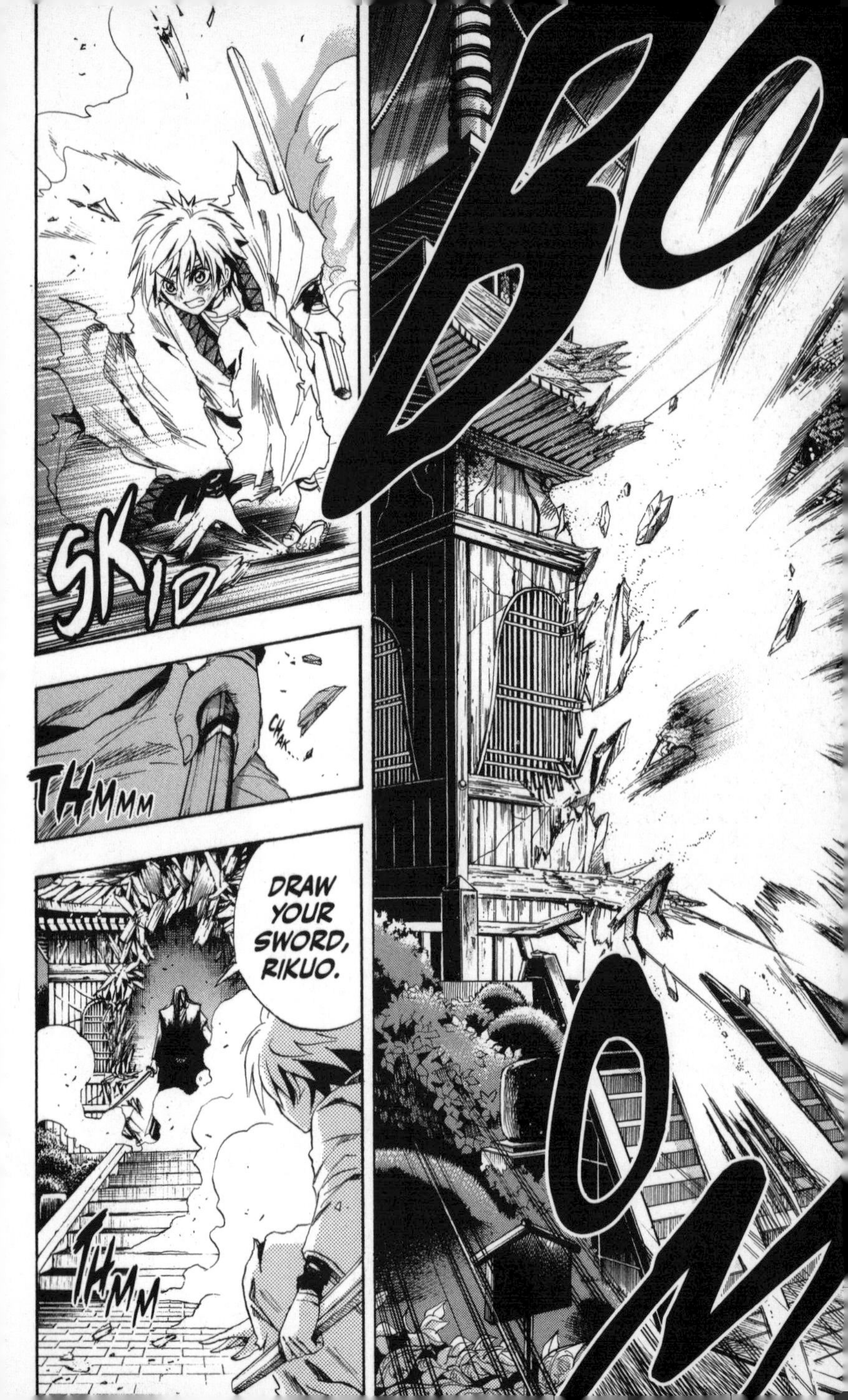
BOOM
SKID
CHAK...
THMMM
DRAW YOUR SWORD, RIKUO.
THMM

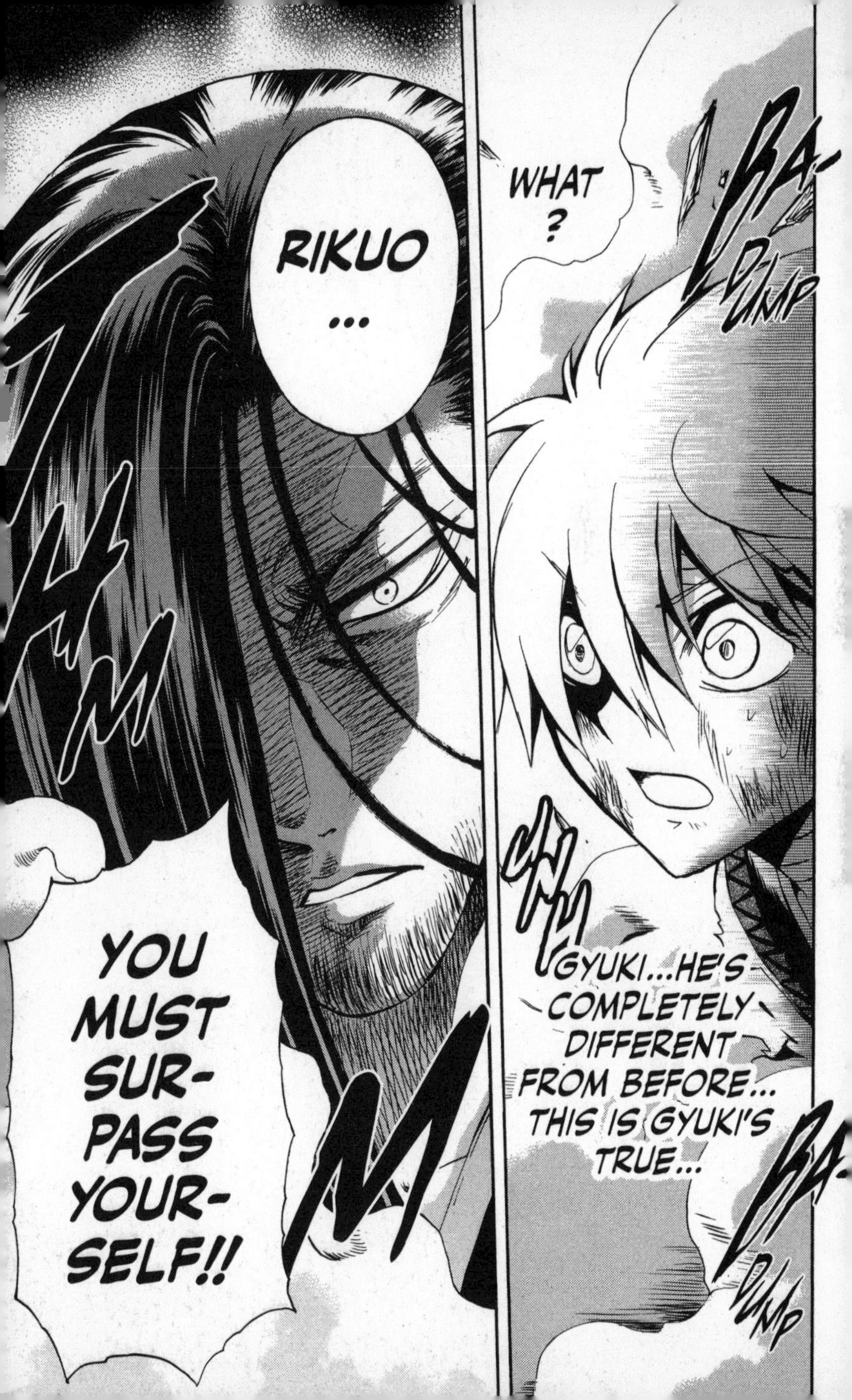
WHAT?
BA-DUMP
GYUKI...HE'S COMPLETELY DIFFERENT FROM BEFORE... THIS IS GYUKI'S TRUE...
BA-DUMP
RIKUO...
YOU MUST SUR-PASS YOUR-SELF!!

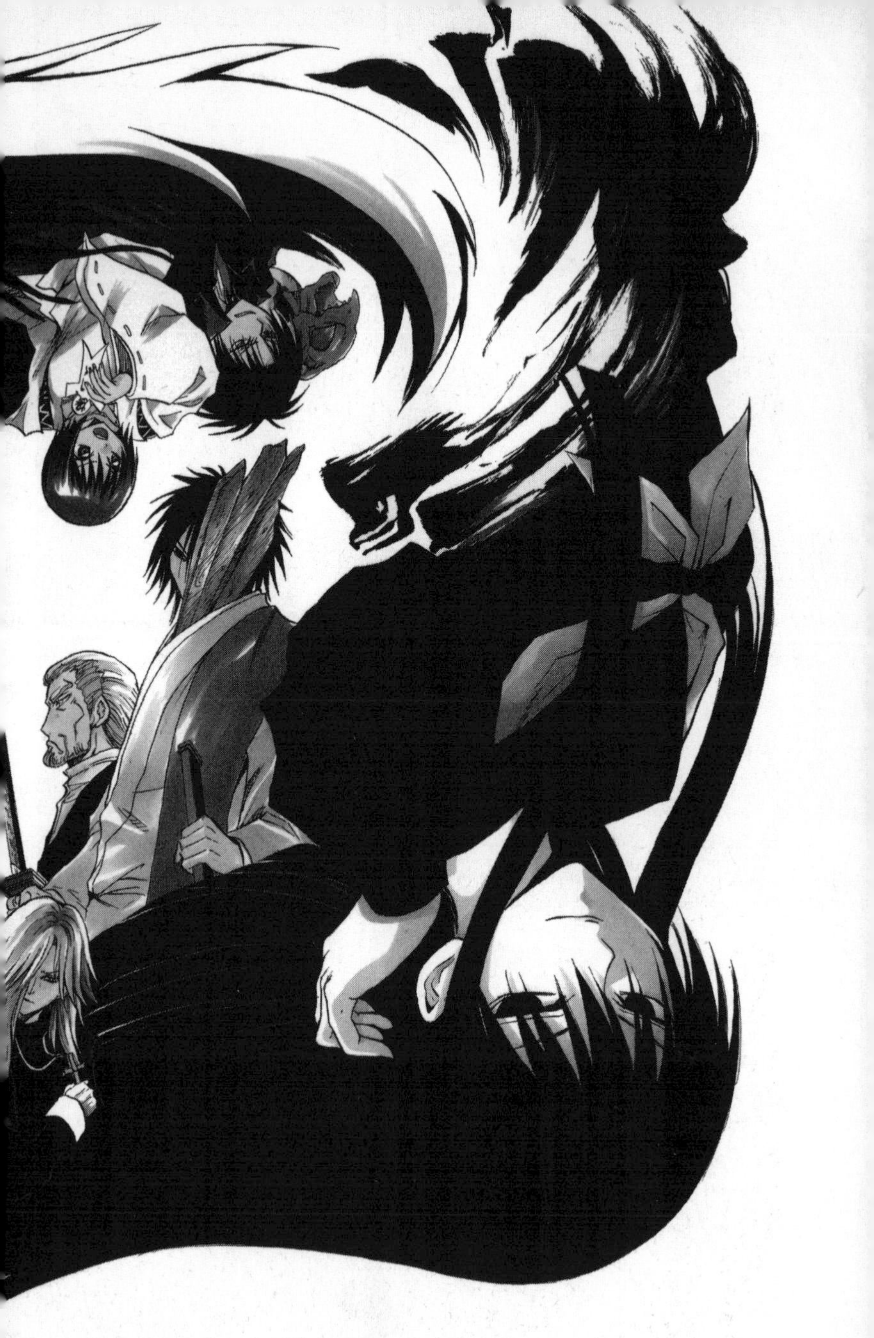

Act 98: Day and Night

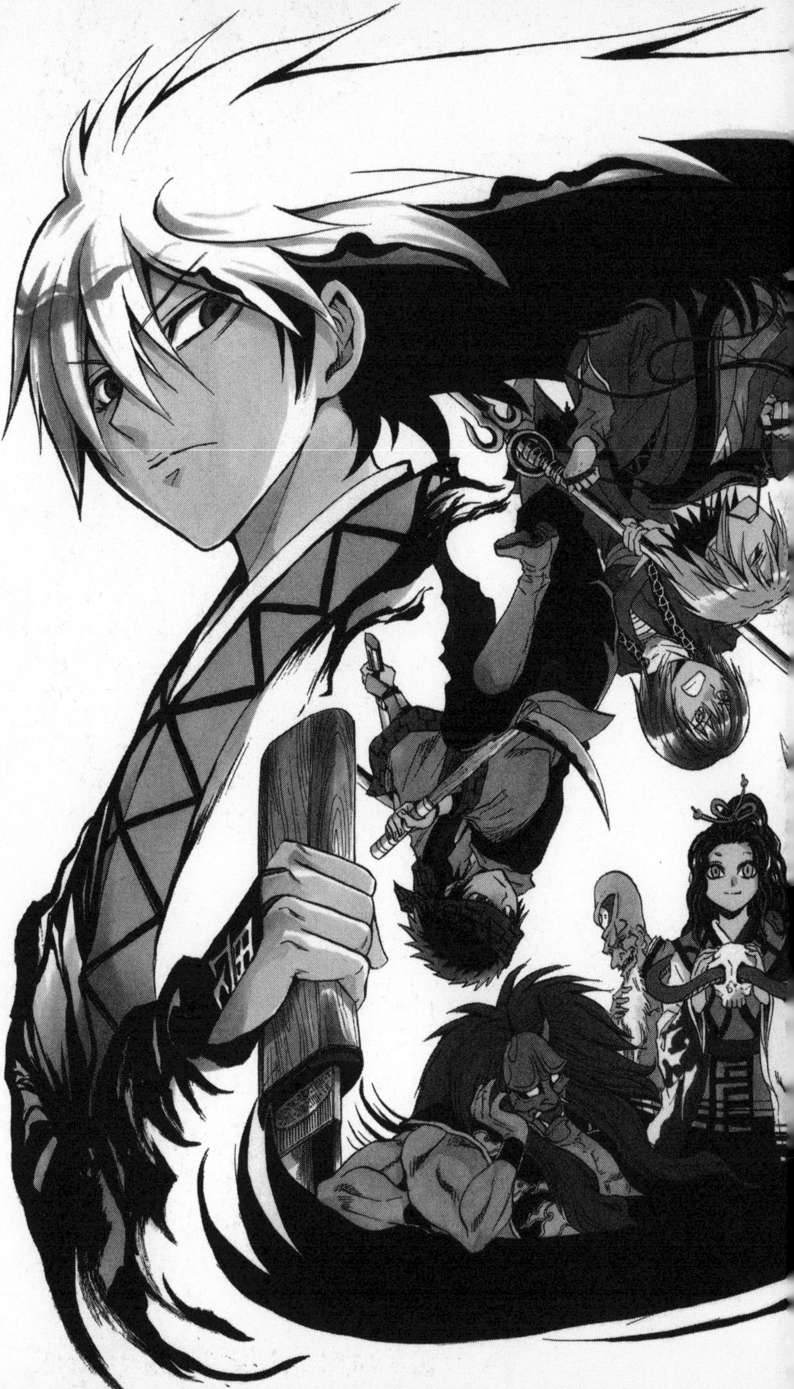

NURA: RISE OF THE YOKAI CLAN

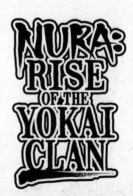

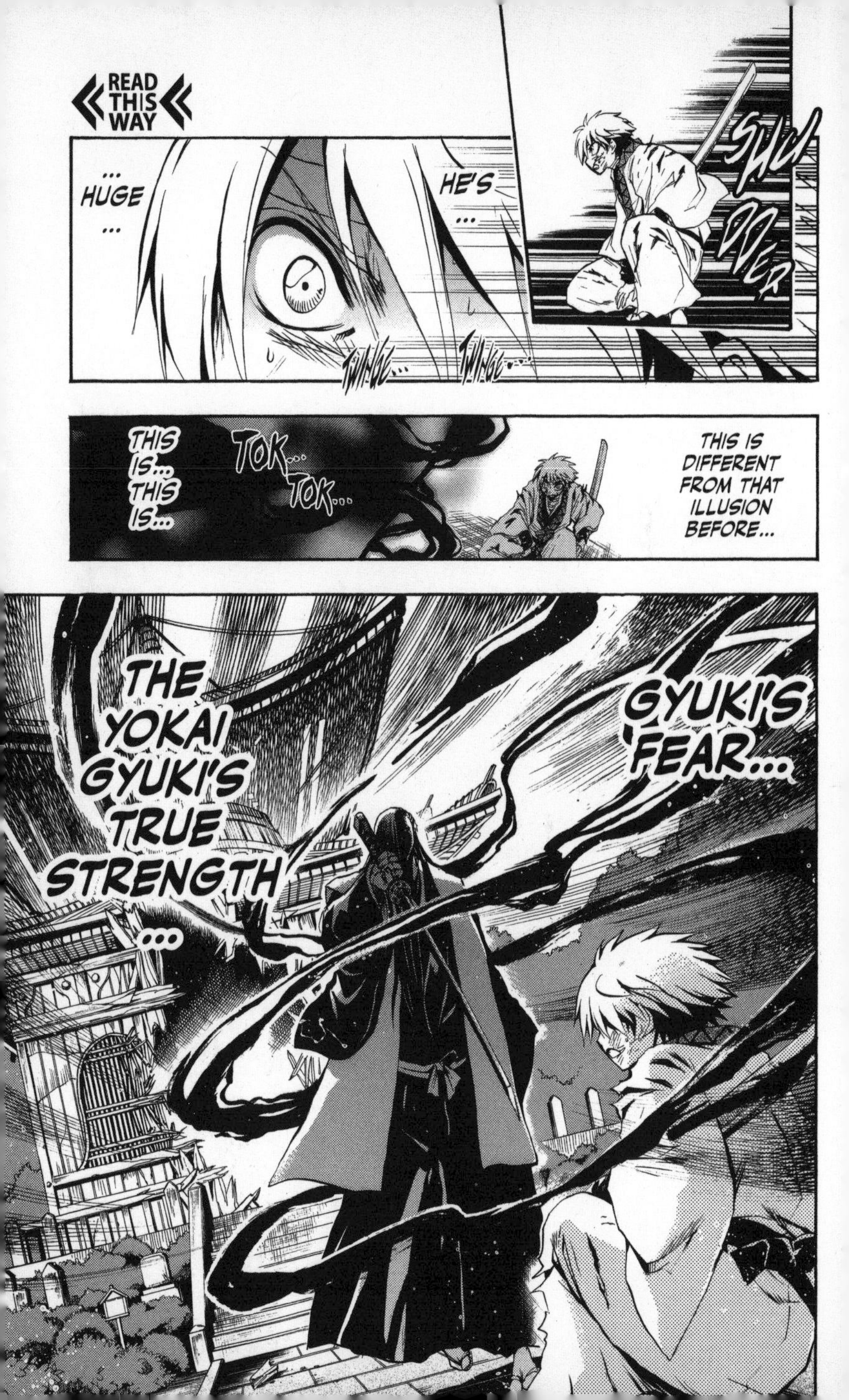
READ THIS WAY
SHUDDER
HE'S ...
... HUGE ...
THIS IS DIFFERENT FROM THAT ILLUSION BEFORE...
TOK... TOK...
THIS IS... THIS IS...
GYUKI'S FEAR...
THE YOKAI GYUKI'S TRUE STRENGTH ...

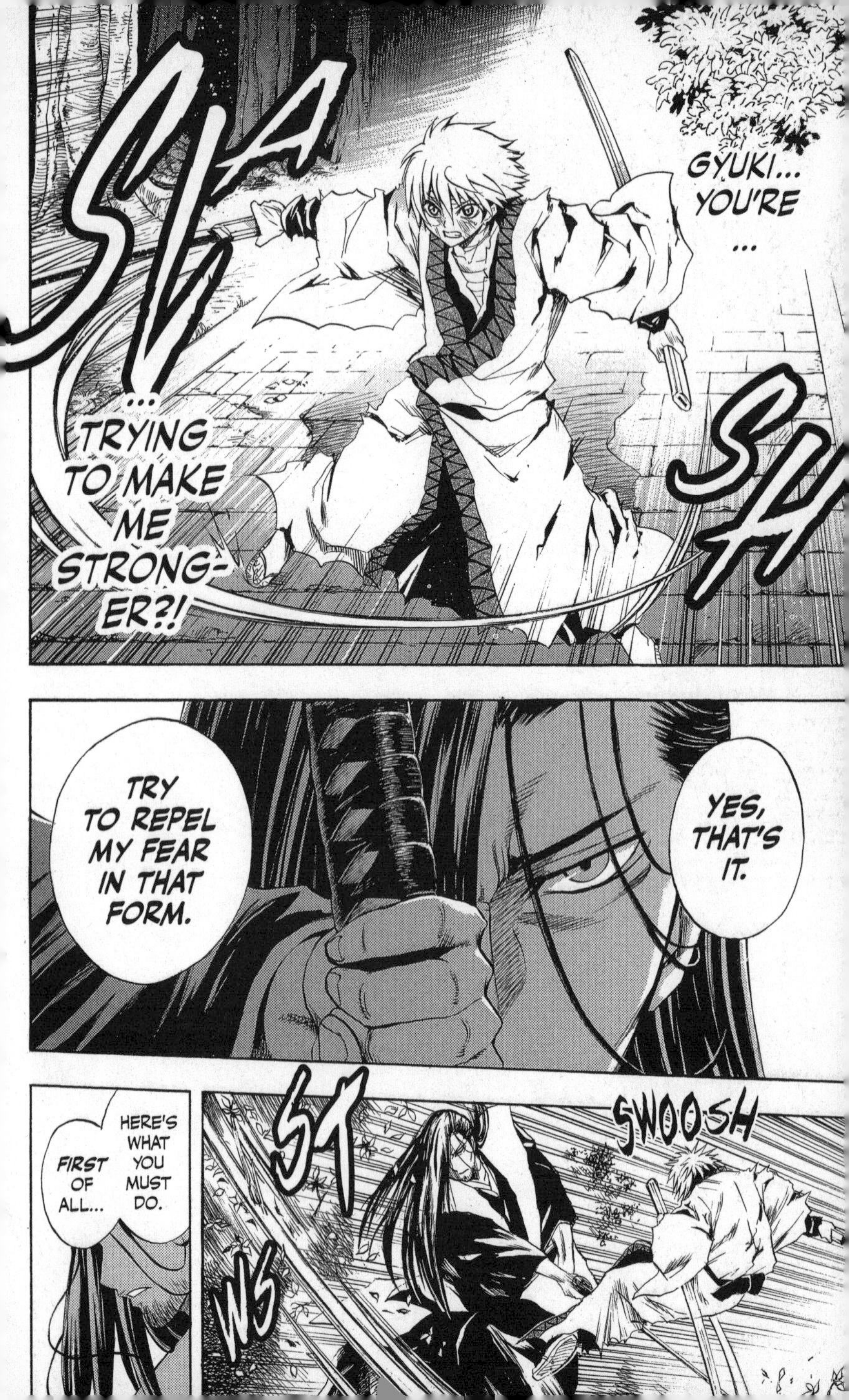
GYUKI... YOU'RE ...
SHA
SH
... TRYING TO MAKE ME STRONGER?!
YES, THAT'S IT.
TRY TO REPEL MY FEAR IN THAT FORM.
SWOOSH
ST
WS
HERE'S WHAT YOU MUST DO.
FIRST OF ALL...

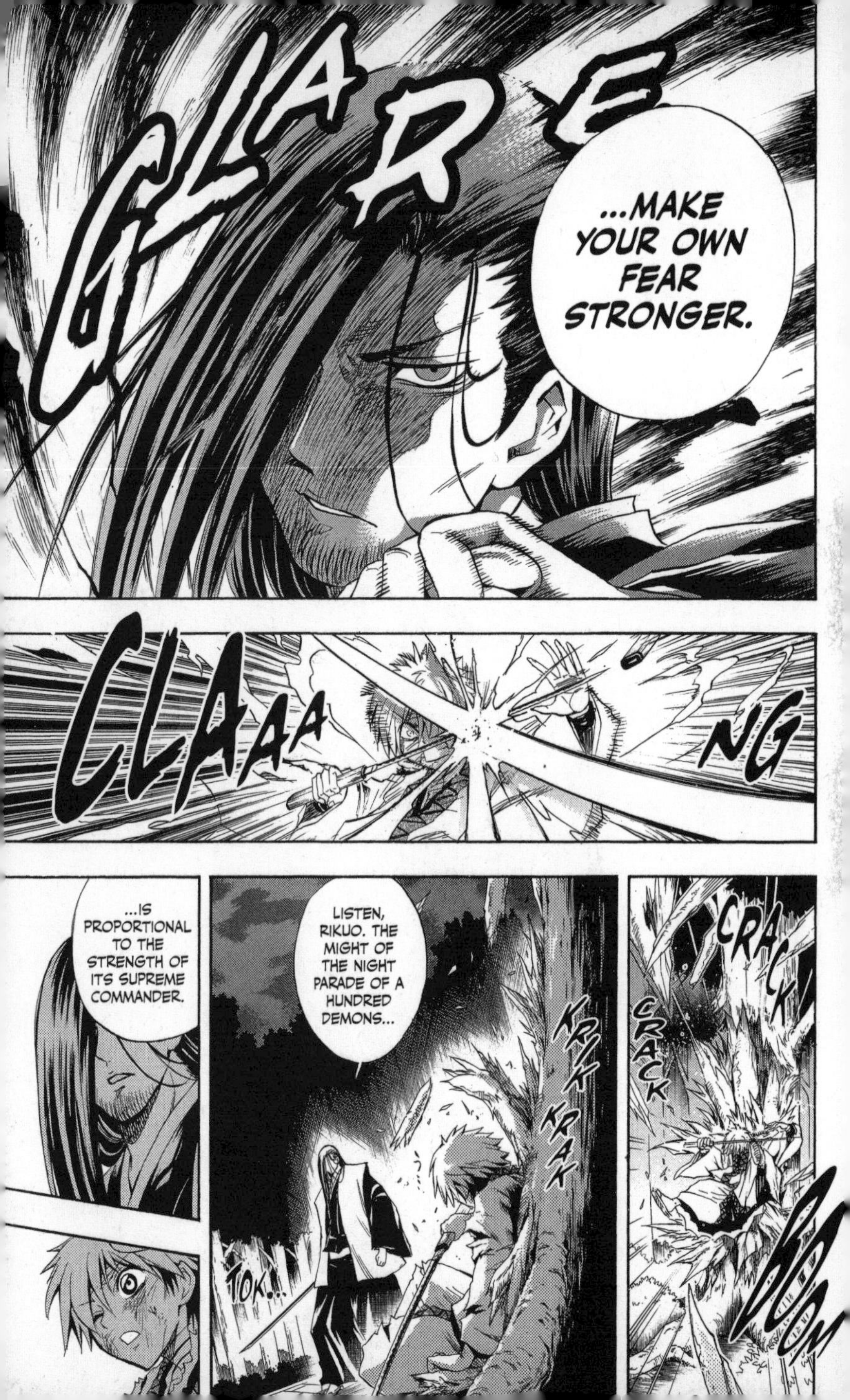
GLARE
...MAKE YOUR OWN FEAR STRONGER.
CLAAAANG
CRACK
CRACK
LISTEN, RIKUO. THE MIGHT OF THE NIGHT PARADE OF A HUNDRED DEMONS...
KRIK KRAK
TOK...
...IS PROPORTIONAL TO THE STRENGTH OF ITS SUPREME COMMANDER.

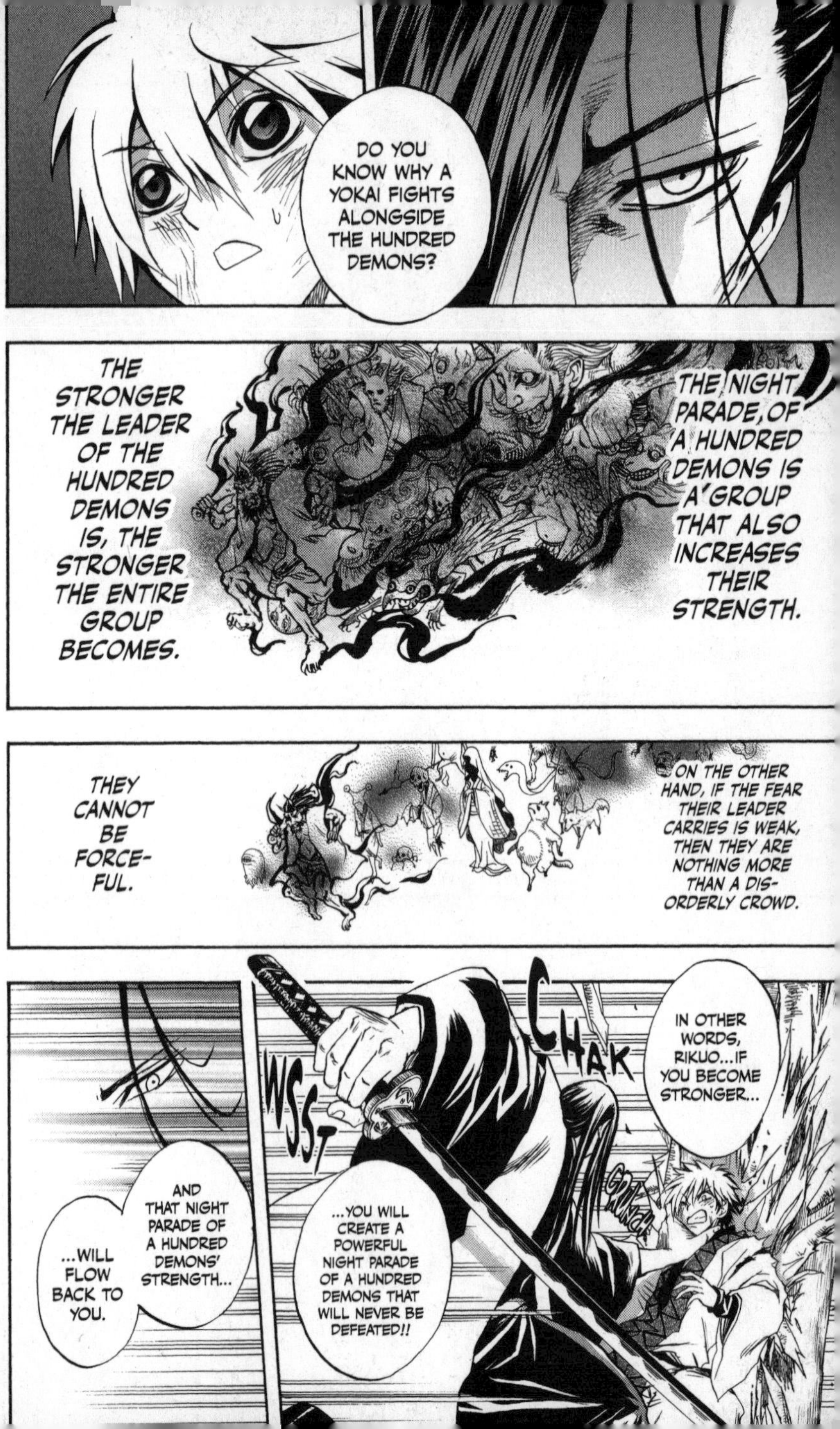
DO YOU KNOW WHY A YOKAI FIGHTS ALONGSIDE THE HUNDRED DEMONS?
THE NIGHT PARADE OF A HUNDRED DEMONS IS A GROUP THAT ALSO INCREASES THEIR STRENGTH.
THE STRONGER THE LEADER OF THE HUNDRED DEMONS IS, THE STRONGER THE ENTIRE GROUP BECOMES.
ON THE OTHER HAND, IF THE FEAR THEIR LEADER CARRIES IS WEAK, THEN THEY ARE NOTHING MORE THAN A DIS-ORDERLY CROWD.
THEY CANNOT BE FORCE-FUL.
CHAK
IN OTHER WORDS, RIKUO...IF YOU BECOME STRONGER...
WSST
...YOU WILL CREATE A POWERFUL NIGHT PARADE OF A HUNDRED DEMONS THAT WILL NEVER BE DEFEATED!!
AND THAT NIGHT PARADE OF A HUNDRED DEMONS' STRENGTH...
...WILL FLOW BACK TO YOU.

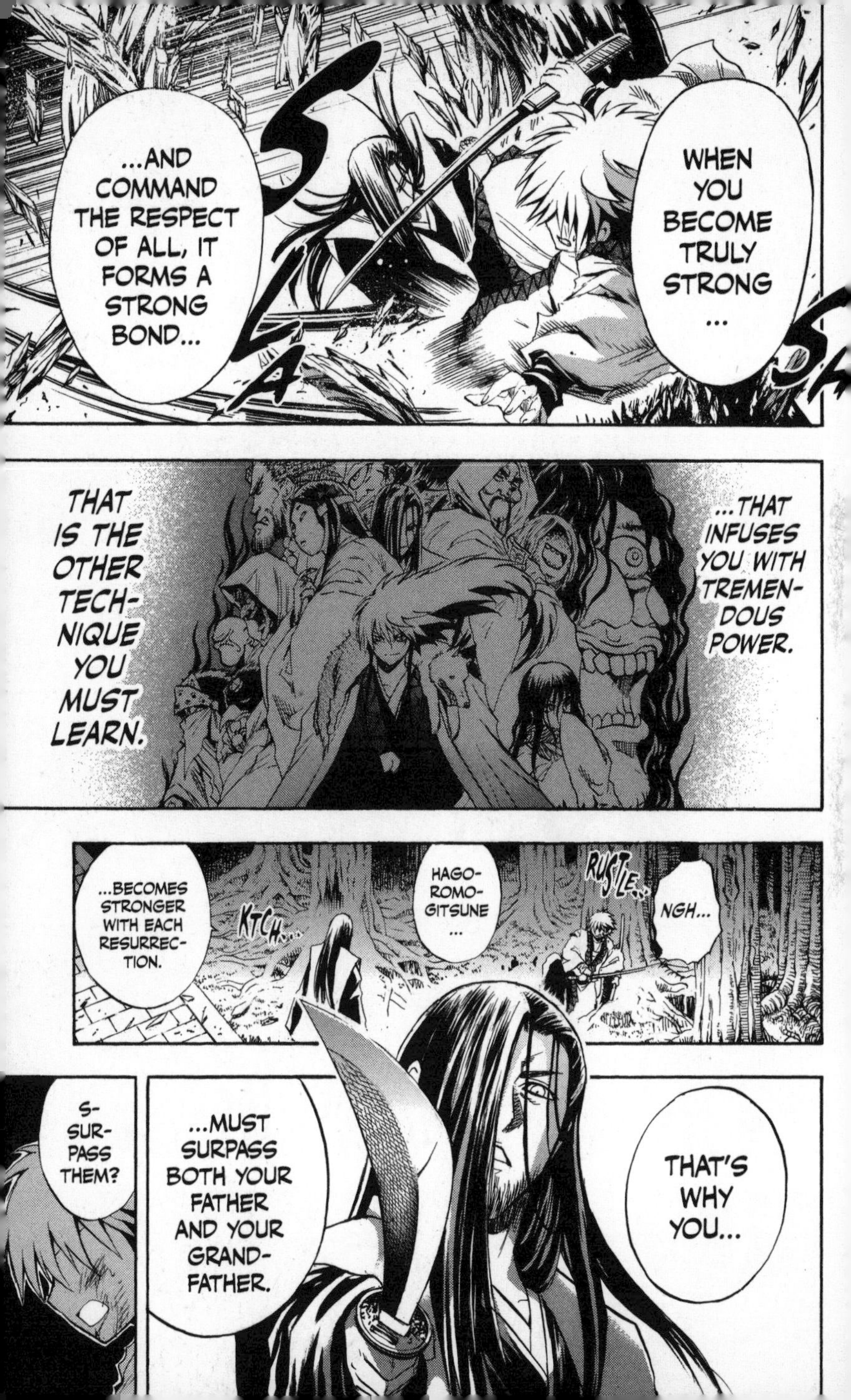
WHEN YOU BECOME TRULY STRONG...
...AND COMMAND THE RESPECT OF ALL, IT FORMS A STRONG BOND...
...THAT INFUSES YOU WITH TREMENDOUS POWER.
THAT IS THE OTHER TECHNIQUE YOU MUST LEARN.
NGH...
RUSTLE...
HAGOROMO-GITSUNE...
KTCH...
...BECOMES STRONGER WITH EACH RESURRECTION.
THAT'S WHY YOU...
...MUST SURPASS BOTH YOUR FATHER AND YOUR GRANDFATHER.
S-SURPASS THEM?

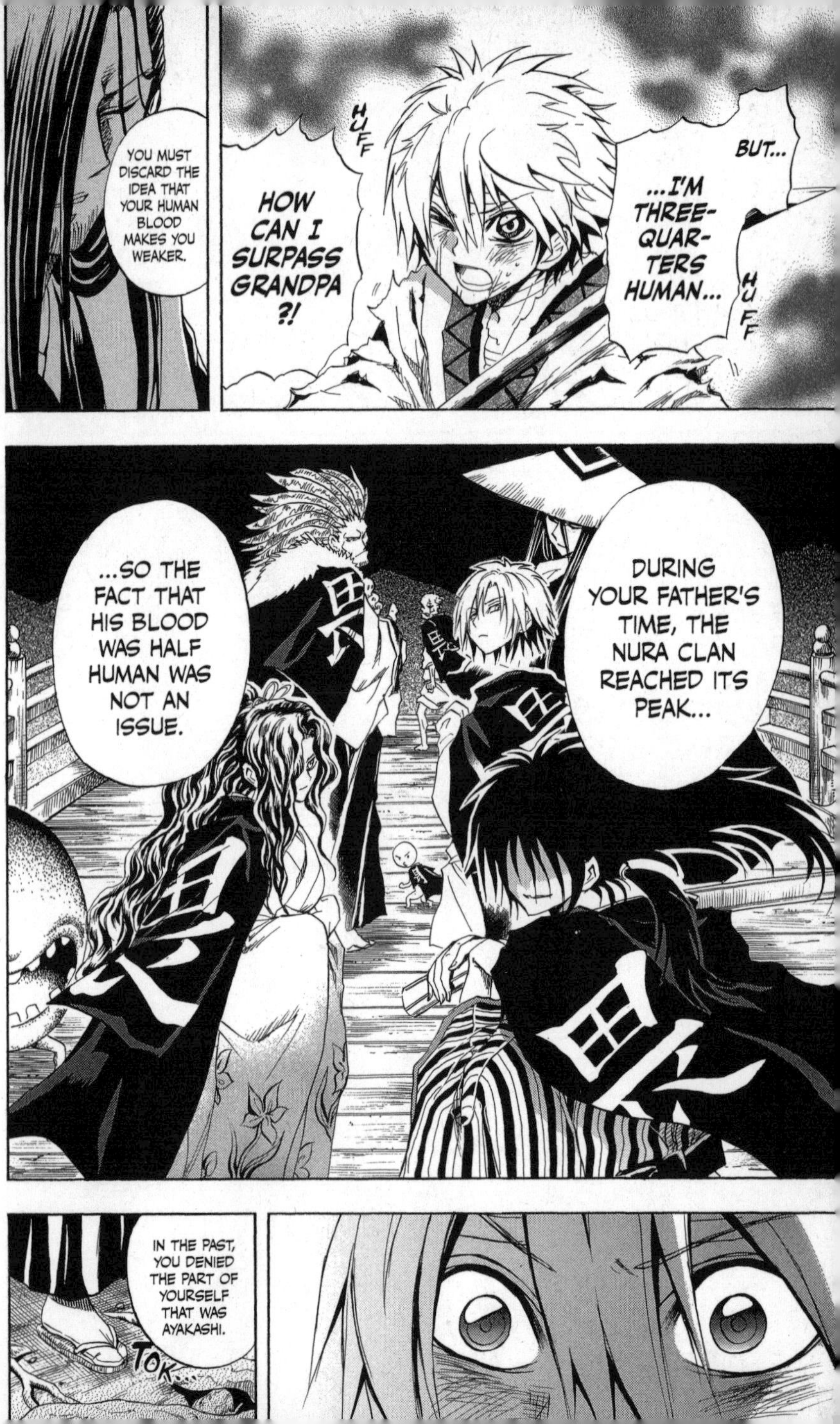
BUT...
...I'M THREE-QUARTERS HUMAN...
HUFF
HUFF
HOW CAN I SURPASS GRANDPA?!
YOU MUST DISCARD THE IDEA THAT YOUR HUMAN BLOOD MAKES YOU WEAKER.
DURING YOUR FATHER'S TIME, THE NURA CLAN REACHED ITS PEAK...
...SO THE FACT THAT HIS BLOOD WAS HALF HUMAN WAS NOT AN ISSUE.
IN THE PAST, YOU DENIED THE PART OF YOURSELF THAT WAS AYAKASHI.
TOK...

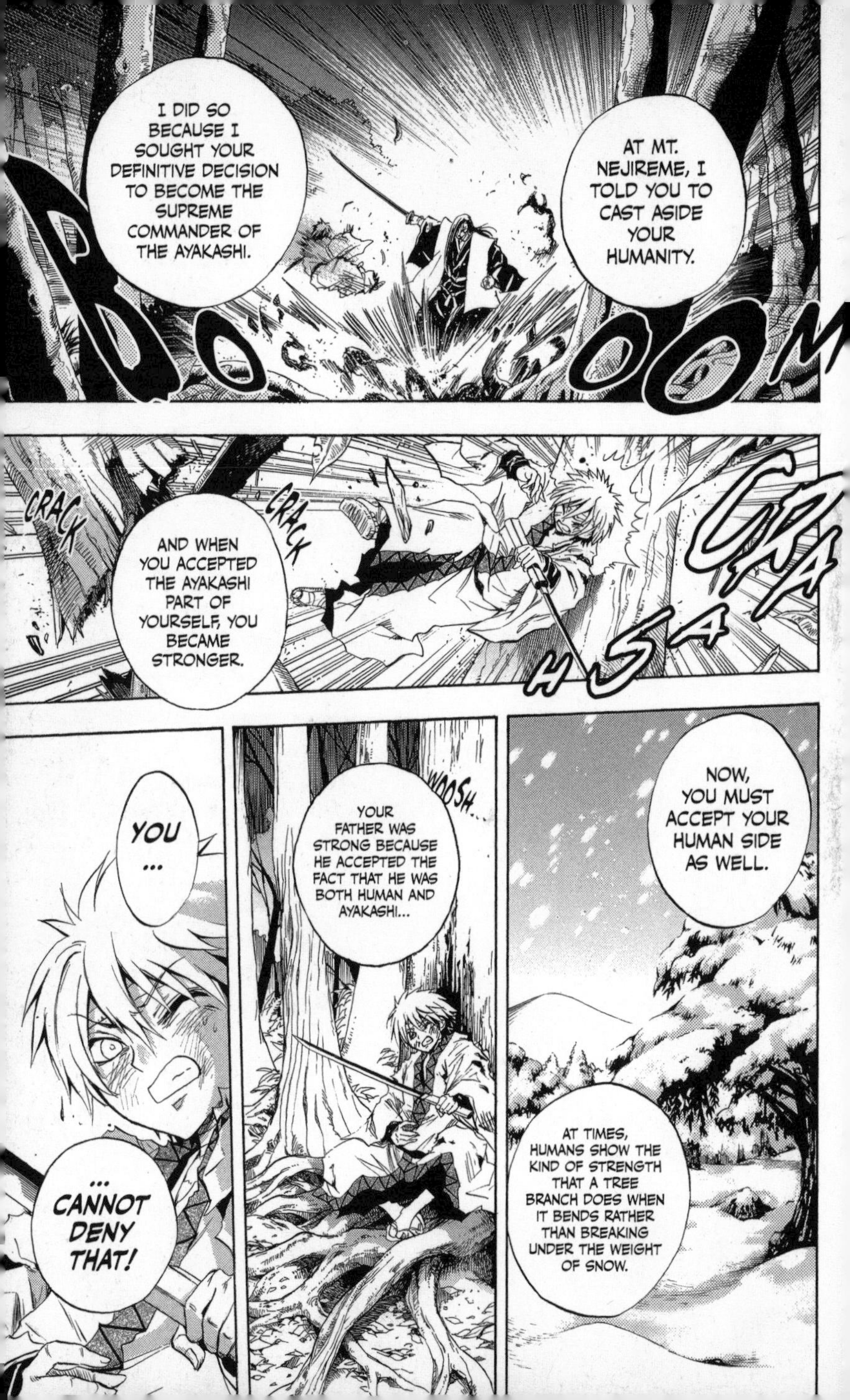

AT MT. NEJIREME, I TOLD YOU TO CAST ASIDE YOUR HUMANITY.
I DID SO BECAUSE I SOUGHT YOUR DEFINITIVE DECISION TO BECOME THE SUPREME COMMANDER OF THE AYAKASHI.
BOOOOOM
CRACK
AND WHEN YOU ACCEPTED THE AYAKASHI PART OF YOURSELF, YOU BECAME STRONGER.
CRACK
NOW, YOU MUST ACCEPT YOUR HUMAN SIDE AS WELL.
AT TIMES, HUMANS SHOW THE KIND OF STRENGTH THAT A TREE BRANCH DOES WHEN IT BENDS RATHER THAN BREAKING UNDER THE WEIGHT OF SNOW.
WOOSH...
YOUR FATHER WAS STRONG BECAUSE HE ACCEPTED THE FACT THAT HE WAS BOTH HUMAN AND AYAKASHI...
YOU ...
... CANNOT DENY THAT!

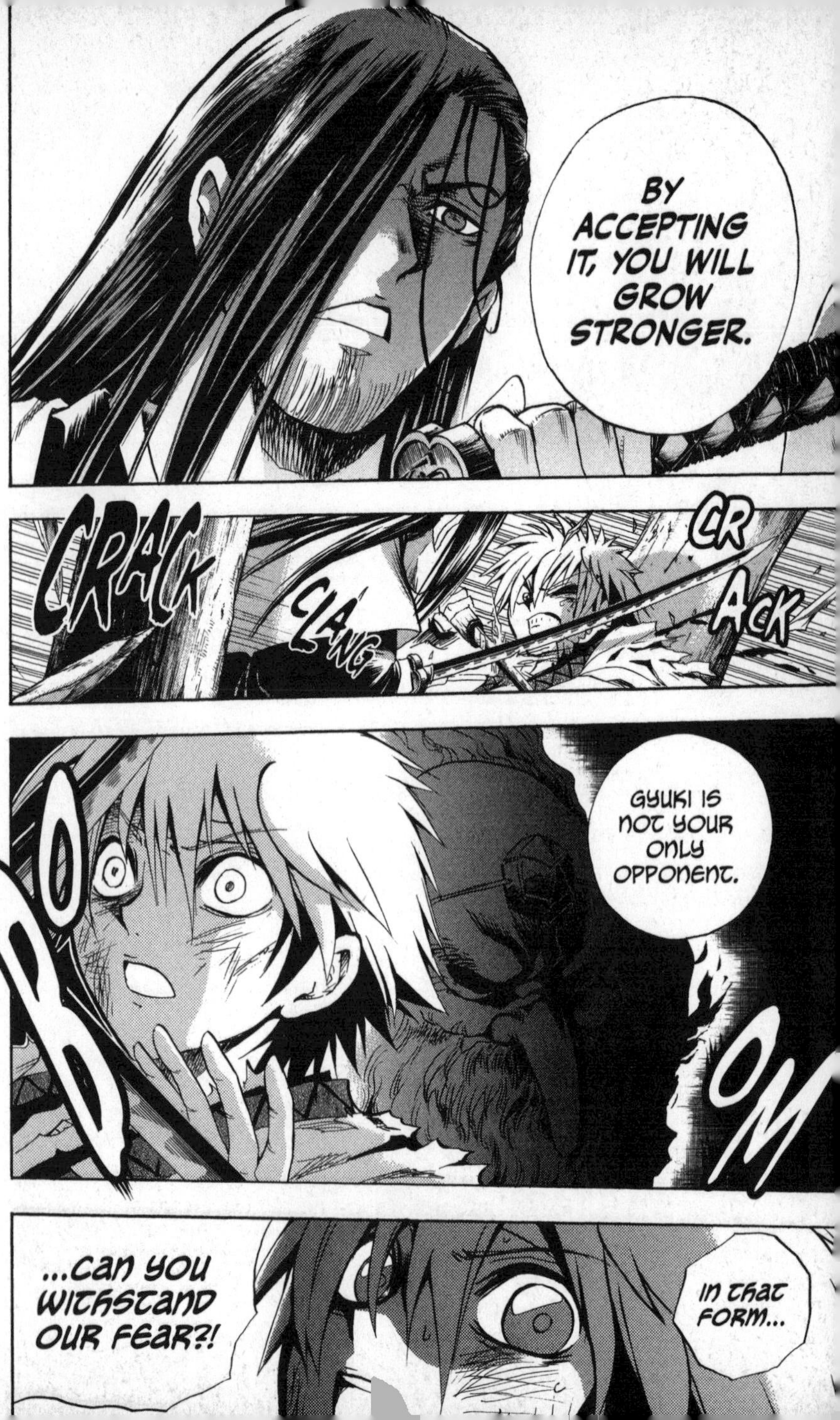
BY ACCEPTING IT, YOU WILL GROW STRONGER.
CR ACK
CLANG
CRACK
GYUKI IS NOT YOUR ONLY OPPONENT.
IN THAT FORM...
...CAN YOU WITHSTAND OUR FEAR?!

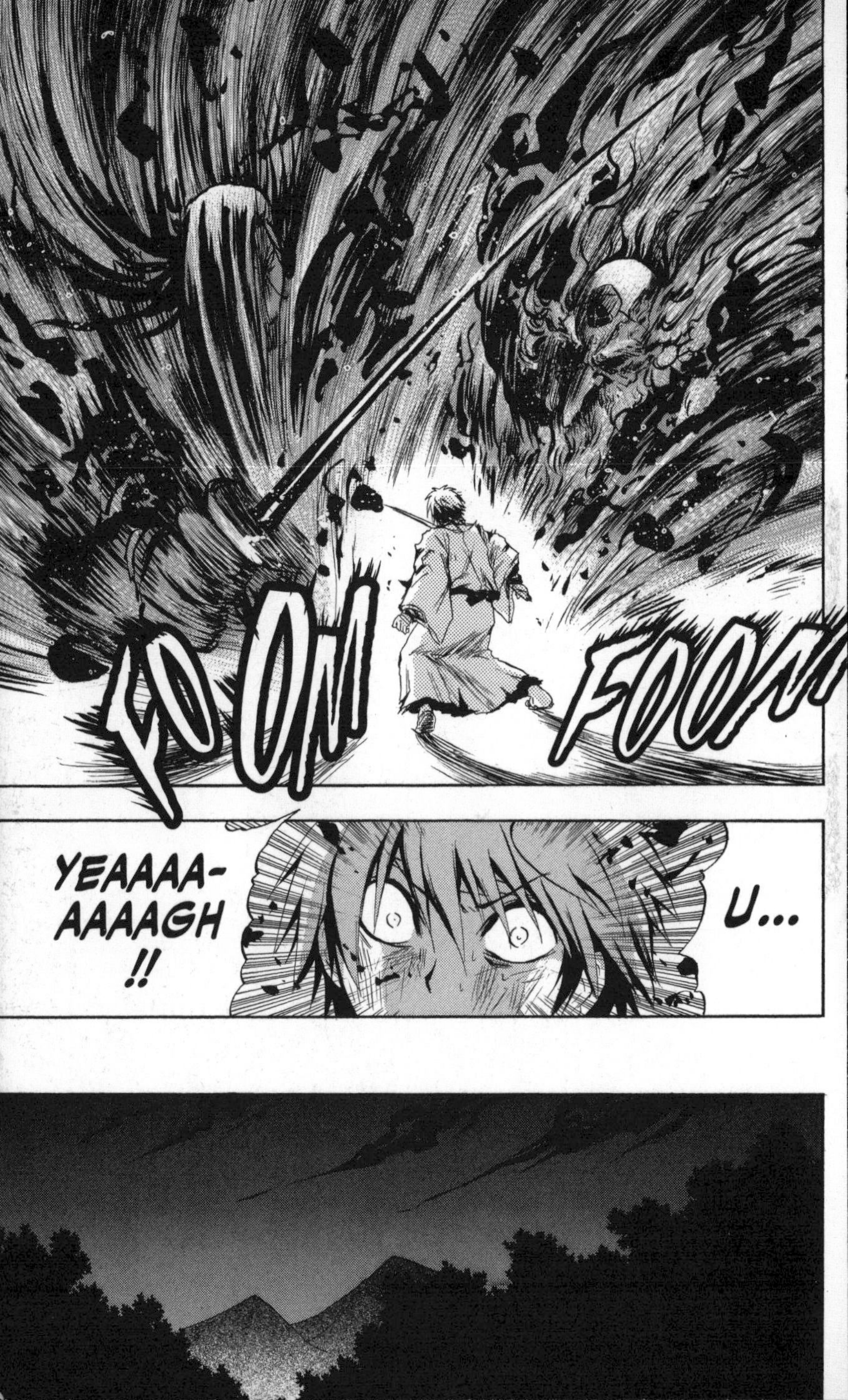
FOOM
ZOOM
U...
YEAAAA-AAAAGH!!

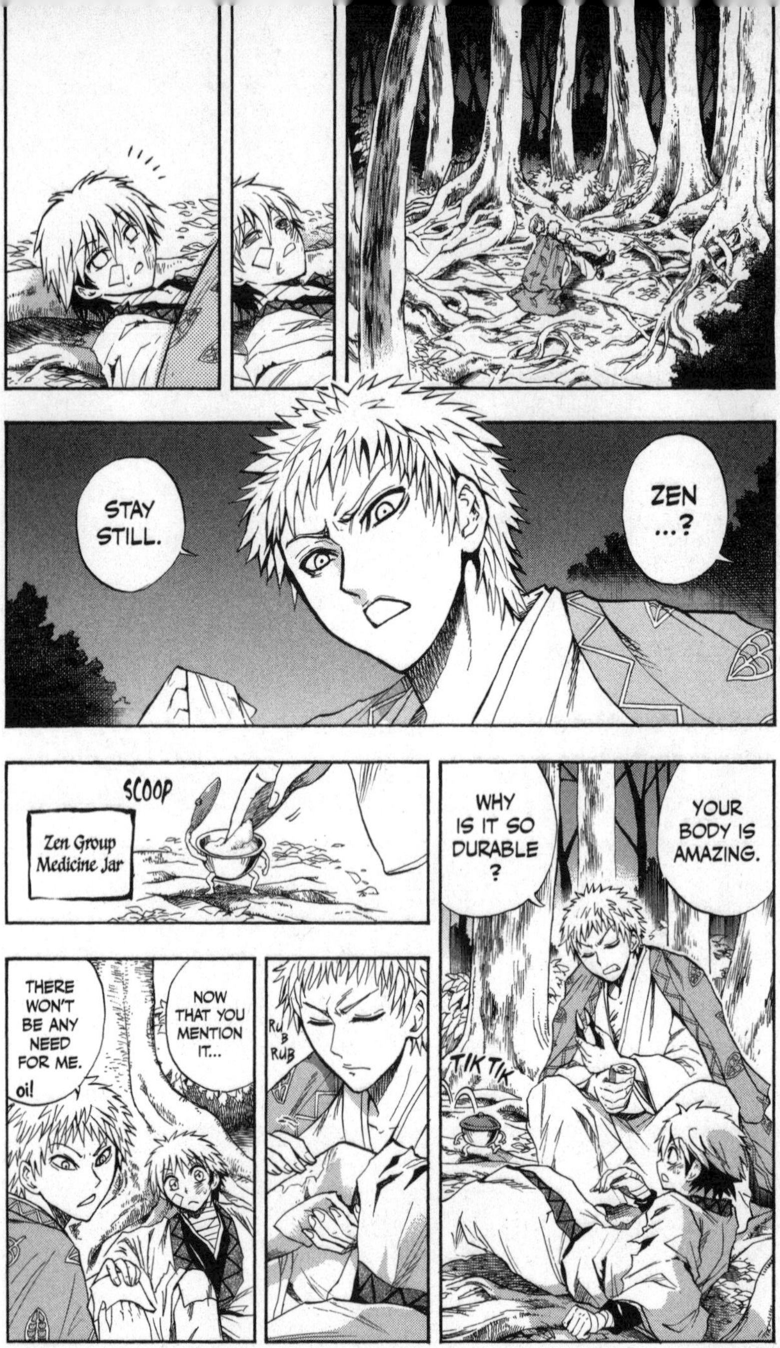
ZEN ...?
STAY STILL.
YOUR BODY IS AMAZING.
WHY IS IT SO DURABLE ?
TIKTIK
SCOOP
Zen Group Medicine Jar
RuB RUB
NOW THAT YOU MENTION IT...
THERE WON'T BE ANY NEED FOR ME.
oi!

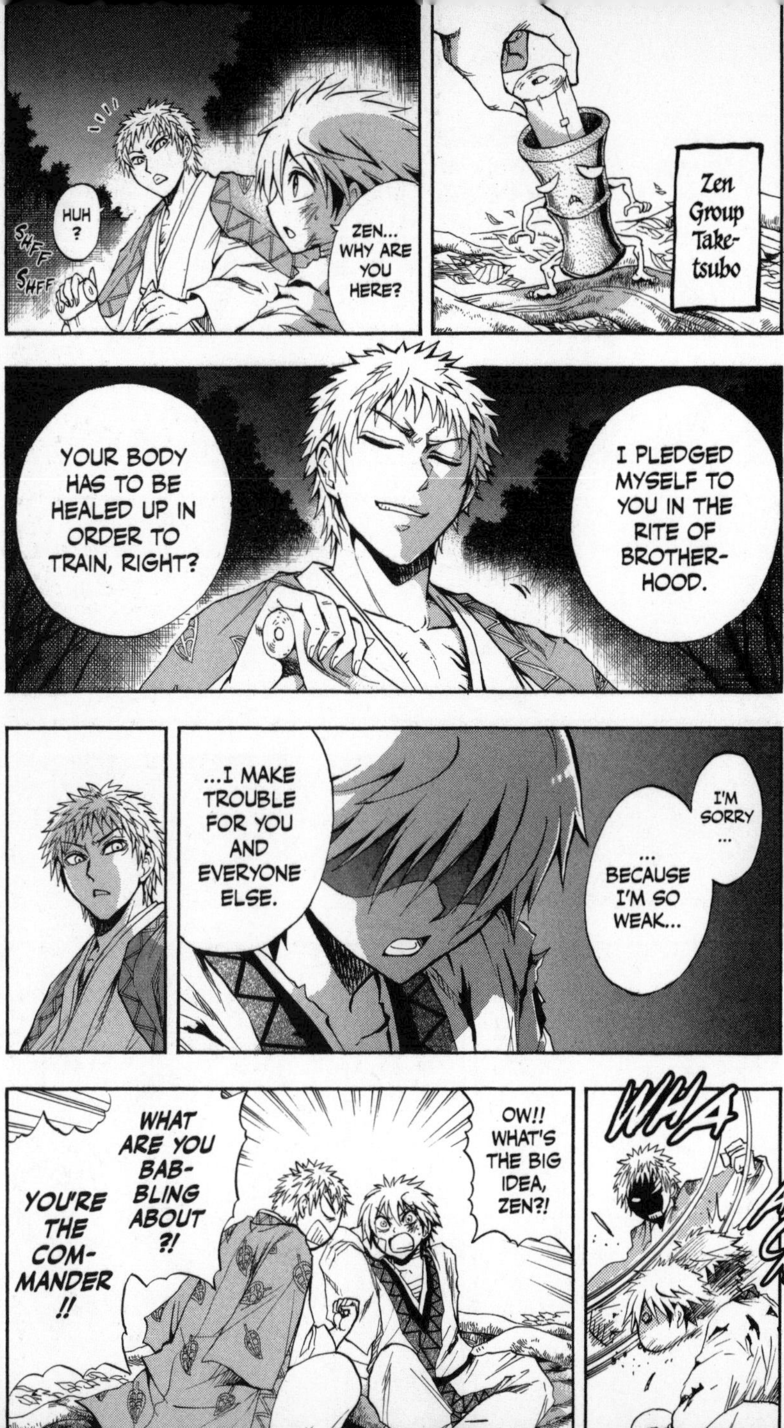
Zen Group Take-tsubo
ZEN... WHY ARE YOU HERE?
HUH ?
SHFF SHFF
I PLEDGED MYSELF TO YOU IN THE RITE OF BROTHER-HOOD.
YOUR BODY HAS TO BE HEALED UP IN ORDER TO TRAIN, RIGHT?
I'M SORRY ...
... BECAUSE I'M SO WEAK...
...I MAKE TROUBLE FOR YOU AND EVERYONE ELSE.
WHA
ACK
OW!! WHAT'S THE BIG IDEA, ZEN?!
WHAT ARE YOU BAB-BLING ABOUT ?!
YOU'RE THE COM-MANDER !!

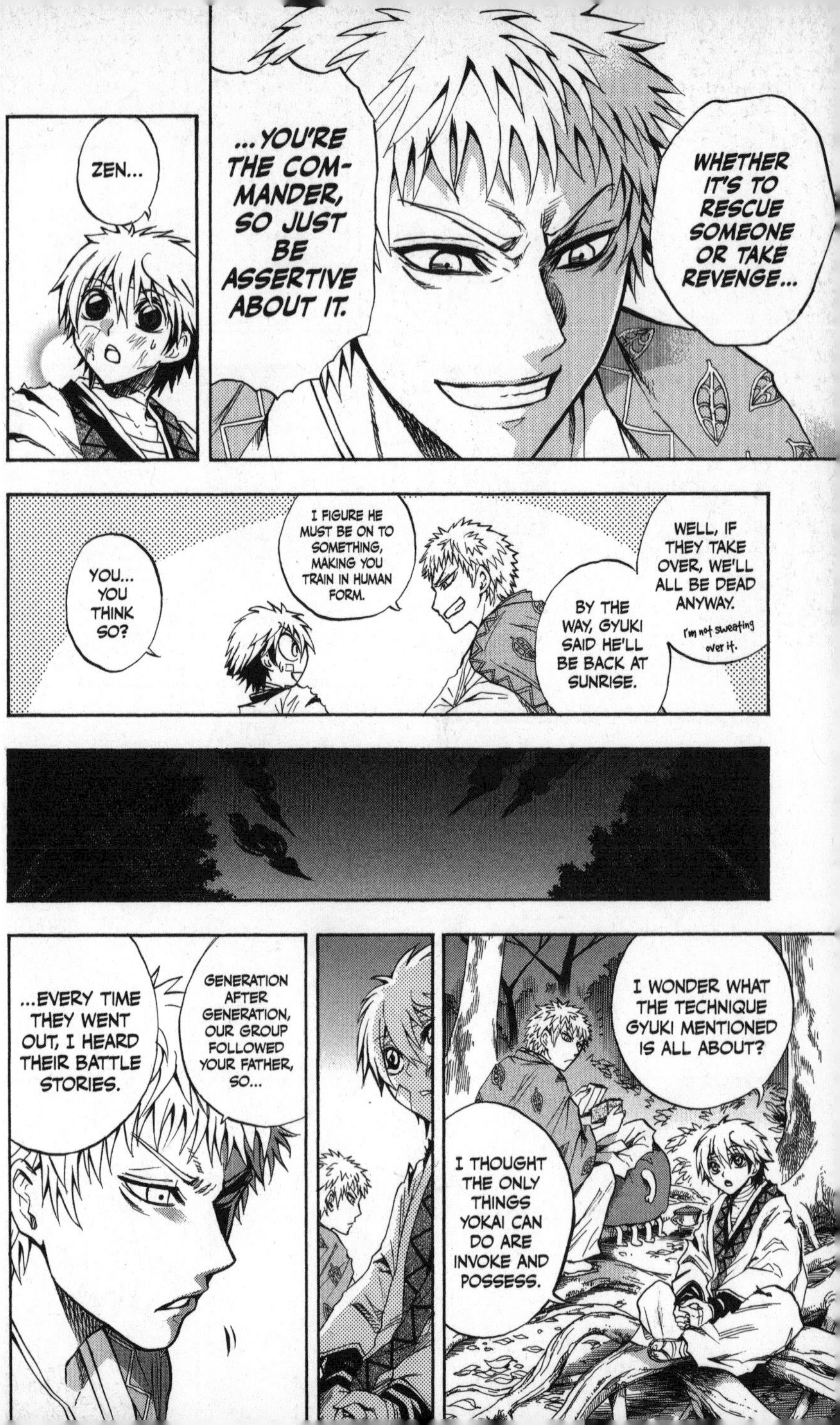
WHETHER IT'S TO RESCUE SOMEONE OR TAKE REVENGE...
...YOU'RE THE COM-MANDER, SO JUST BE ASSERTIVE ABOUT IT.
ZEN...
WELL, IF THEY TAKE OVER, WE'LL ALL BE DEAD ANYWAY.
I'm not sweating over it.
BY THE WAY, GYUKI SAID HE'LL BE BACK AT SUNRISE.
I FIGURE HE MUST BE ON TO SOMETHING, MAKING YOU TRAIN IN HUMAN FORM.
YOU... YOU THINK SO?
I WONDER WHAT THE TECHNIQUE GYUKI MENTIONED IS ALL ABOUT?
I THOUGHT THE ONLY THINGS YOKAI CAN DO ARE INVOKE AND POSSESS.
GENERATION AFTER GENERATION, OUR GROUP FOLLOWED YOUR FATHER, SO...
...EVERY TIME THEY WENT OUT, I HEARD THEIR BATTLE STORIES.

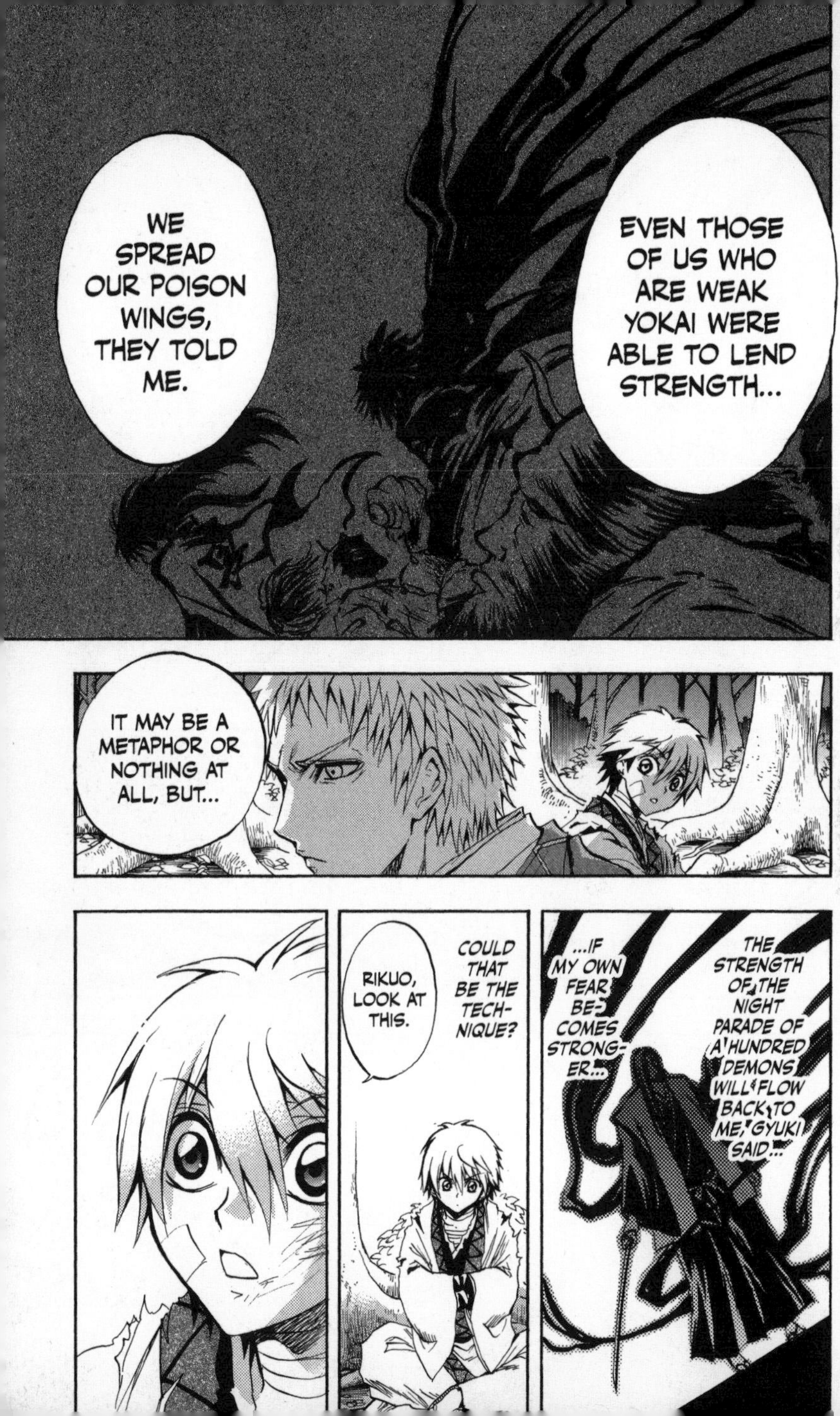

EVEN THOSE OF US WHO ARE WEAK YOKAI WERE ABLE TO LEND STRENGTH...
WE SPREAD OUR POISON WINGS, THEY TOLD ME.
IT MAY BE A METAPHOR OR NOTHING AT ALL, BUT...
THE STRENGTH OF THE NIGHT PARADE OF A HUNDRED DEMONS WILL FLOW BACK TO ME, GYUKI SAID...
...IF MY OWN FEAR BE-COMES STRONG-ER...
COULD THAT BE THE TECH-NIQUE?
RIKUO, LOOK AT THIS.

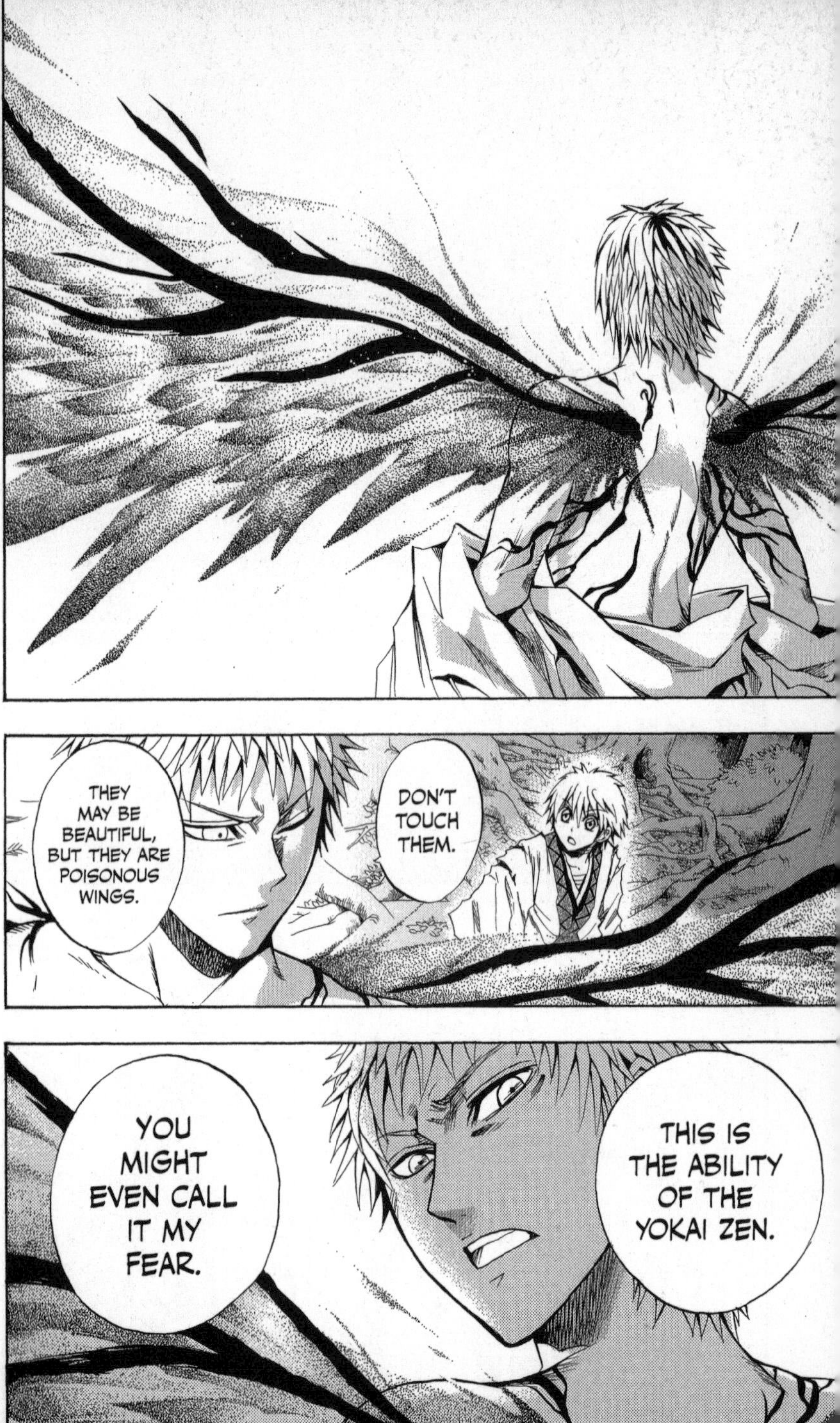
DON'T TOUCH THEM.
THEY MAY BE BEAUTIFUL, BUT THEY ARE POISONOUS WINGS.
THIS IS THE ABILITY OF THE YOKAI ZEN.
YOU MIGHT EVEN CALL IT MY FEAR.

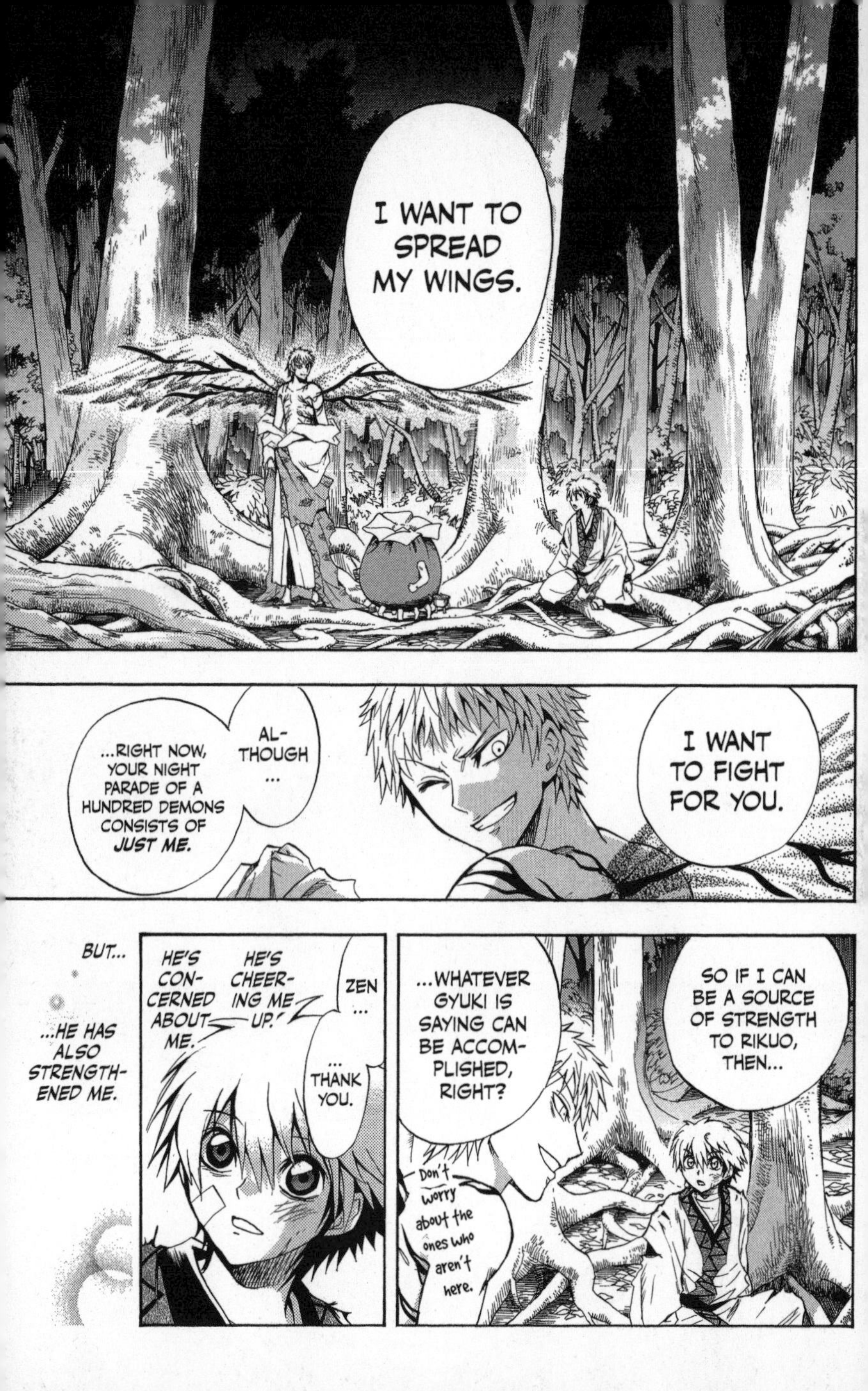
I WANT TO SPREAD MY WINGS.
I WANT TO FIGHT FOR YOU.
AL-THOUGH...
...RIGHT NOW, YOUR NIGHT PARADE OF A HUNDRED DEMONS CONSISTS OF JUST ME.
SO IF I CAN BE A SOURCE OF STRENGTH TO RIKUO, THEN...
...WHATEVER GYUKI IS SAYING CAN BE ACCOM-PLISHED, RIGHT?
Don't worry about the ones who aren't here.
ZEN...
...THANK YOU.
HE'S CHEER-ING ME UP.
HE'S CON-CERNED ABOUT ME.
BUT...
...HE HAS ALSO STRENGTH-ENED ME.

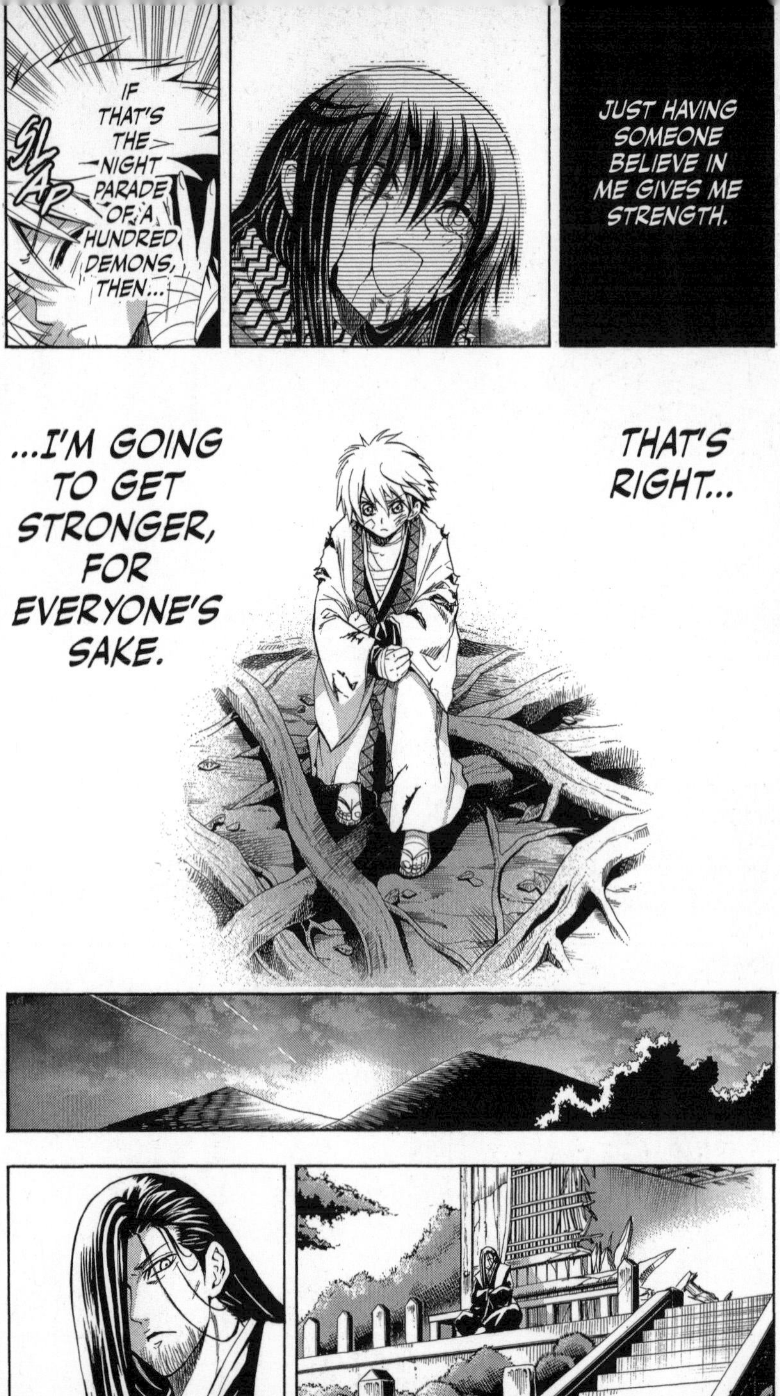
JUST HAVING SOMEONE BELIEVE IN ME GIVES ME STRENGTH.
IF THAT'S THE NIGHT PARADE OF A HUNDRED DEMONS, THEN...
SLAP
THAT'S RIGHT...
...I'M GOING TO GET STRONGER, FOR EVERYONE'S SAKE.

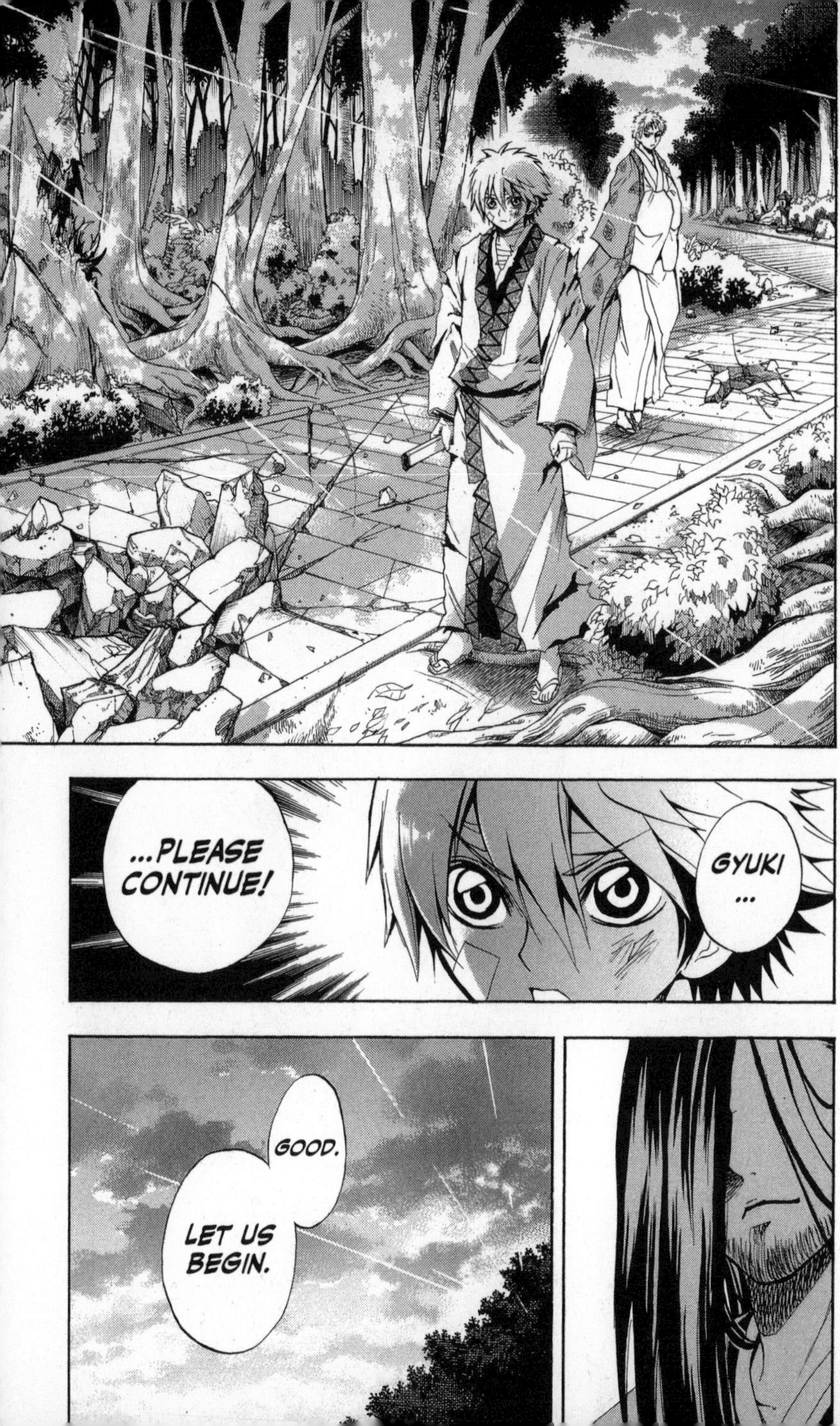
GYUKI ...
...PLEASE CONTINUE!
GOOD.
LET US BEGIN.

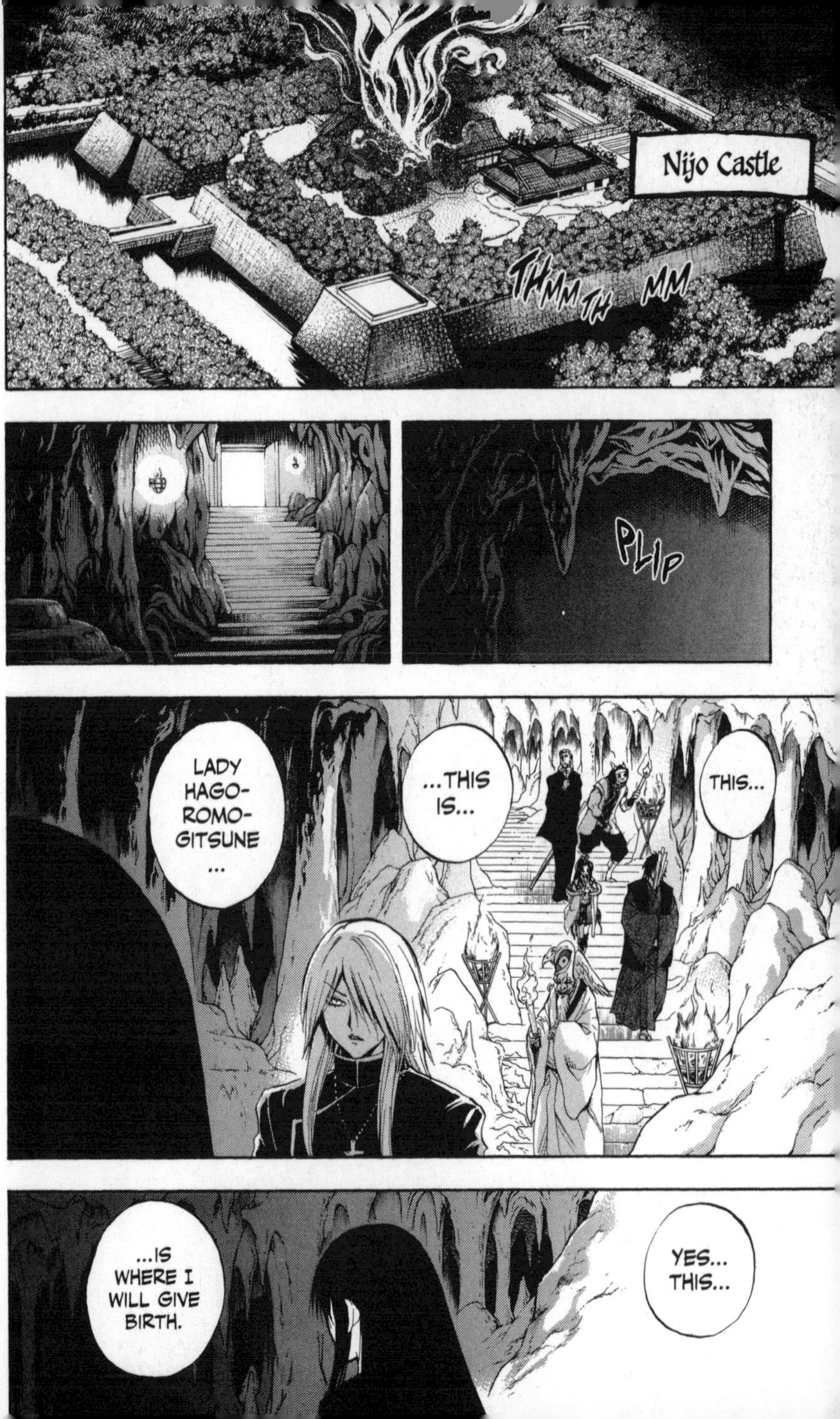
Nijo Castle
THMM TH MM
PLIP
THIS...
...THIS IS...
LADY HAGO-ROMO-GITSUNE...
YES... THIS...
...IS WHERE I WILL GIVE BIRTH.

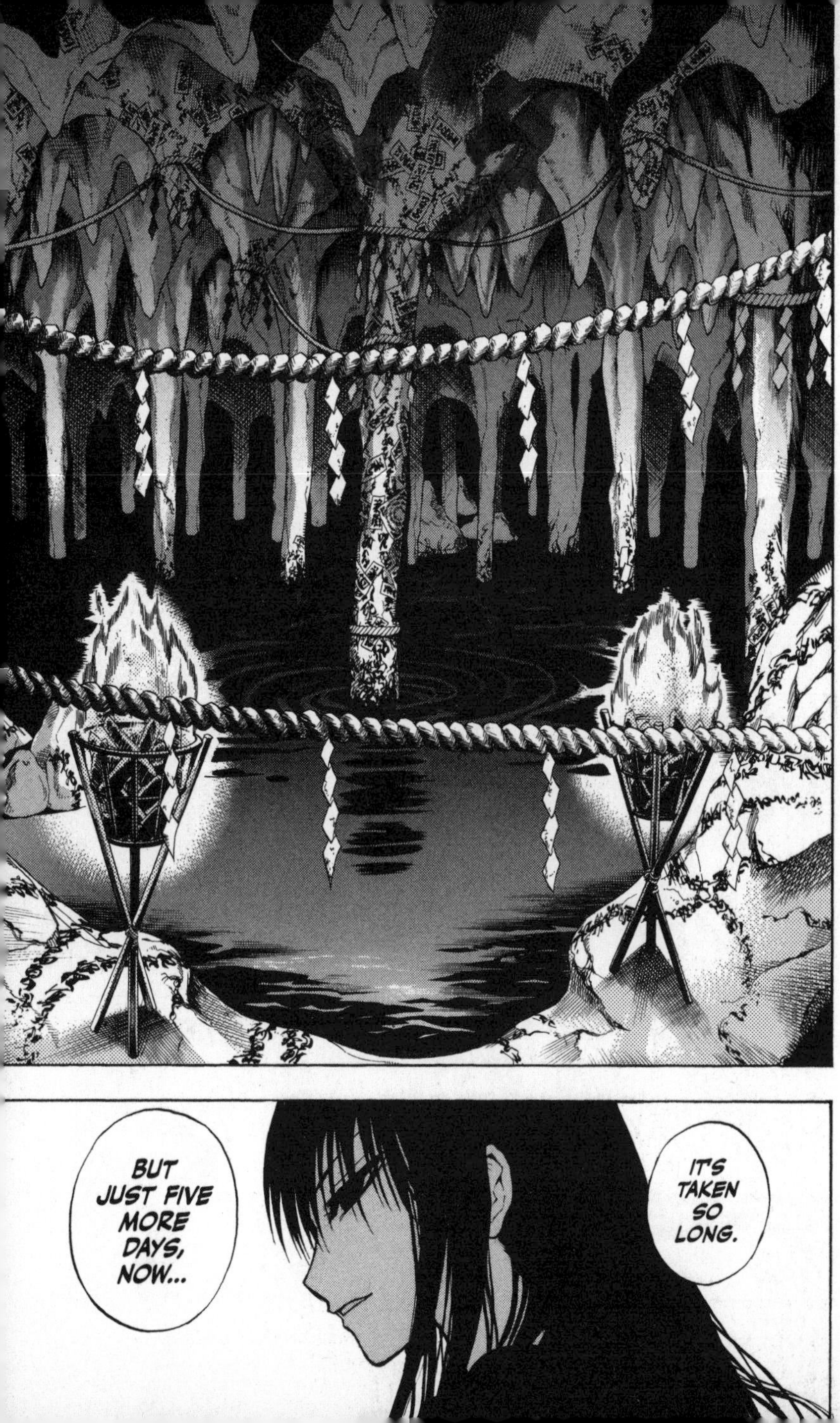
IT'S TAKEN SO LONG.
BUT JUST FIVE MORE DAYS, NOW...

The Return

Special 4 HAGOROMOMOMO

By Kana Yoshimura

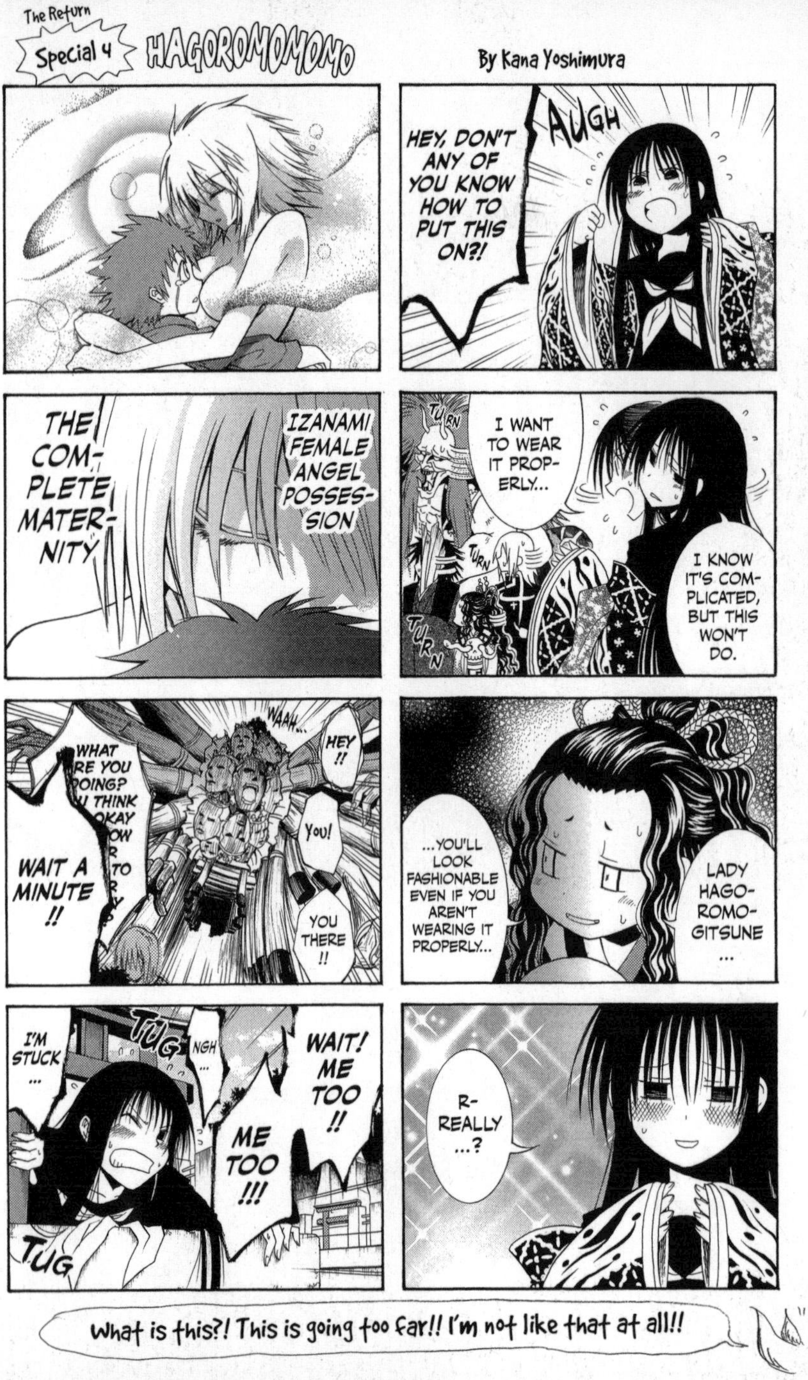
AUGH
HEY, DON'T ANY OF YOU KNOW HOW TO PUT THIS ON?!
TURN
TURN
TURN
I WANT TO WEAR IT PROPERLY...
I KNOW IT'S COMPLICATED, BUT THIS WON'T DO.
IZANAMI FEMALE ANGEL POSSESSION
THE COMPLETE MATERNITY
LADY HAGOROMO-GITSUNE...
...YOU'LL LOOK FASHIONABLE EVEN IF YOU AREN'T WEARING IT PROPERLY...
WAAH...
HEY!!
You!
YOU THERE!!
WAIT A MINUTE!!
R-REALLY...?
WAIT! ME TOO!!
ME TOO!!!
NGH...
TUG
I'M STUCK...
TUG

What is this?! This is going too far!! I'm not like that at all!!

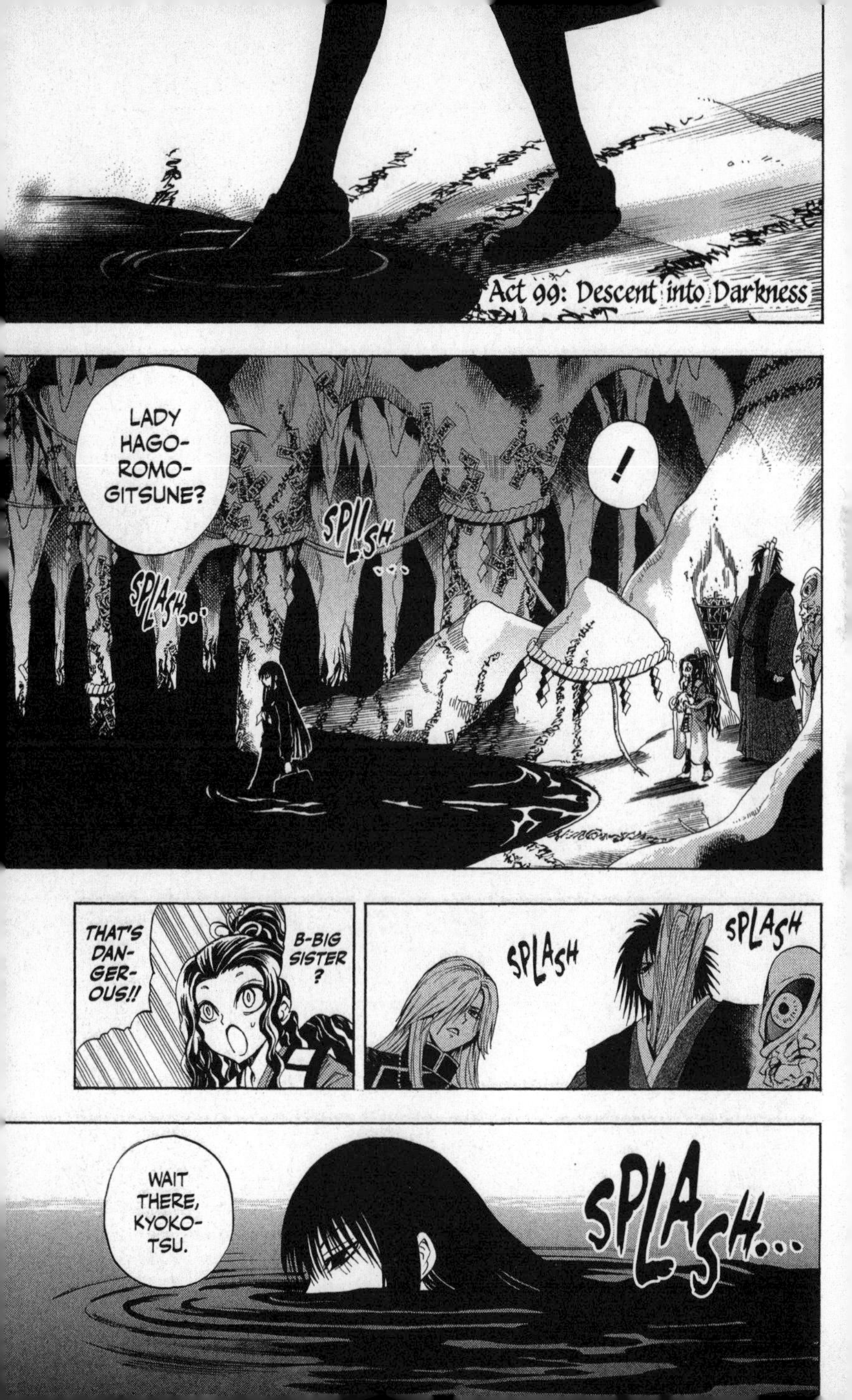
Act 99: Descent into Darkness
!
LADY HAGO-ROMO-GITSUNE?
SPLISH
SPLASH
SPLASH
SPLASH
B-BIG SISTER?
THAT'S DAN-GER-OUS!!
SPLASH...
WAIT THERE, KYOKO-TSU.

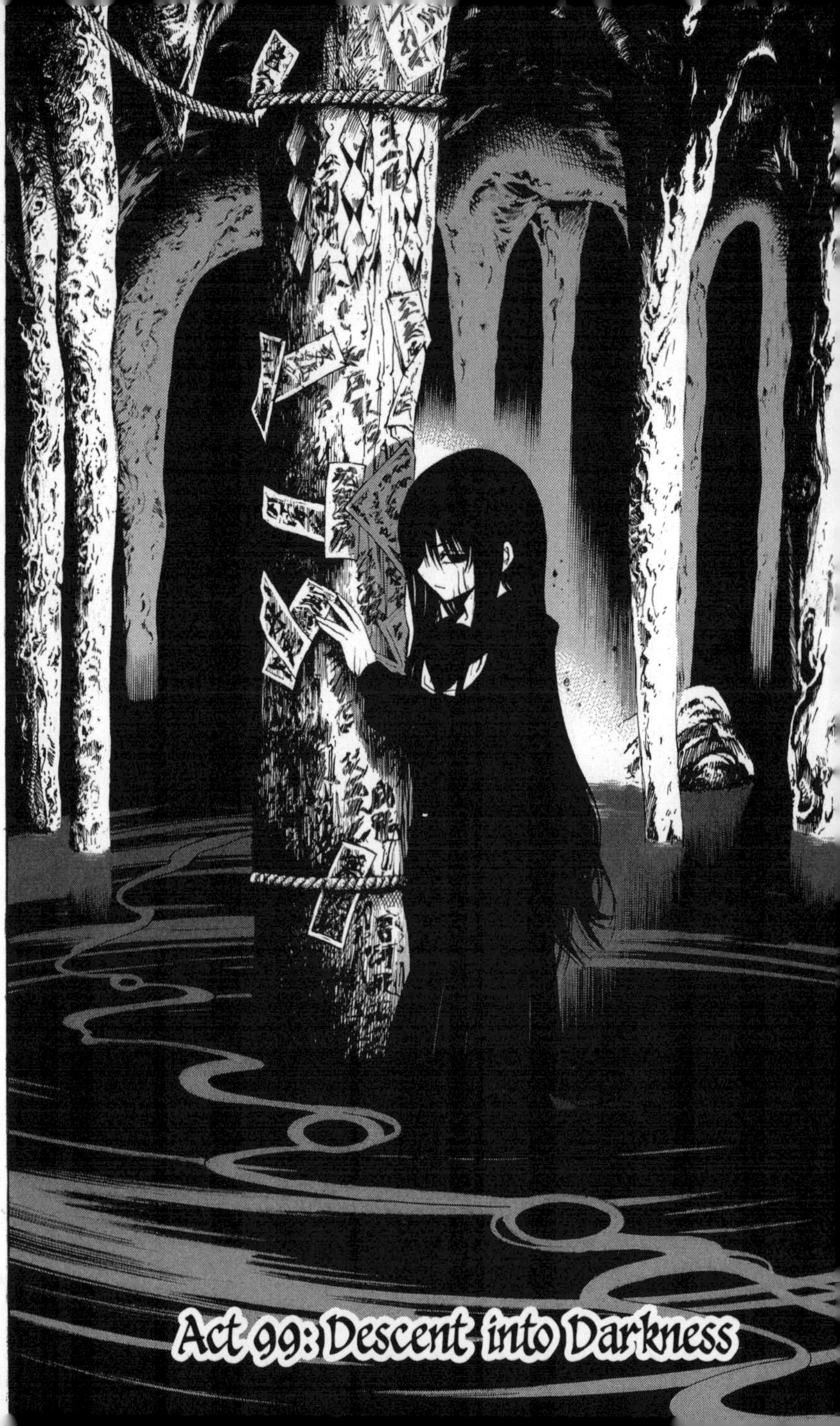
Act 99: Descent into Darkness

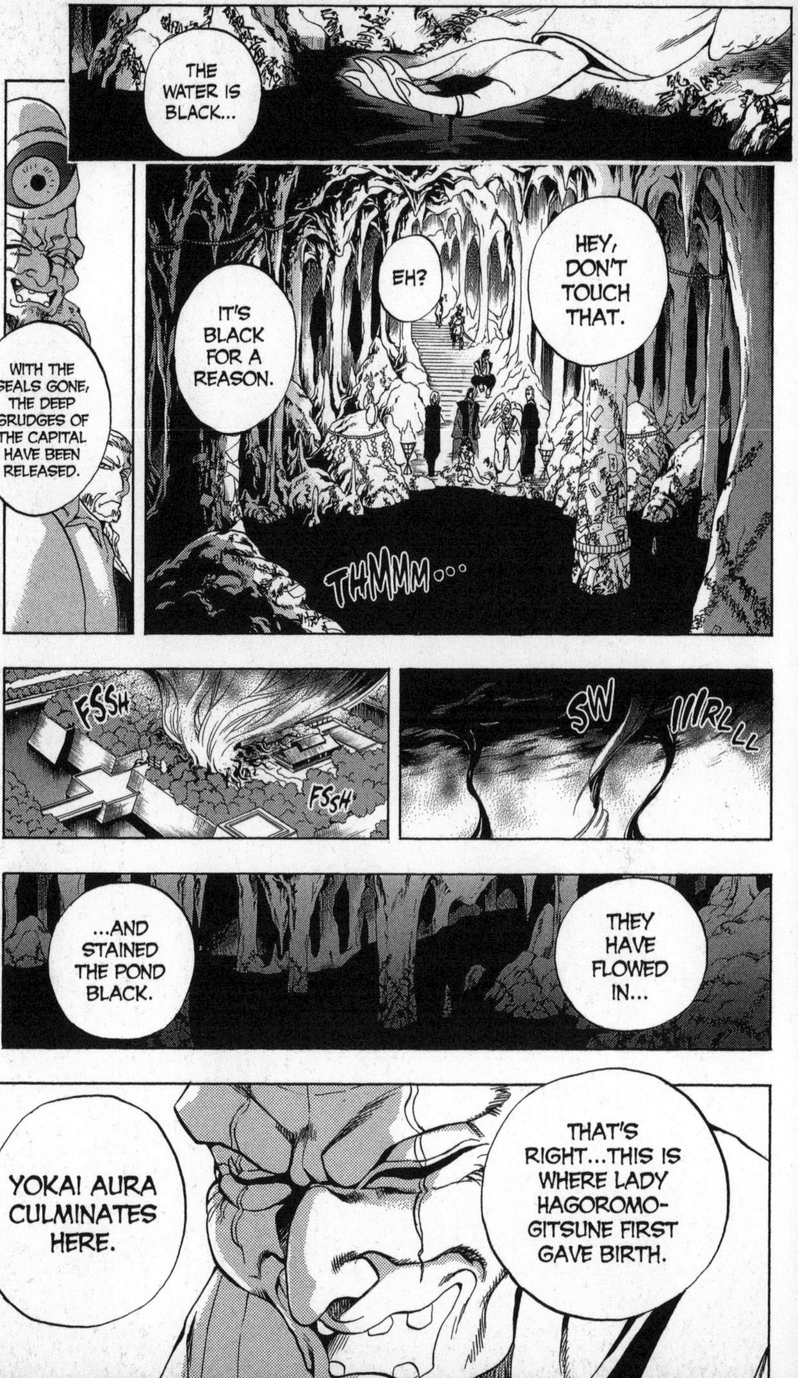
THE WATER IS BLACK...
HEY, DON'T TOUCH THAT.
EH?
IT'S BLACK FOR A REASON.
THMMM...
WITH THE SEALS GONE, THE DEEP GRUDGES OF THE CAPITAL HAVE BEEN RELEASED.
SWIIRLLL
FSSH
FSSH
THEY HAVE FLOWED IN...
...AND STAINED THE POND BLACK.
THAT'S RIGHT...THIS IS WHERE LADY HAGOROMO-GITSUNE FIRST GAVE BIRTH.
YOKAI AURA CULMINATES HERE.

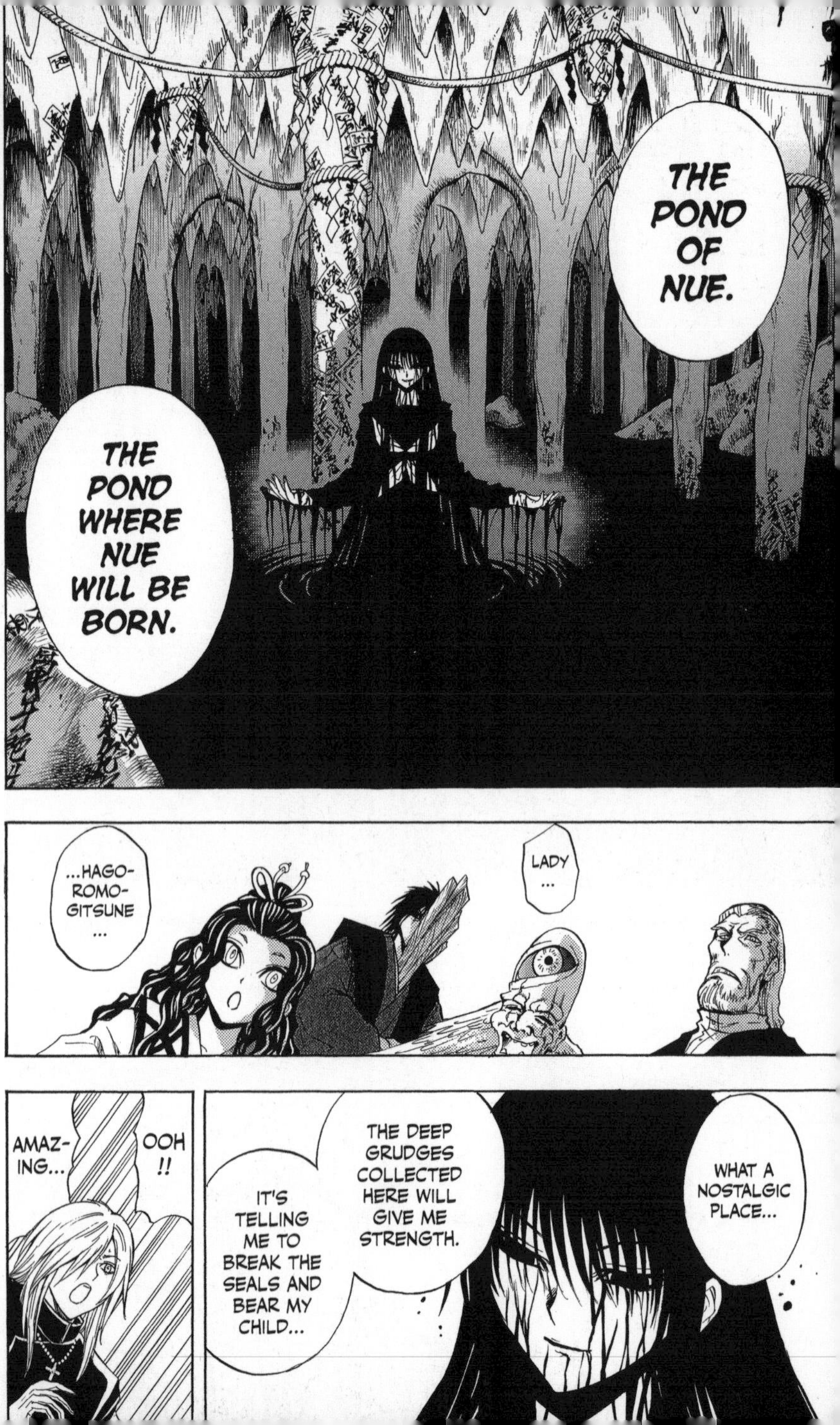
THE POND OF NUE.
THE POND WHERE NUE WILL BE BORN.
LADY ...
...HAGO-ROMO-GITSUNE ...
WHAT A NOSTALGIC PLACE...
THE DEEP GRUDGES COLLECTED HERE WILL GIVE ME STRENGTH.
IT'S TELLING ME TO BREAK THE SEALS AND BEAR MY CHILD...
OOH !!
AMAZ-ING...

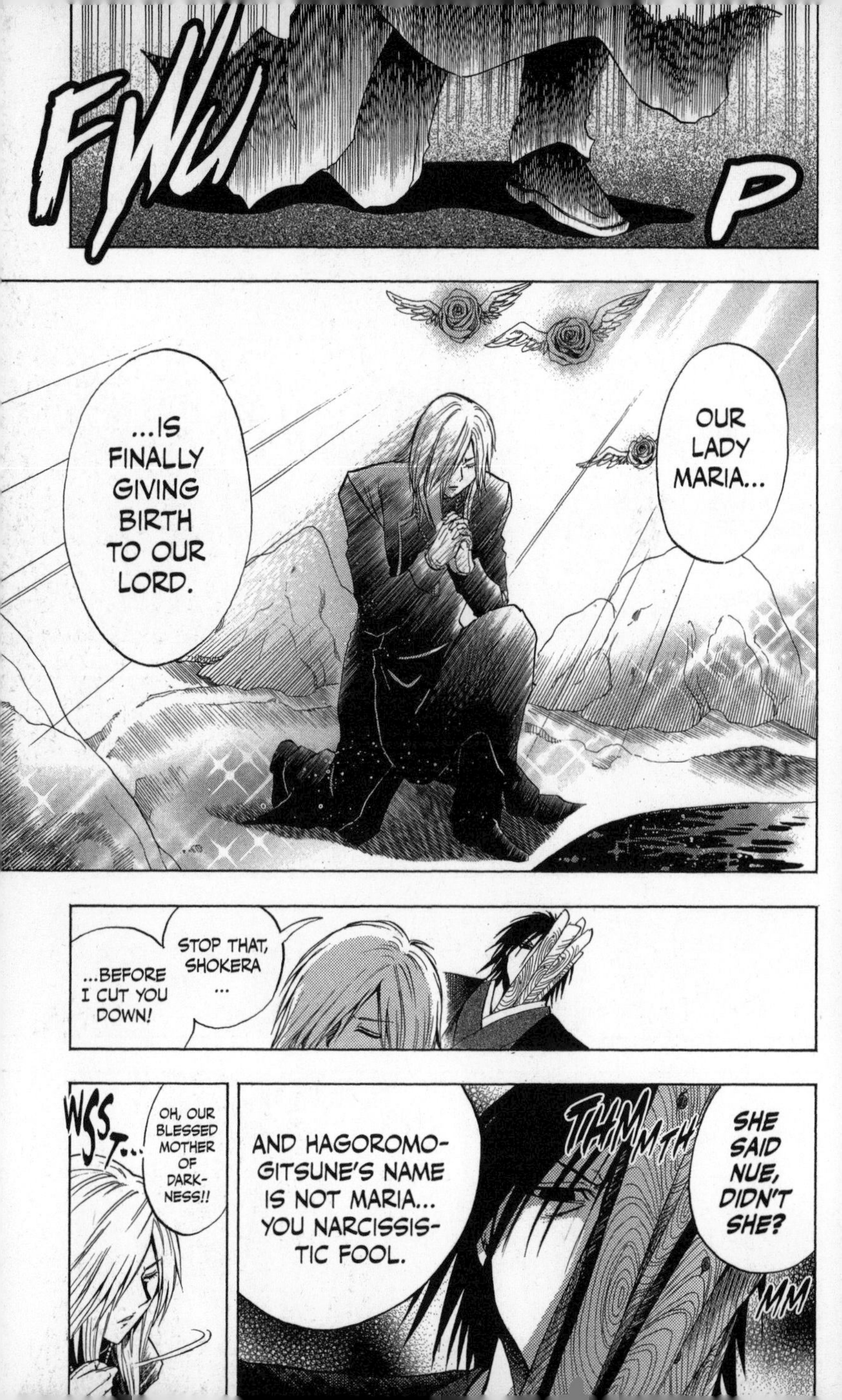
FWU
P
OUR LADY MARIA...
...IS FINALLY GIVING BIRTH TO OUR LORD.
STOP THAT, SHOKERA ...
...BEFORE I CUT YOU DOWN!
THMMMTH
SHE SAID NUE, DIDN'T SHE?
MM
AND HAGOROMO-GITSUNE'S NAME IS NOT MARIA... YOU NARCISSIS-TIC FOOL.
WSST...
OH, OUR BLESSED MOTHER OF DARK-NESS!!

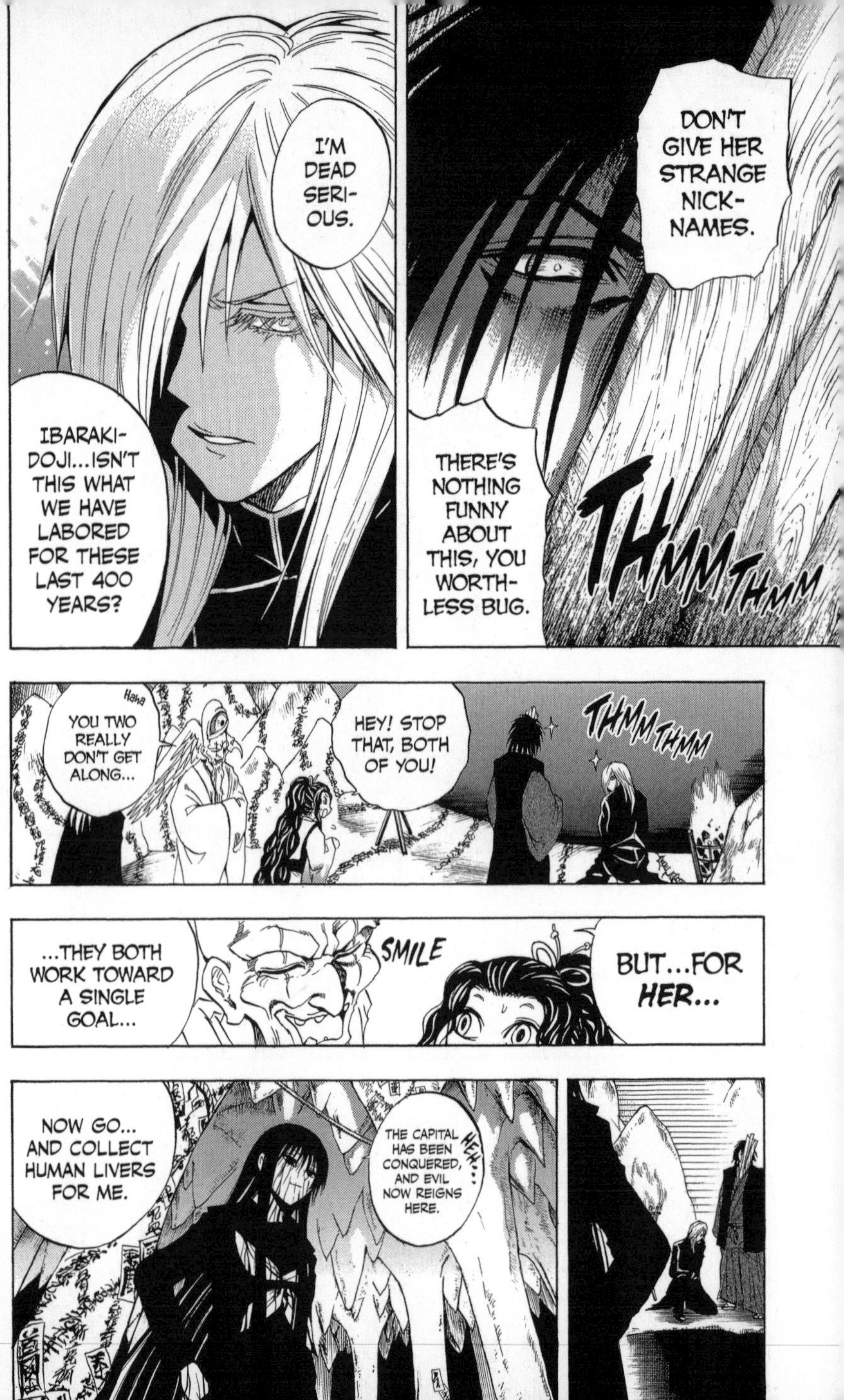
DON'T GIVE HER STRANGE NICK-NAMES.
THMM THMM
THERE'S NOTHING FUNNY ABOUT THIS, YOU WORTH-LESS BUG.
I'M DEAD SERI-OUS.
IBARAKI-DOJI...ISN'T THIS WHAT WE HAVE LABORED FOR THESE LAST 400 YEARS?
THMM THMM
HEY! STOP THAT, BOTH OF YOU!
Haha
YOU TWO REALLY DON'T GET ALONG...
BUT...FOR HER...
SMILE
...THEY BOTH WORK TOWARD A SINGLE GOAL...
HEH...
THE CAPITAL HAS BEEN CONQUERED, AND EVIL NOW REIGNS HERE.
NOW GO... AND COLLECT HUMAN LIVERS FOR ME.

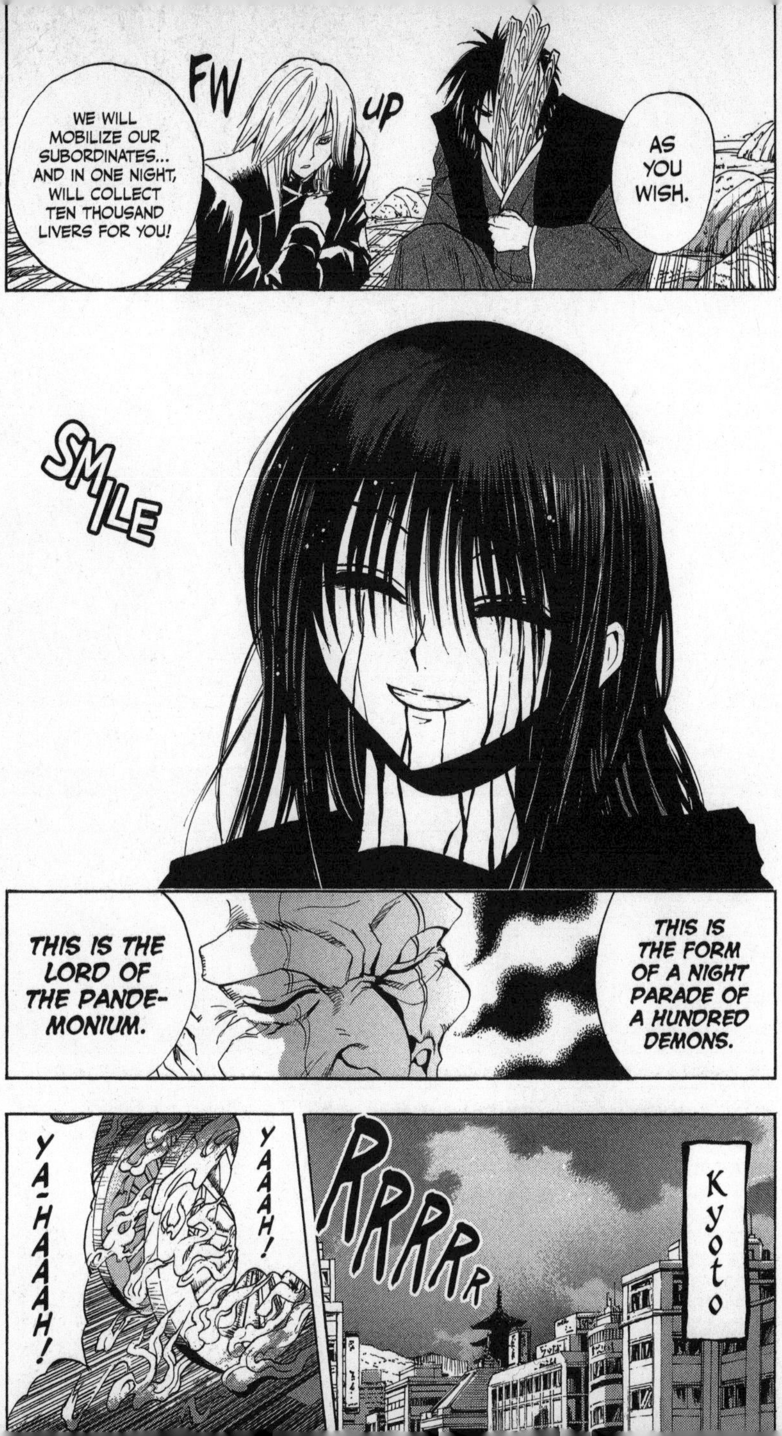
AS YOU WISH.
UP
FW
WE WILL MOBILIZE OUR SUBORDINATES... AND IN ONE NIGHT, WILL COLLECT TEN THOUSAND LIVERS FOR YOU!
SMILE
THIS IS THE FORM OF A NIGHT PARADE OF A HUNDRED DEMONS.
THIS IS THE LORD OF THE PANDE-MONIUM.
Kyoto
RRRRRR
YAAAH!
YA-HAAAAAH!

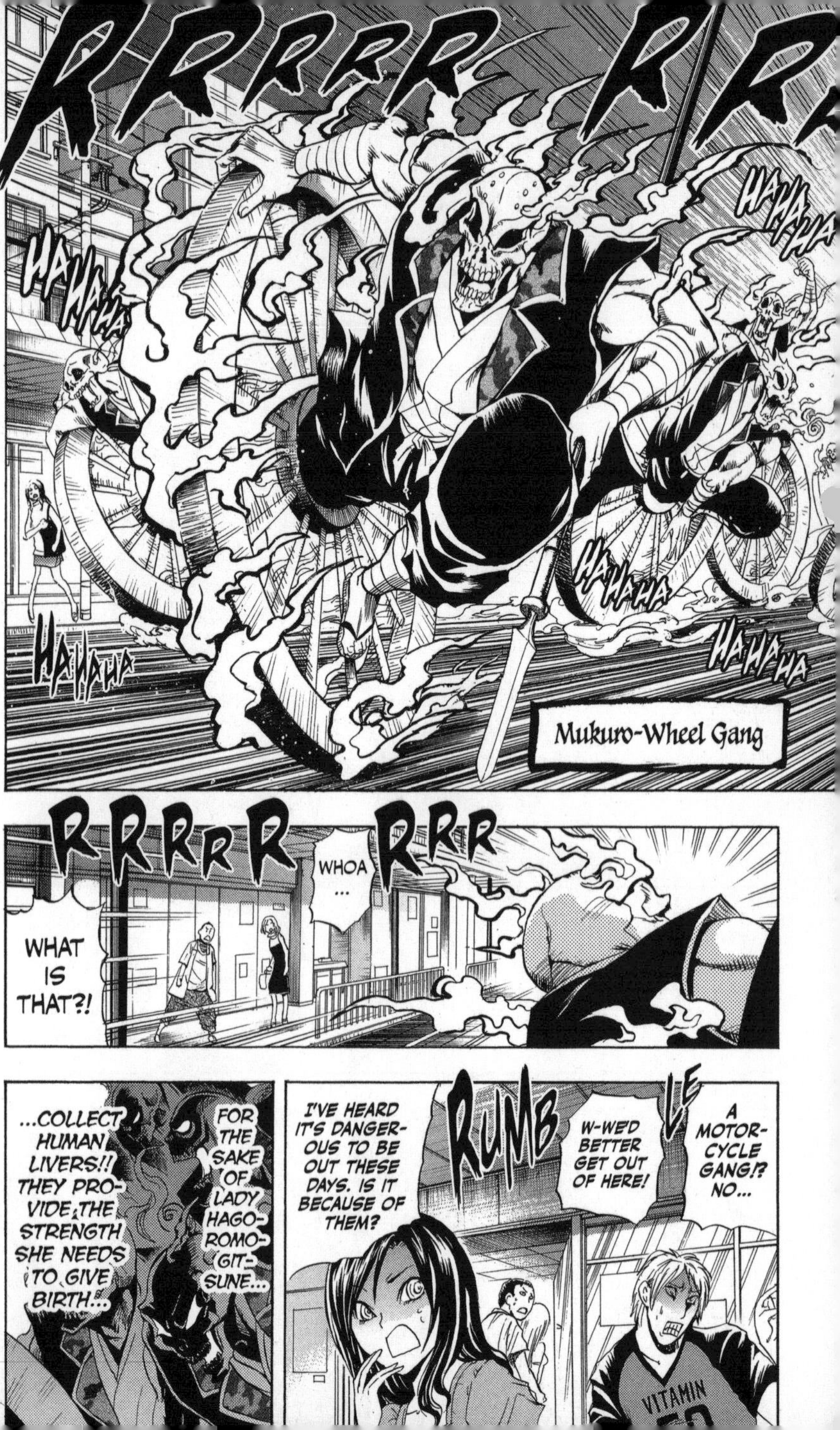
RRRRRR... RRR
HAHAHA
HAHAHA
HAHAHA
HAHAHA
HAHAHA
Mukuro-Wheel Gang
RRRRR RRR
WHOA ...
WHAT IS THAT?!
A MOTORCYCLE GANG!? NO...
W-WE'D BETTER GET OUT OF HERE!
RUMBLE
I'VE HEARD IT'S DANGEROUS TO BE OUT THESE DAYS. IS IT BECAUSE OF THEM?
FOR THE SAKE OF LADY HAGOROMO-GITSUNE...
...COLLECT HUMAN LIVERS!! THEY PROVIDE THE STRENGTH SHE NEEDS TO GIVE BIRTH...

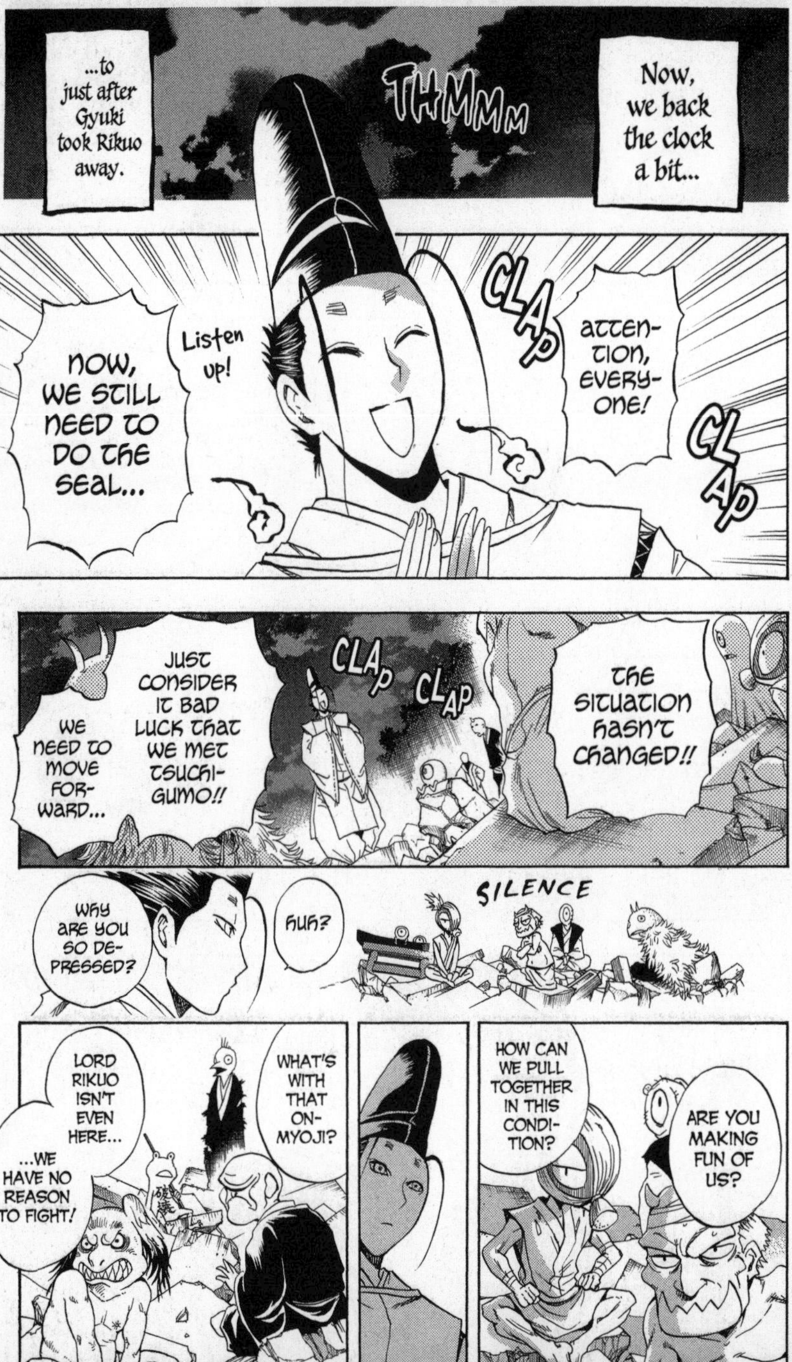
Now, we back the clock a bit...
...to just after Gyuki took Rikuo away.
THMMM
CLAP
ATTENTION, EVERYONE!
CLAP
Listen up!
NOW, WE STILL NEED TO DO THE SEAL...
THE SITUATION HASN'T CHANGED!!
CLAP CLAP
JUST CONSIDER IT BAD LUCK THAT WE MET TSUCHIGUMO!!
WE NEED TO MOVE FORWARD...
SILENCE
HUH?
WHY ARE YOU SO DEPRESSED?
ARE YOU MAKING FUN OF US?
HOW CAN WE PULL TOGETHER IN THIS CONDITION?
WHAT'S WITH THAT ONMYOJI?
LORD RIKUO ISN'T EVEN HERE...
...WE HAVE NO REASON TO FIGHT!

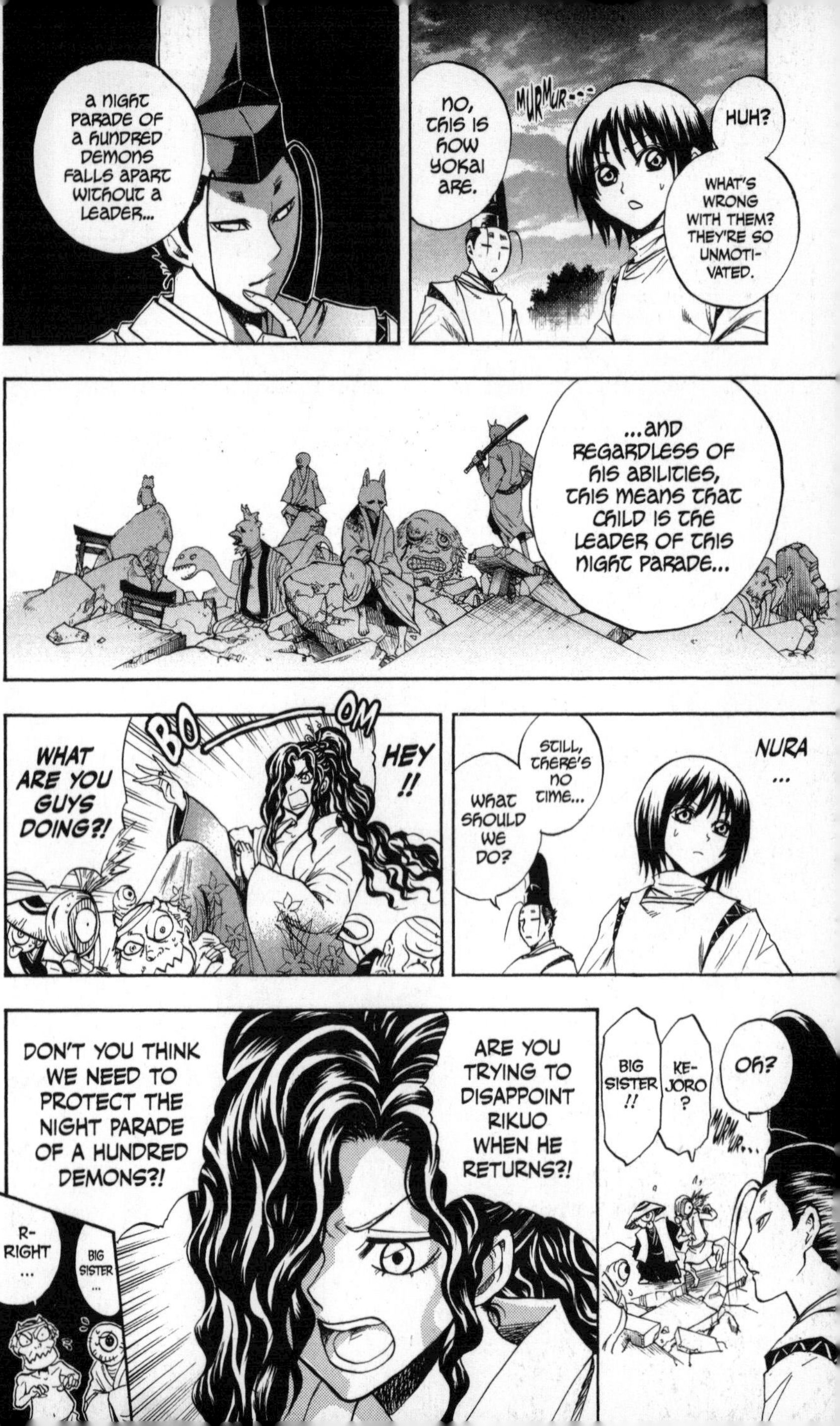
HUH?
WHAT'S WRONG WITH THEM? THEY'RE SO UNMOTIVATED.
MURMUR...
NO, THIS IS HOW YOKAI ARE.
A NIGHT PARADE OF A HUNDRED DEMONS FALLS APART WITHOUT A LEADER...
...AND REGARDLESS OF HIS ABILITIES, THIS MEANS THAT CHILD IS THE LEADER OF THIS NIGHT PARADE...
NURA...
STILL, THERE'S NO TIME...
WHAT SHOULD WE DO?
BO——OM
HEY!!
WHAT ARE YOU GUYS DOING?!
OH?
KE-JORO?
BIG SISTER!!
MURMUR...
ARE YOU TRYING TO DISAPPOINT RIKUO WHEN HE RETURNS?!
DON'T YOU THINK WE NEED TO PROTECT THE NIGHT PARADE OF A HUNDRED DEMONS?!
BIG SISTER...
R-RIGHT...

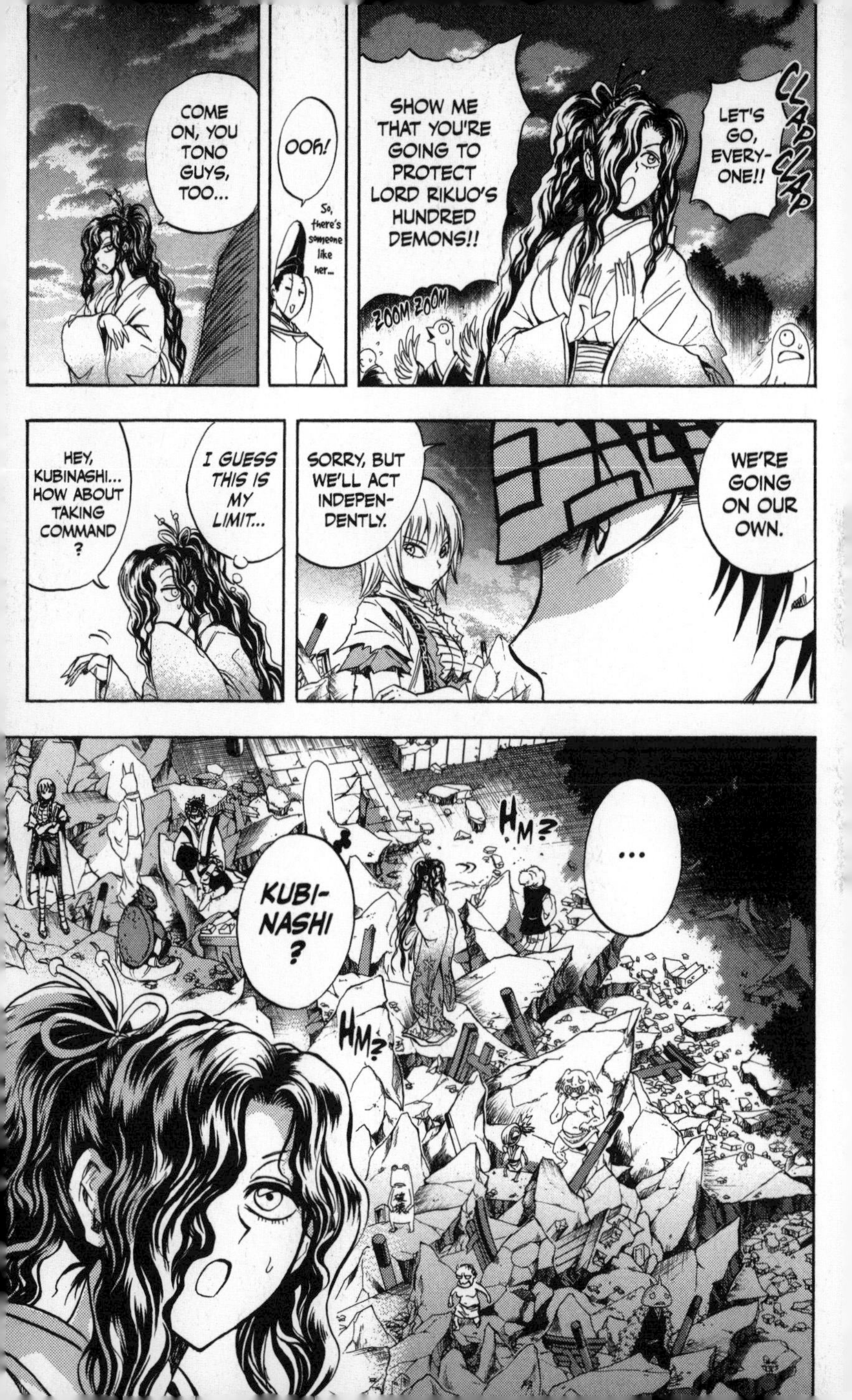
CLAP CLAP
LET'S GO, EVERY-ONE!!
SHOW ME THAT YOU'RE GOING TO PROTECT LORD RIKUO'S HUNDRED DEMONS!!
ZOOM ZOOM
OOH!
So, there's someone like her...
COME ON, YOU TONO GUYS, TOO...
WE'RE GOING ON OUR OWN.
SORRY, BUT WE'LL ACT INDEPEN-DENTLY.
I GUESS THIS IS MY LIMIT...
HEY, KUBINASHI... HOW ABOUT TAKING COMMAND?
...
HM?
KUBI-NASHI?
HM?

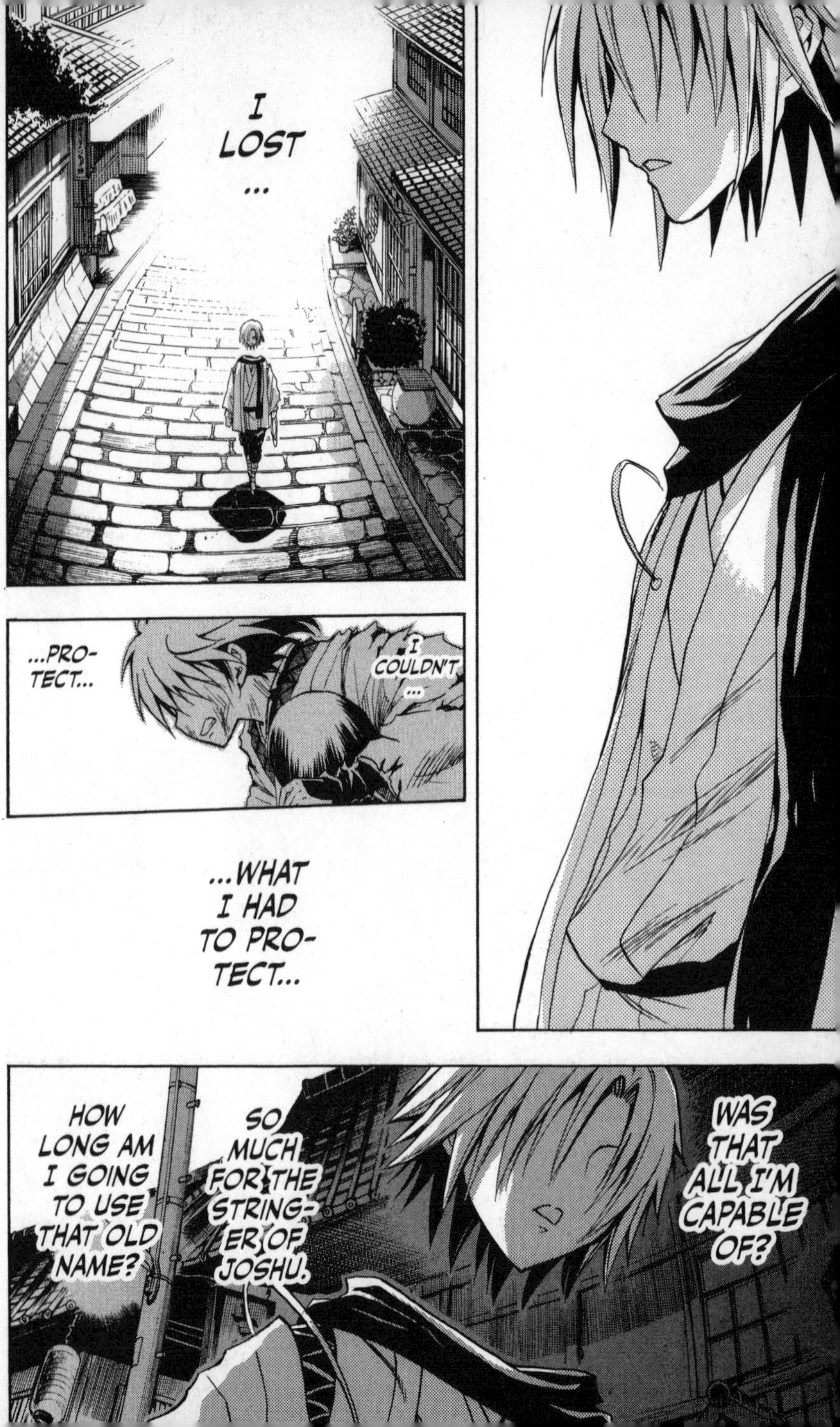
I LOST ...
I COULDN'T ...
...PRO-TECT...
...WHAT I HAD TO PRO-TECT...
WAS THAT ALL I'M CAPABLE OF?
SO MUCH FOR THE STRING-ER OF JOSHU.
HOW LONG AM I GOING TO USE THAT OLD NAME?

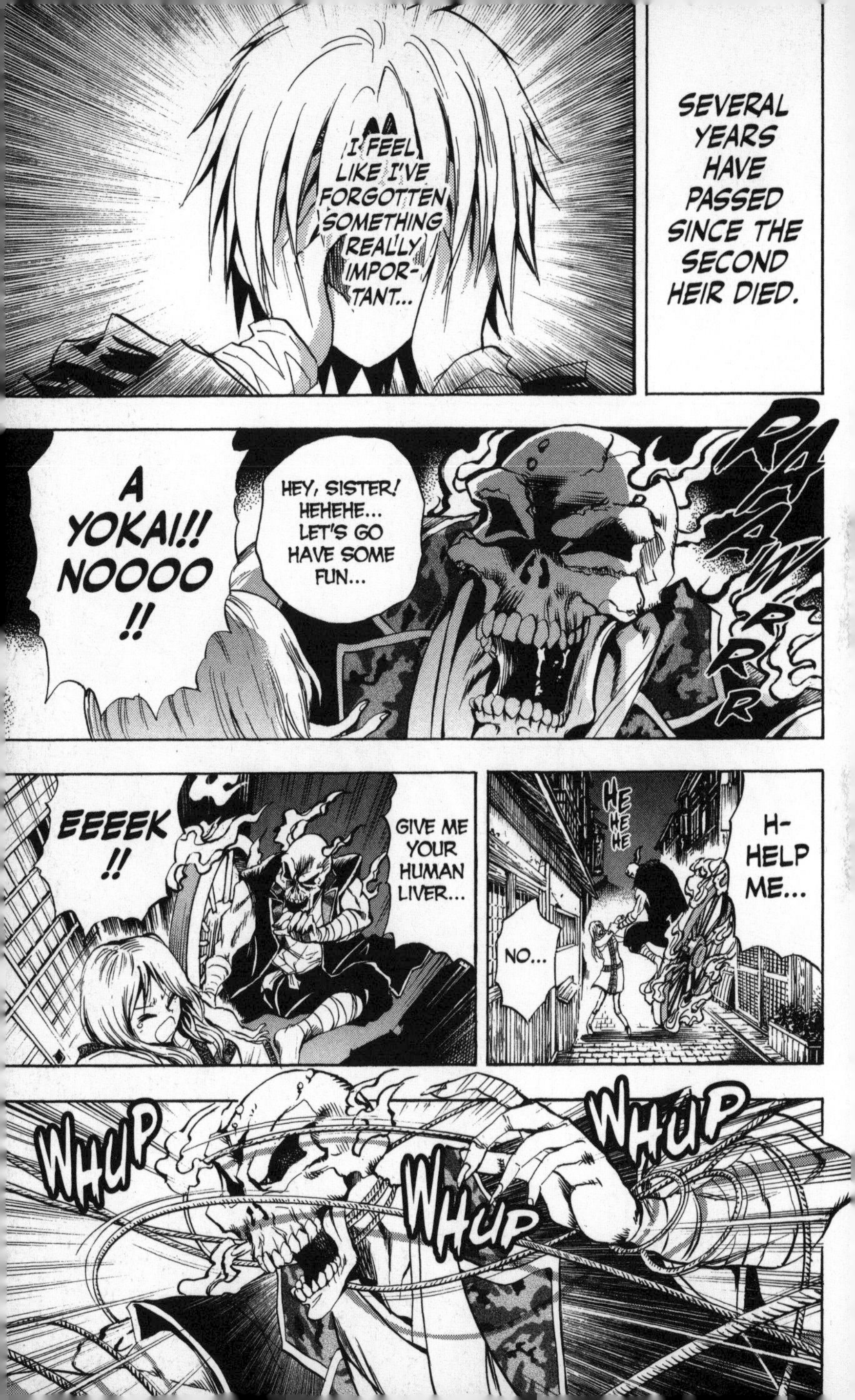
SEVERAL YEARS HAVE PASSED SINCE THE SECOND HEIR DIED.
I FEEL LIKE I'VE FORGOTTEN SOMETHING REALLY IMPORTANT...
RAAWRRRR
HEY, SISTER! HEHEHE... LET'S GO HAVE SOME FUN...
A YOKAI!! NOOOO!!
H-HELP ME...
HEHEHE
NO...
GIVE ME YOUR HUMAN LIVER...
EEEEK!!
WHUP
WHUP
WHUP

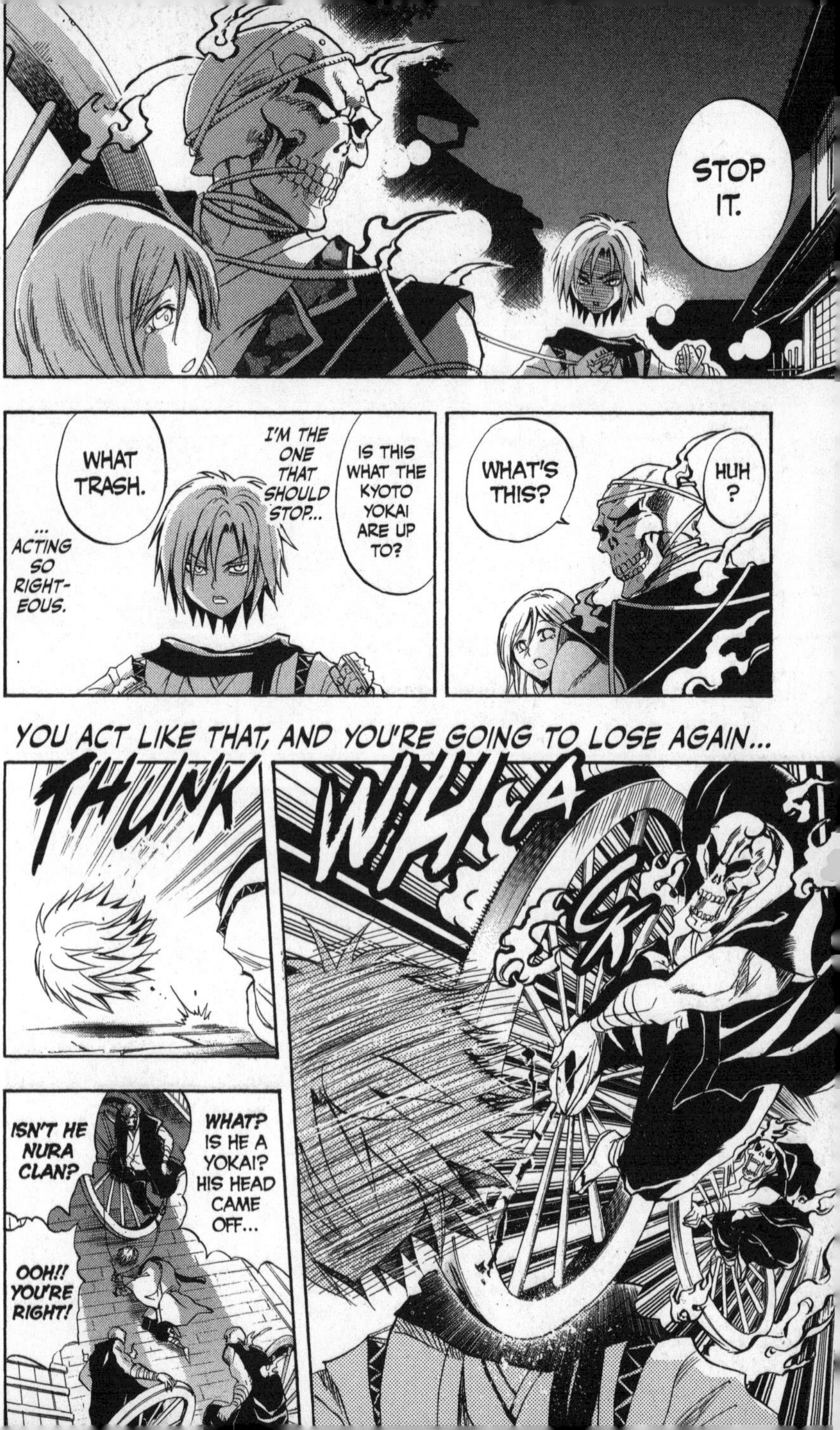
STOP IT.
HUH ?
WHAT'S THIS?
IS THIS WHAT THE KYOTO YOKAI ARE UP TO?
I'M THE ONE THAT SHOULD STOP...
WHAT TRASH.
...ACTING SO RIGHTEOUS.
YOU ACT LIKE THAT, AND YOU'RE GOING TO LOSE AGAIN...
WHACK
THUNK
WHAT? IS HE A YOKAI? HIS HEAD CAME OFF...
ISN'T HE NURA CLAN?
OOH!! YOU'RE RIGHT!

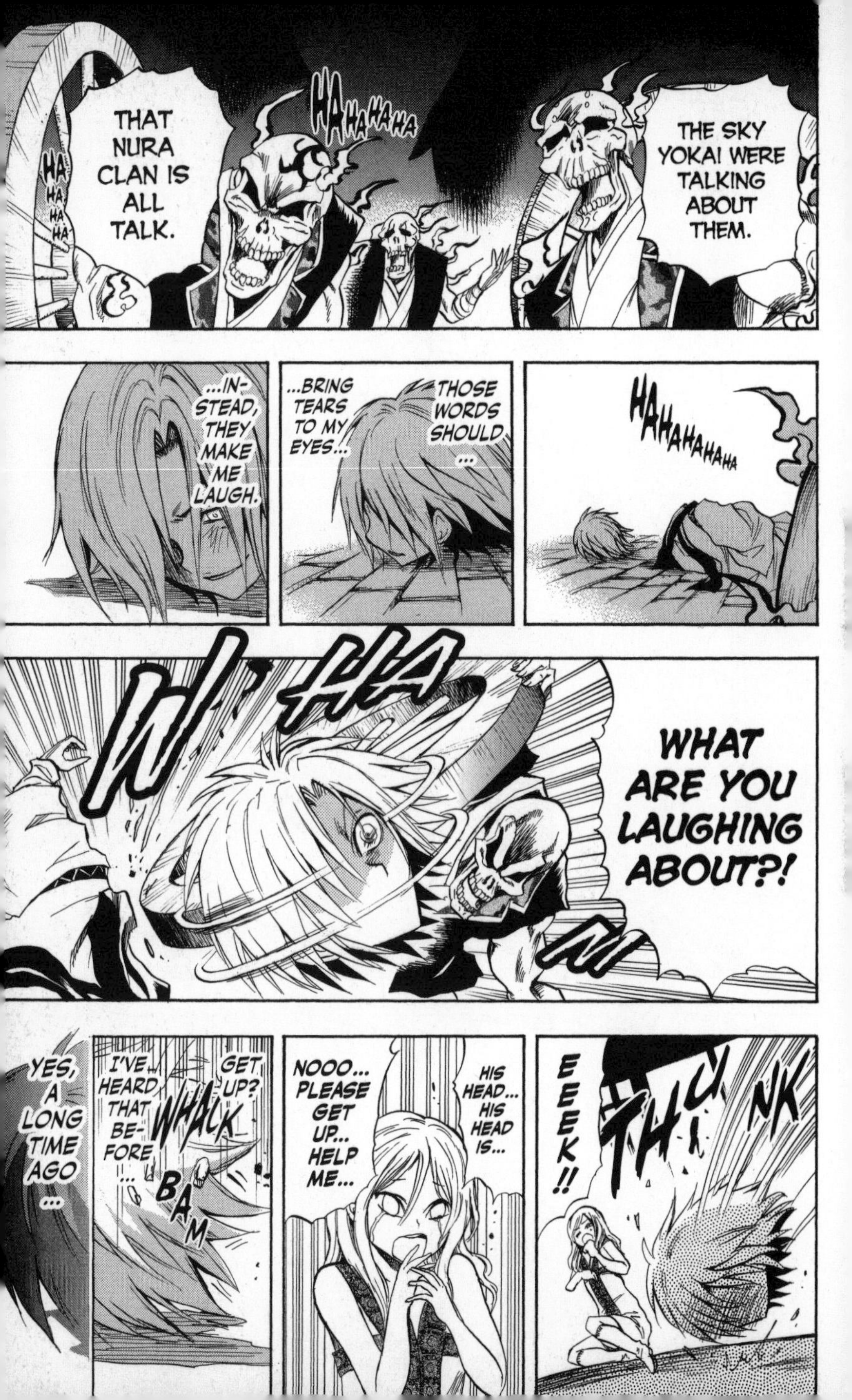
THE SKY YOKAI WERE TALKING ABOUT THEM.
HAHAHAHAHA
THAT NURA CLAN IS ALL TALK.
HA HA HA HA
HAHAHAHAHAHA
THOSE WORDS SHOULD ...
...BRING TEARS TO MY EYES...
...IN-STEAD, THEY MAKE ME LAUGH.
WHAT ARE YOU LAUGHING ABOUT?!
EEEEK!!
THUNK
HIS HEAD... HIS HEAD IS...
NOOO... PLEASE GET UP... HELP ME...
GET UP?
I'VE HEARD THAT BE-FORE!...
WHACK
BAM
YES, A LONG TIME AGO...

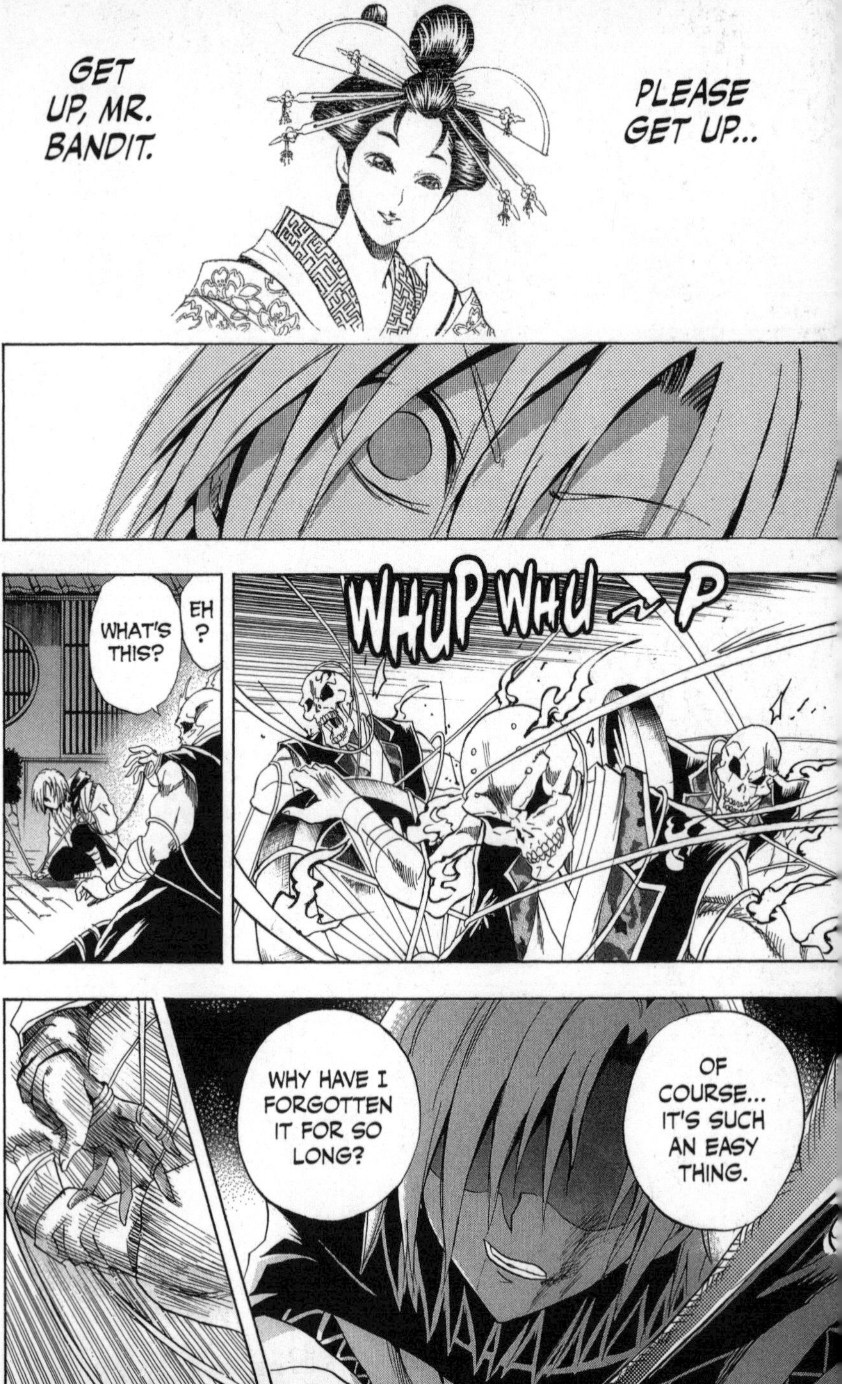
PLEASE GET UP...
GET UP, MR. BANDIT.
WHUP WHU ~ P
EH ?
WHAT'S THIS?
OF COURSE... IT'S SUCH AN EASY THING.
WHY HAVE I FORGOTTEN IT FOR SO LONG?

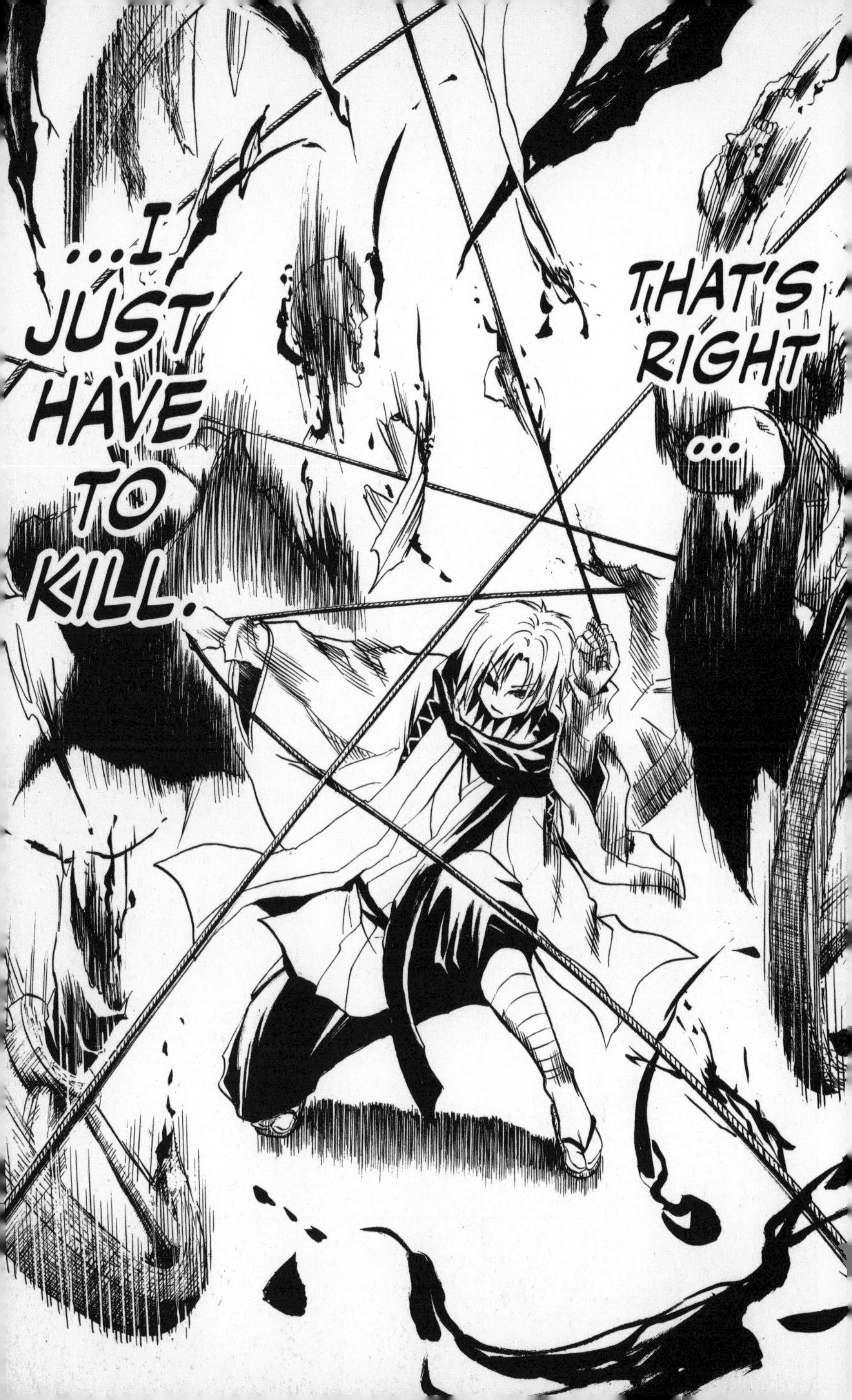
THAT'S RIGHT...
...I JUST HAVE TO KILL.

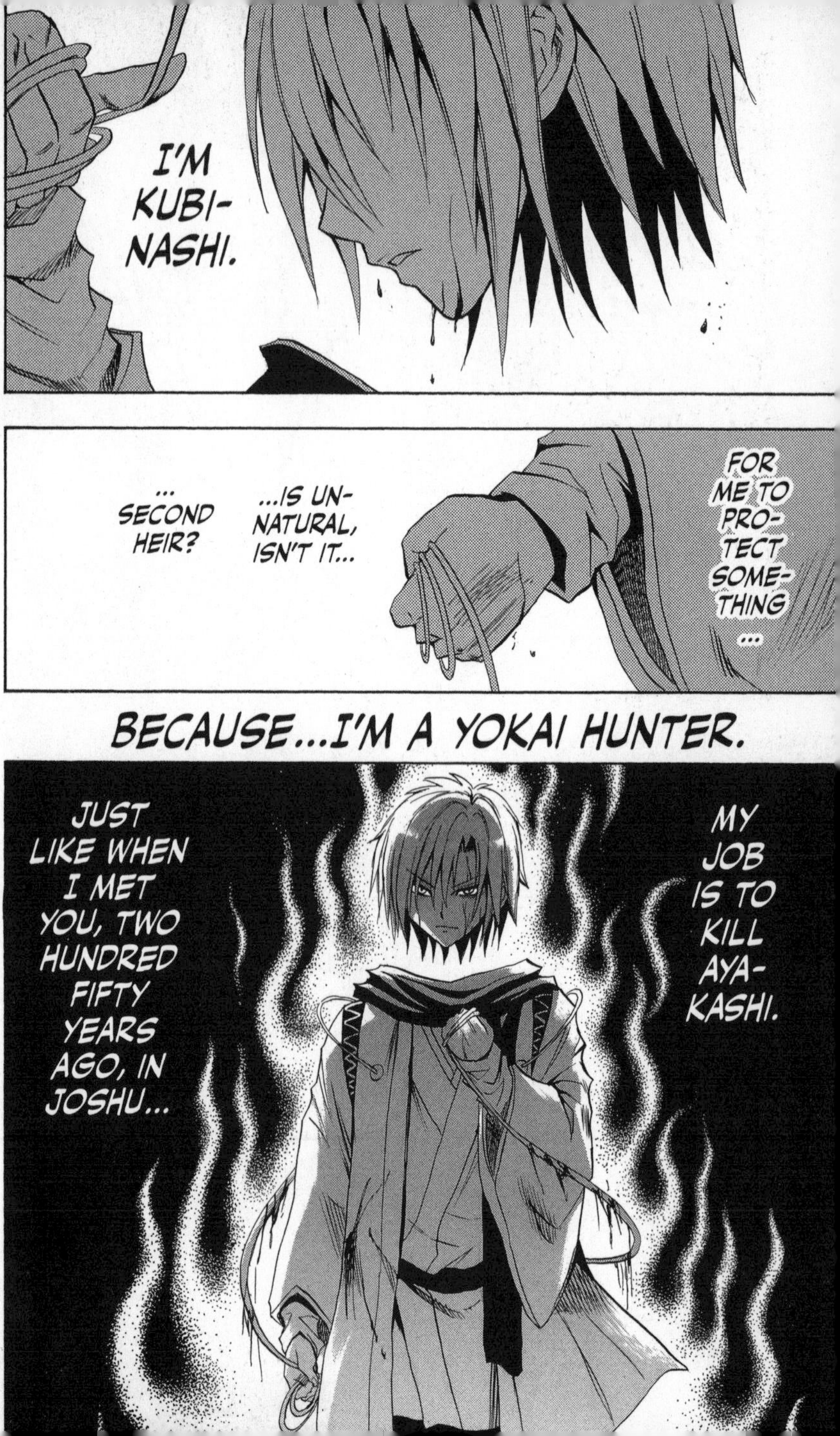
I'M KUBI-NASHI.
FOR ME TO PRO-TECT SOME-THING...
...IS UN-NATURAL, ISN'T IT...
...SECOND HEIR?
BECAUSE...I'M A YOKAI HUNTER.
MY JOB IS TO KILL AYA-KASHI.
JUST LIKE WHEN I MET YOU, TWO HUNDRED FIFTY YEARS AGO, IN JOSHU...

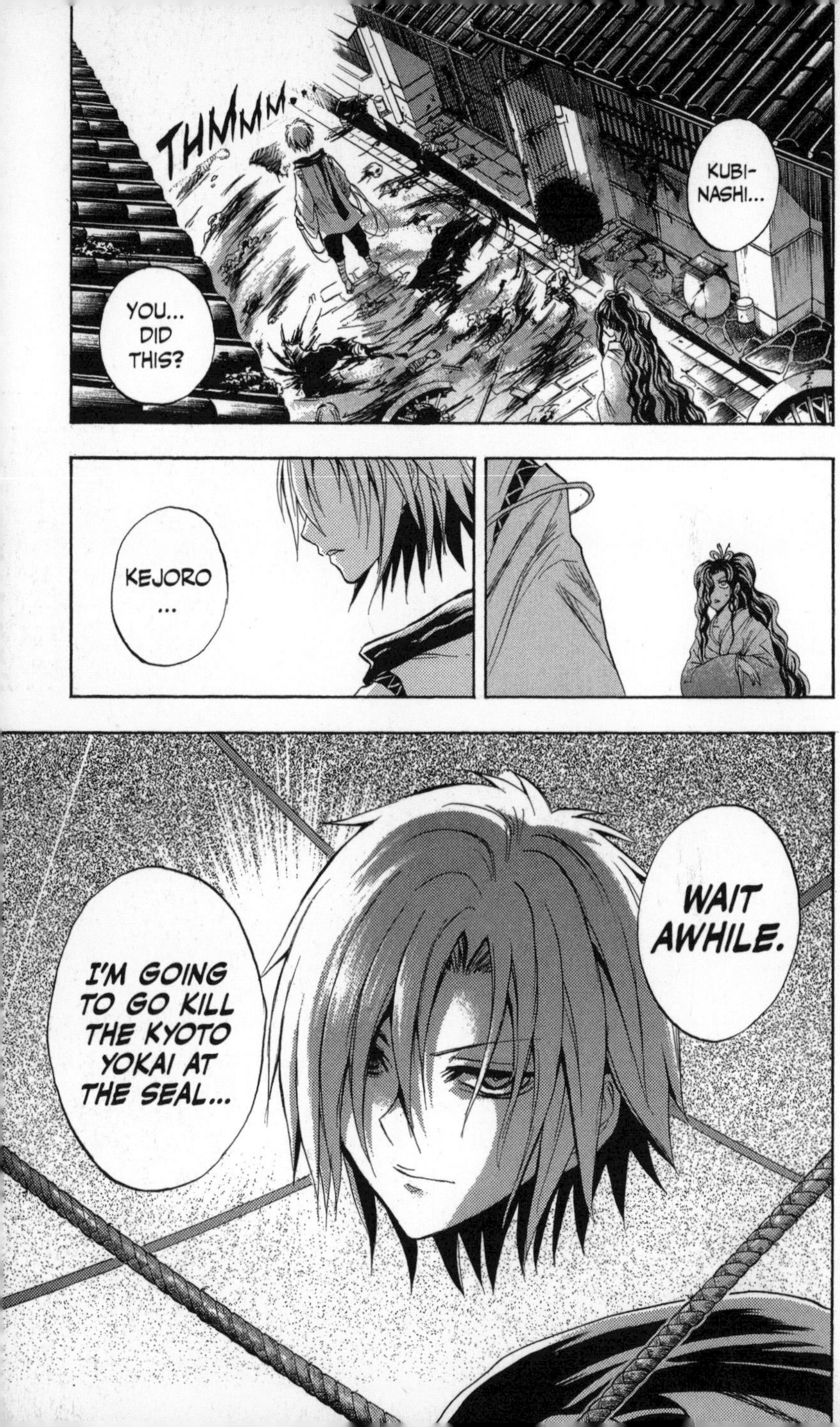
KUBI-NASHI...
THMMM...
YOU... DID THIS?
KEJORO ...
WAIT AWHILE.
I'M GOING TO GO KILL THE KYOTO YOKAI AT THE SEAL...

NURA: RISE OF THE YOKAI CLAN

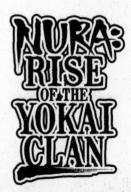

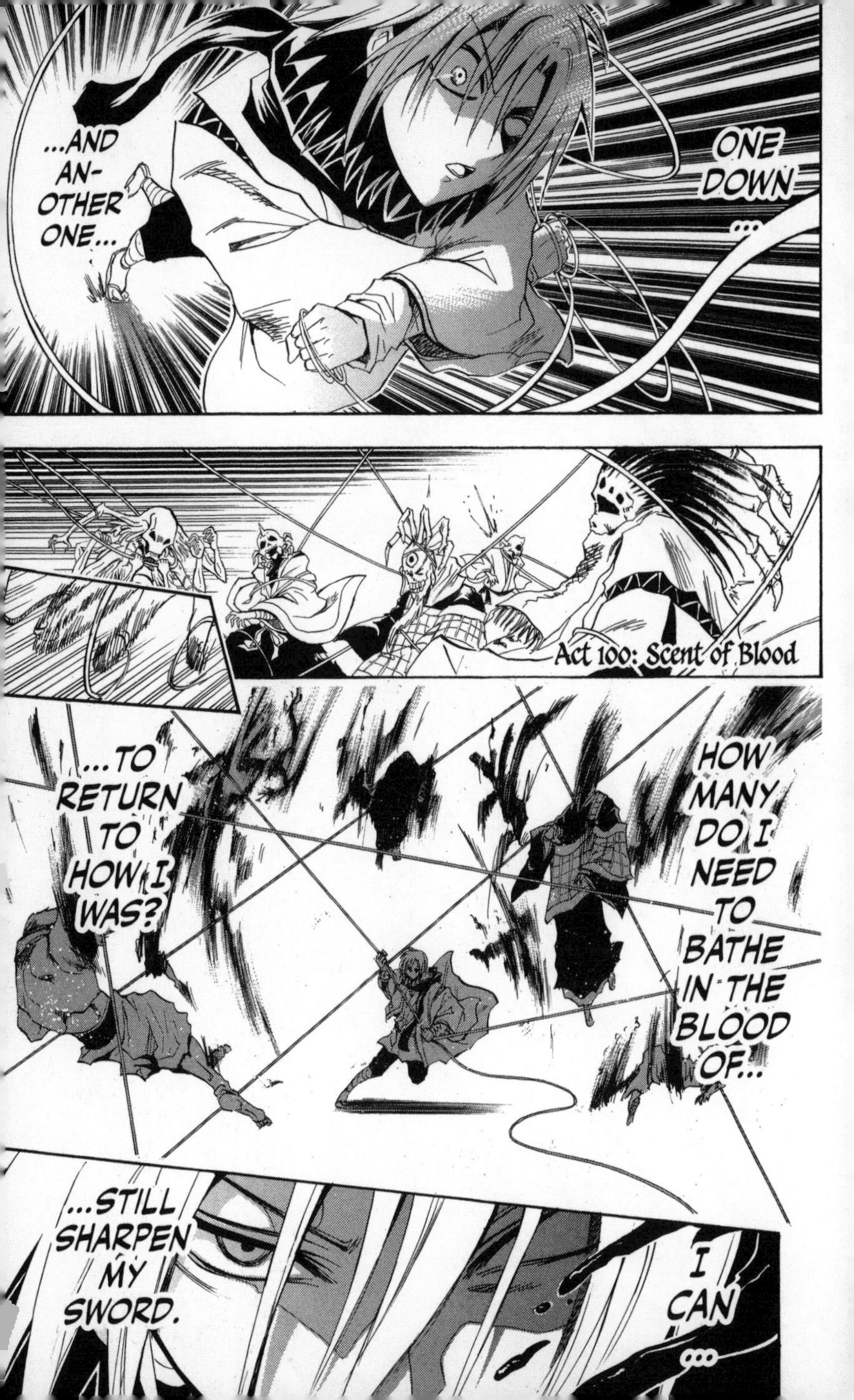
ONE DOWN...
...AND ANOTHER ONE...
Act 100: Scent of Blood
HOW MANY DO I NEED TO BATHE IN THE BLOOD OF...
...TO RETURN TO HOW I WAS?
I CAN...
...STILL SHARPEN MY SWORD.

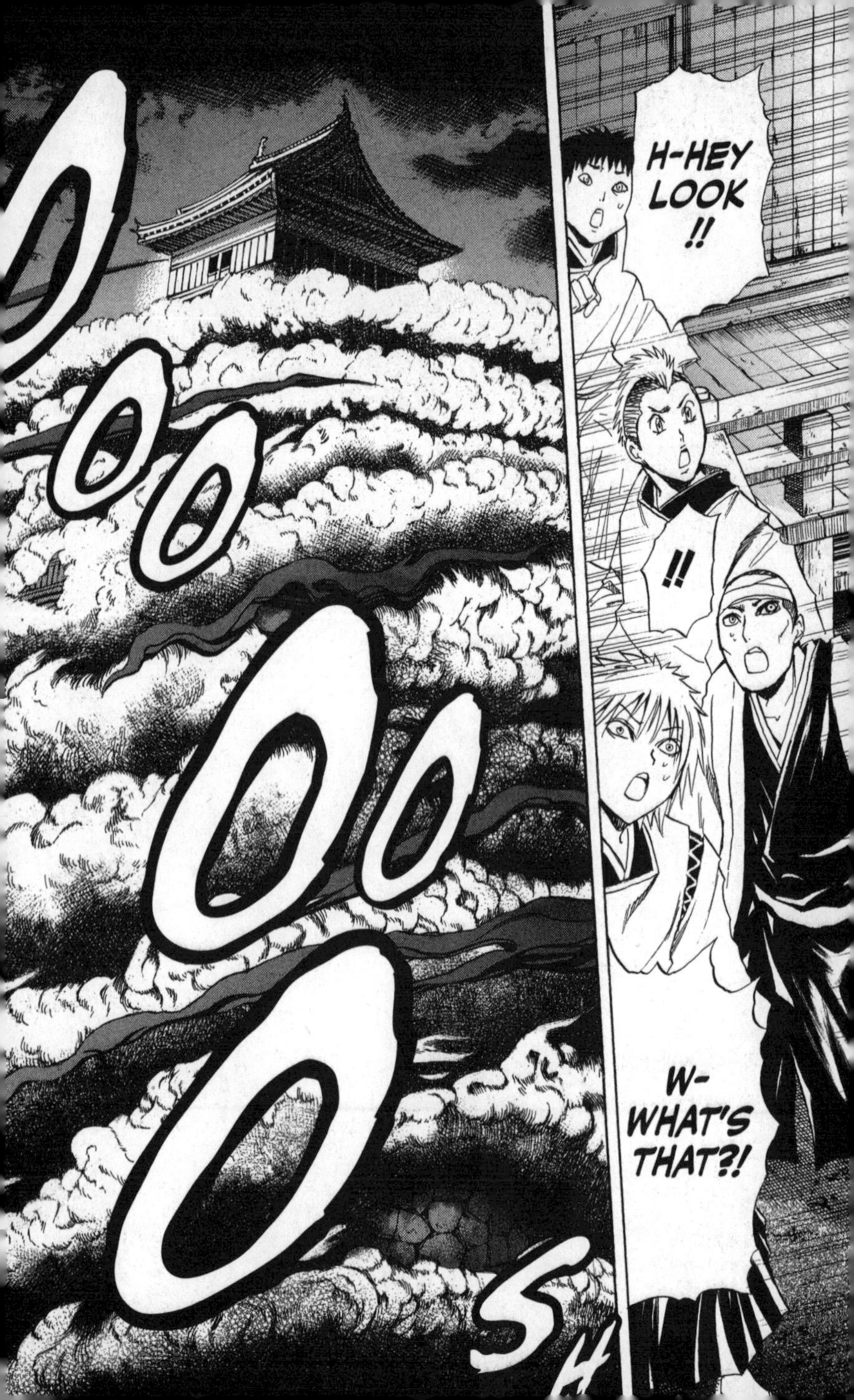
H-HEY LOOK !!
!!
W-WHAT'S THAT?!
OOOOOOSH

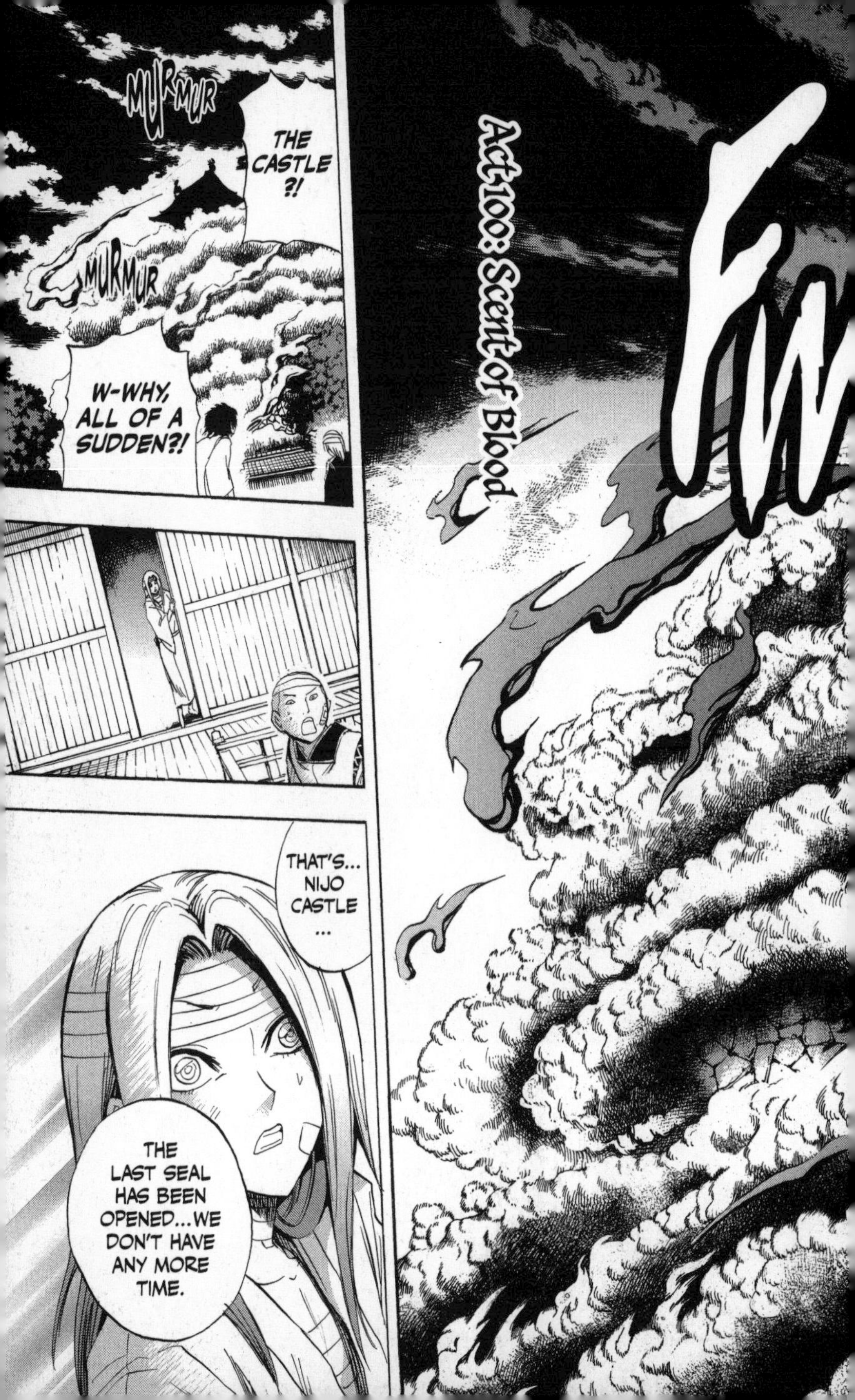
Act100: Scent of Blood
MURMUR
THE CASTLE ?!
MURMUR
W-WHY, ALL OF A SUDDEN?!
THAT'S... NIJO CASTLE ...
THE LAST SEAL HAS BEEN OPENED...WE DON'T HAVE ANY MORE TIME.

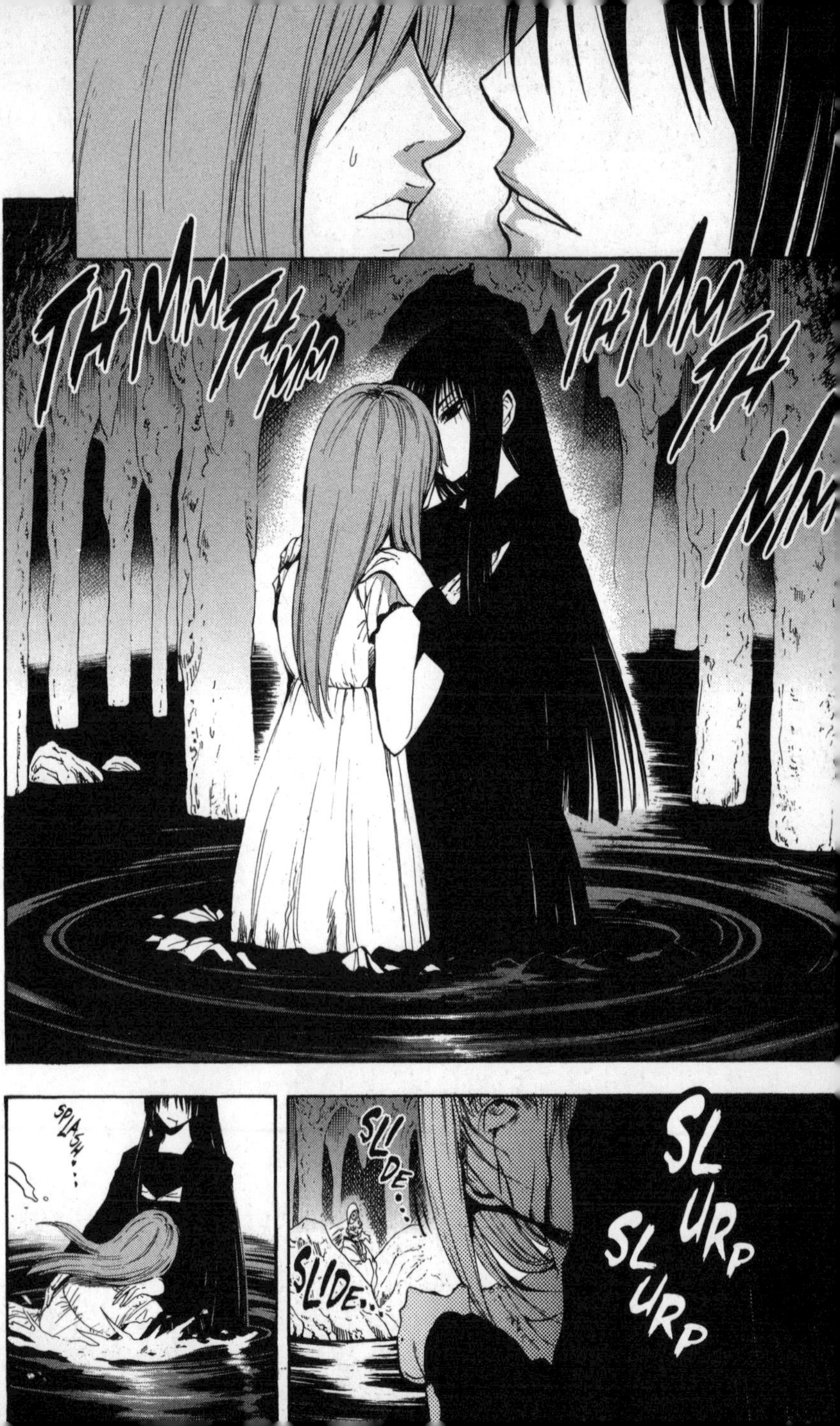
THMM THMM
THMM THMM
SLURP SLURP
SLIDE...
SLIDE...
SPLASH...

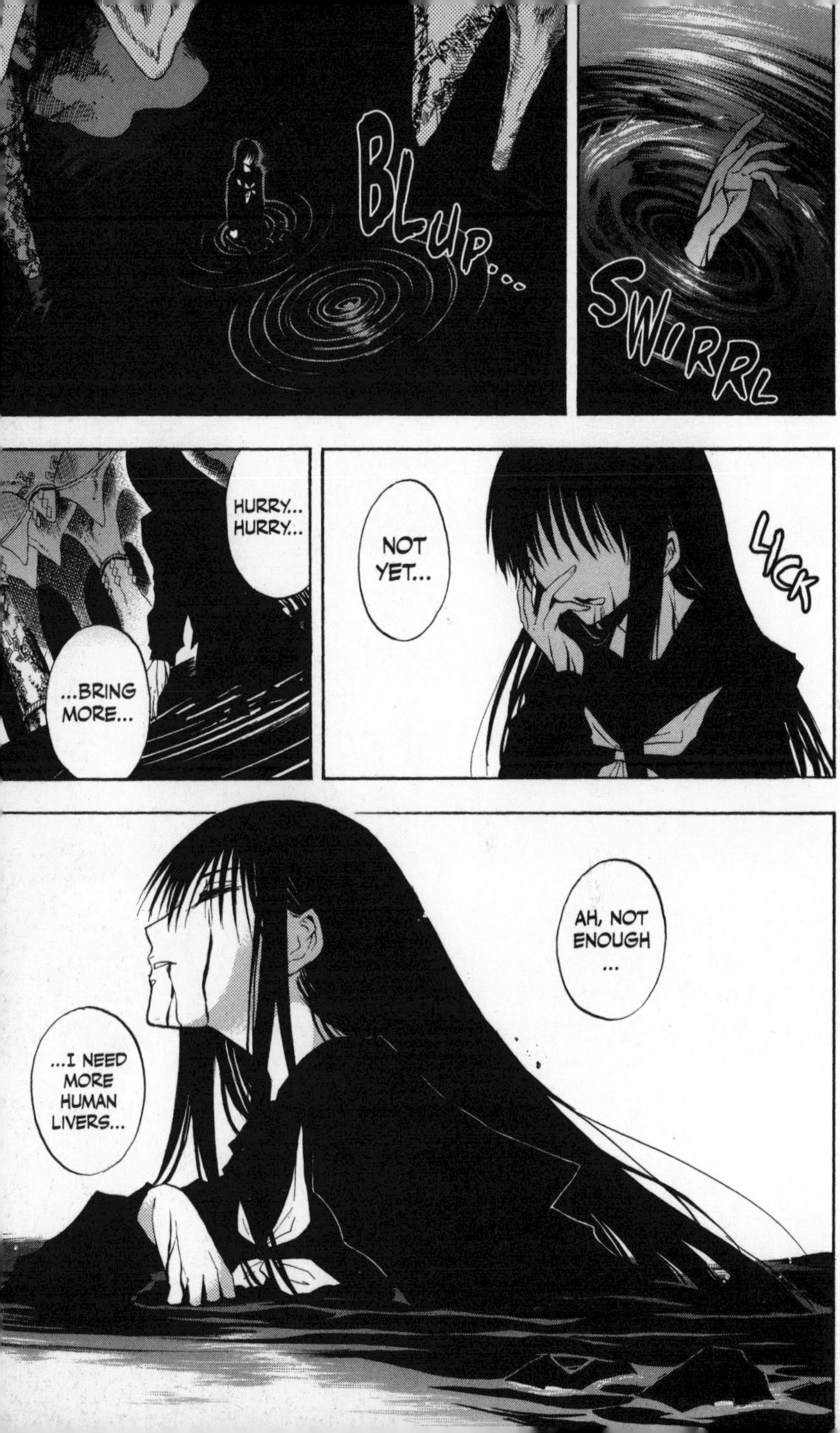
SWIRRL
BLUP...
LICK
NOT YET...
HURRY... HURRY...
...BRING MORE...
AH, NOT ENOUGH ...
...I NEED MORE HUMAN LIVERS...

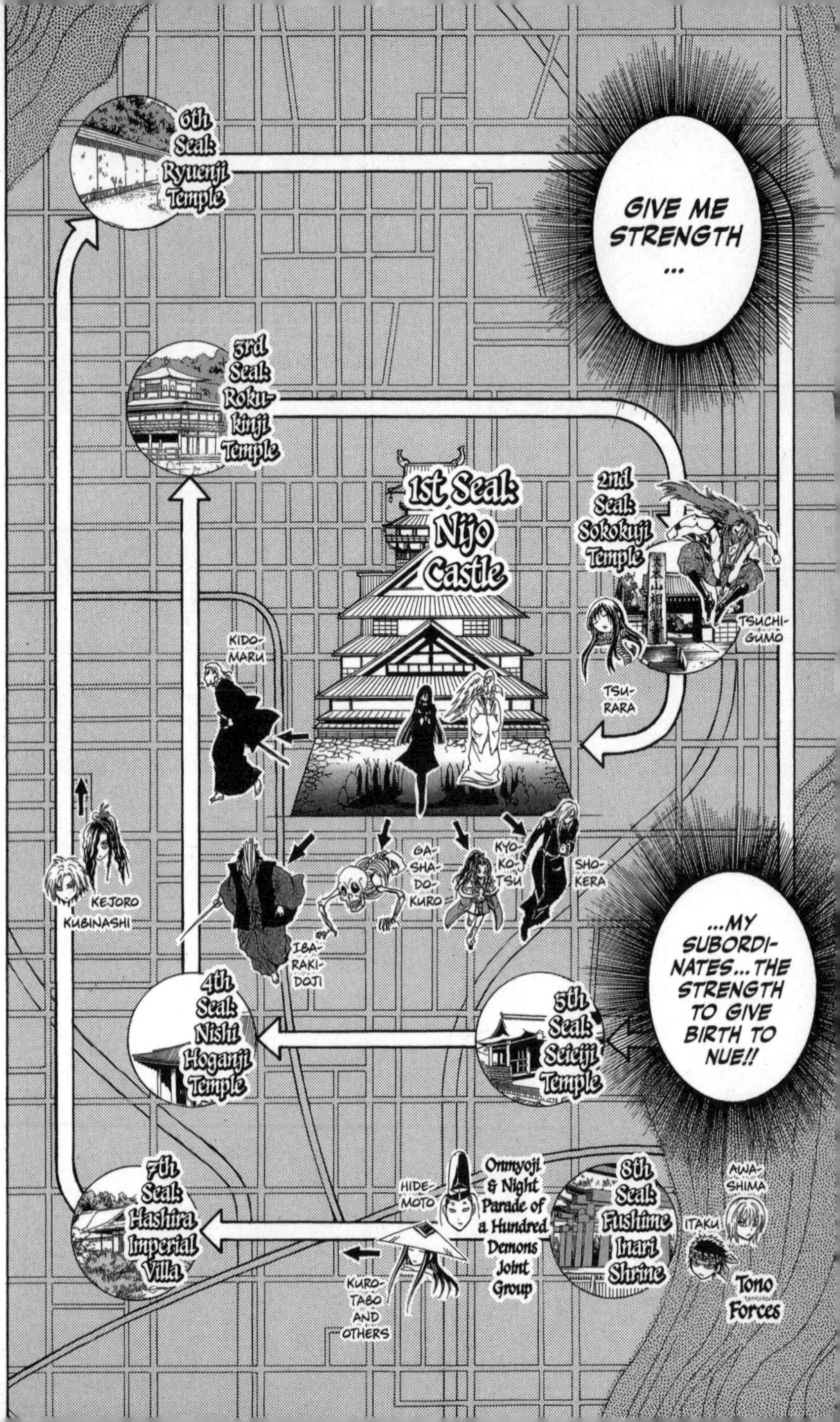
GIVE ME STRENGTH ...
6th Seal: Ryuenji Temple
3rd Seal: Rokukinji Temple
2nd Seal: Sokokuji Temple
1st Seal: Nijo Castle
TSUCHIGUMO
TSURARA
KIDOMARU
SHOKERA
KYOKOTSU
GASHADOKURO
IBARAKIDOJI
KEJORO
KUBINASHI
...MY SUBORDINATES...THE STRENGTH TO GIVE BIRTH TO NUE!!
5th Seal: Seieiji Temple
4th Seal: Nishi Hoganji Temple
AWASHIMA
ITAKU
Tono Forces
8th Seal: Fushime Inari Shrine
Onmyoji & Night Parade of a Hundred Demons Joint Group
HIDEMOTO
KUROTABO AND OTHERS
7th Seal: Hashira Imperial Villa

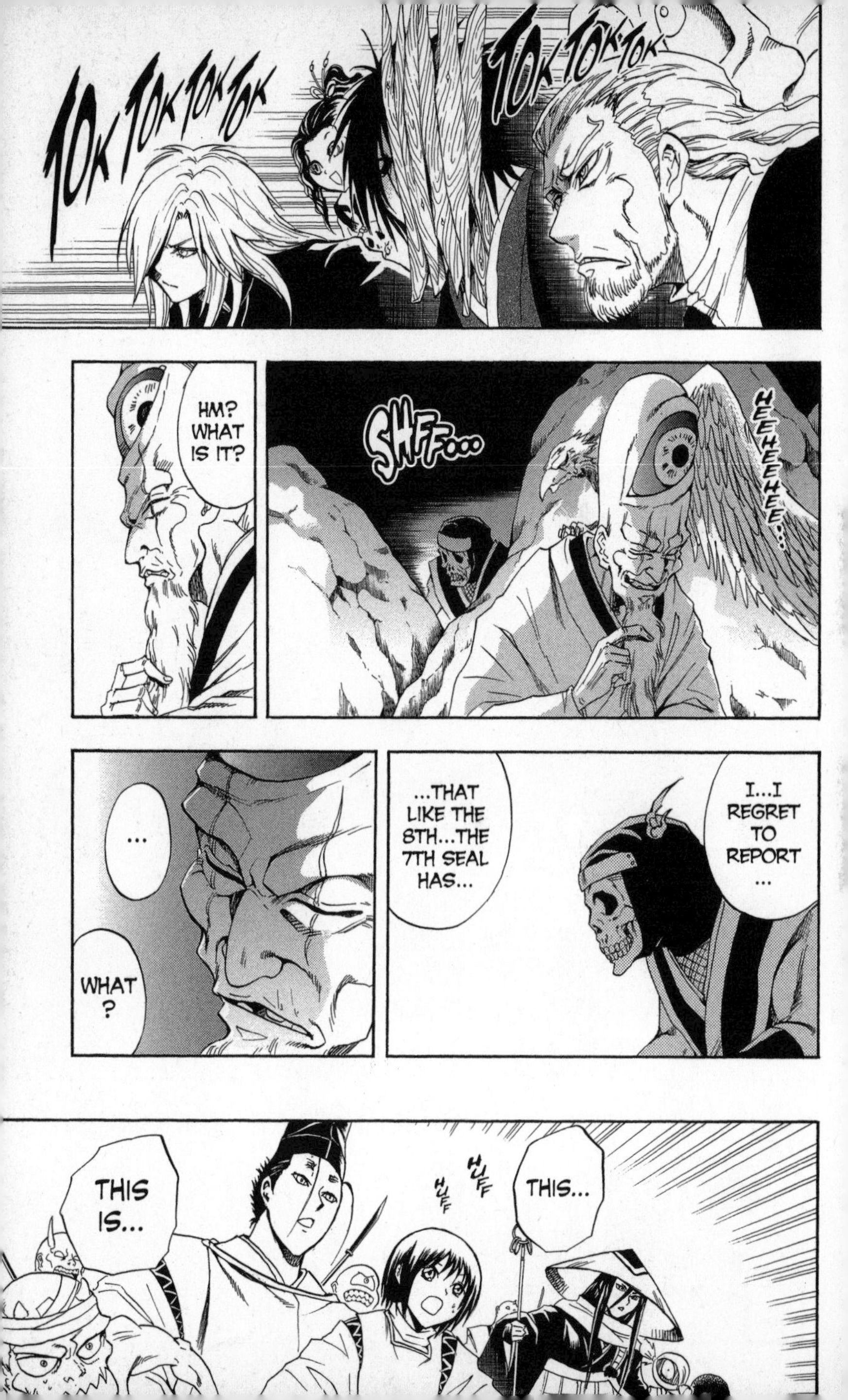

TOK TOK TOK
TOK TOK TOK TOK
HEEHEEHEE...
SHFFOOO
HM? WHAT IS IT?
I...I REGRET TO REPORT...
...THAT LIKE THE 8TH...THE 7TH SEAL HAS...
...
WHAT?
THIS...
HUFF HUFF
THIS IS...

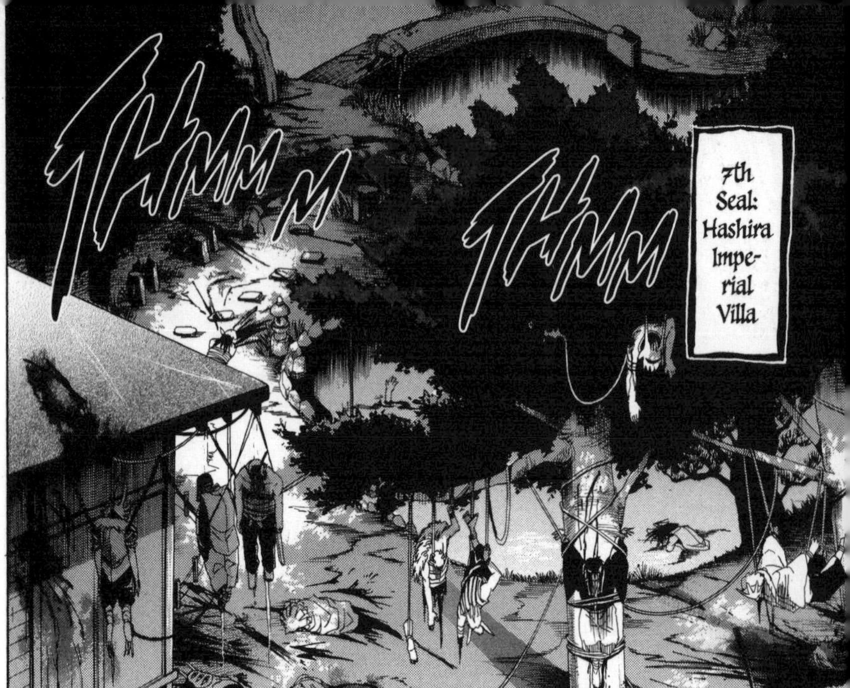
7th Seal: Hashira Imperial Villa
THMMM
THMMM
THMM
THMM

*WINNING TEAM

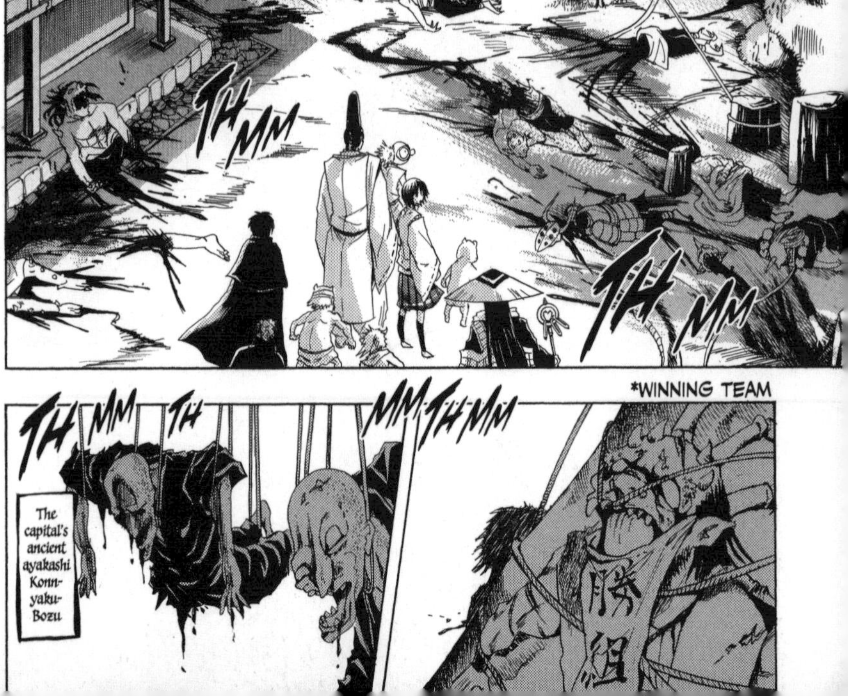
THMM THMM THMM
The capital's ancient ayakashi Konn-yaku-Bozu

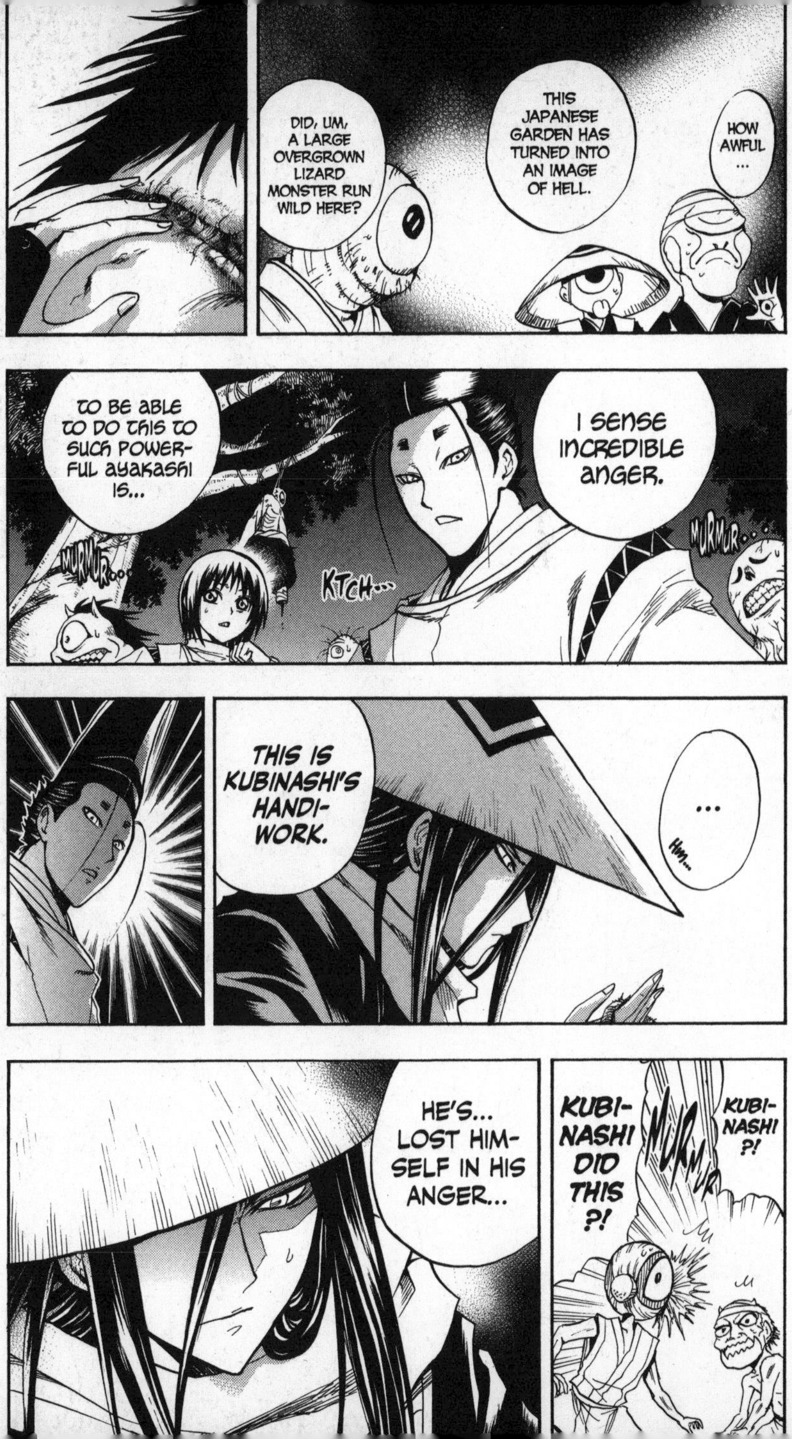
HOW AWFUL ...
THIS JAPANESE GARDEN HAS TURNED INTO AN IMAGE OF HELL.
DID, UM, A LARGE OVERGROWN LIZARD MONSTER RUN WILD HERE?
MURMUR...
I SENSE INCREDIBLE ANGER.
KTCH...
TO BE ABLE TO DO THIS TO SUCH POWERFUL AYAKASHI IS...
MURMUR...
...
HM...
THIS IS KUBINASHI'S HANDIWORK.
KUBINASHI?!
MURMUR
KUBINASHI DID THIS?!
HE'S... LOST HIMSELF IN HIS ANGER...

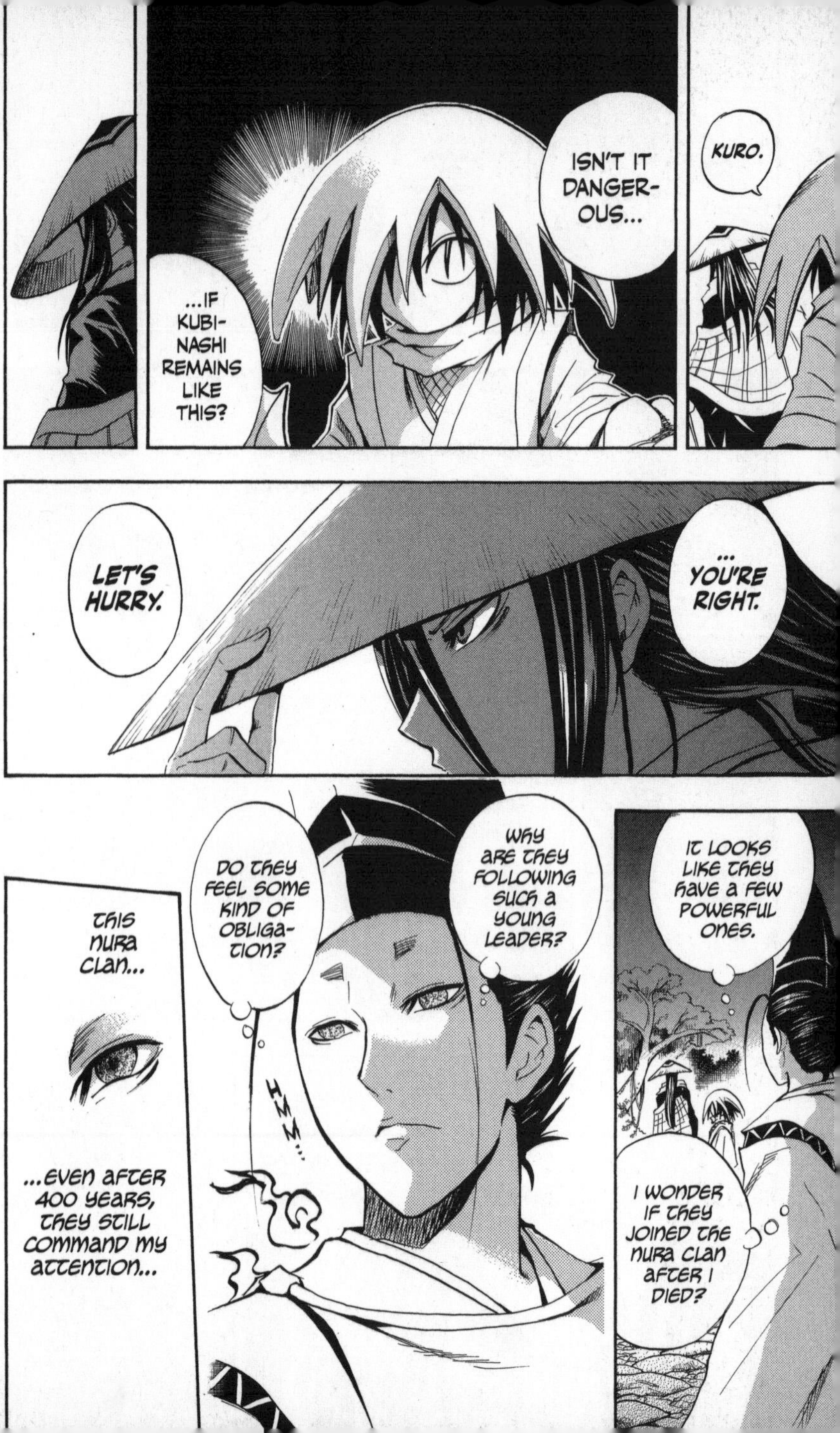
KURO.
ISN'T IT DANGEROUS...
...IF KUBINASHI REMAINS LIKE THIS?
...YOU'RE RIGHT.
LET'S HURRY.
IT LOOKS LIKE THEY HAVE A FEW POWERFUL ONES.
I WONDER IF THEY JOINED THE NURA CLAN AFTER I DIED?
WHY ARE THEY FOLLOWING SUCH A YOUNG LEADER?
DO THEY FEEL SOME KIND OF OBLIGATION?
HMM...
THIS NURA CLAN...
...EVEN AFTER 400 YEARS, THEY STILL COMMAND MY ATTENTION...

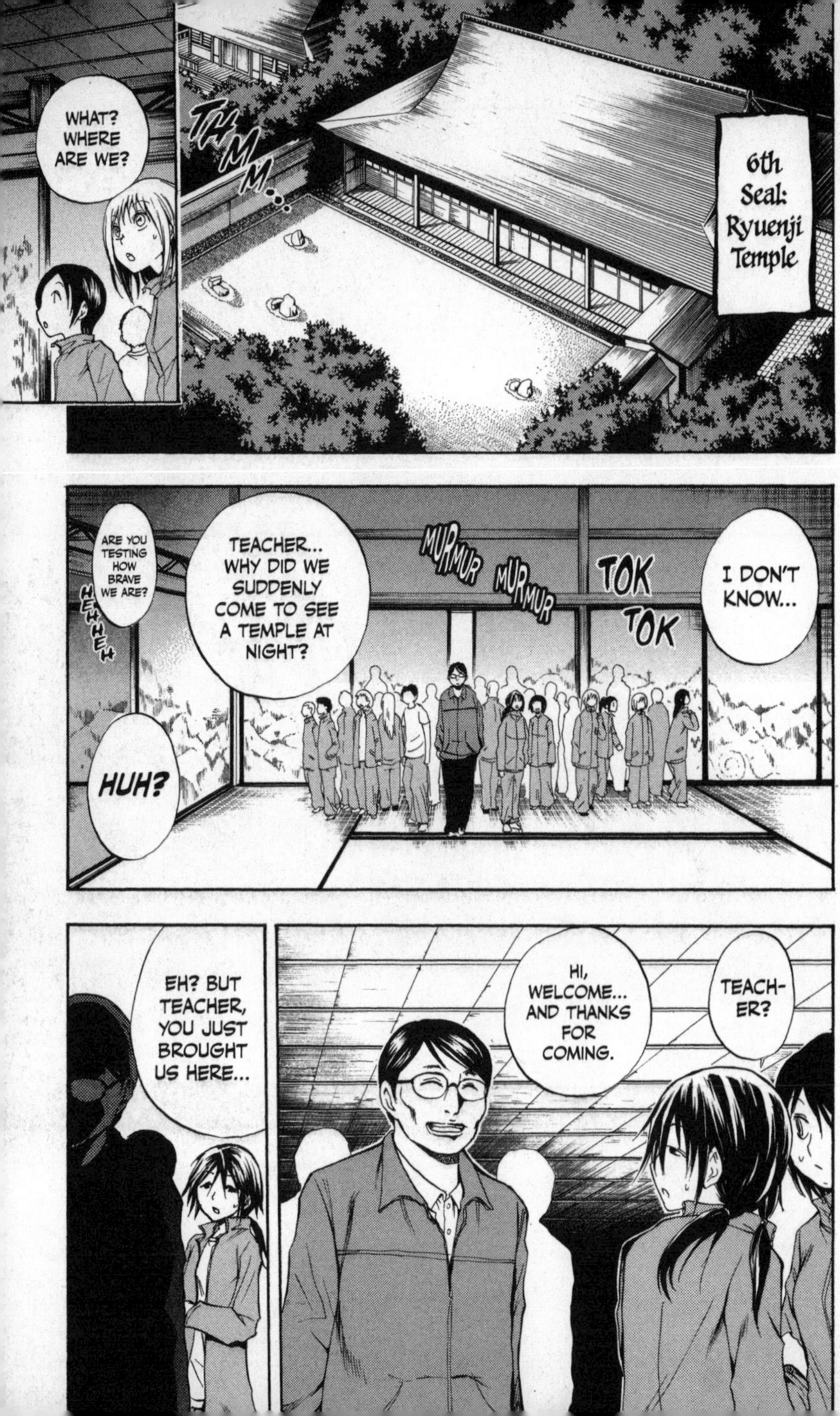
6th Seal: Ryuenji Temple
THMM..
WHAT? WHERE ARE WE?
I DON'T KNOW...
TOK TOK
MURMUR MURMUR
TEACHER... WHY DID WE SUDDENLY COME TO SEE A TEMPLE AT NIGHT?
ARE YOU TESTING HOW BRAVE WE ARE?
HEH HEH
HUH?
TEACH-ER?
HI, WELCOME... AND THANKS FOR COMING.
EH? BUT TEACHER, YOU JUST BROUGHT US HERE...

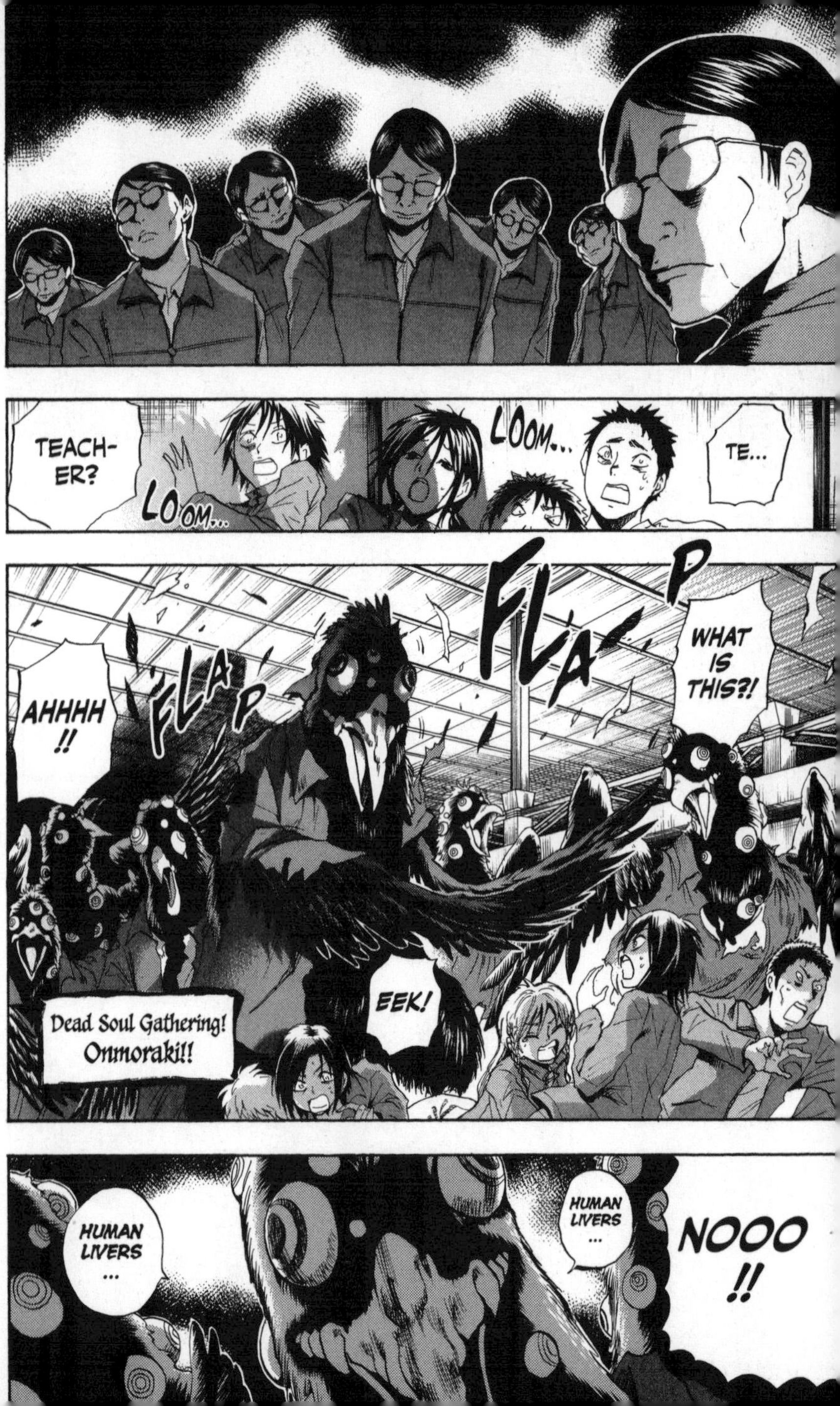
TE...
LOOM...
TEACHER?
LOOM...
FLAP
WHAT IS THIS?!
FLAP
AHHHH!!
EEK!
Dead Soul Gathering! Onmoraki!!
NOOO!!
HUMAN LIVERS...
HUMAN LIVERS...

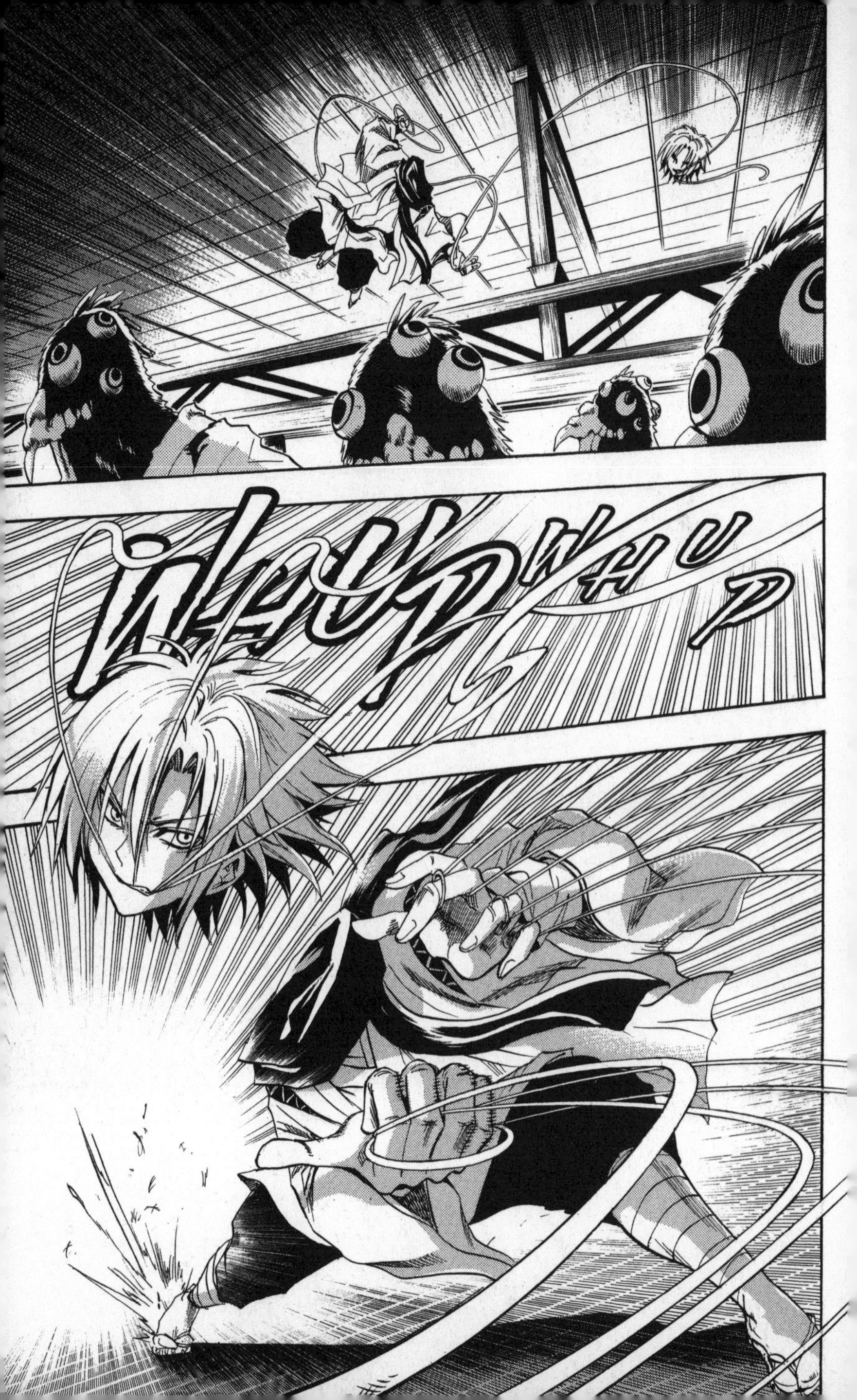
WHUPWHUP

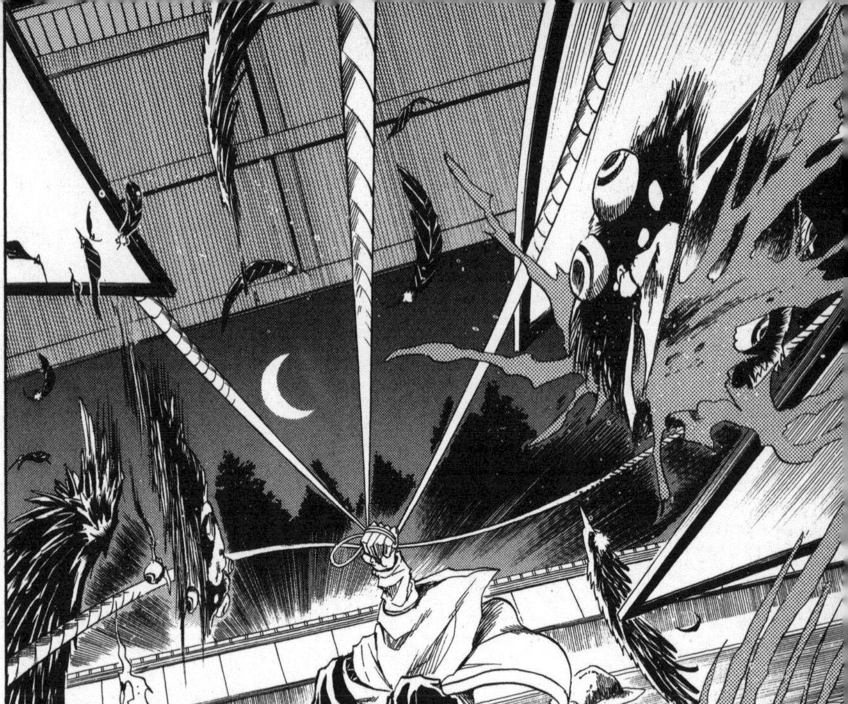

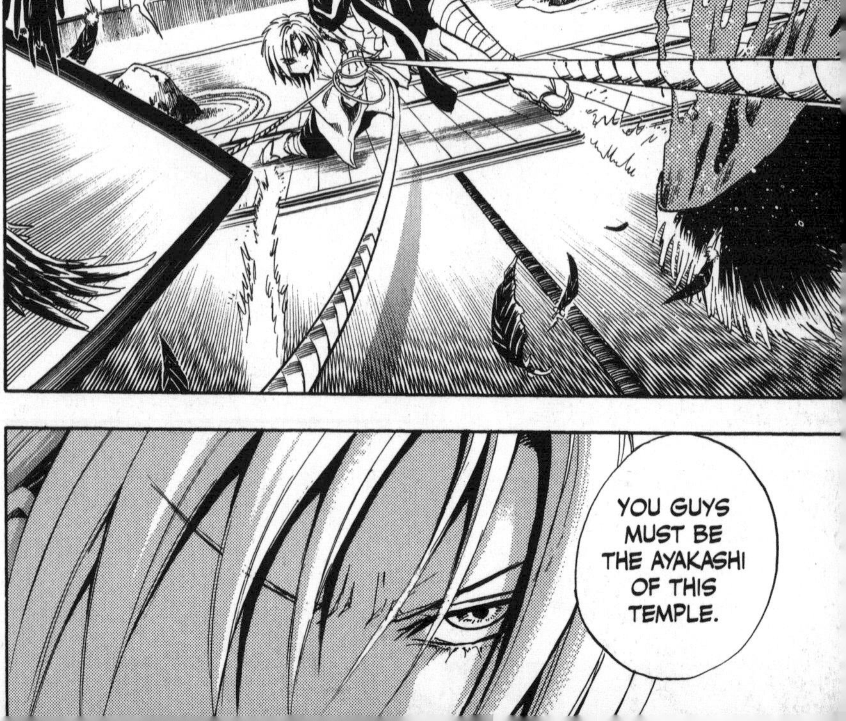
YOU GUYS MUST BE THE AYAKASHI OF THIS TEMPLE.

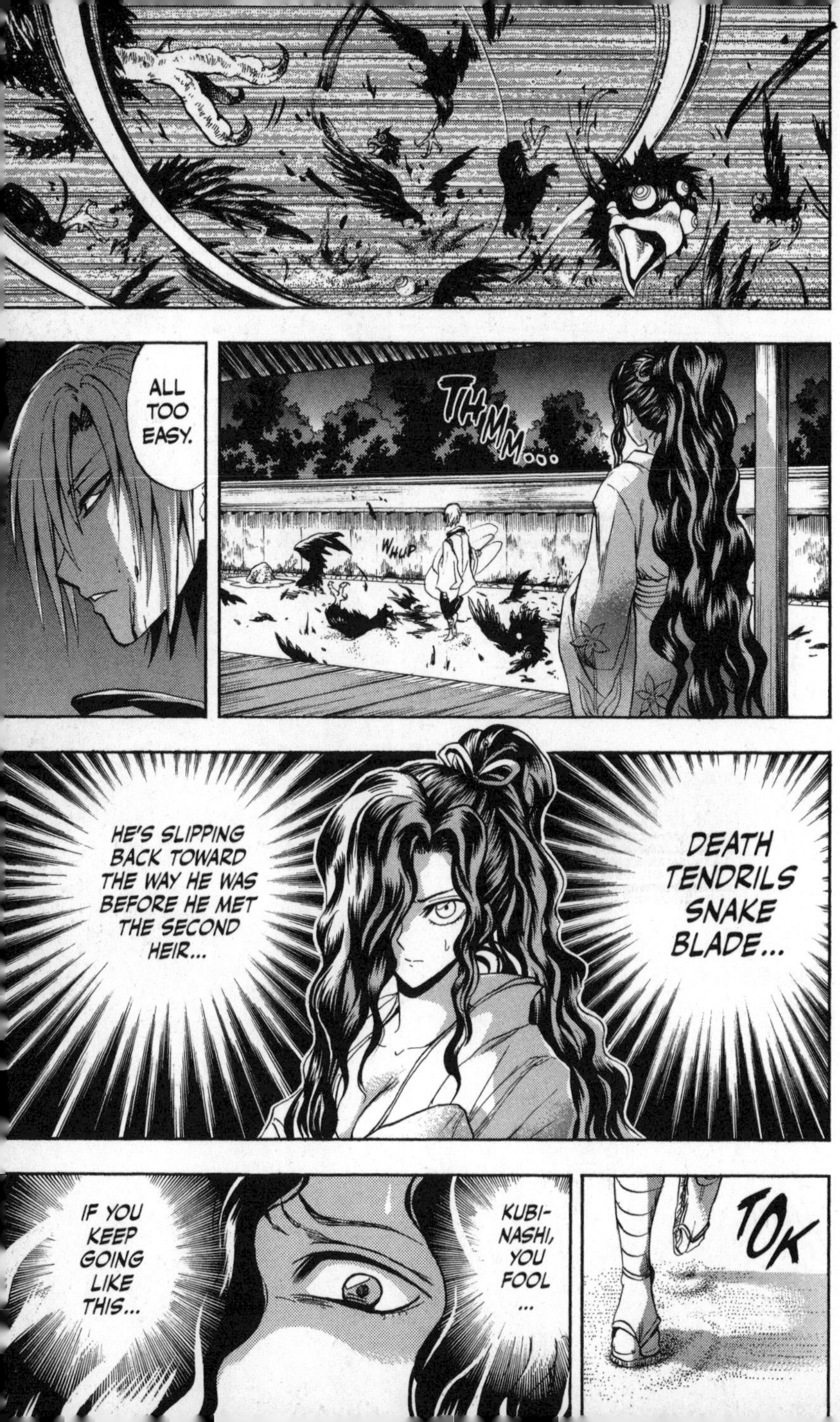
THMM...
WHUP
ALL TOO EASY.
DEATH TENDRILS SNAKE BLADE...
HE'S SLIPPING BACK TOWARD THE WAY HE WAS BEFORE HE MET THE SECOND HEIR...
TOK
KUBI-NASHI, YOU FOOL...
IF YOU KEEP GOING LIKE THIS...

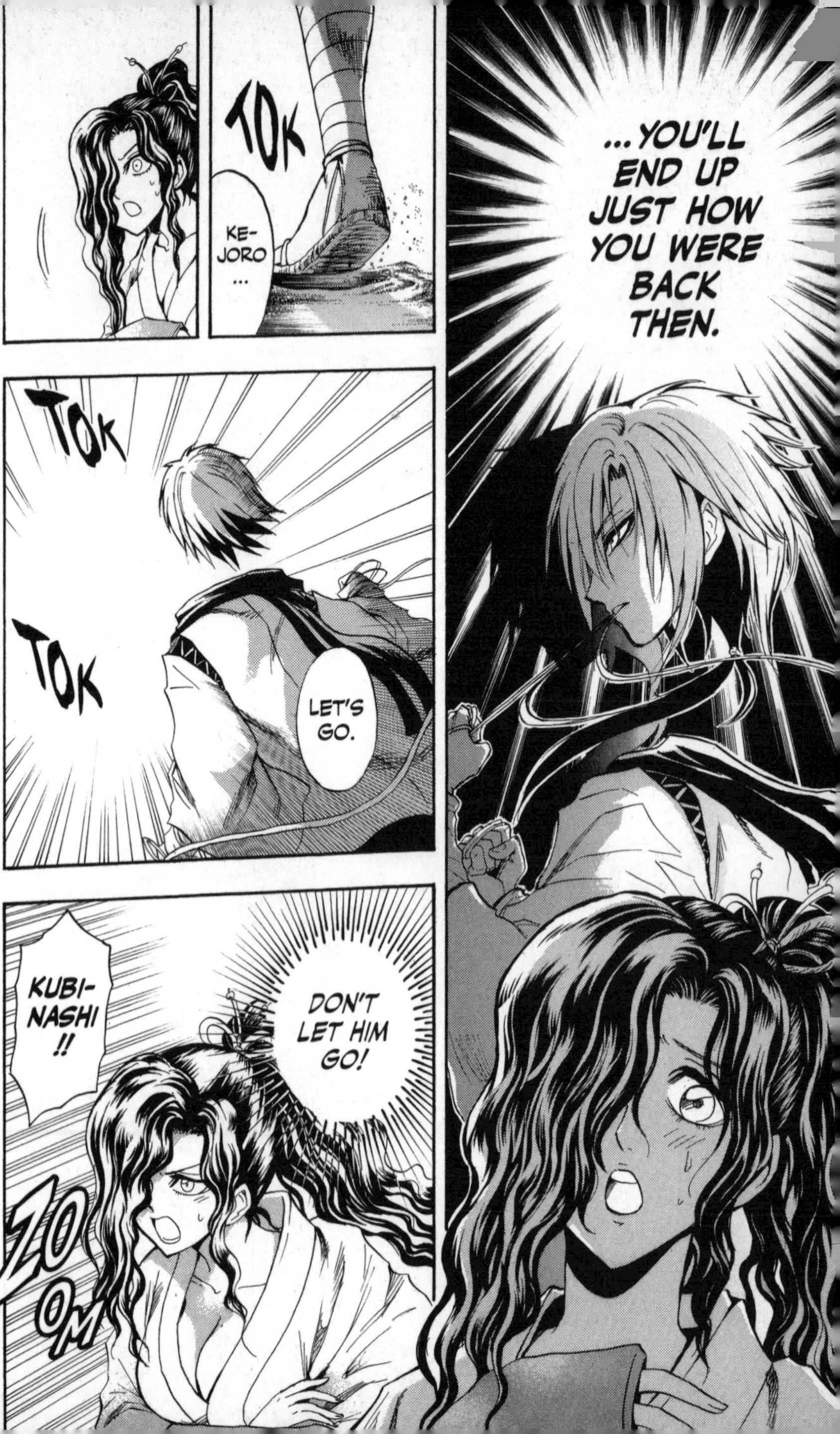
...YOU'LL END UP JUST HOW YOU WERE BACK THEN.
TOK
KE-JORO ...
TOK
TOK
LET'S GO.
DON'T LET HIM GO!
KUBI-NASHI !!
ZOOM

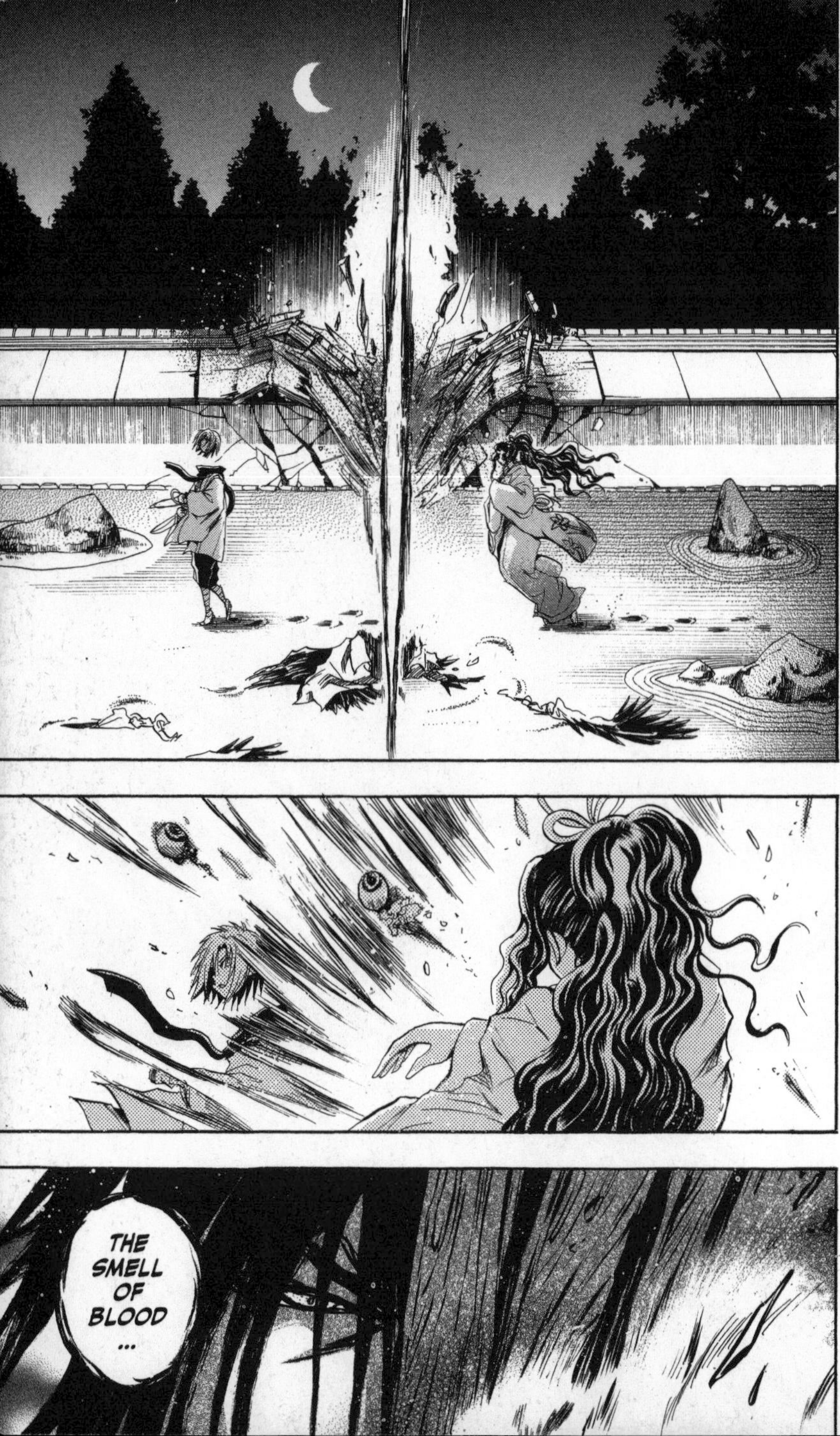
THE SMELL OF BLOOD ...

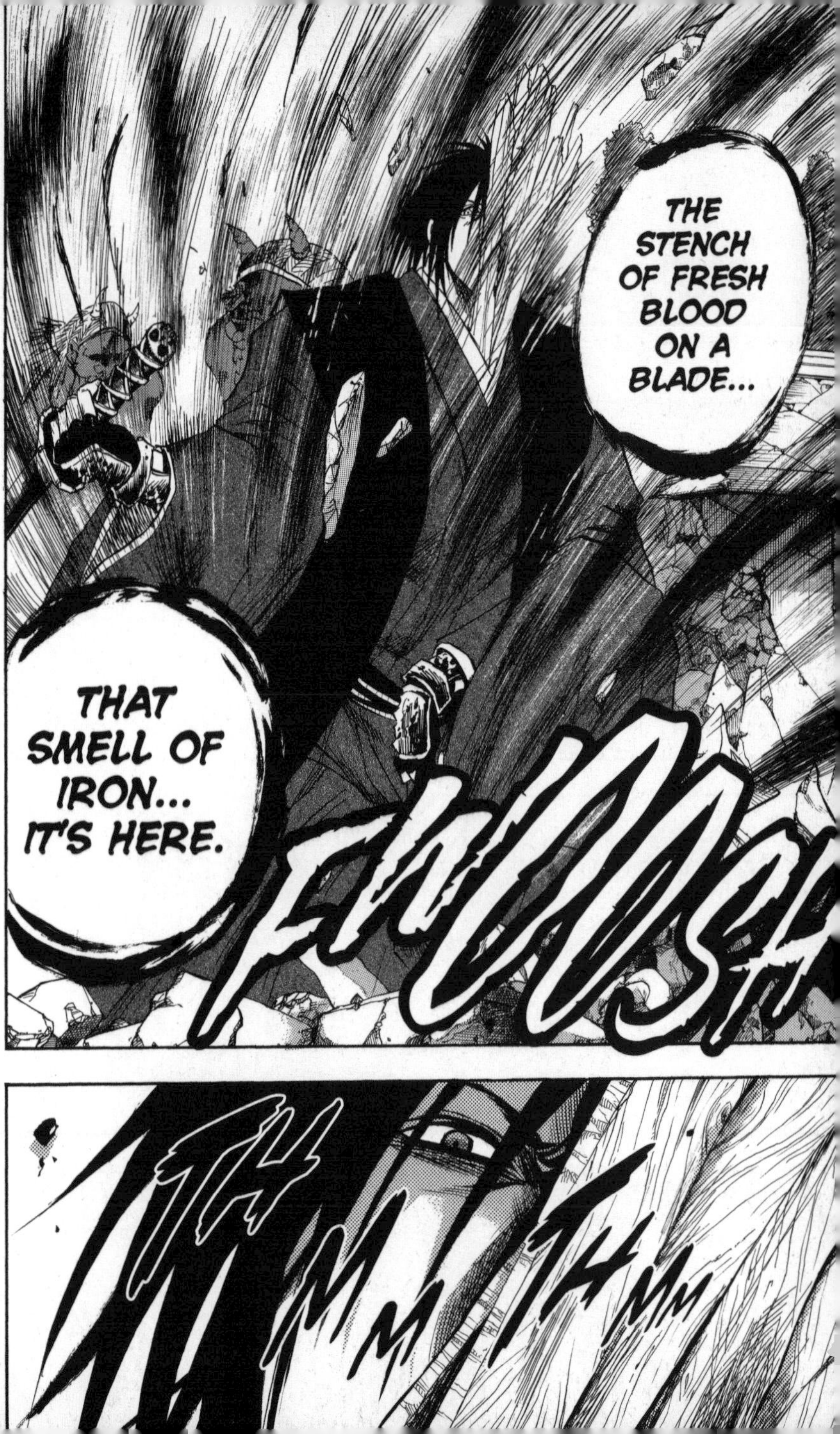
THE STENCH OF FRESH BLOOD ON A BLADE...
THAT SMELL OF IRON... IT'S HERE.

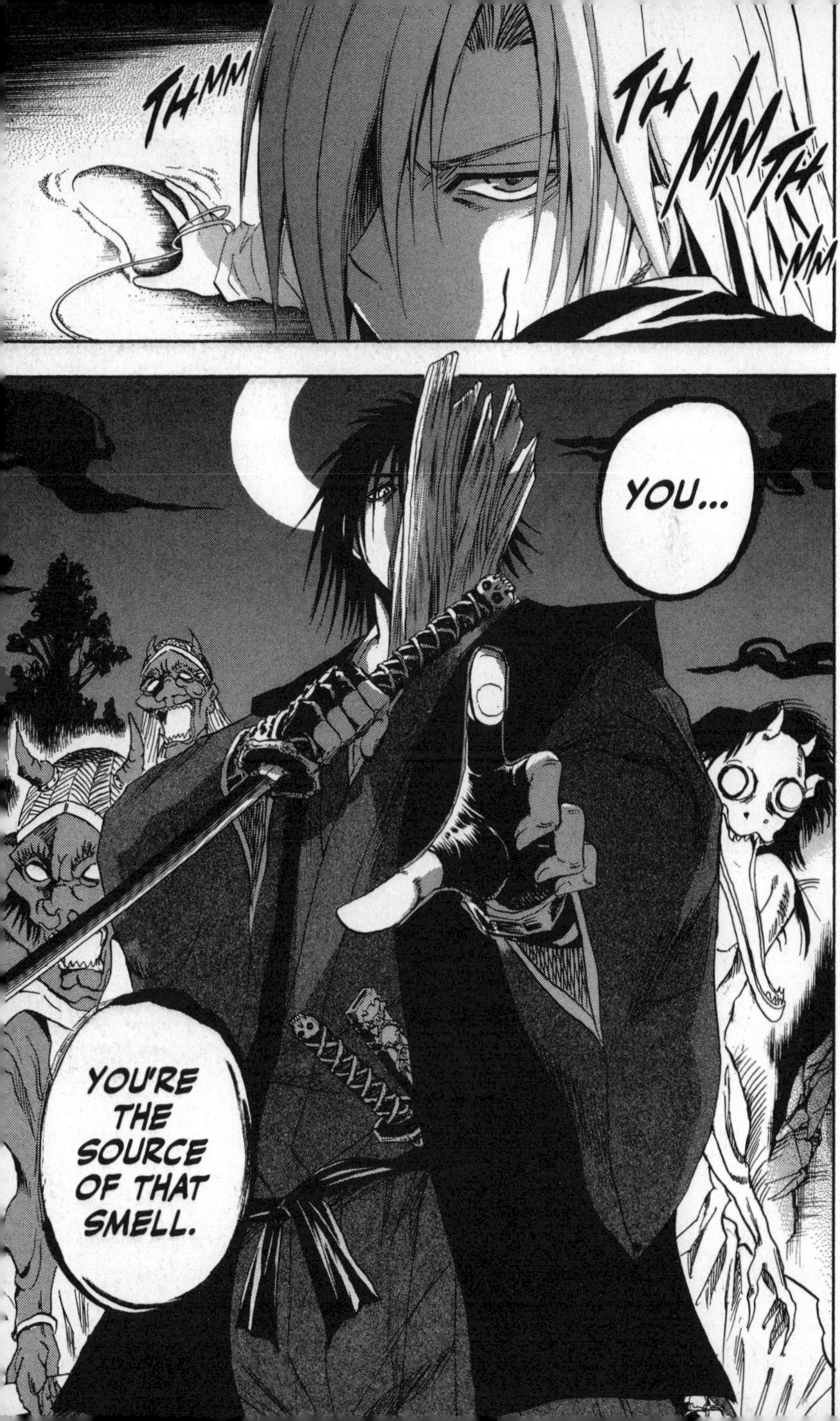
THMM THMM
THMM
YOU...
YOU'RE THE SOURCE OF THAT SMELL.

Relentless 4-panels

HAGOROMOMOMOMO!!

By Kana Yoshimura

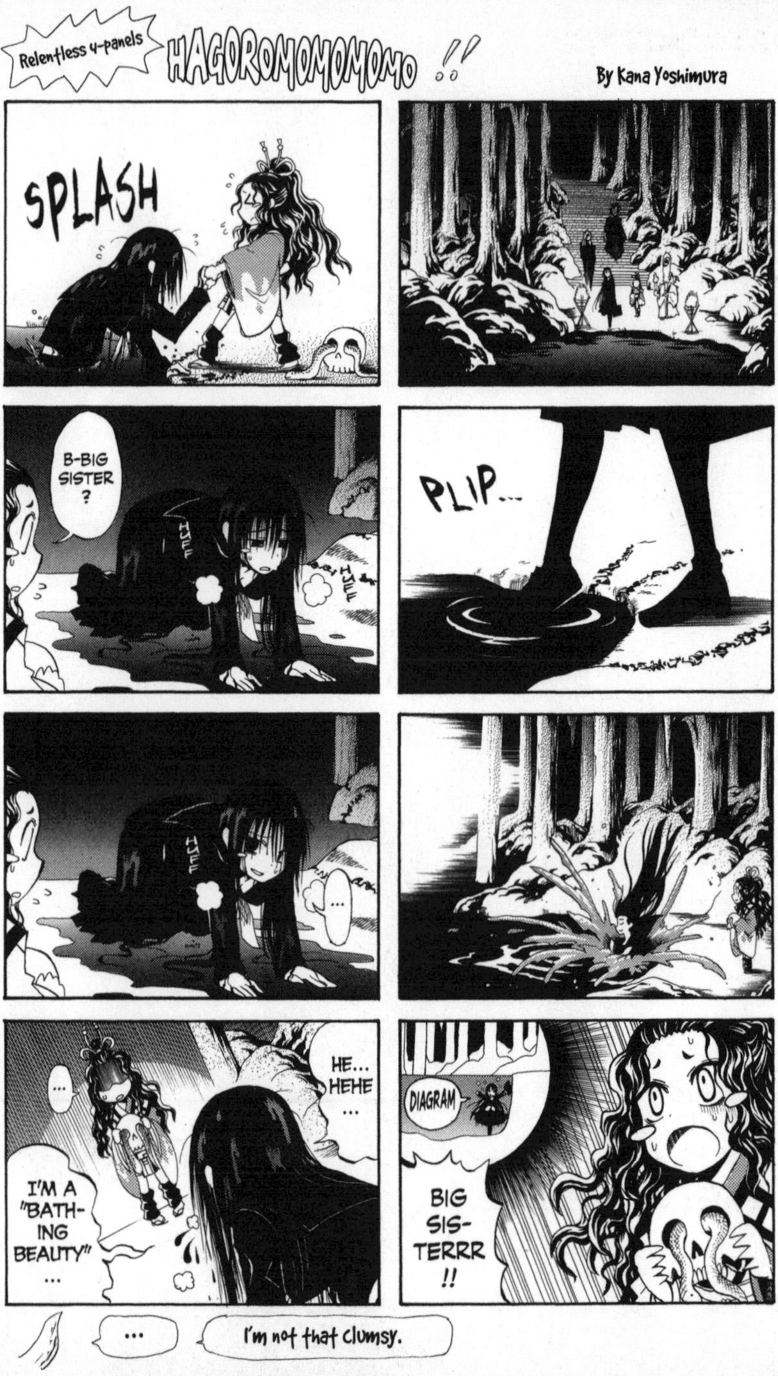
PLIP...
DIAGRAM
BIG SIS-TERRR!!
SPLASH
B-BIG SISTER?
HUFF
HUFF
HUFF
...
HE... HEHE...
...
I'M A "BATH-ING BEAUTY"...

... I'm not that clumsy.

Act 101: Devil's Drum

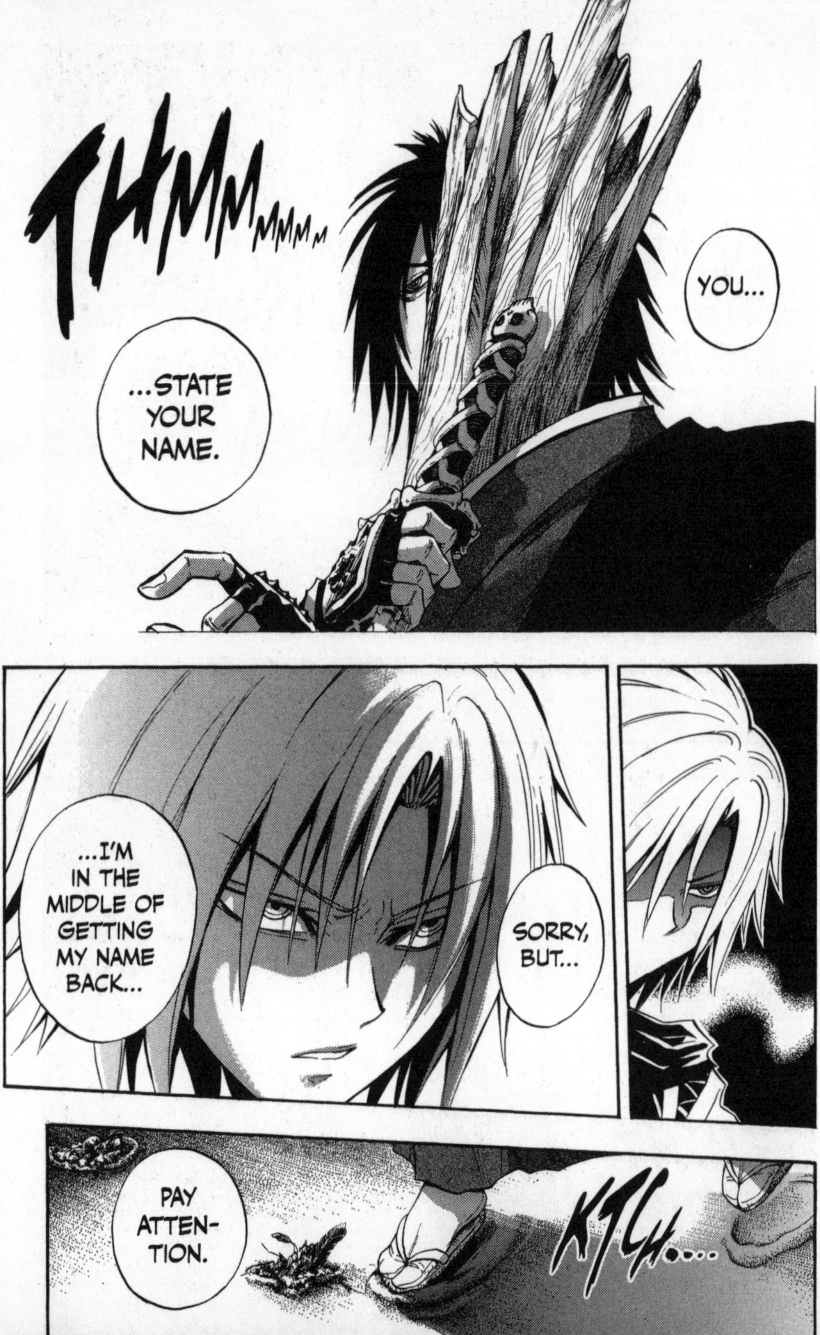
THMMMMMM
YOU...
...STATE YOUR NAME.
SORRY, BUT...
...I'M IN THE MIDDLE OF GETTING MY NAME BACK...
KTCH....
PAY ATTENTION.

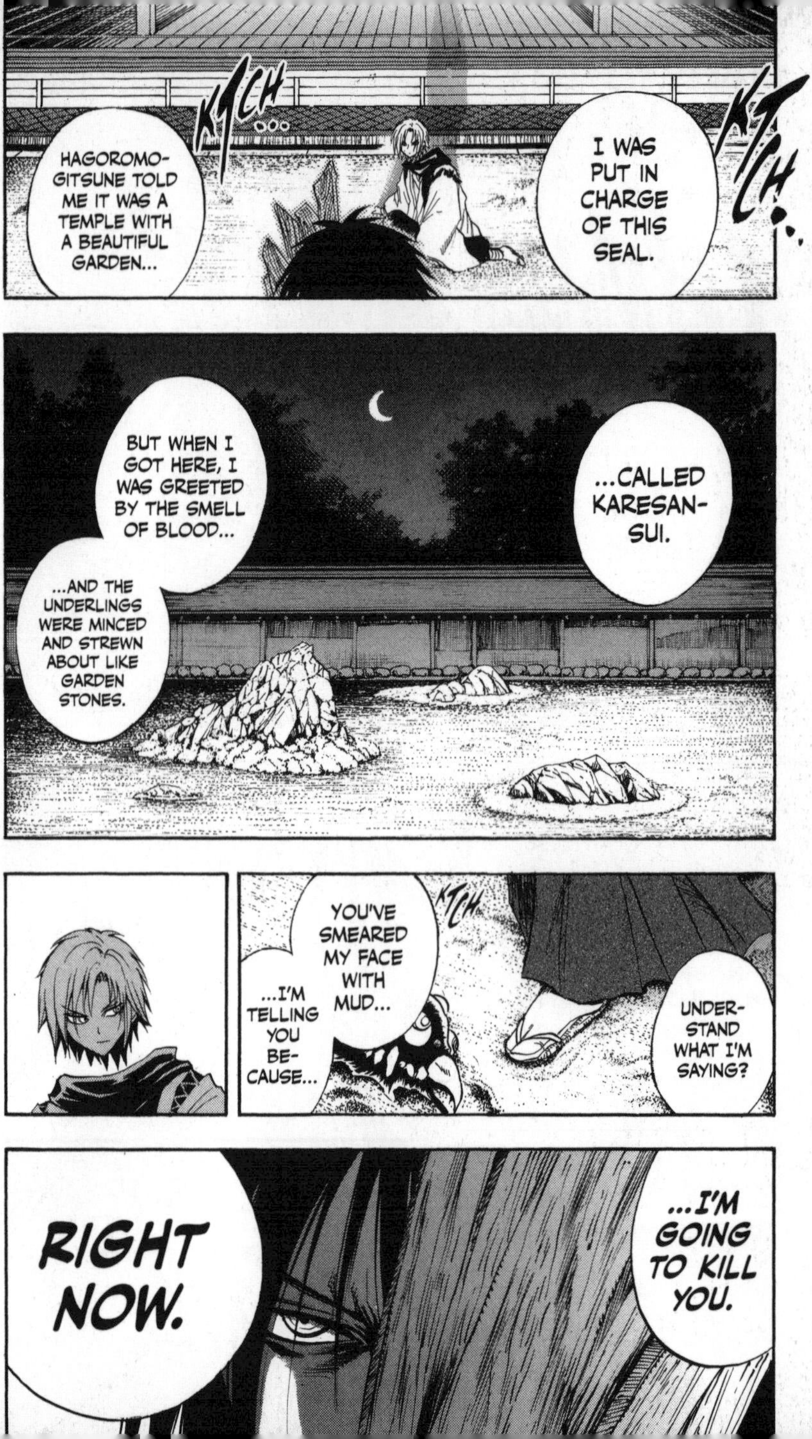
KTCH...
I WAS PUT IN CHARGE OF THIS SEAL.
KTCH
HAGOROMO-GITSUNE TOLD ME IT WAS A TEMPLE WITH A BEAUTIFUL GARDEN...
...CALLED KARESAN-SUI.
BUT WHEN I GOT HERE, I WAS GREETED BY THE SMELL OF BLOOD...
...AND THE UNDERLINGS WERE MINCED AND STREWN ABOUT LIKE GARDEN STONES.
UNDER-STAND WHAT I'M SAYING?
KTCH
YOU'VE SMEARED MY FACE WITH MUD...
...I'M TELLING YOU BE-CAUSE...
...I'M GOING TO KILL YOU.
RIGHT NOW.

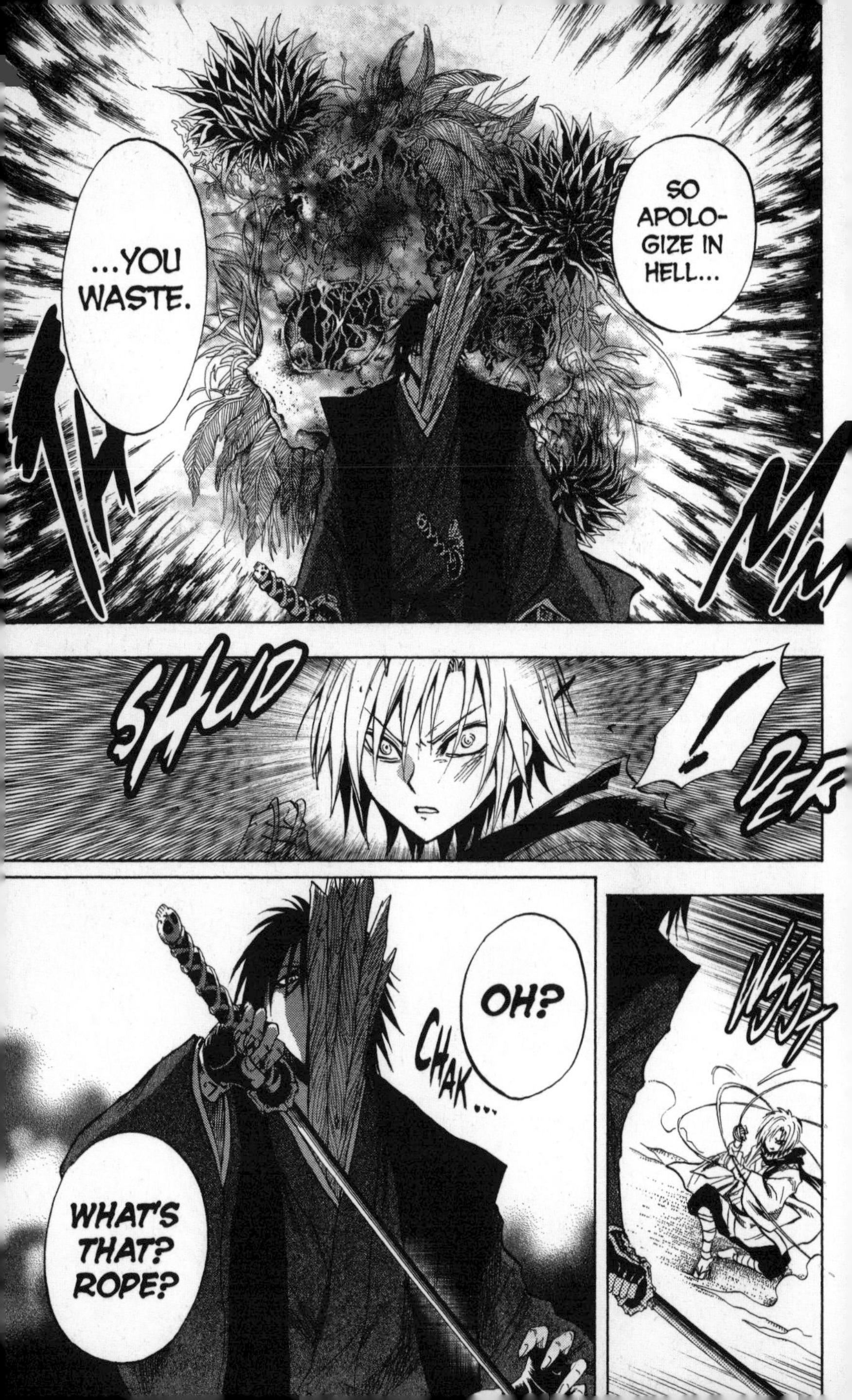
SO APOLOGIZE IN HELL...
...YOU WASTE.
OH?
CHAK...
WHAT'S THAT? ROPE?

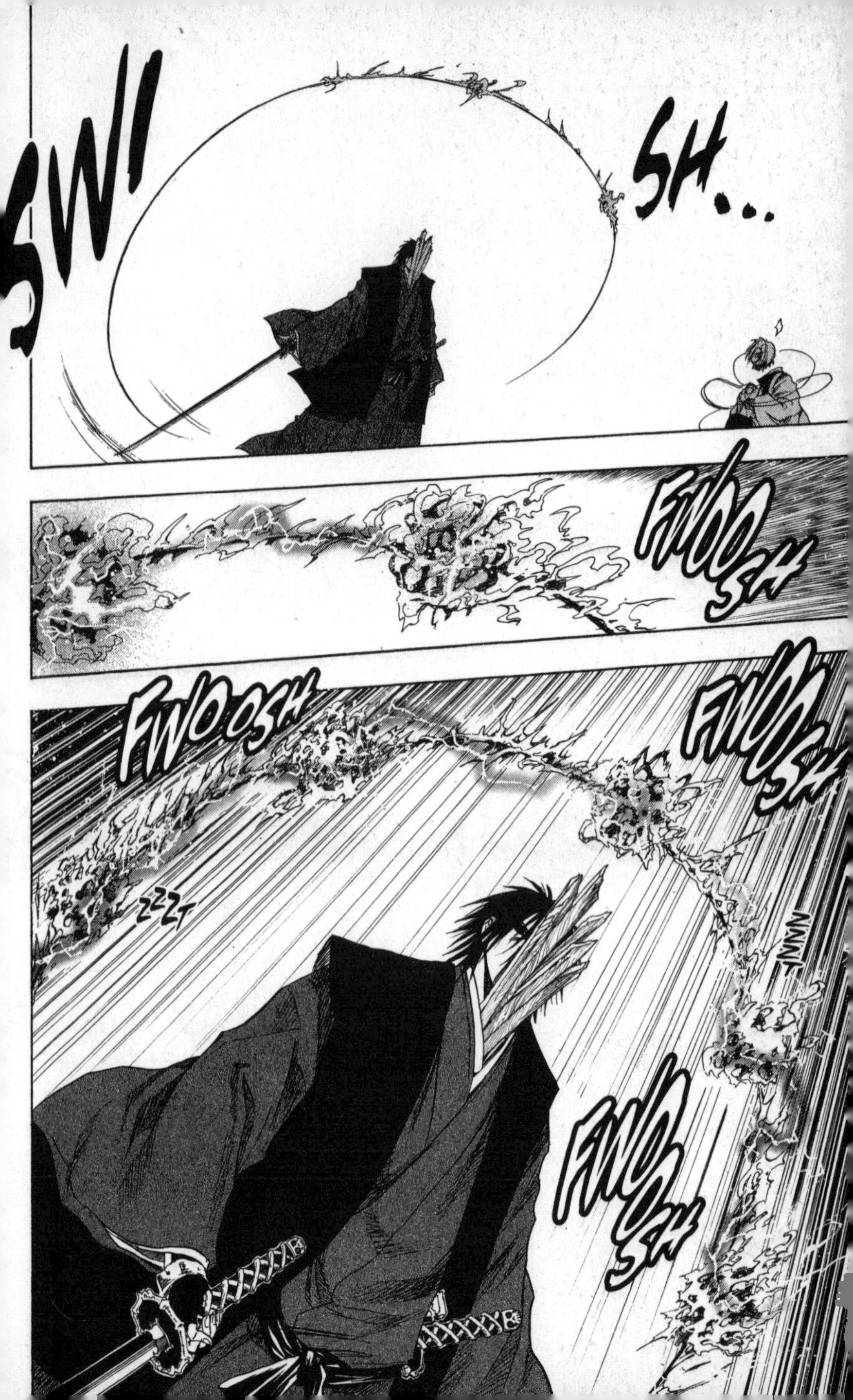
SWI
SH...
FWOOSH
FWOOSH
FWOOSH
ZZZT
NNNN
FWOOSH

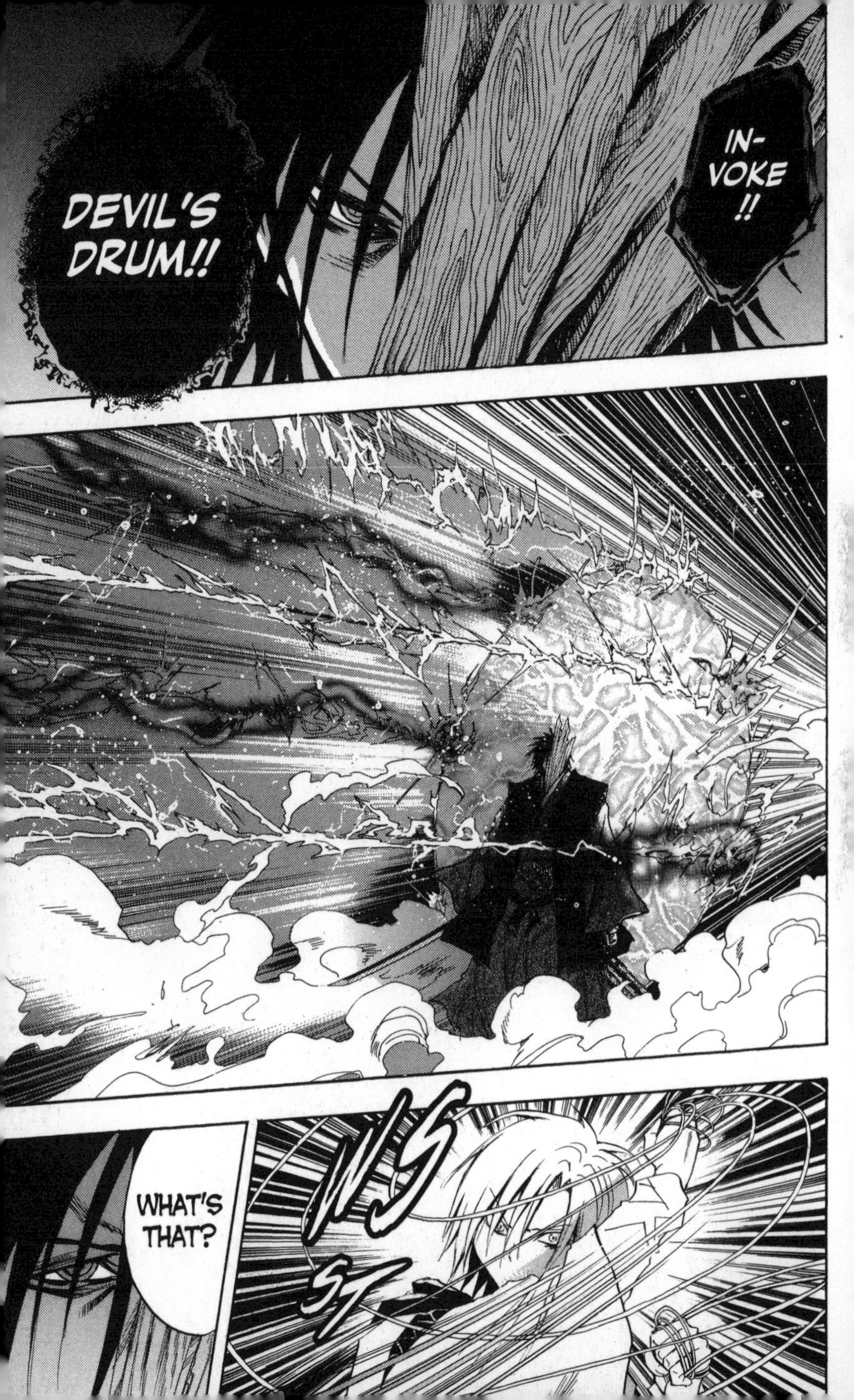
IN-VOKE!!
DEVIL'S DRUM!!
WHS
ST
WHAT'S THAT?

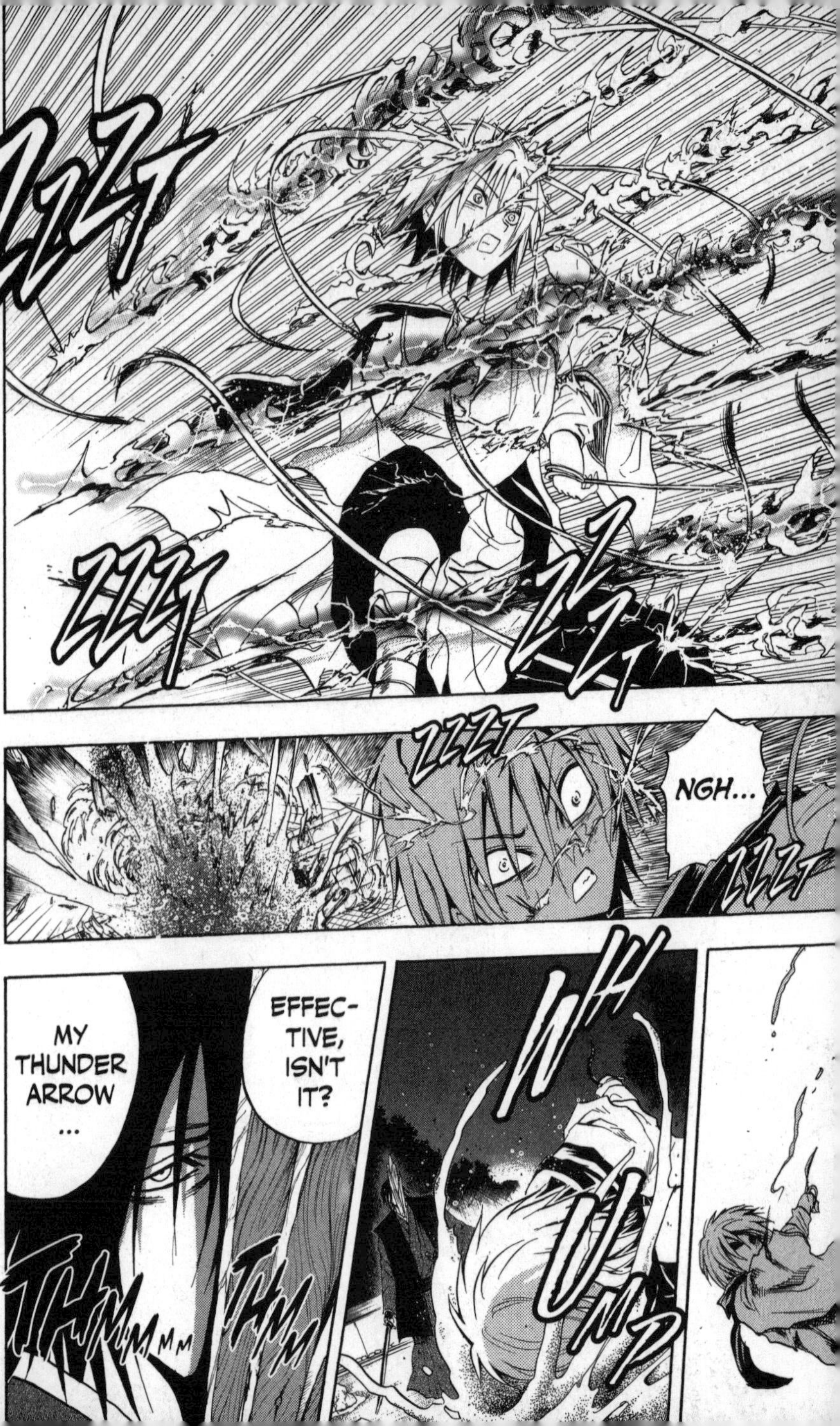
ZZZT
ZZZT
ZZZT
ZZZT
NGH...
ZZZT
MY THUNDER ARROW ...
EFFECTIVE, ISN'T IT?
THMMMMM
THMM
WHUMP

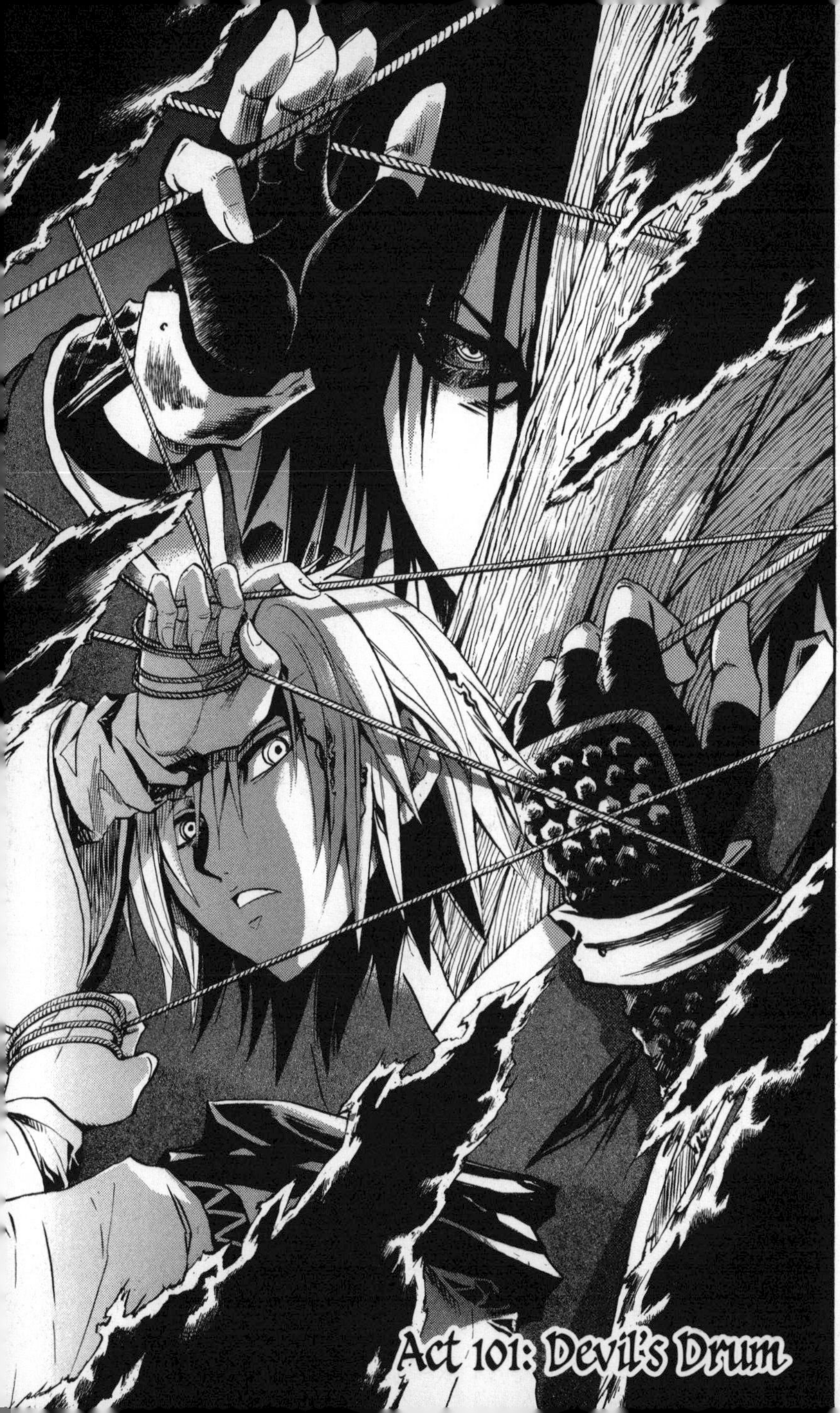
Act 101: Devil's Drum

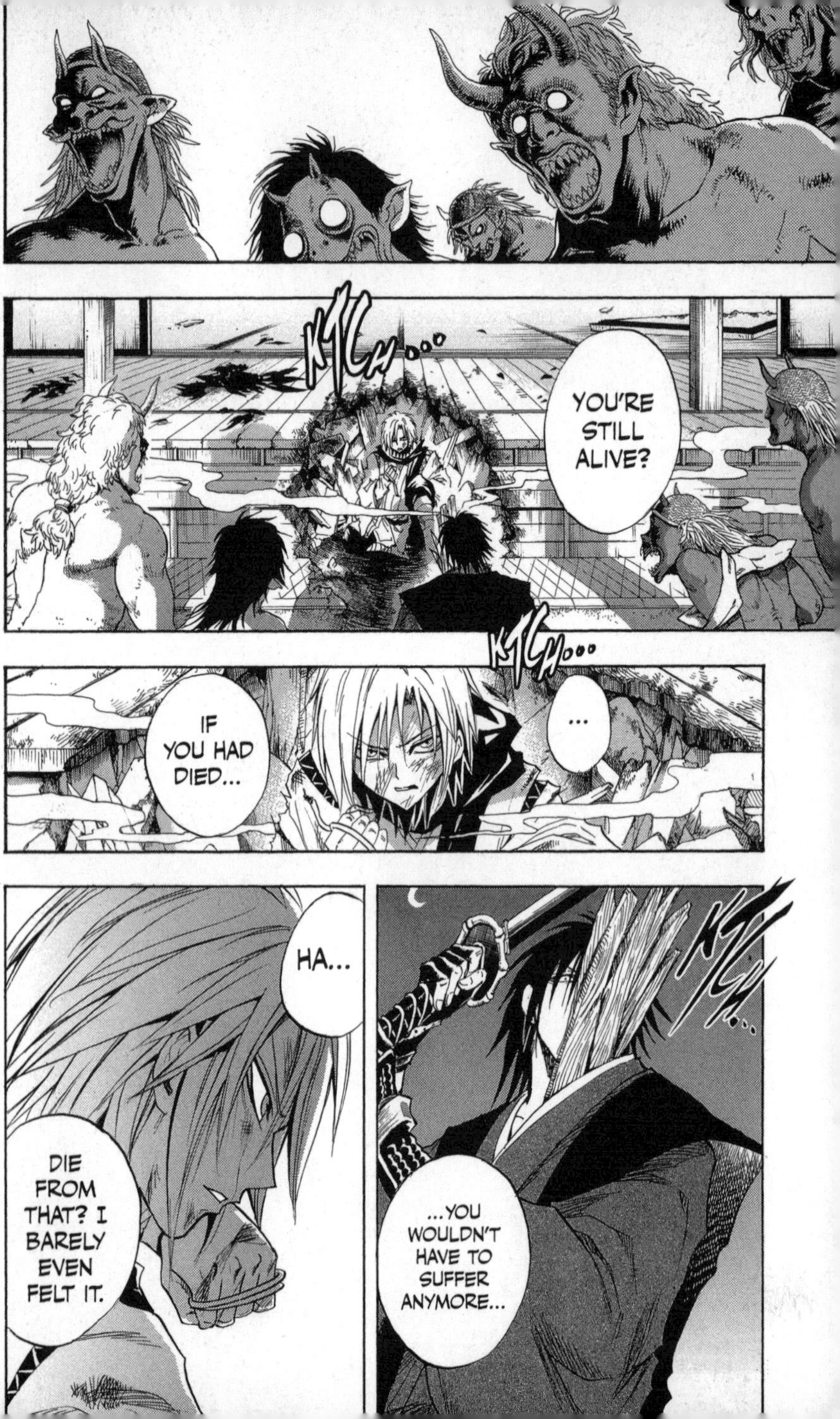
KTCH...
YOU'RE STILL ALIVE?
KTCH...
...
IF YOU HAD DIED...
KTCH...
...YOU WOULDN'T HAVE TO SUFFER ANYMORE...
HA...
DIE FROM THAT? I BARELY EVEN FELT IT.

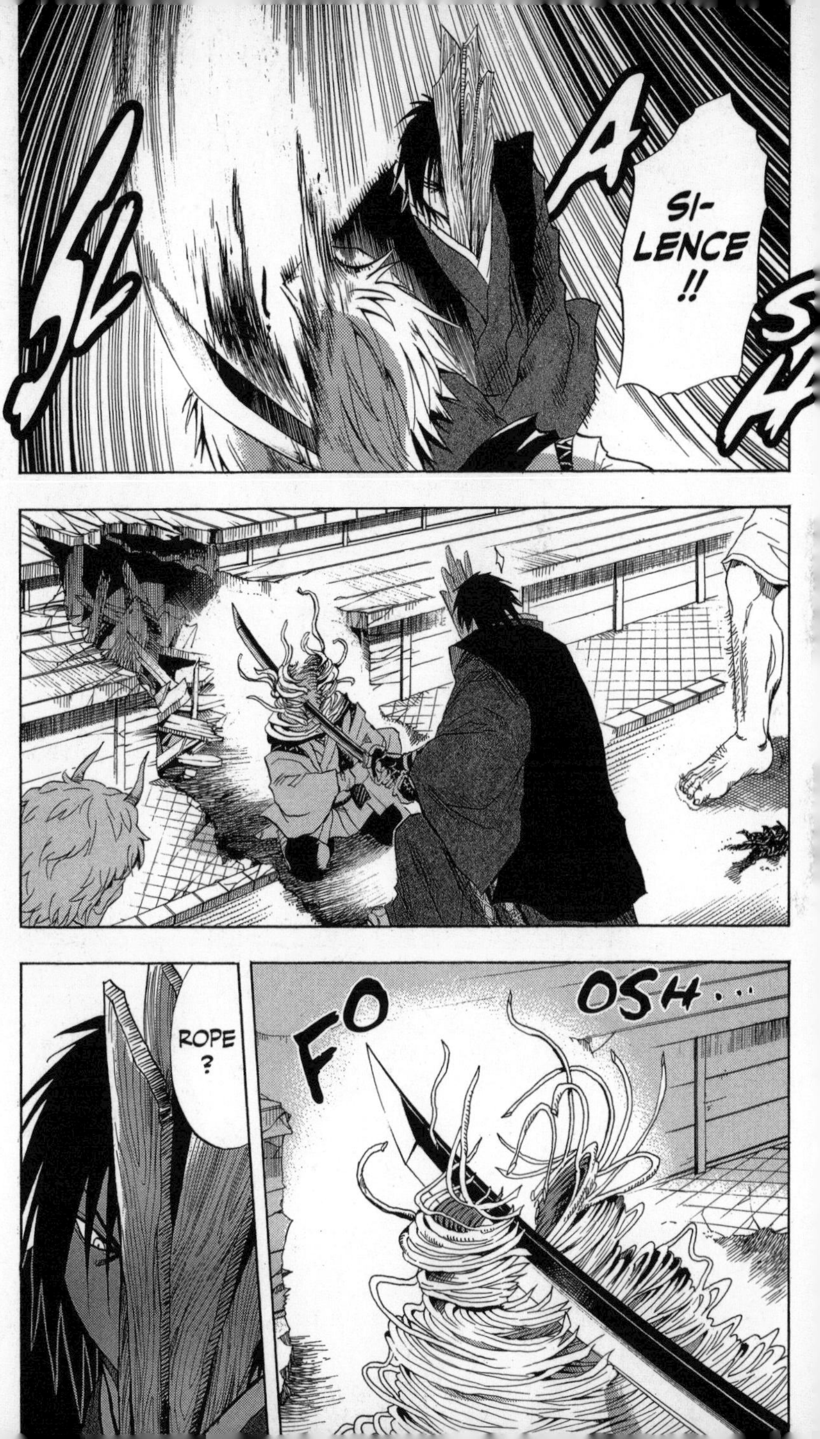
SI-
LENCE
!!
FO
OSH...
ROPE
?

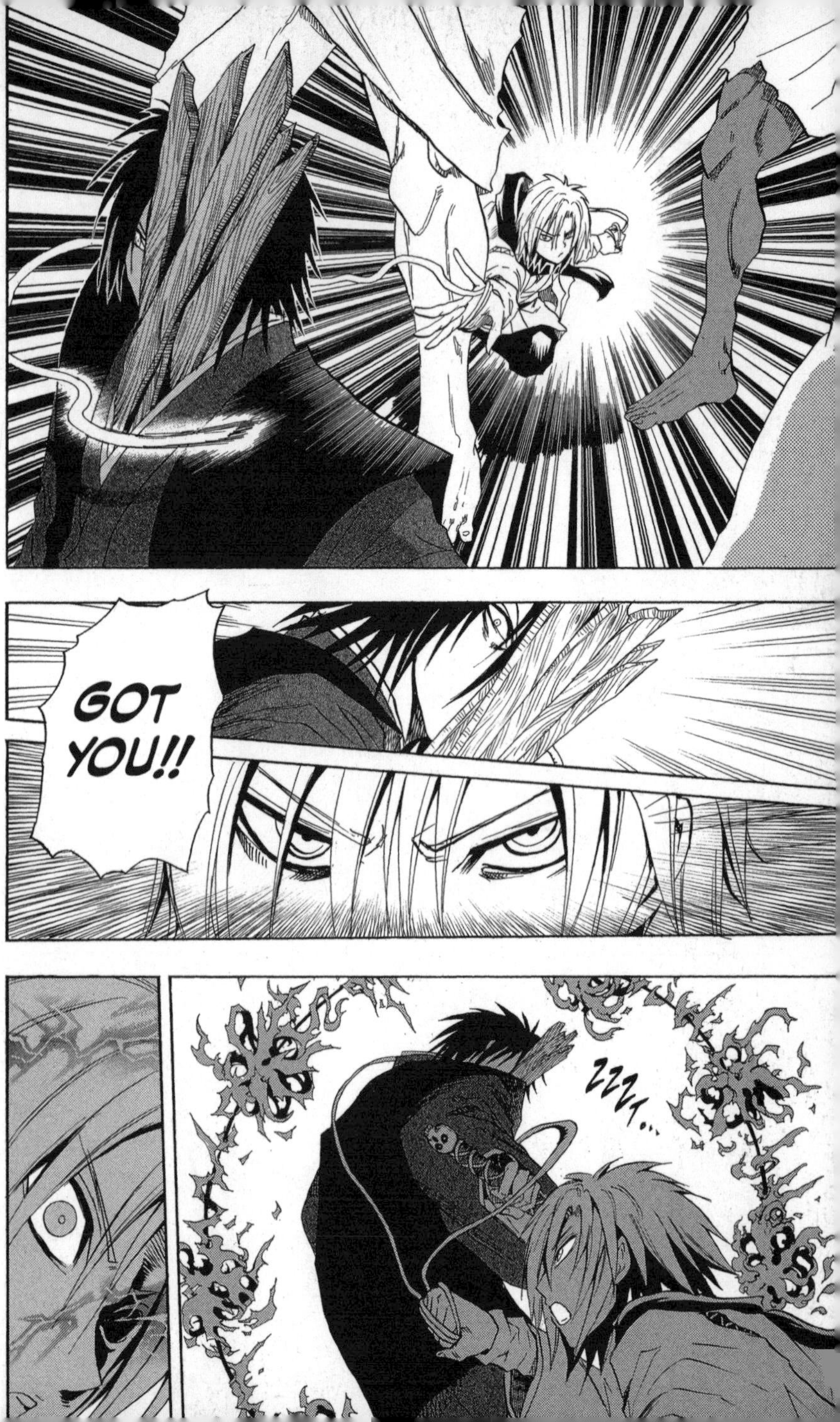
GOT YOU!!
ZZZZ...

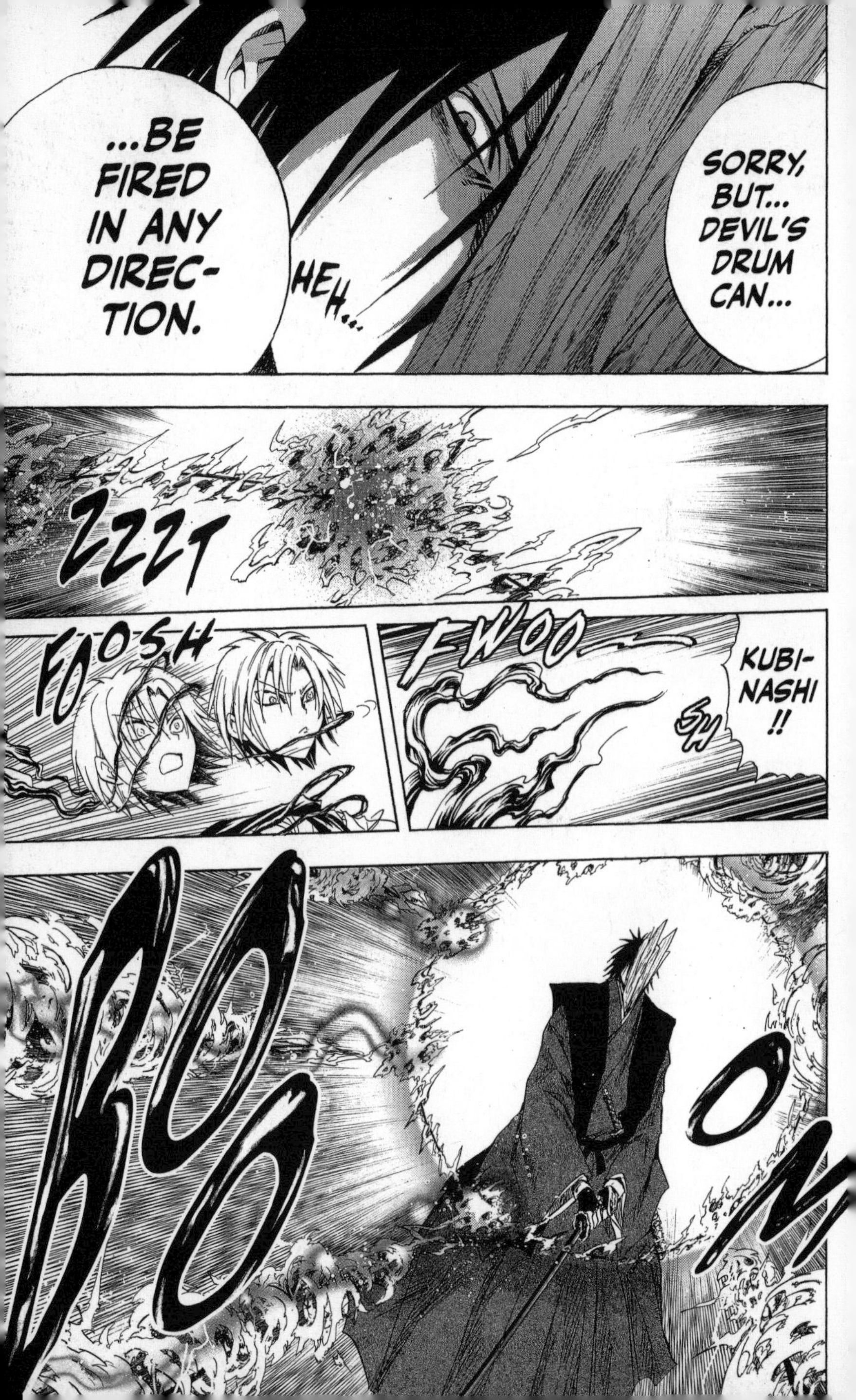
SORRY, BUT... DEVIL'S DRUM CAN...
HEH...
...BE FIRED IN ANY DIREC-TION.
ZZZT
FWOO
SH
KUBI-NASHI!!
FOOSH
KBOOM

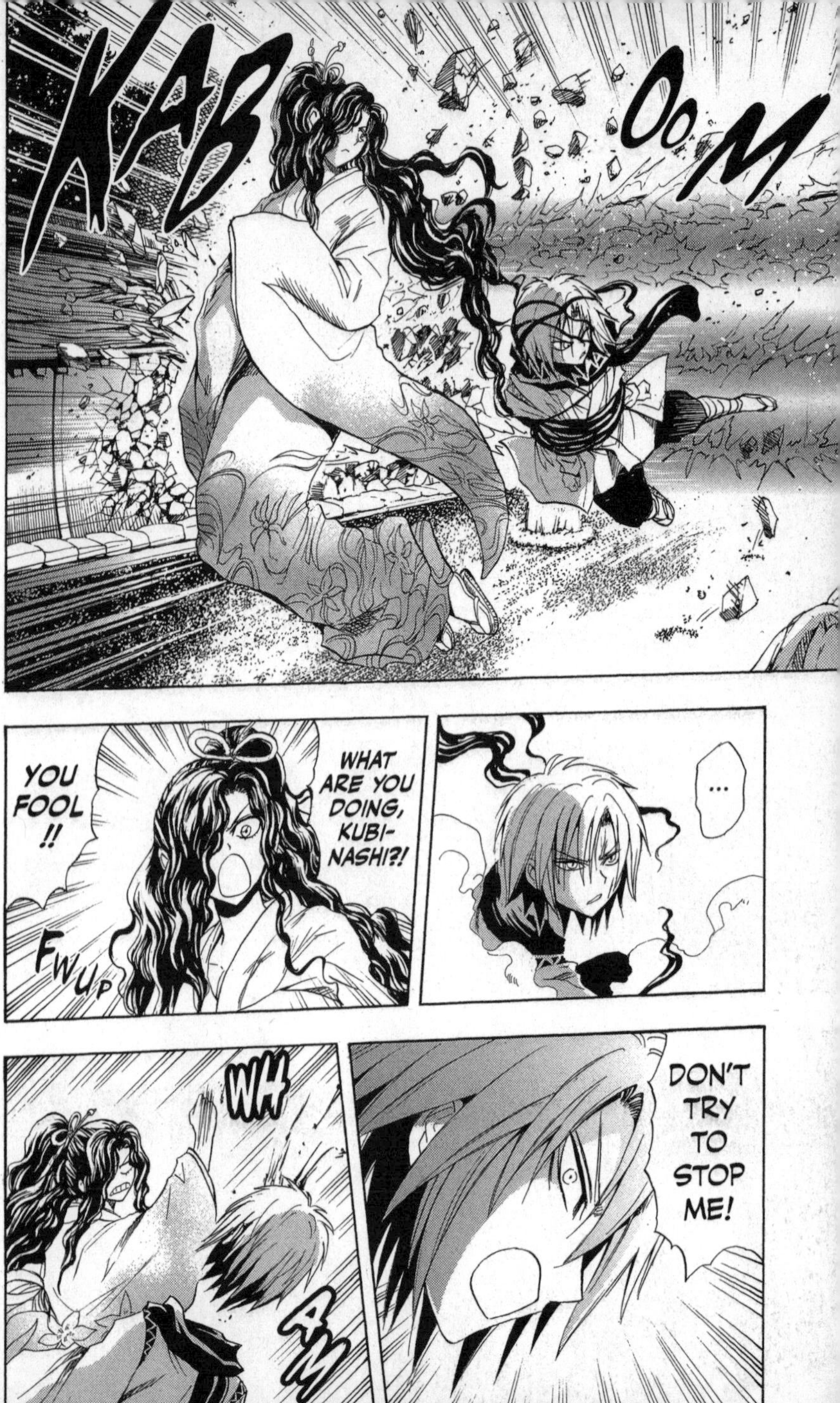
KAB
OOM
...
WHAT ARE YOU DOING, KUBI-NASHI?!
YOU FOOL!!
FWUP
DON'T TRY TO STOP ME!
WH
AM

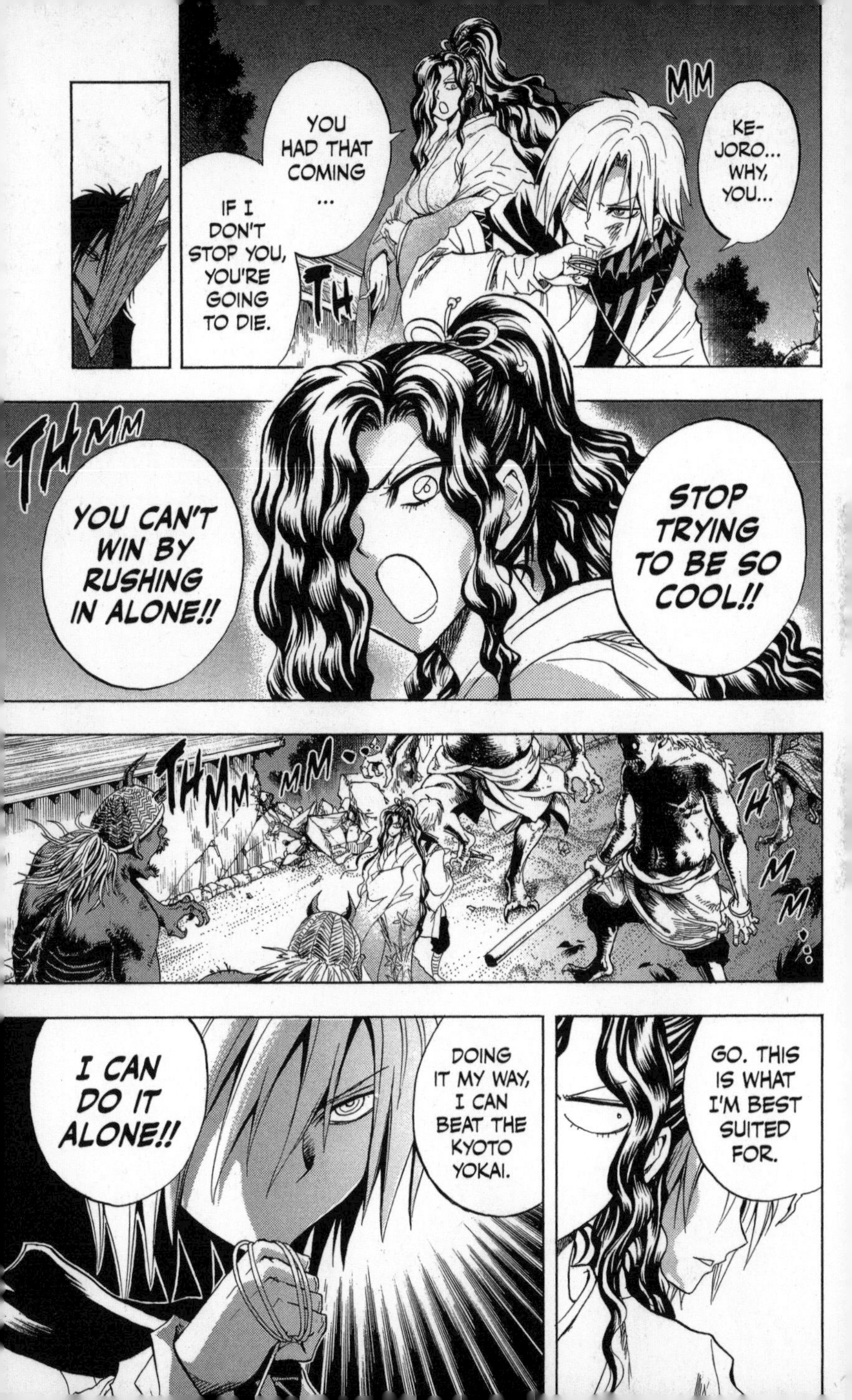
MM
KE-JORO... WHY, YOU...
YOU HAD THAT COMING ...
IF I DON'T STOP YOU, YOU'RE GOING TO DIE.
TH
STOP TRYING TO BE SO COOL!!
YOU CAN'T WIN BY RUSHING IN ALONE!!
THMM
THMM...
THMM MM...
GO. THIS IS WHAT I'M BEST SUITED FOR.
DOING IT MY WAY, I CAN BEAT THE KYOTO YOKAI.
I CAN DO IT ALONE!!

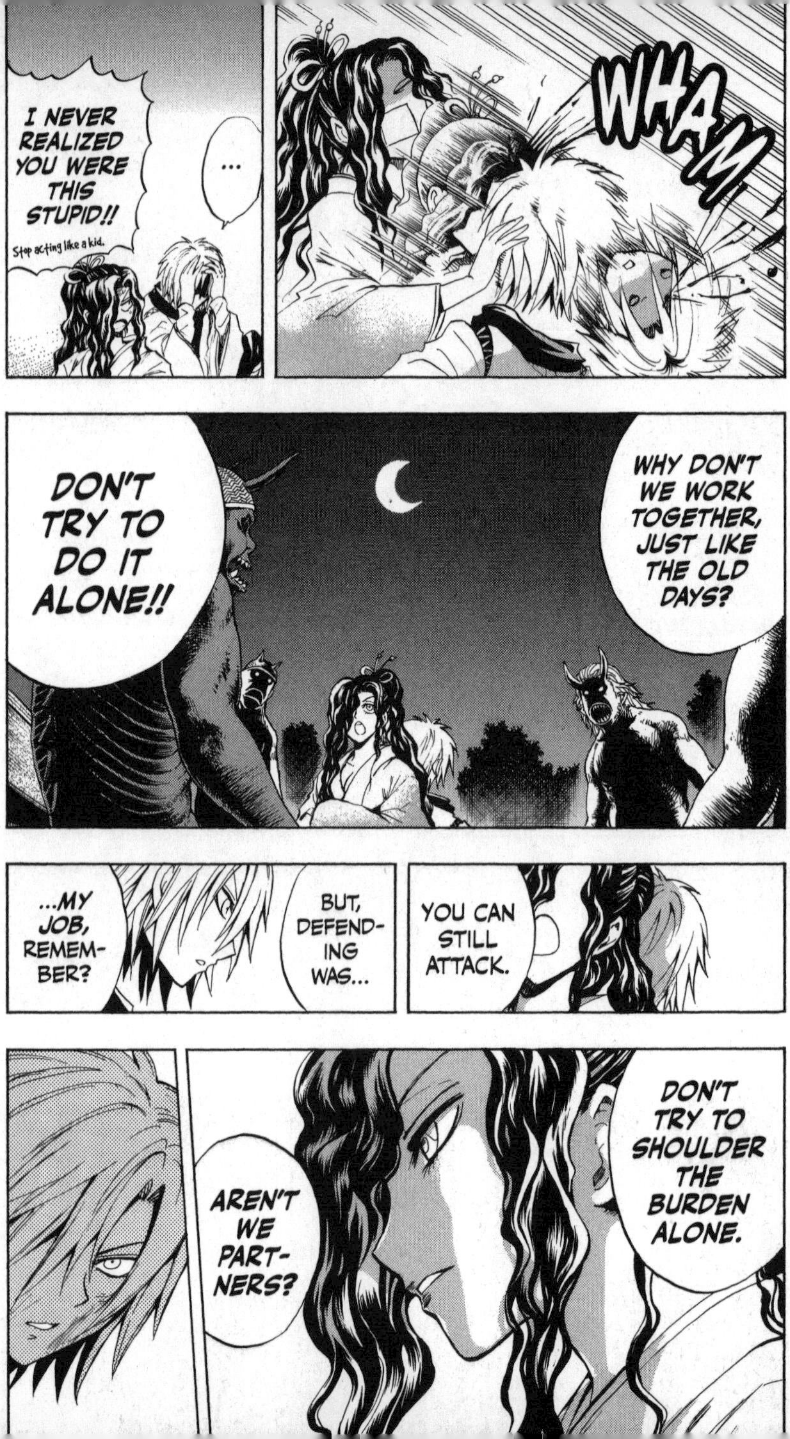
WHAM
...
I NEVER REALIZED YOU WERE THIS STUPID!!
Stop acting like a kid.
WHY DON'T WE WORK TOGETHER, JUST LIKE THE OLD DAYS?
DON'T TRY TO DO IT ALONE!!
YOU CAN STILL ATTACK.
BUT, DEFENDING WAS...
...MY JOB, REMEMBER?
DON'T TRY TO SHOULDER THE BURDEN ALONE.
AREN'T WE PARTNERS?

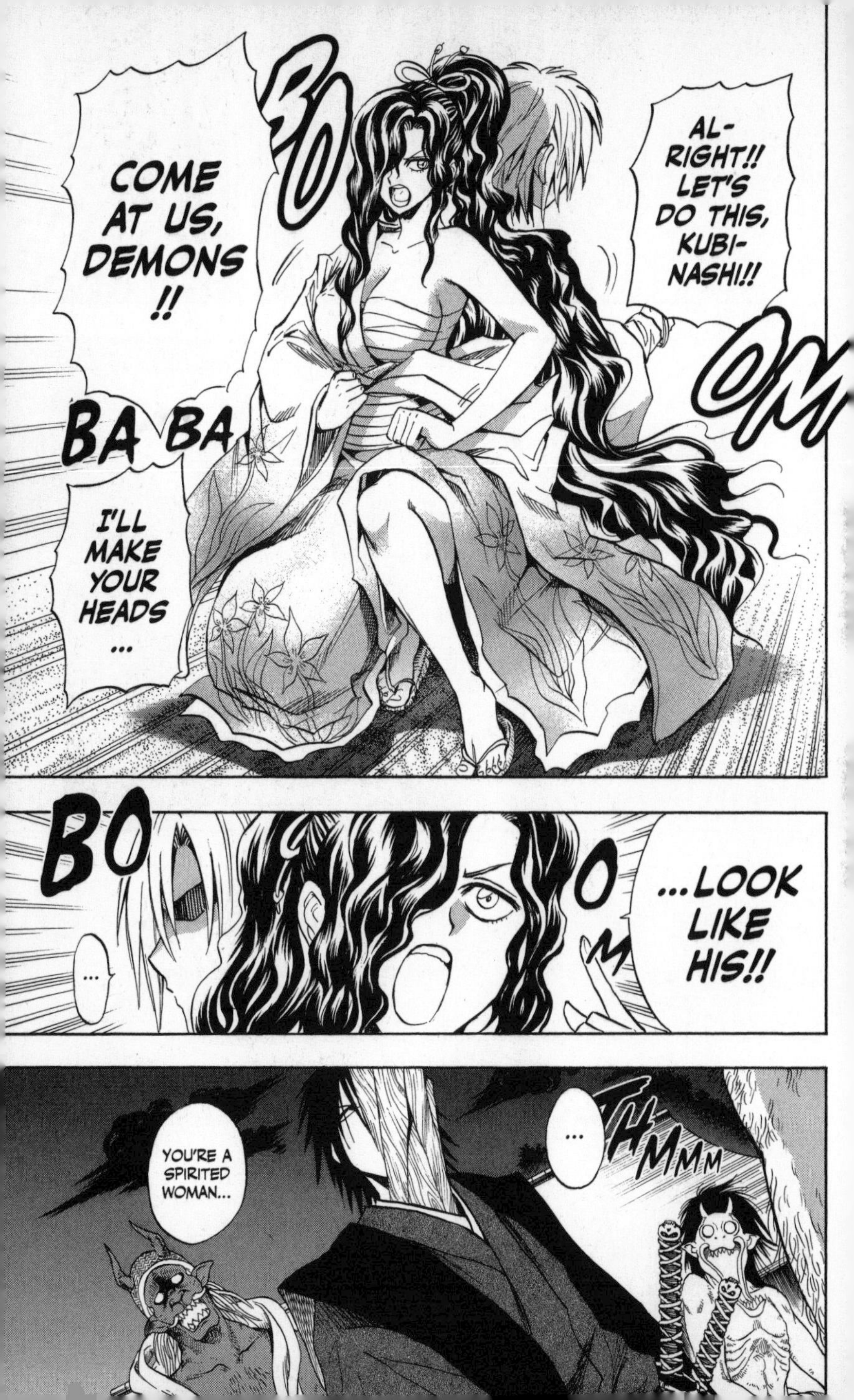

AL-RIGHT!! LET'S DO THIS, KUBI-NASHI!!
BO
OM
COME AT US, DEMONS!!
BA BA
I'LL MAKE YOUR HEADS...
...LOOK LIKE HIS!!
BO O M
...
...
THMMM
YOU'RE A SPIRITED WOMAN...

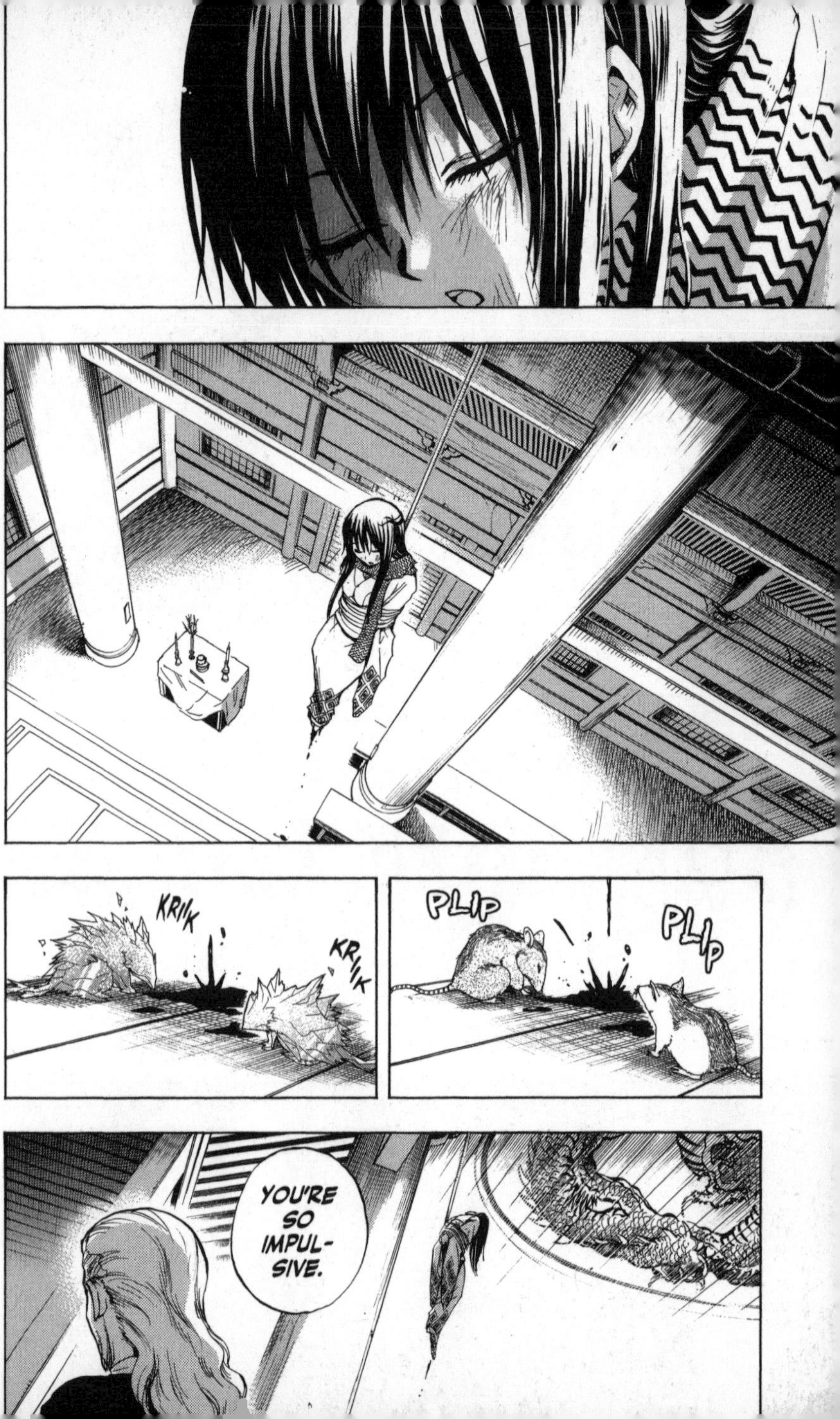
PLIP
PLIP
KRIK
KRIK
YOU'RE SO IMPUL-SIVE.

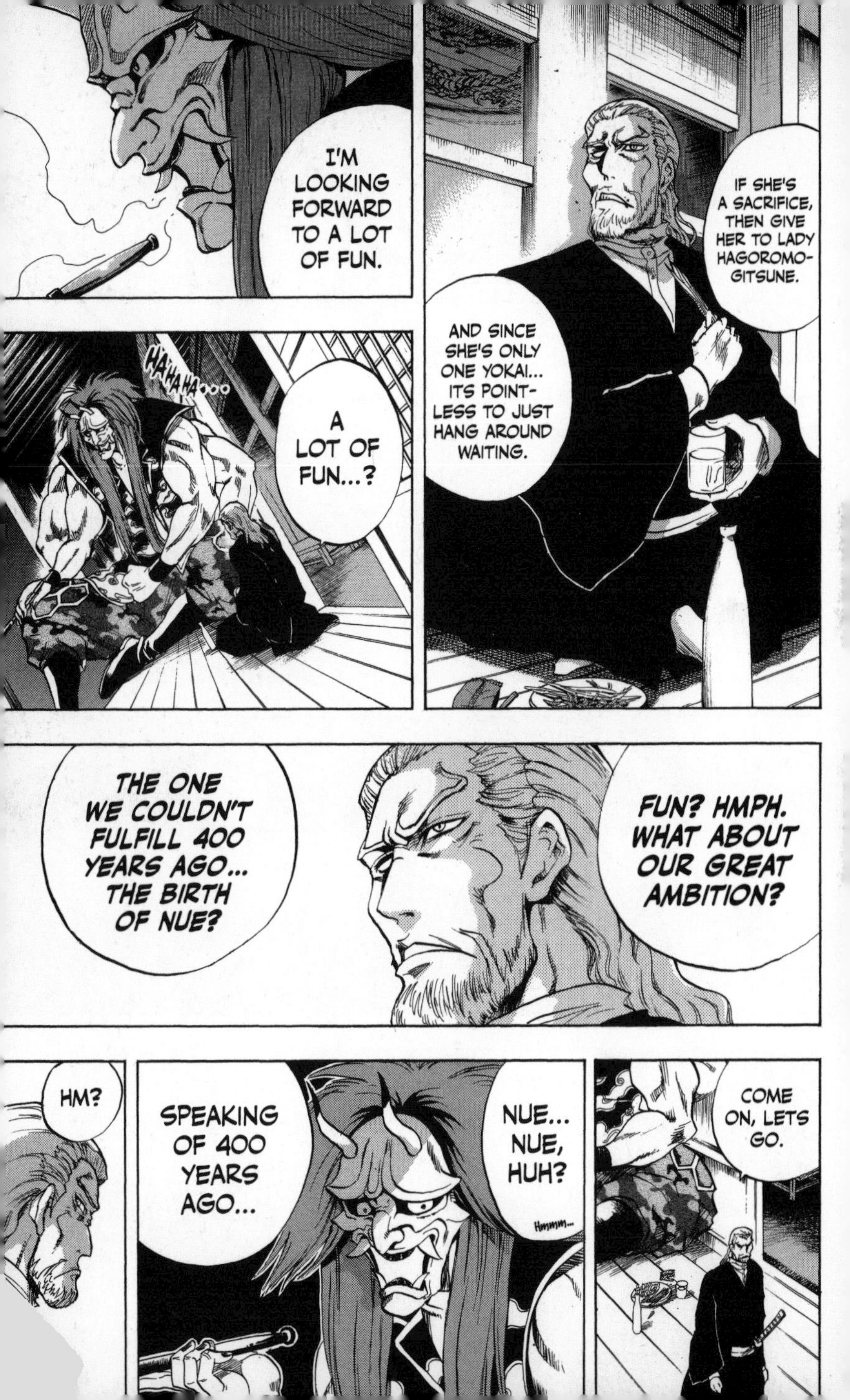
IF SHE'S A SACRIFICE, THEN GIVE HER TO LADY HAGOROMO-GITSUNE.
AND SINCE SHE'S ONLY ONE YOKAI... ITS POINT-LESS TO JUST HANG AROUND WAITING.
I'M LOOKING FORWARD TO A LOT OF FUN.
HA HA HA...
A LOT OF FUN...?
FUN? HMPH. WHAT ABOUT OUR GREAT AMBITION?
THE ONE WE COULDN'T FULFILL 400 YEARS AGO... THE BIRTH OF NUE?
COME ON, LETS GO.
NUE... NUE, HUH?
Hmmm...
SPEAKING OF 400 YEARS AGO...
HM?

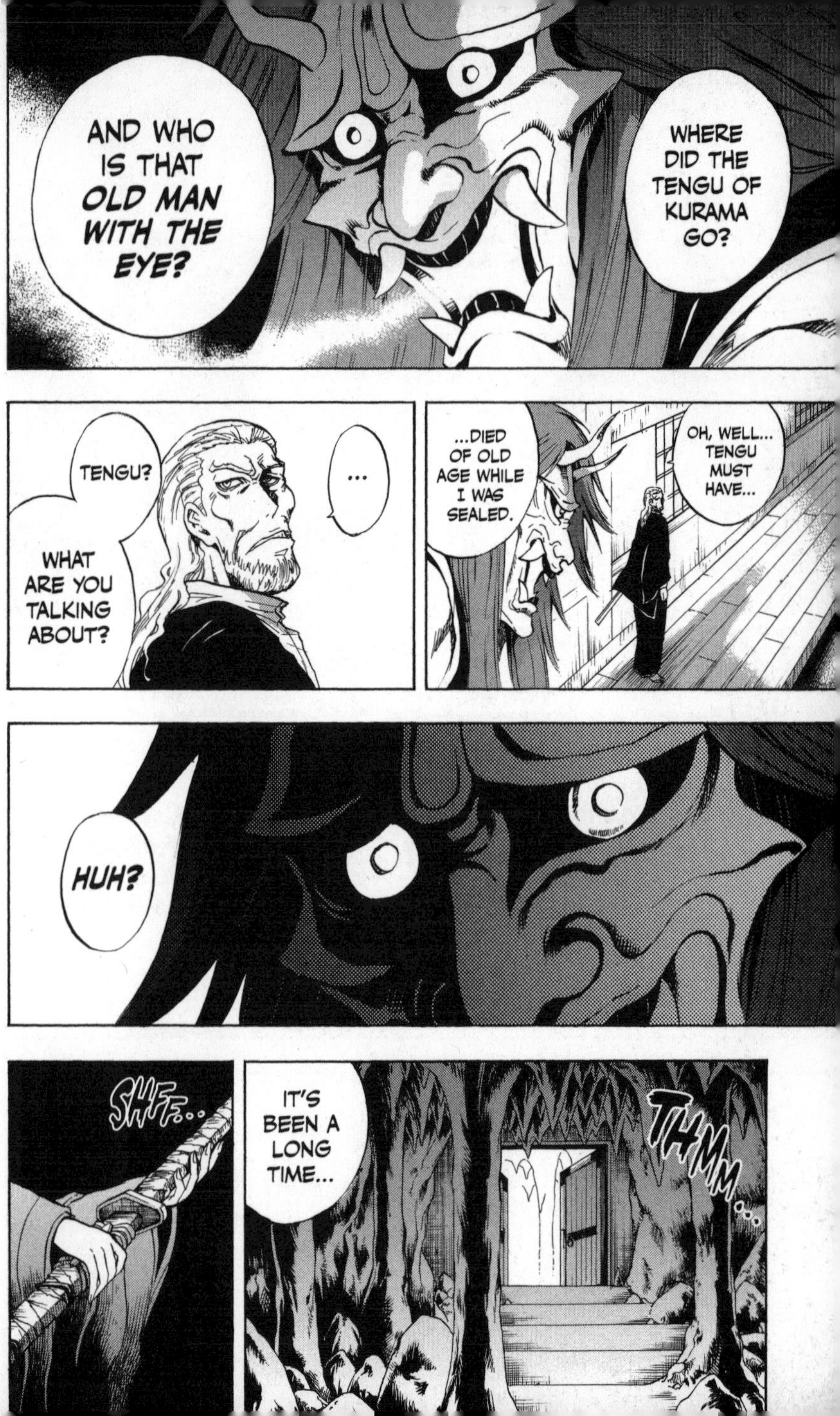
WHERE DID THE TENGU OF KURAMA GO?
AND WHO IS THAT OLD MAN WITH THE EYE?
OH, WELL... TENGU MUST HAVE...
...DIED OF OLD AGE WHILE I WAS SEALED.
...
TENGU?
WHAT ARE YOU TALKING ABOUT?
HUH?
THMM...
IT'S BEEN A LONG TIME...
SHFF...

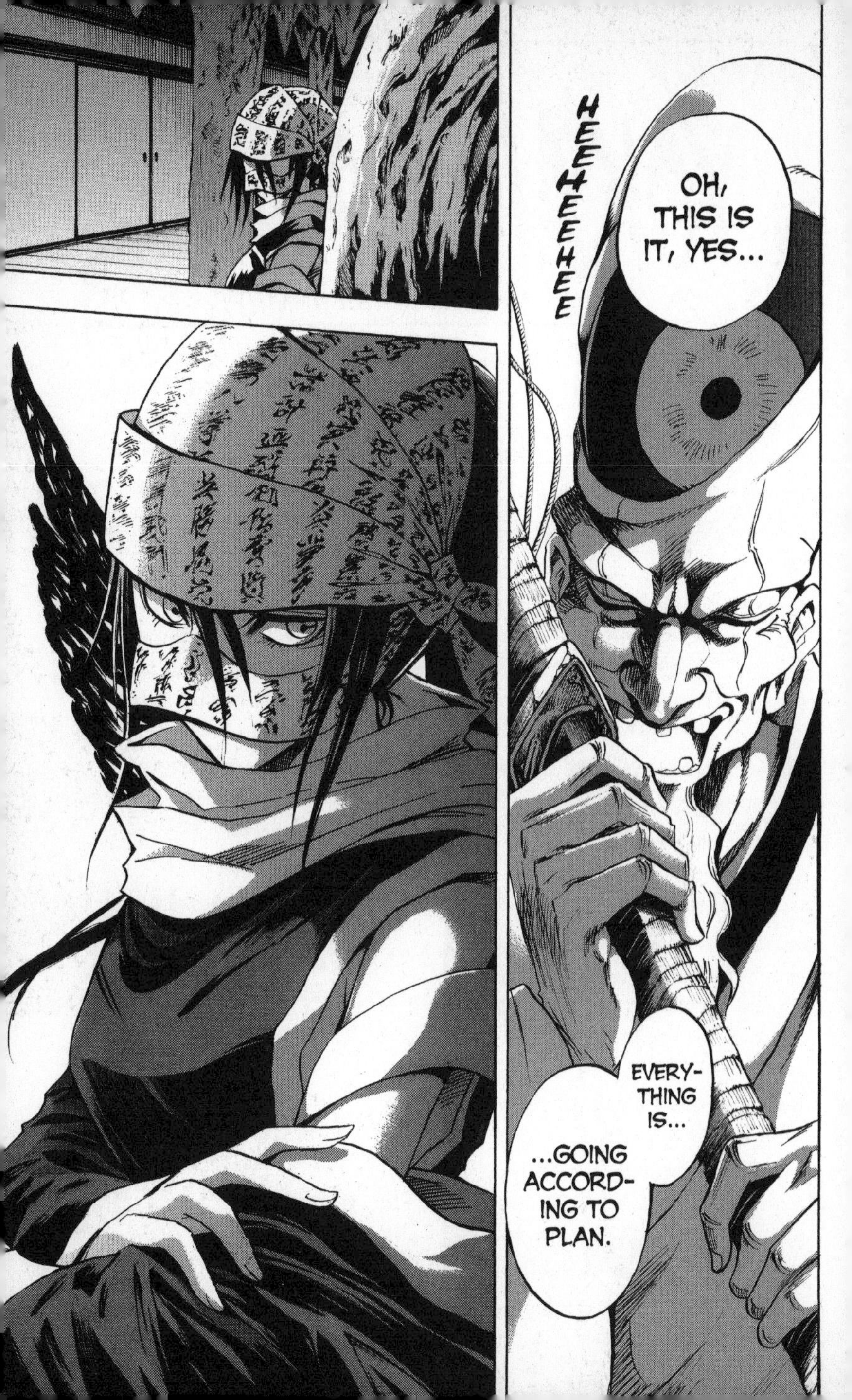
HEEHEEHEEHEE
OH, THIS IS IT, YES...
EVERY-THING IS...
...GOING ACCORD-ING TO PLAN.

KIYOTSUGU'S
QUESTION CORNER EDITION
YOKAI BRAIN
#11 BY KIYO

Question 1: This question is for Kuromaru. How many hours do you patrol Ukiyoe Town at night? —*Yukina Imafuku, Kanagawa Prefecture*

Kuromaru: It's actually supposed to have been done by three of us in three-hour shifts, but...because Dad gives us so much work to do, I've been doing the patrol by myself. In Ukiyoe Town we have a lot of crows as subordinates, so it's not like I have to cover the whole area every day.

Question 2: What is the difference between Kappa and Numa-Gappa? —*Benizakura*

Kappa: Hm? I'm not sure...

Amezo: I was born in the swamp, so I'm a Numa-Gappa. We're basically the same, even though we look very different!

Question 3: How long can Kejoro's hair grow? —*Deppi, Fukushima Prefecture*

Kejoro: Eh? Me? Oh, my...I have no idea...because I've never let it grow to its limit... But I do like it that even if it gets cut, it grows back right away! ♡

Question 4: Why is Gozumaru's left eye hidden? —*Yukimaru, Tokyo*

Gozumaru: It's not hidden.

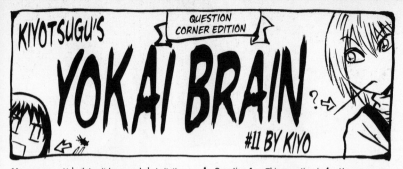

Mezumaru: He's doing it because he's imitating Lord Gyuki!! But it's actually on the opposite side... ♪

Gozumaru: Shut up, stupid!! I'm gonna punch you!!

Mezumaru: Don't hit me from above!! Now I can't see where I'm going!!

Gyuki: ...

Question 5: What kind of foods would Yura absolutely refuse to eat? —*Nurasato, Wakayama Prefecture*

Yura: Crickets and dragonflies. There's no way I would eat those...

Ryuji: Try them once. They're good. (smile)

Yura: Eh? Really?

Question 6: What's that thing in Awashima's mouth? —*Potechi, Fukushima Prefecture*

Awashima: Oh! A question for me? I thought people would have asked more about my body. This thing is...um...the stem of a single flower I found growing along the road!!

Rikuo: In other words, the stem of a weed, right...?

Awashima: Watch it, Rikuo!! Huh? Y-you're in human form...so it must be day now.

Rikuo: Don't use me as a substitute for a clock! Check out your own body.

Awashima: Rikuo...you have such a dirty mind...

Rikuo: Huh?!

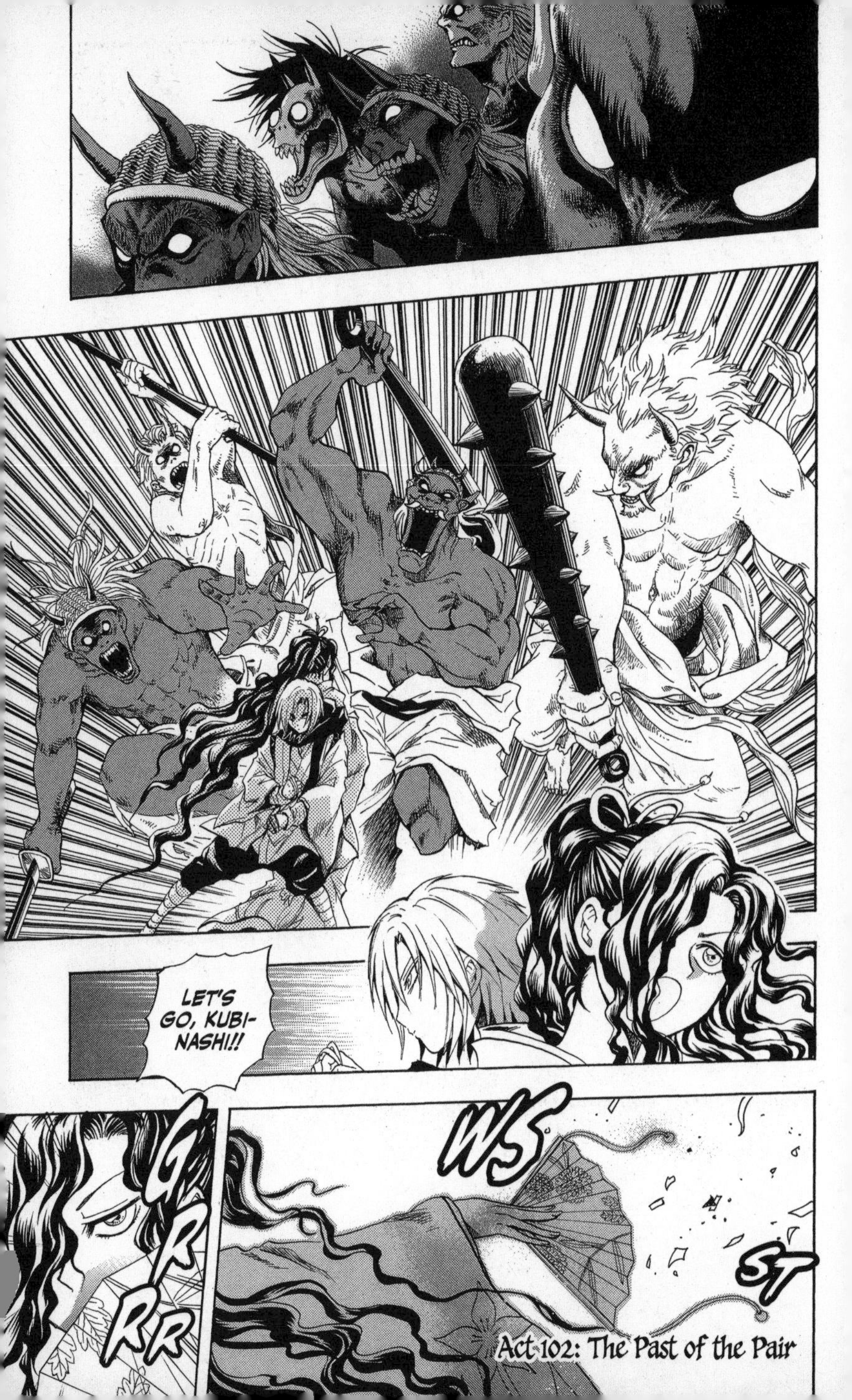
LET'S GO, KUBI-NASHI!!
WS
ST
Act 102: The Past of the Pair
GRRRR

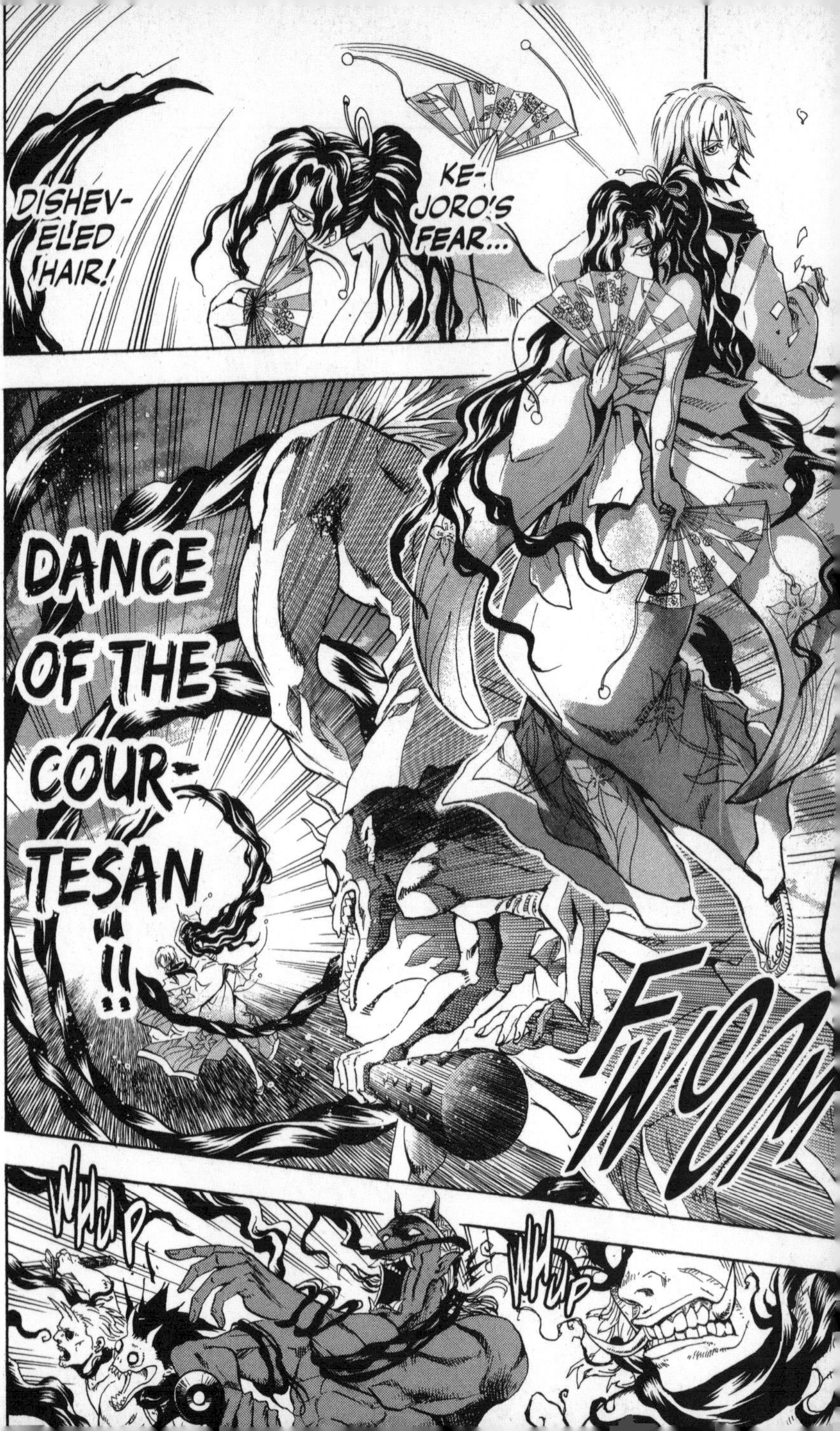
KE-JORO'S FEAR...
DISHEV-ELED HAIR!
DANCE OF THE COUR-TESAN!!
FWOOM
WHIP
WHIP

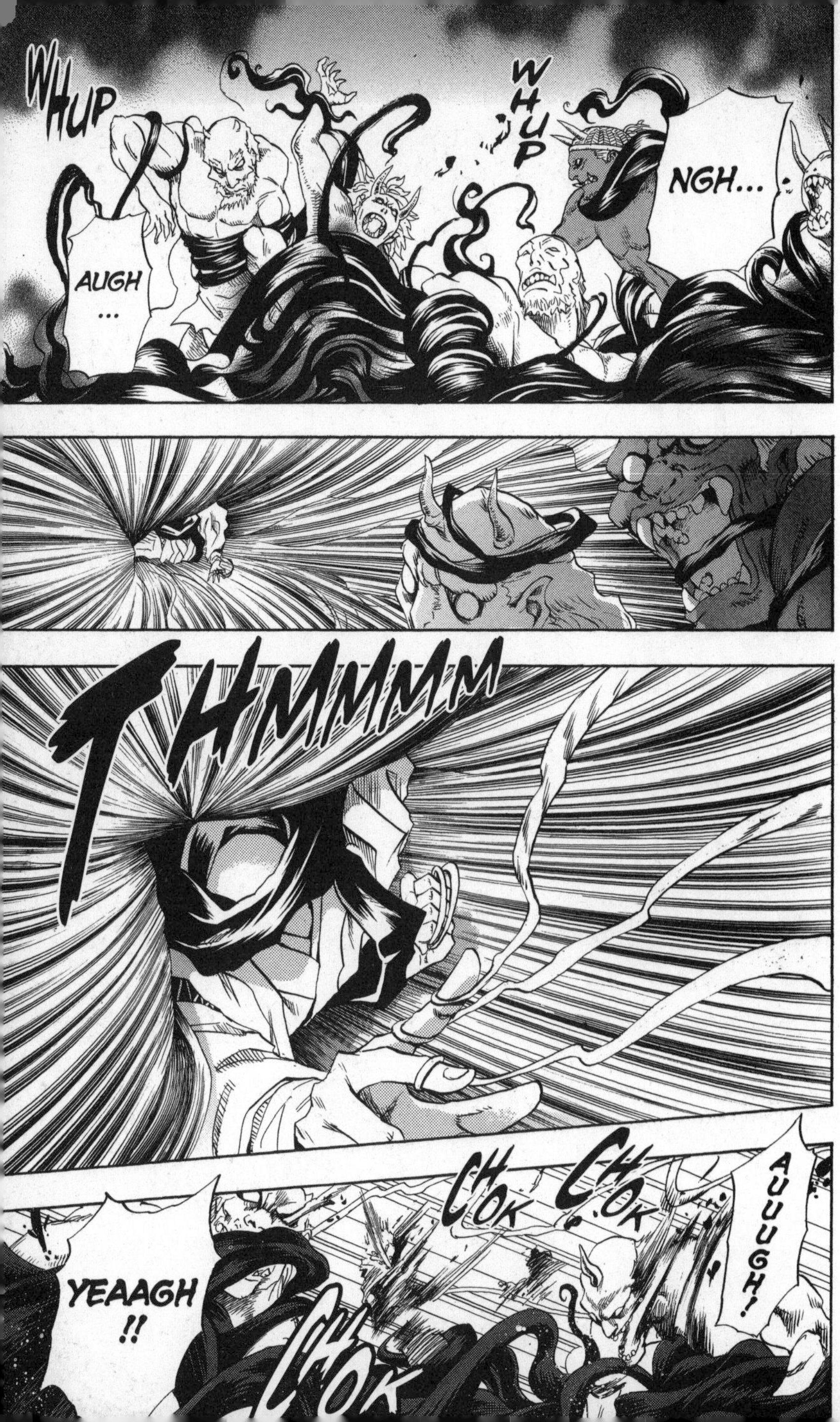
NGH...
WHUP
WHUP
AUGH ...
THMMMM
AUUUGH!
CHOK
CHOK
YEAAGH !!
CHOK

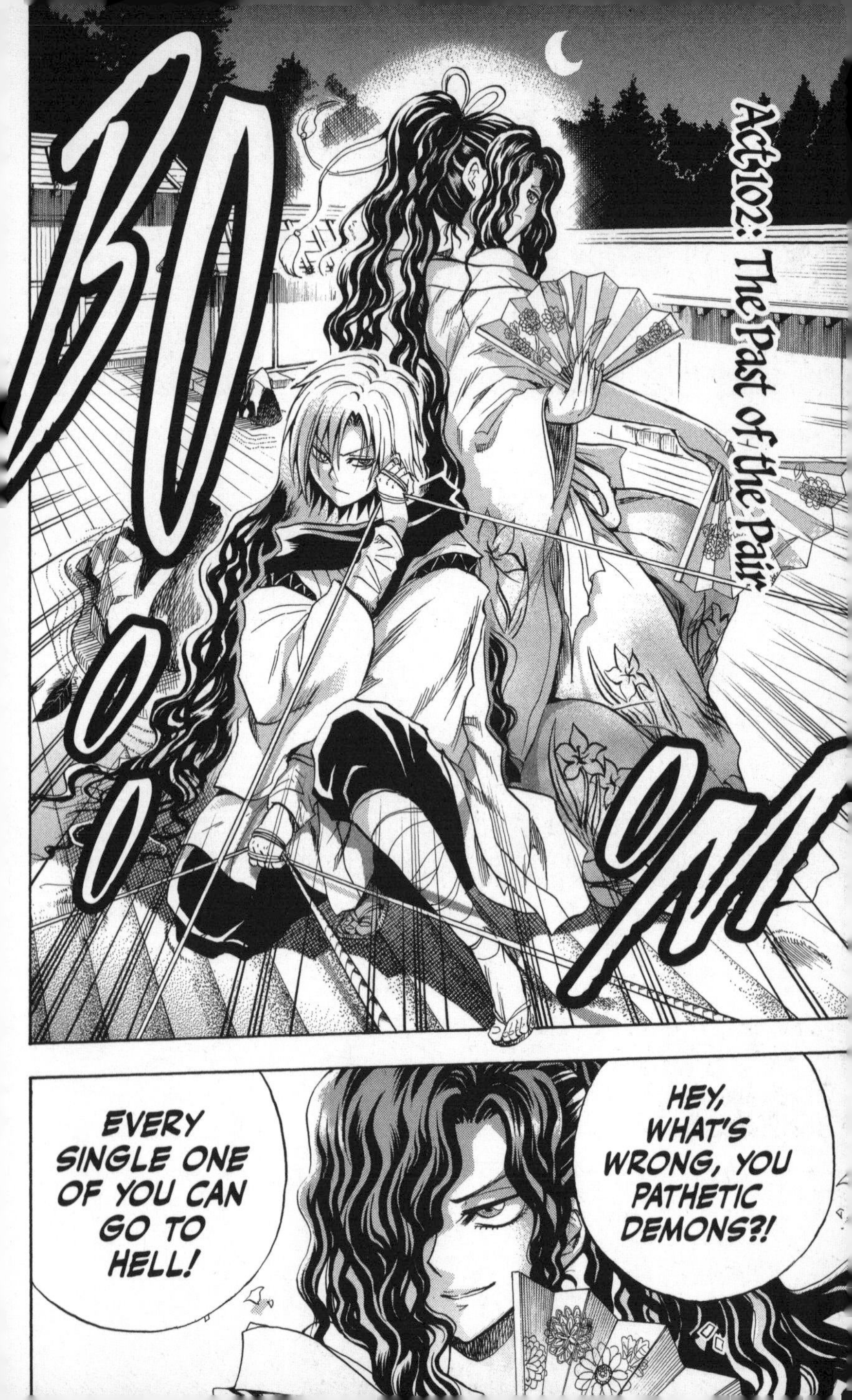
Act 102: The Past of the Pair
BOOOM
HEY, WHAT'S WRONG, YOU PATHETIC DEMONS?!
EVERY SINGLE ONE OF YOU CAN GO TO HELL!

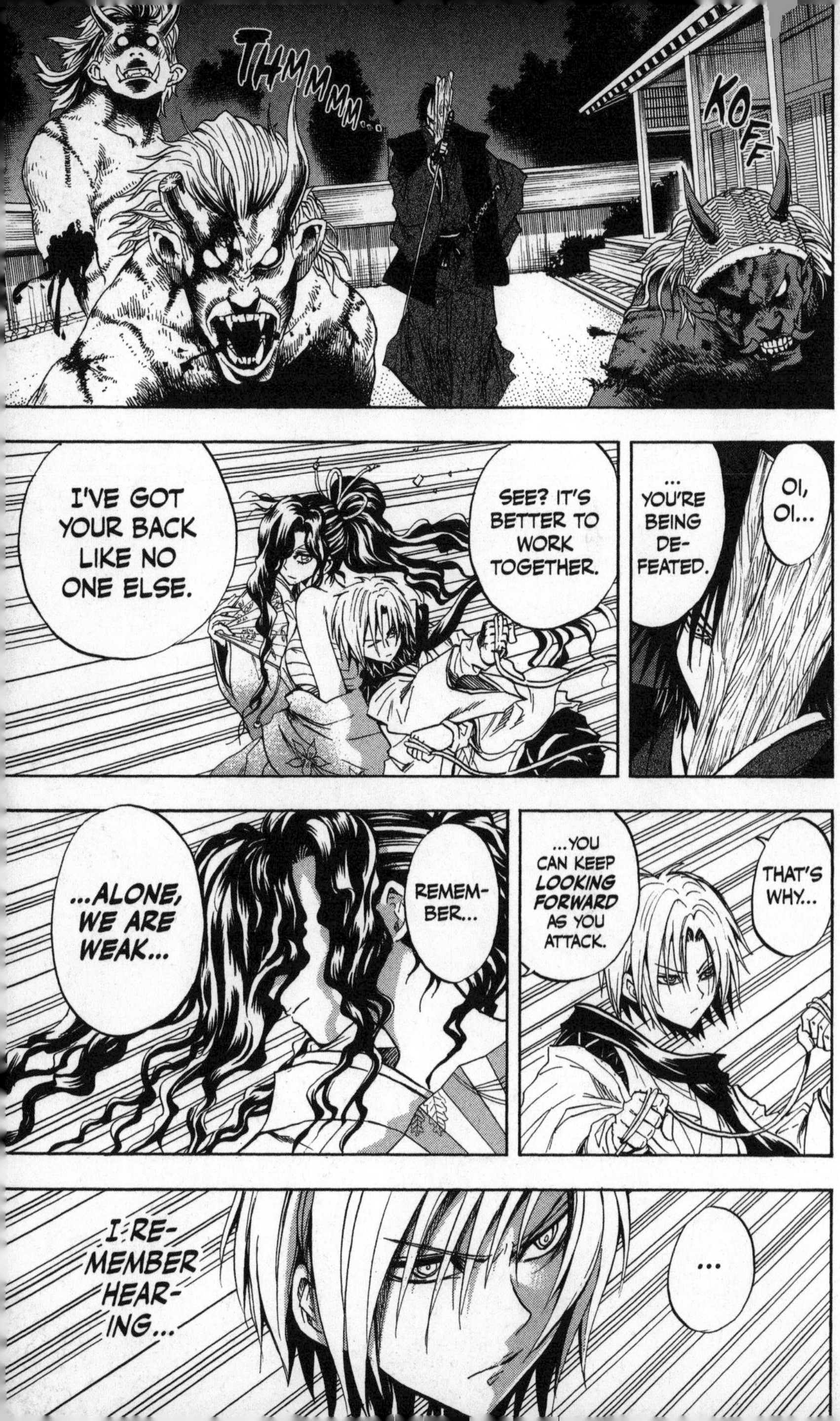
KOFF
THMMMM...
OI, OI...
... YOU'RE BEING DE-FEATED.
SEE? IT'S BETTER TO WORK TOGETHER.
I'VE GOT YOUR BACK LIKE NO ONE ELSE.
THAT'S WHY...
...YOU CAN KEEP *LOOKING FORWARD* AS YOU ATTACK.
REMEM-BER...
...ALONE, WE ARE WEAK...
...
I RE-MEMBER HEAR-ING...

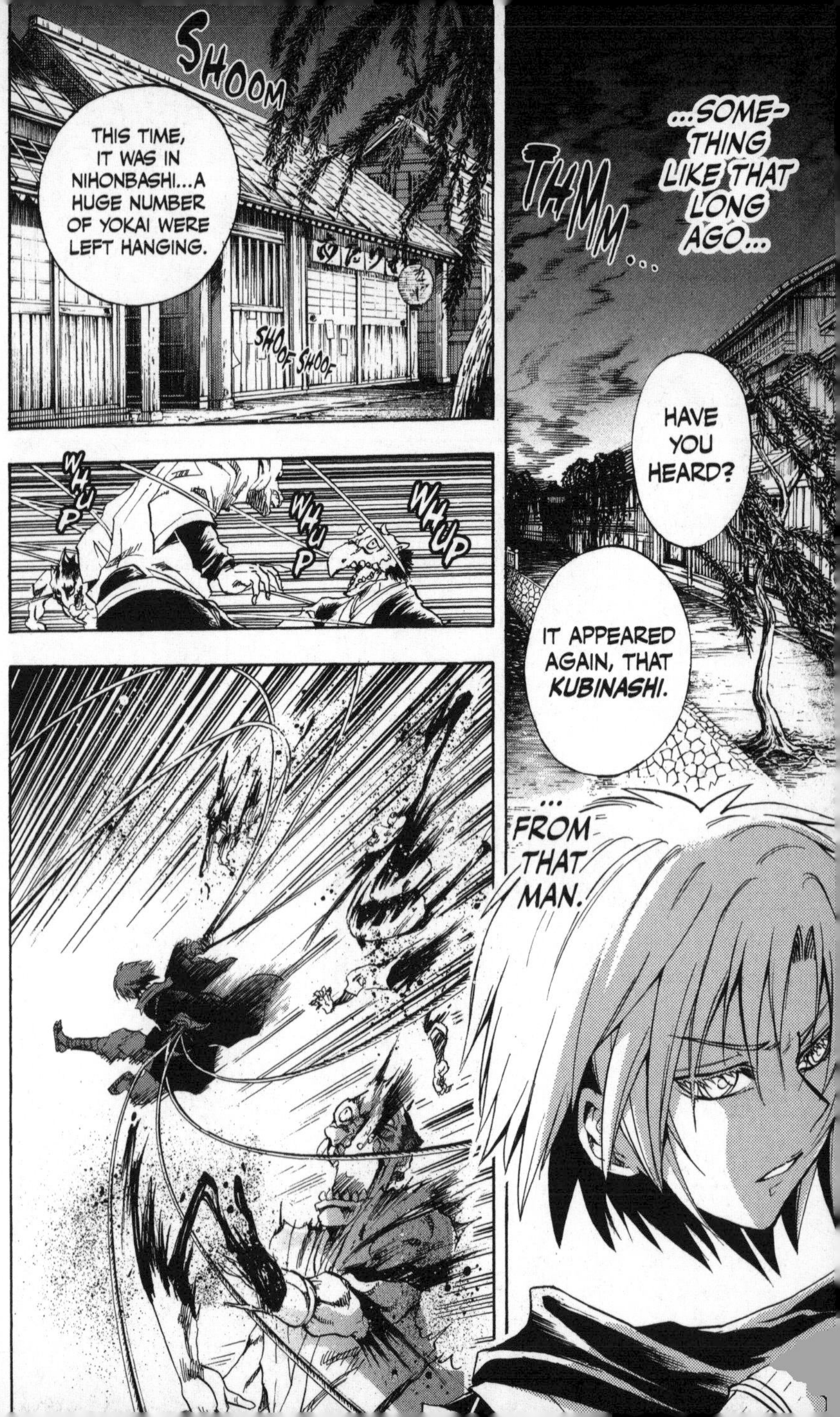
...SOME-THING LIKE THAT LONG AGO...
THMM...
HAVE YOU HEARD?
IT APPEARED AGAIN, THAT KUBINASHI.
...FROM THAT MAN.
SHOOM
THIS TIME, IT WAS IN NIHONBASHI...A HUGE NUMBER OF YOKAI WERE LEFT HANGING.
SHOOF SHOOF
WHUP
WHUP
WHUP

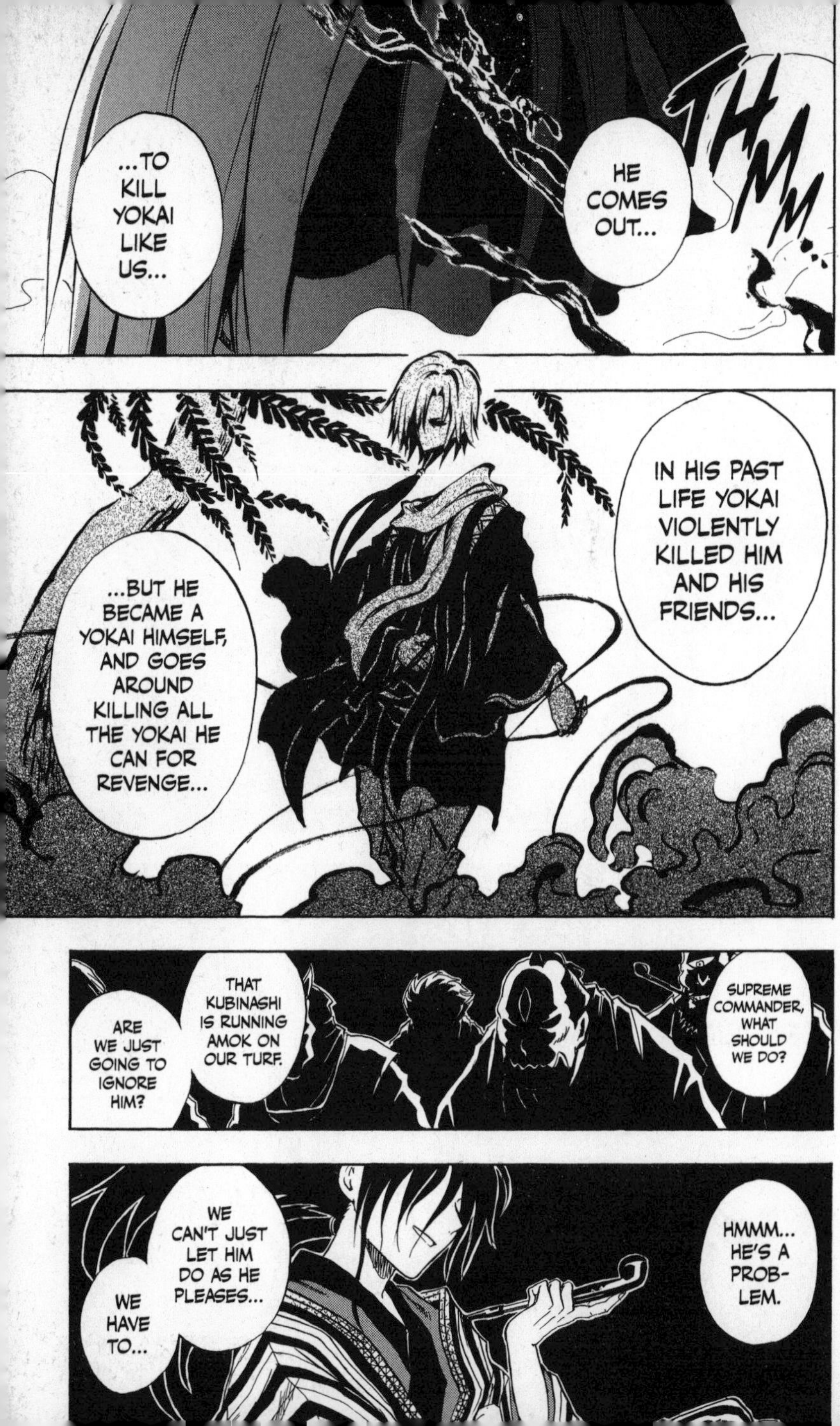
THMM
HE COMES OUT...
...TO KILL YOKAI LIKE US...
IN HIS PAST LIFE YOKAI VIOLENTLY KILLED HIM AND HIS FRIENDS...
...BUT HE BECAME A YOKAI HIMSELF, AND GOES AROUND KILLING ALL THE YOKAI HE CAN FOR REVENGE...
SUPREME COMMANDER, WHAT SHOULD WE DO?
THAT KUBINASHI IS RUNNING AMOK ON OUR TURF.
ARE WE JUST GOING TO IGNORE HIM?
HMMM... HE'S A PROB-LEM.
WE CAN'T JUST LET HIM DO AS HE PLEASES...
WE HAVE TO...

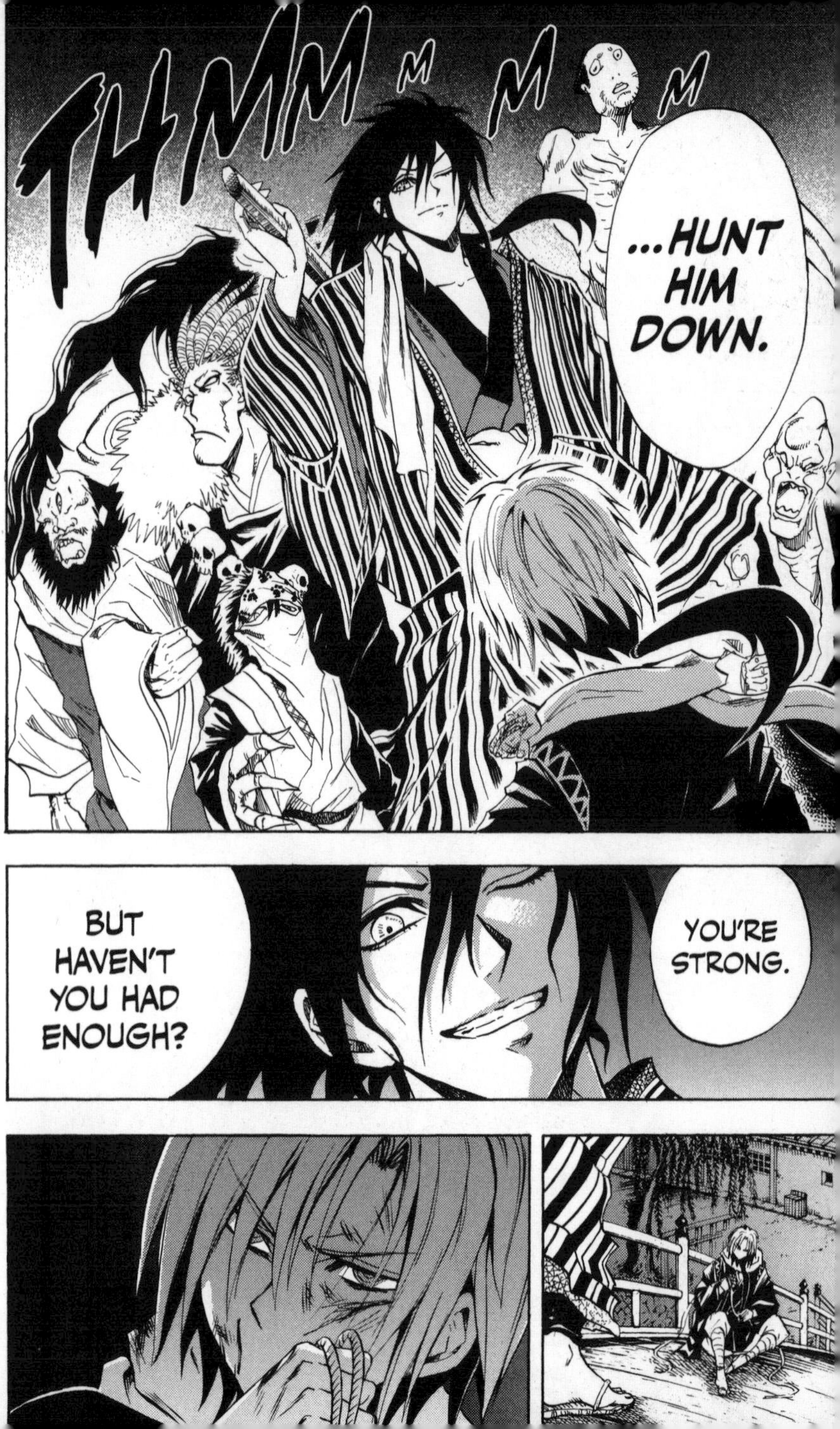
THMMMMM
...HUNT HIM DOWN.
YOU'RE STRONG.
BUT HAVEN'T YOU HAD ENOUGH?

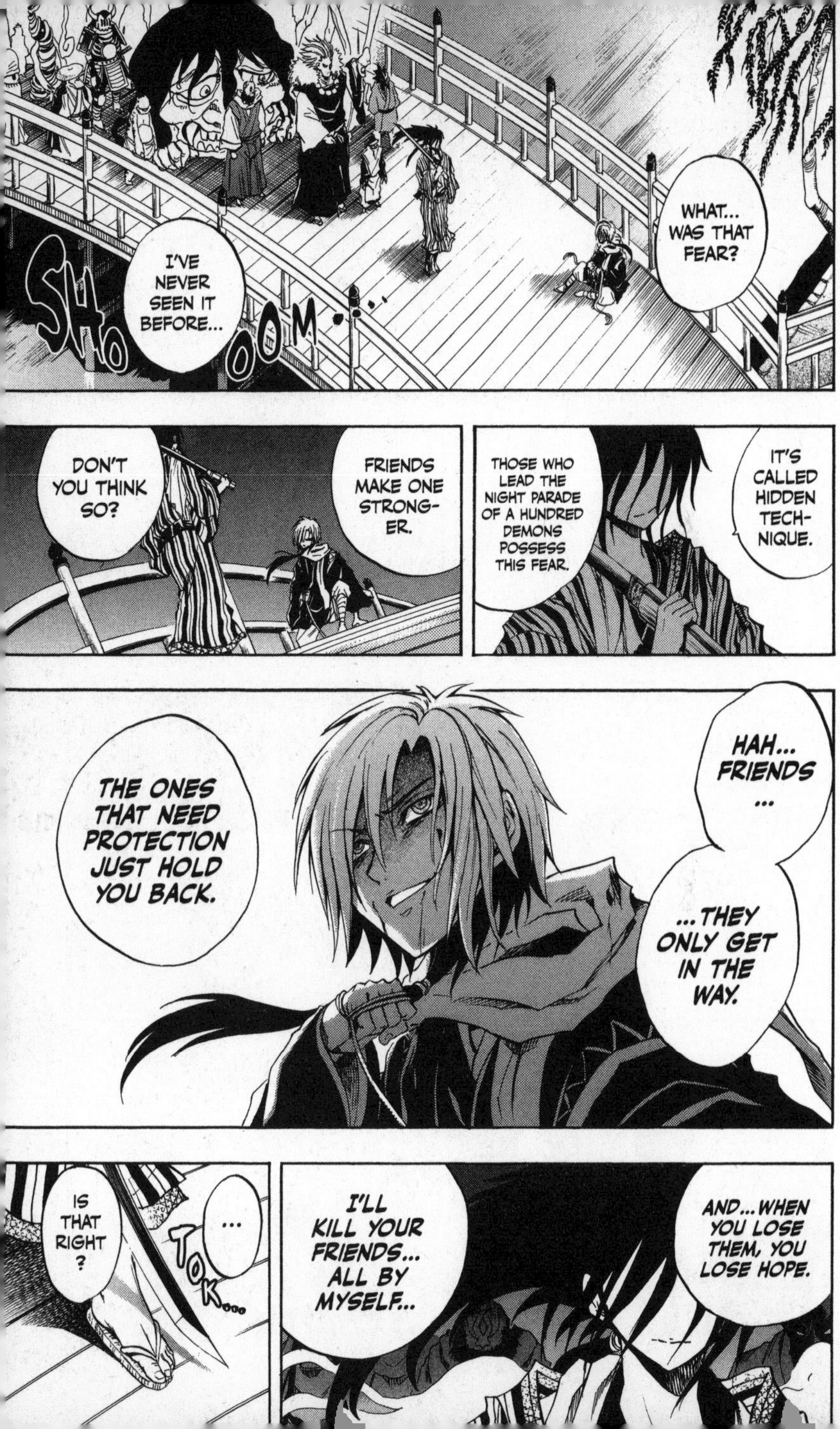
WHAT... WAS THAT FEAR?
I'VE NEVER SEEN IT BEFORE...
SHOOOM
IT'S CALLED HIDDEN TECH-NIQUE.
THOSE WHO LEAD THE NIGHT PARADE OF A HUNDRED DEMONS POSSESS THIS FEAR.
FRIENDS MAKE ONE STRONG-ER.
DON'T YOU THINK SO?
HAH... FRIENDS...
...THEY ONLY GET IN THE WAY.
THE ONES THAT NEED PROTECTION JUST HOLD YOU BACK.
AND... WHEN YOU LOSE THEM, YOU LOSE HOPE.
I'LL KILL YOUR FRIENDS... ALL BY MYSELF...
...
IS THAT RIGHT?
TOK...

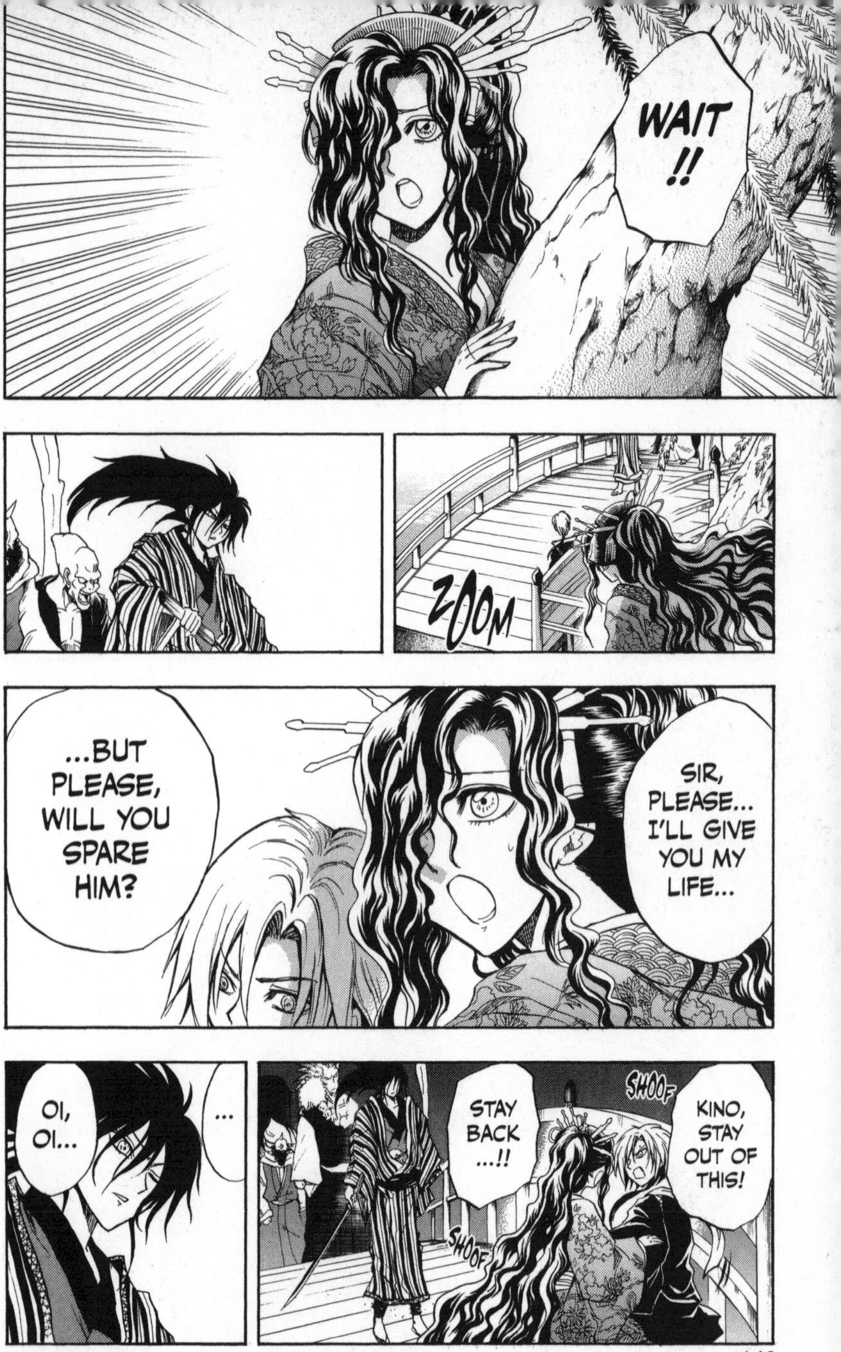
WAIT!!
ZOOM
SIR, PLEASE... I'LL GIVE YOU MY LIFE...
...BUT PLEASE, WILL YOU SPARE HIM?
SHOOF
KINO, STAY OUT OF THIS!
STAY BACK ...!!
SHOOF
...
OI, OI...

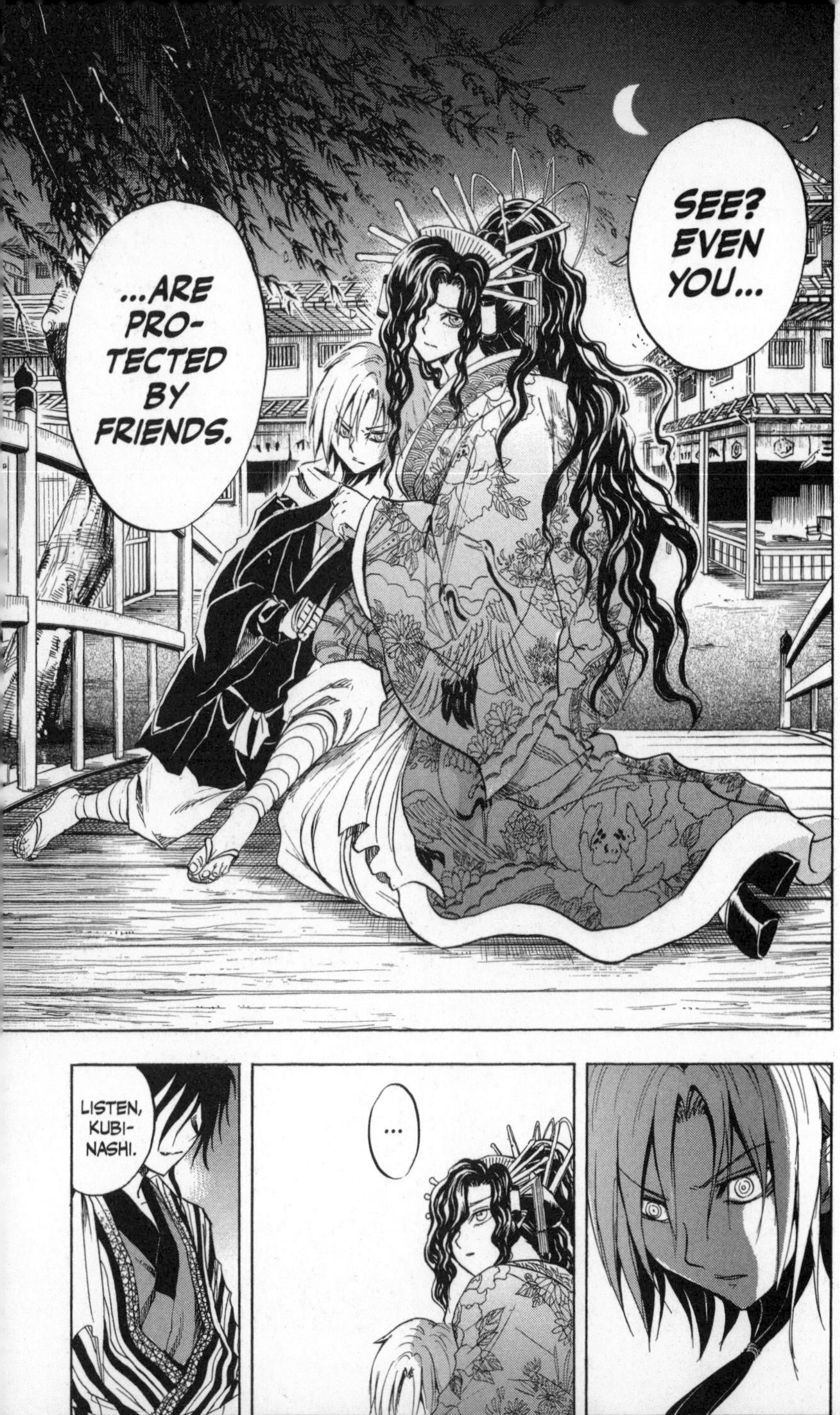
SEE? EVEN YOU...
...ARE PRO-TECTED BY FRIENDS.
...
LISTEN, KUBI-NASHI.

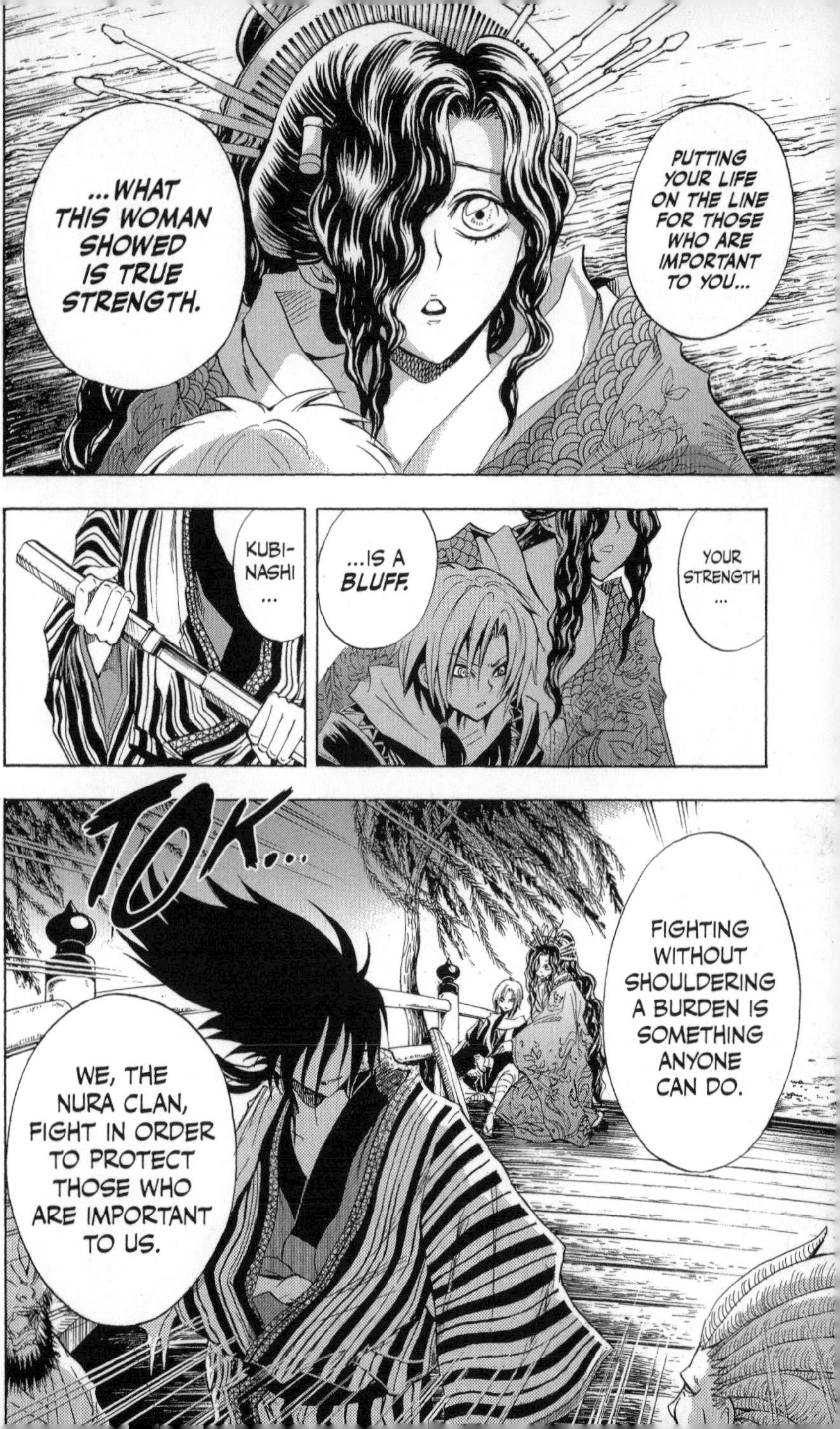
PUTTING YOUR LIFE ON THE LINE FOR THOSE WHO ARE IMPORTANT TO YOU...
...WHAT THIS WOMAN SHOWED IS TRUE STRENGTH.
YOUR STRENGTH ...
...IS A BLUFF.
KUBI-NASHI ...
TOK...
FIGHTING WITHOUT SHOULDERING A BURDEN IS SOMETHING ANYONE CAN DO.
WE, THE NURA CLAN, FIGHT IN ORDER TO PROTECT THOSE WHO ARE IMPORTANT TO US.

READ THIS WAY

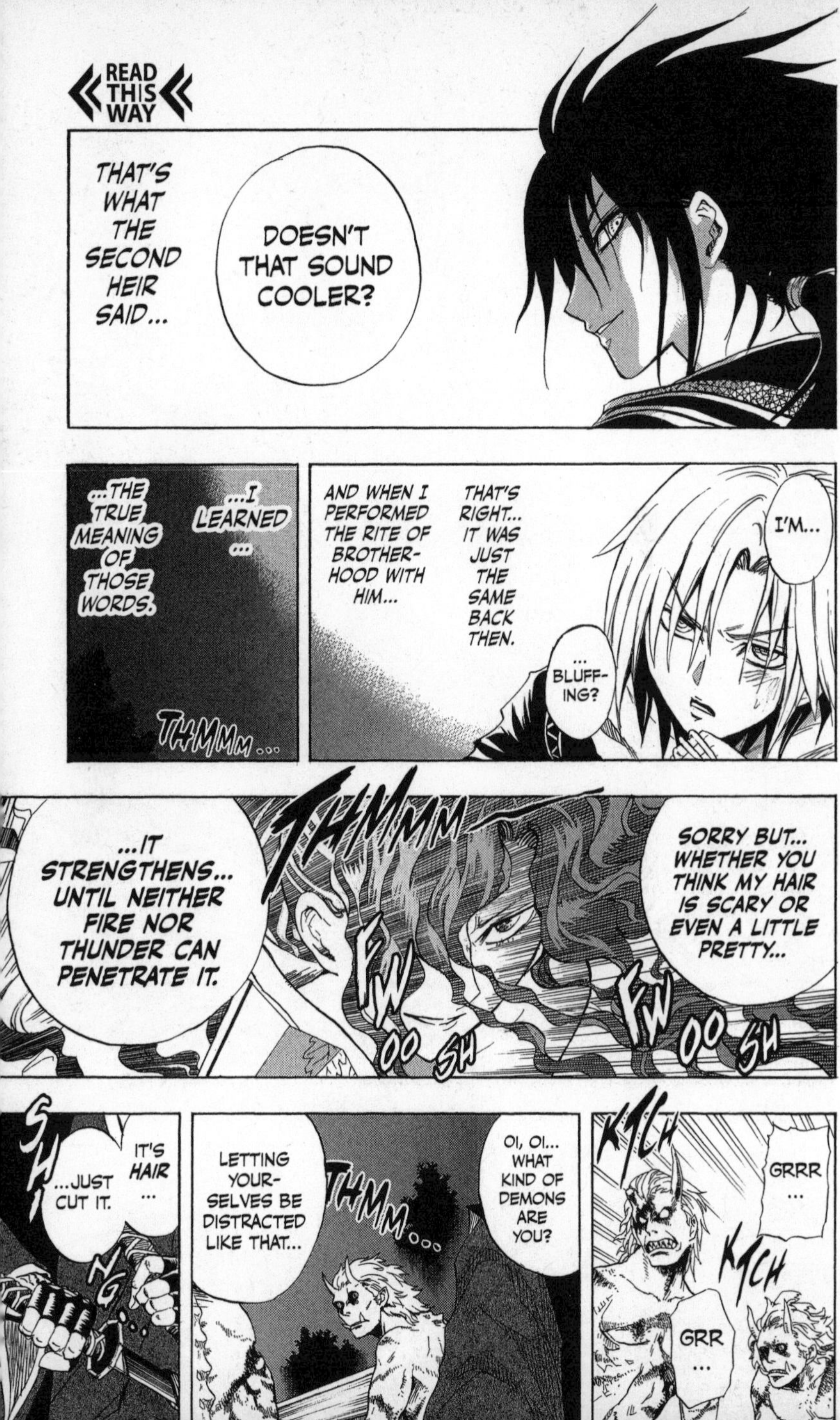
DOESN'T THAT SOUND COOLER?
THAT'S WHAT THE SECOND HEIR SAID...
I'M...
...BLUFFING?
THAT'S RIGHT... IT WAS JUST THE SAME BACK THEN.
AND WHEN I PERFORMED THE RITE OF BROTHER-HOOD WITH HIM...
...I LEARNED...
...THE TRUE MEANING OF THOSE WORDS.
THMMM...
SORRY BUT... WHETHER YOU THINK MY HAIR IS SCARY OR EVEN A LITTLE PRETTY...
FWOOSH
THMMM
FWOOSH
...IT STRENGTHENS... UNTIL NEITHER FIRE NOR THUNDER CAN PENETRATE IT.
GRRR...
GRR...
OI, OI... WHAT KIND OF DEMONS ARE YOU?
LETTING YOUR-SELVES BE DISTRACTED LIKE THAT...
THMM...
IT'S HAIR...
...JUST CUT IT.

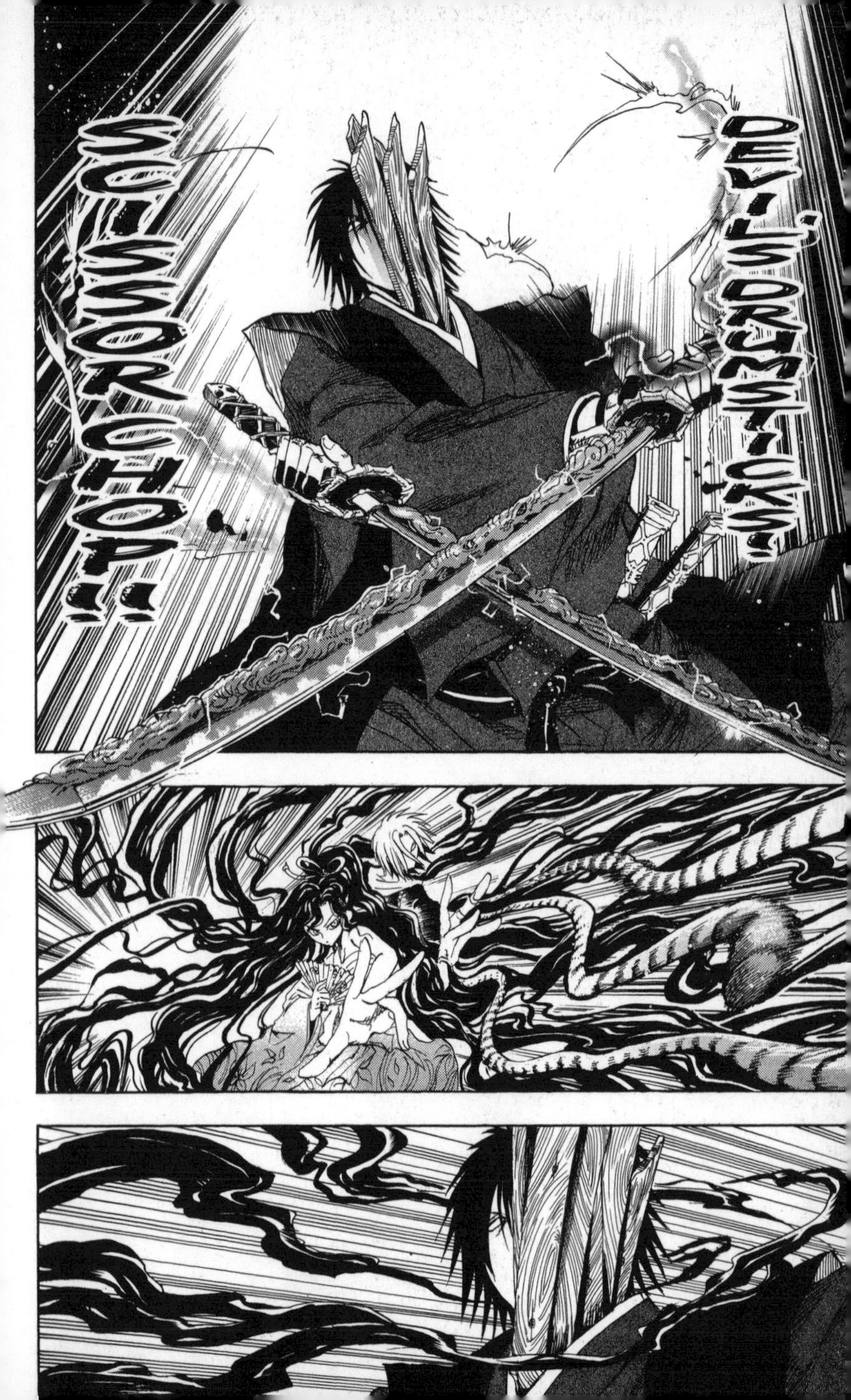
DEVIL'S DRUMSTICKS!
SCISSOR CHOP!!

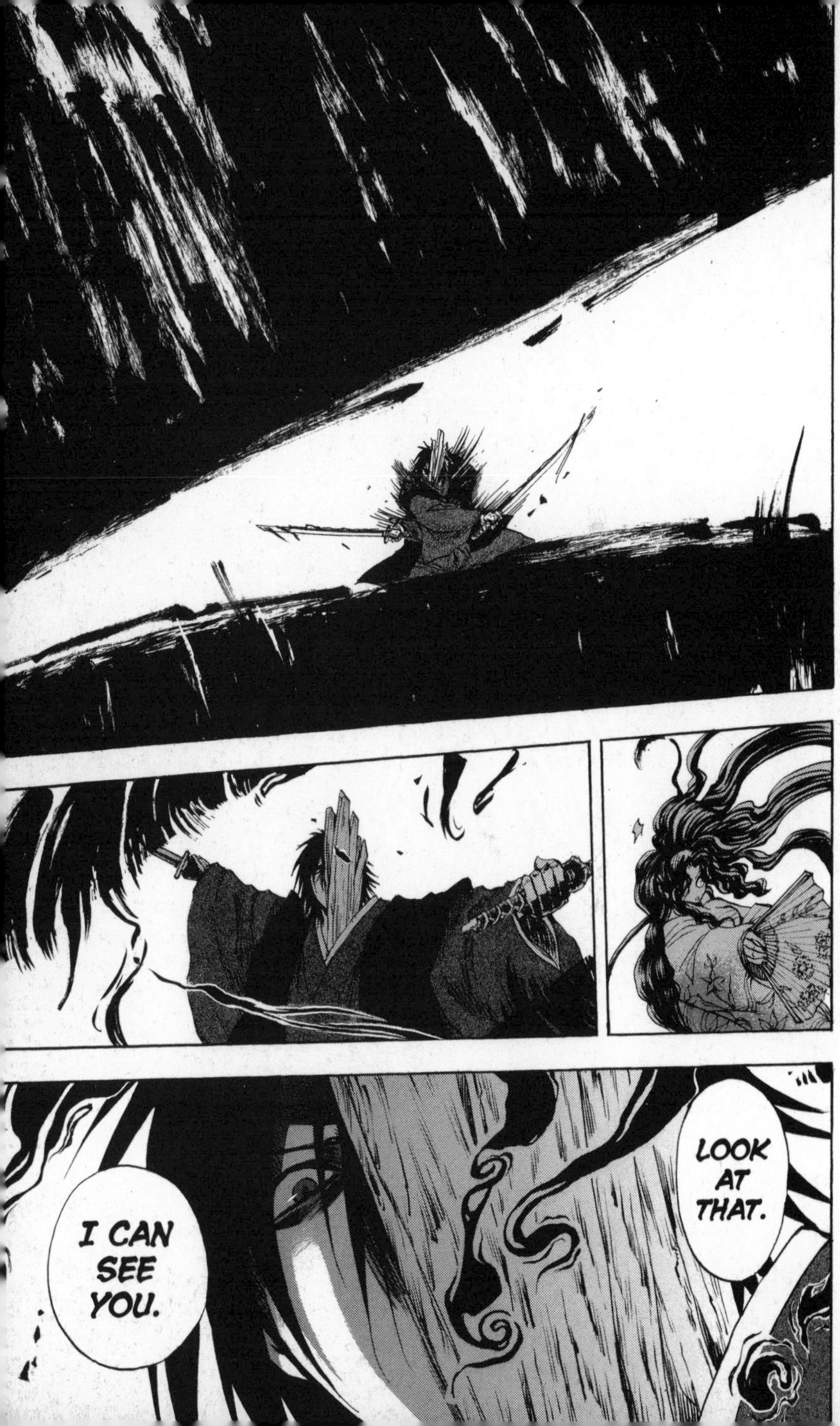
LOOK AT THAT.
I CAN SEE YOU.

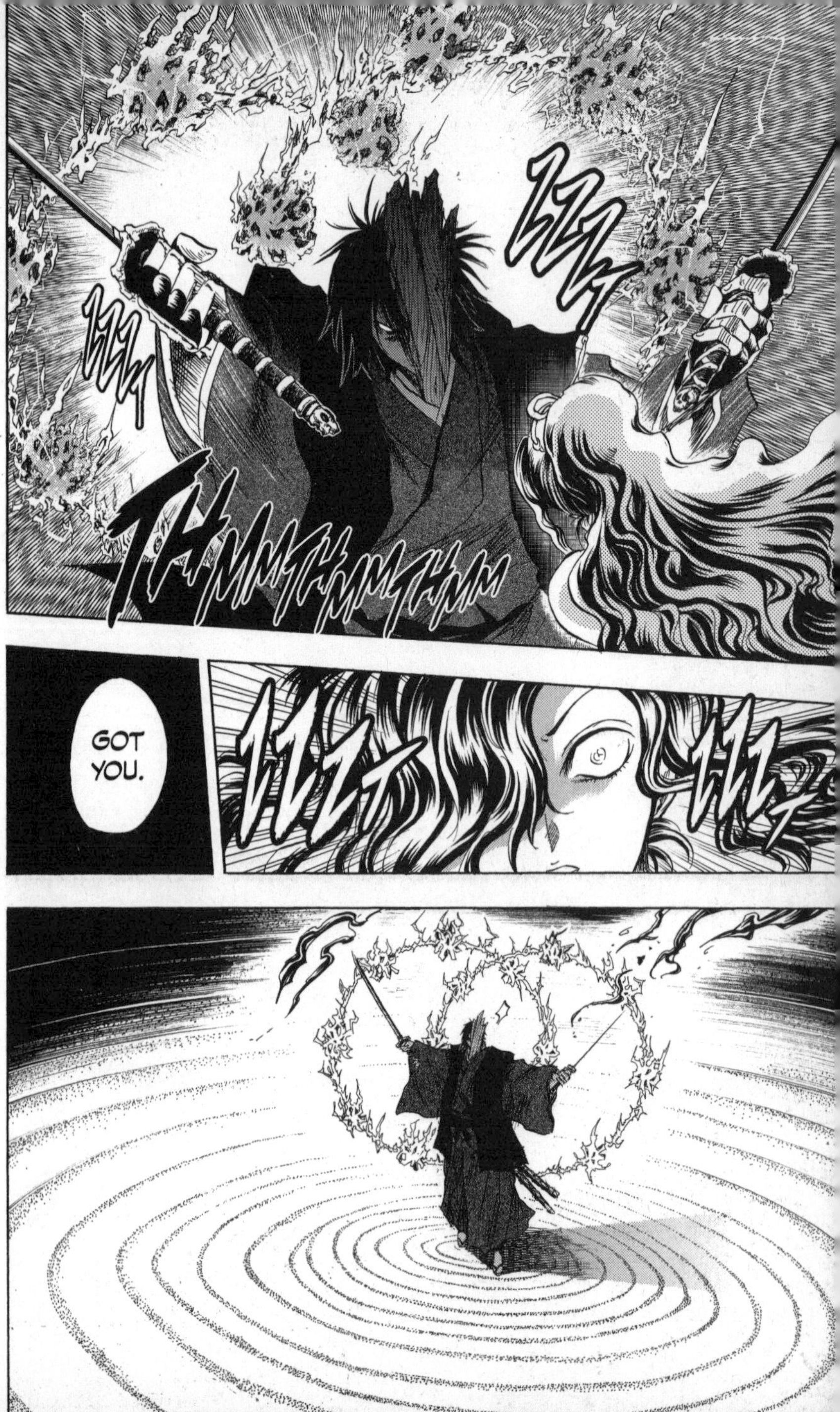
GOT YOU.

...?!
WHAT? WHAT IS THIS PATTERN ON THE GROUND?
KARE-SAN-SUI ...?
NO...IT ISN'T.
WHY HAS THE SAND ENCIRCLED ME?
DEATH TENDRILS !!
SPIRAL BLADE !!

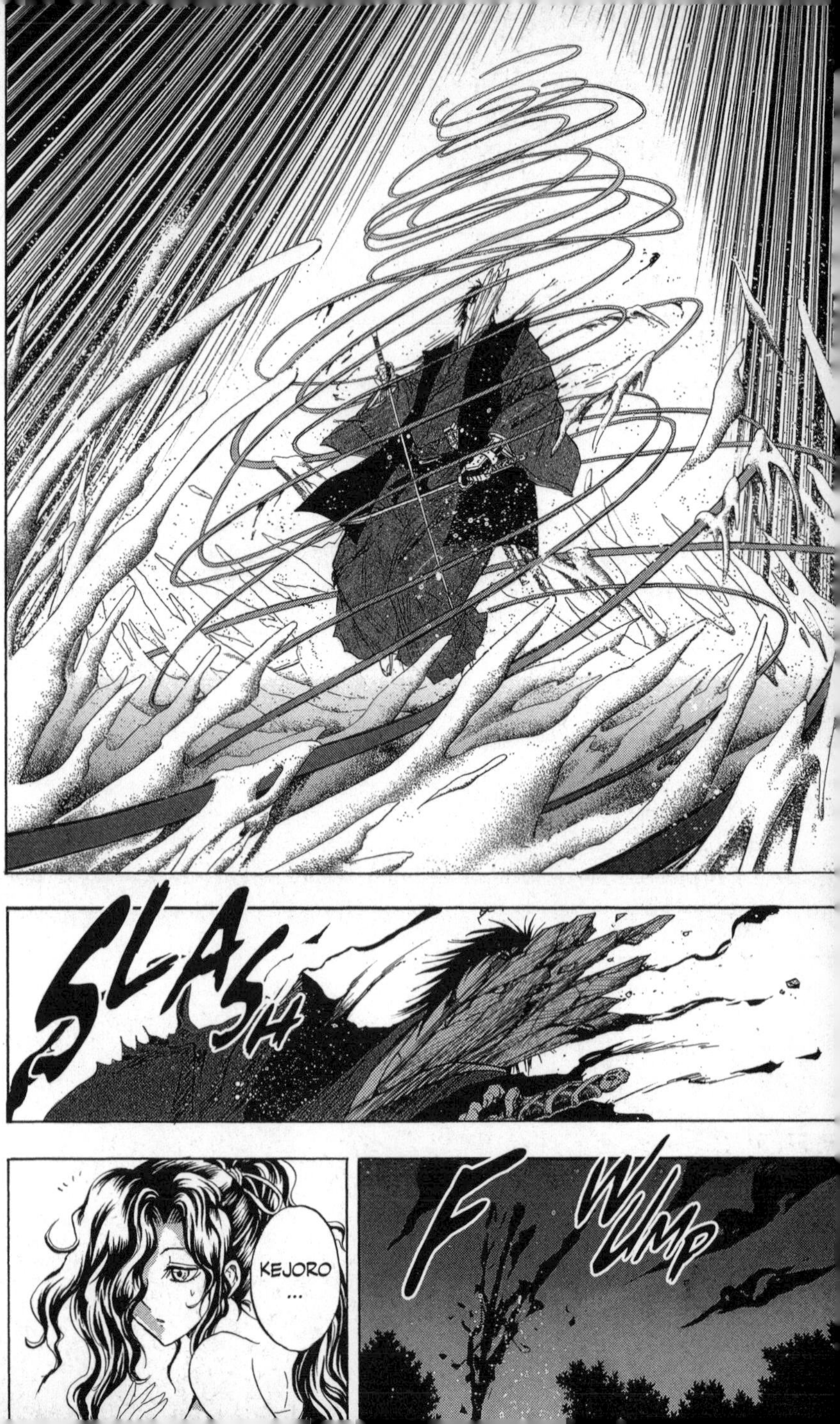
SLASH
FWUMP
KEJORO
...

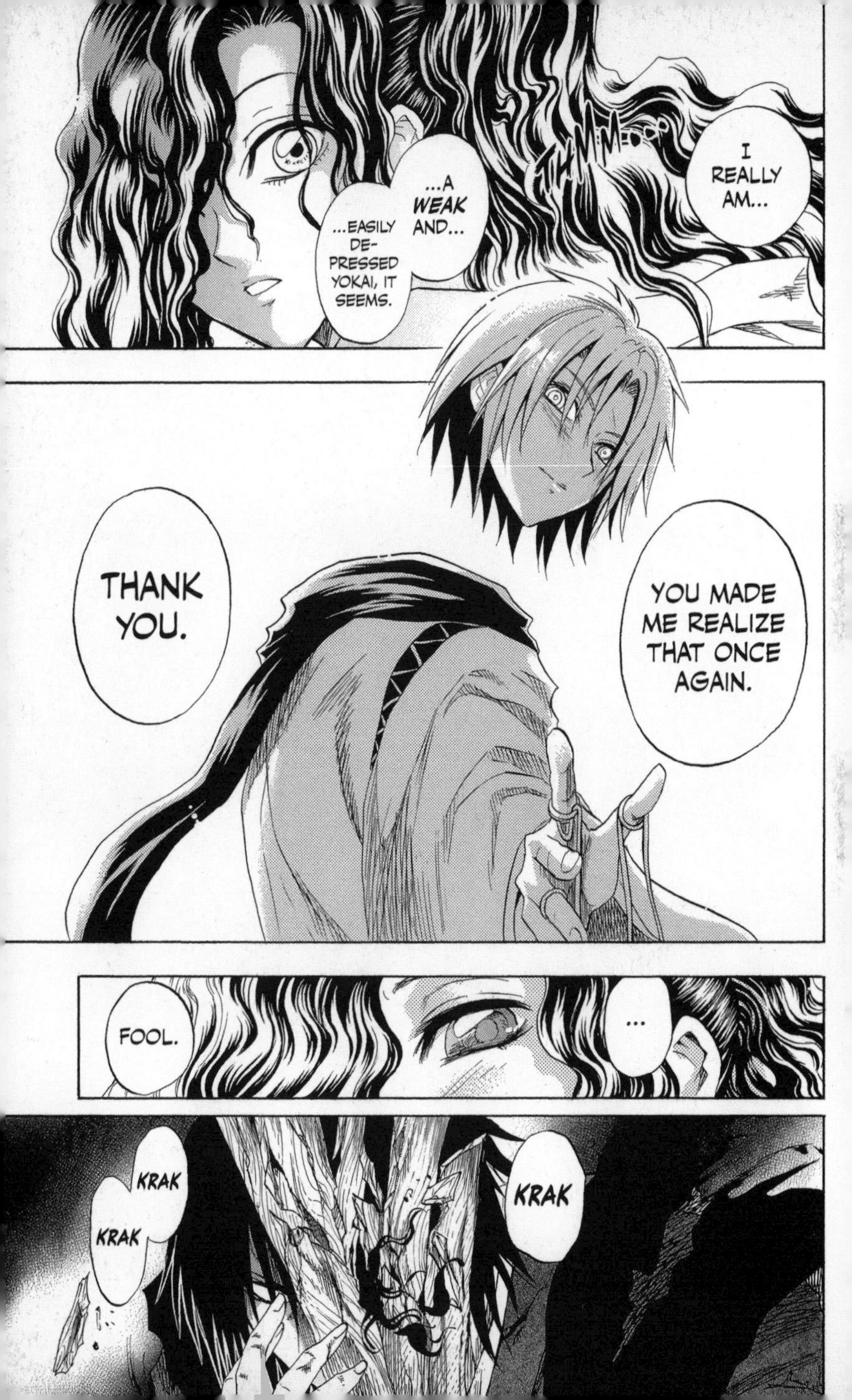
I REALLY AM...
...A WEAK AND...
...EASILY DE-PRESSED YOKAI, IT SEEMS.
YOU MADE ME REALIZE THAT ONCE AGAIN.
THANK YOU.
...
FOOL.
KRAK
KRAK
KRAK

Act 103: Strength and Strength

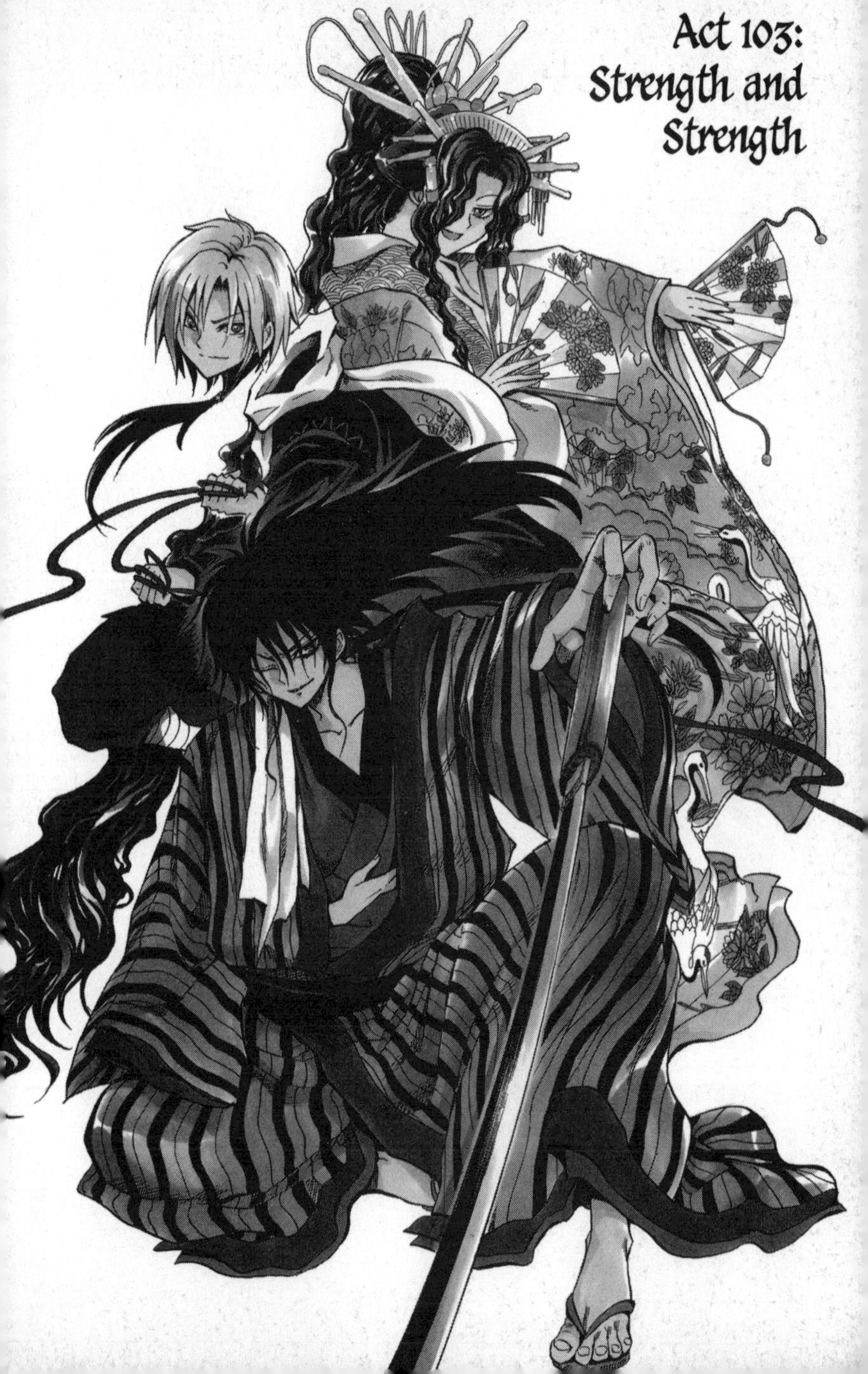

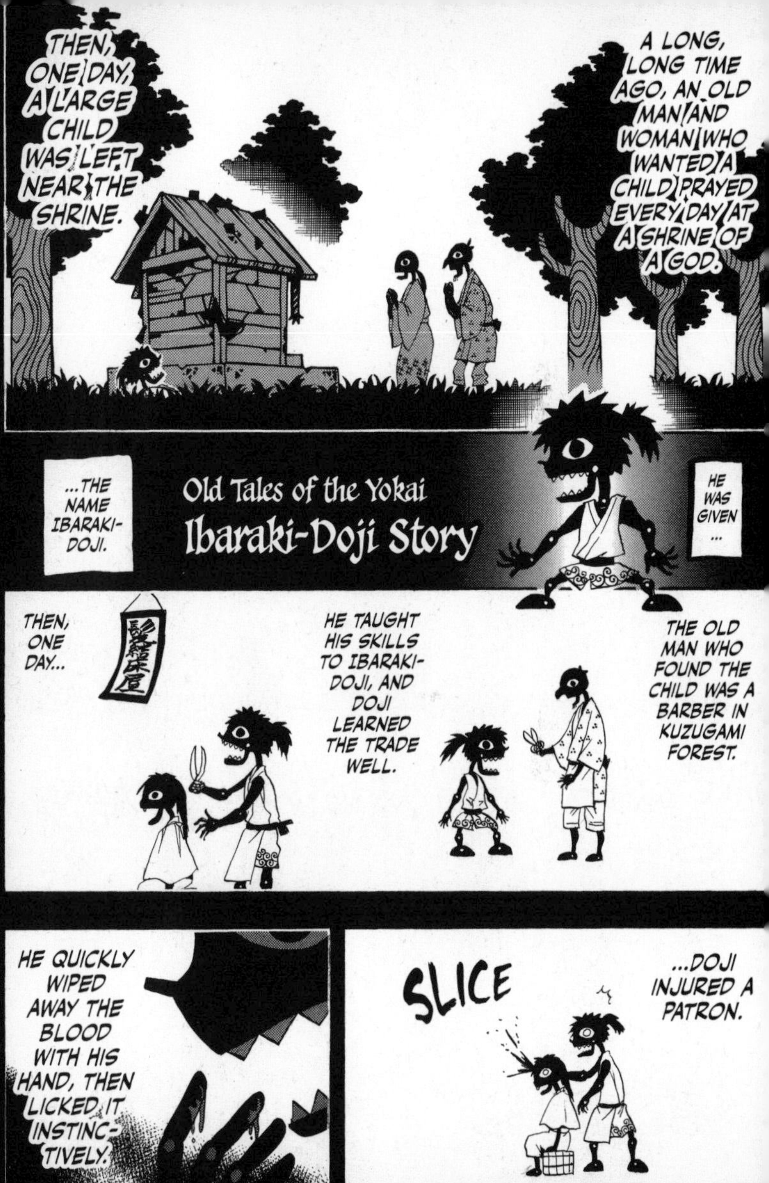
A LONG, LONG TIME AGO, AN OLD MAN AND WOMAN WHO WANTED A CHILD PRAYED EVERY DAY AT A SHRINE OF A GOD.
THEN, ONE DAY, A LARGE CHILD WAS LEFT NEAR THE SHRINE.
HE WAS GIVEN ...
Old Tales of the Yokai
Ibaraki-Doji Story
...THE NAME IBARAKI-DOJI.
THE OLD MAN WHO FOUND THE CHILD WAS A BARBER IN KUZUGAMI FOREST.
HE TAUGHT HIS SKILLS TO IBARAKI-DOJI, AND DOJI LEARNED THE TRADE WELL.
THEN, ONE DAY...
...DOJI INJURED A PATRON.
SLICE
HE QUICKLY WIPED AWAY THE BLOOD WITH HIS HAND, THEN LICKED IT INSTINCTIVELY.

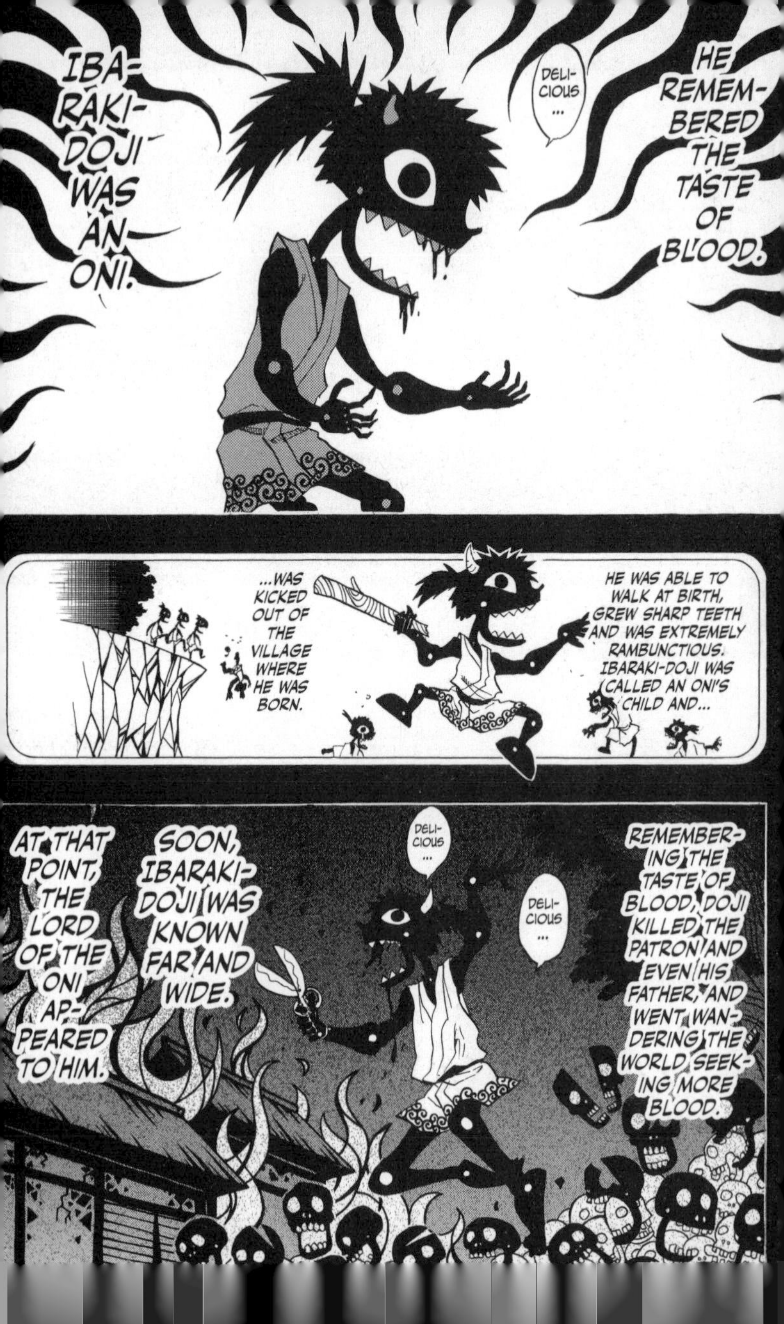
HE REMEMBERED THE TASTE OF BLOOD.
DELICIOUS...
IBARAKI-DOJI WAS AN ONI.
HE WAS ABLE TO WALK AT BIRTH, GREW SHARP TEETH AND WAS EXTREMELY RAMBUNCTIOUS. IBARAKI-DOJI WAS CALLED AN ONI'S CHILD AND...
...WAS KICKED OUT OF THE VILLAGE WHERE HE WAS BORN.
REMEMBERING THE TASTE OF BLOOD, DOJI KILLED THE PATRON AND EVEN HIS FATHER, AND WENT WANDERING THE WORLD SEEKING MORE BLOOD.
DELICIOUS...
DELICIOUS...
SOON, IBARAKI-DOJI WAS KNOWN FAR AND WIDE.
AT THAT POINT, THE LORD OF THE ONI APPEARED TO HIM.

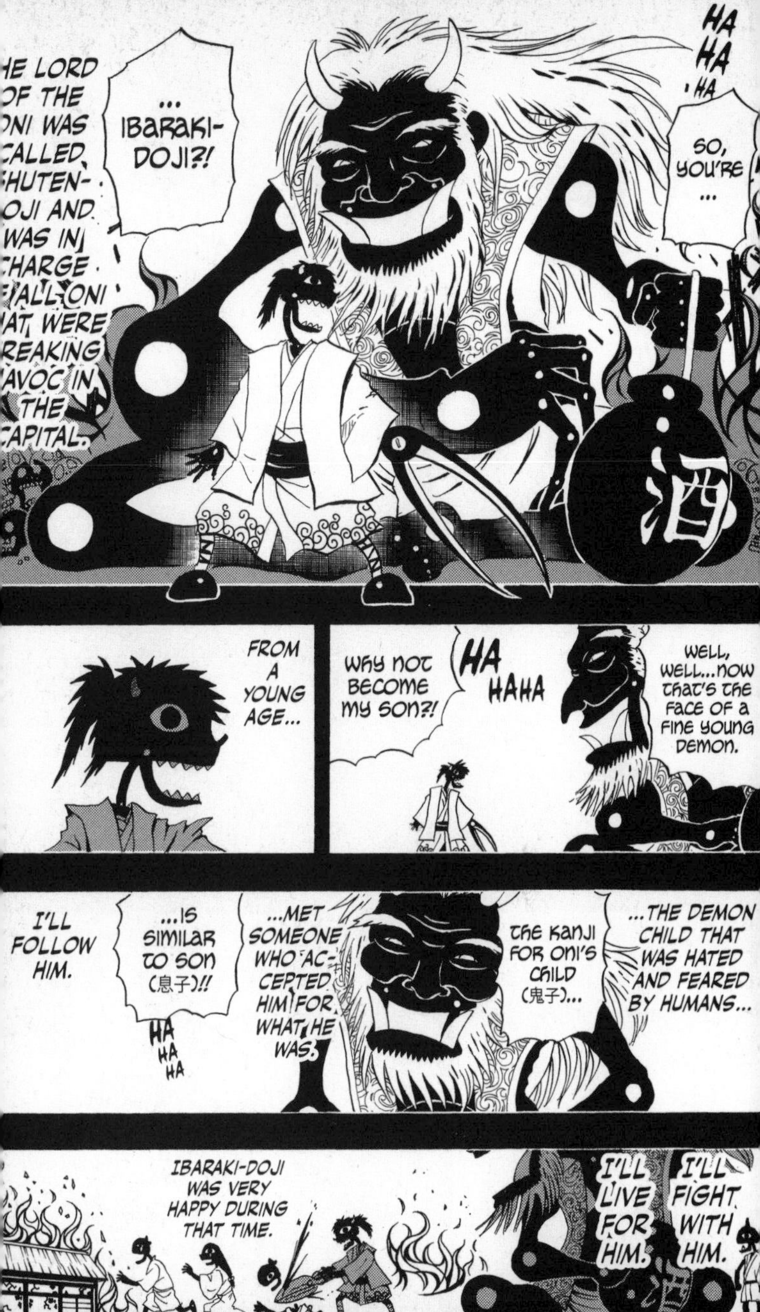
HA HA HA
SO, YOU'RE ...
... IBARAKI-DOJI?!
HE LORD OF THE ONI WAS CALLED HUTEN-OJI AND WAS IN CHARGE F ALL ONI AT WERE REAKING AVOC IN THE CAPITAL.
WELL, WELL...NOW THAT'S THE FACE OF A FINE YOUNG DEMON.
HA HAHA
WHY NOT BECOME MY SON?!
FROM A YOUNG AGE...
...THE DEMON CHILD THAT WAS HATED AND FEARED BY HUMANS...
THE KANJI FOR ONI'S CHILD (鬼子)...
...MET SOMEONE WHO ACCEPTED HIM FOR WHAT HE WAS.
...IS SIMILAR TO SON (息子)!!
HA HA HA
I'LL FOLLOW HIM.
I'LL FIGHT WITH HIM.
I'LL LIVE FOR HIM.
IBARAKI-DOJI WAS VERY HAPPY DURING THAT TIME.

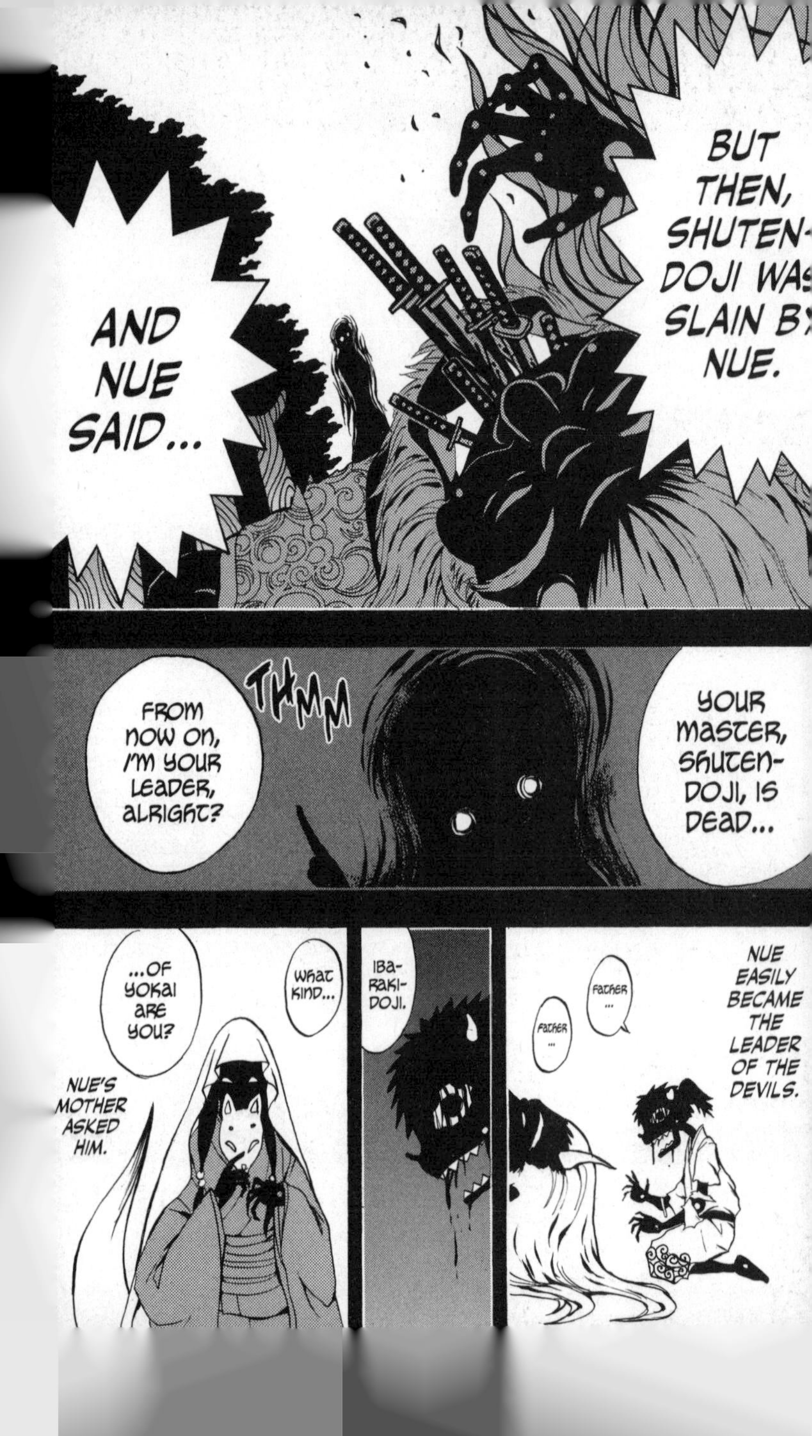
BUT THEN, SHUTEN-DOJI WAS SLAIN BY NUE.
AND NUE SAID...
YOUR MASTER, SHUTEN-DOJI, IS DEAD...
THMM
FROM NOW ON, I'M YOUR LEADER, ALRIGHT?
NUE EASILY BECAME THE LEADER OF THE DEVILS.
FATHER...
FATHER...
IBA-RAKI-DOJI.
WHAT KIND...
...OF YOKAI ARE YOU?
NUE'S MOTHER ASKED HIM.

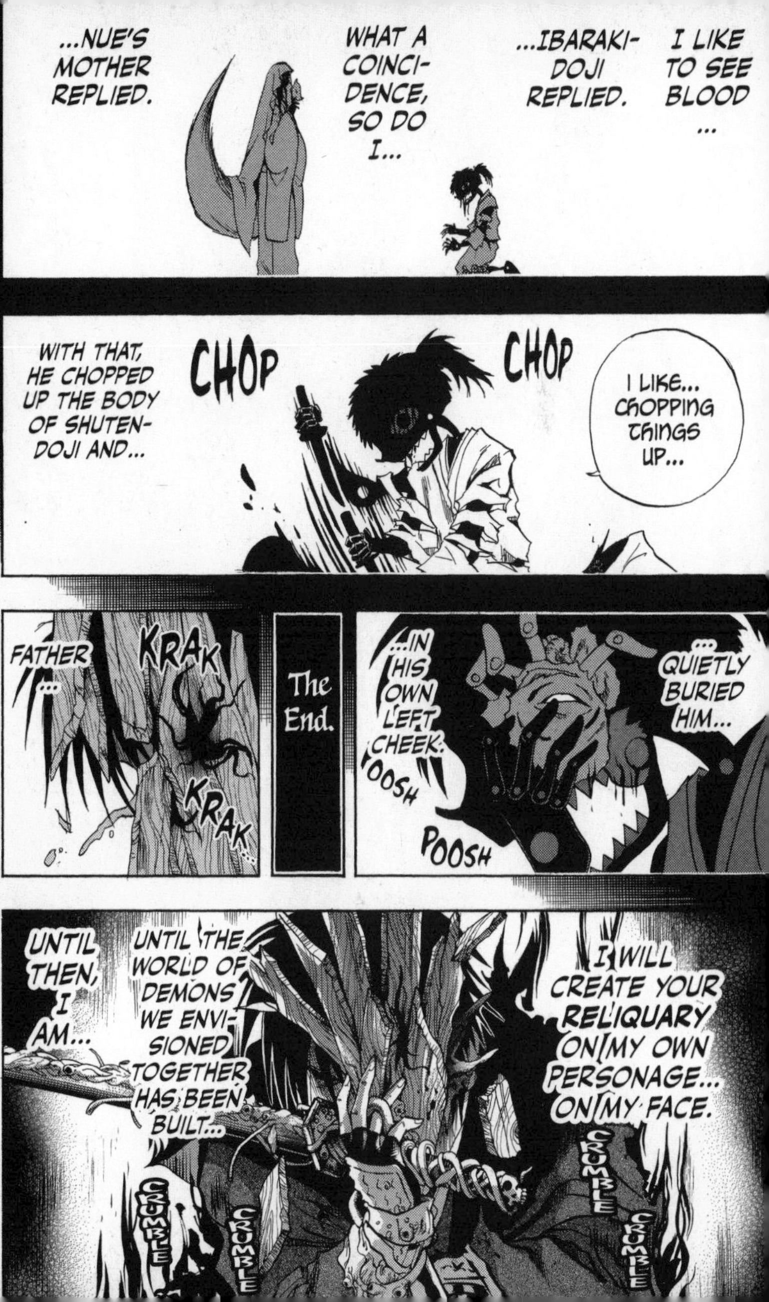
I LIKE TO SEE BLOOD ...
...IBARAKI-DOJI REPLIED.
WHAT A COINCIDENCE, SO DO I...
...NUE'S MOTHER REPLIED.
I LIKE... CHOPPING THINGS UP...
CHOP
CHOP
WITH THAT, HE CHOPPED UP THE BODY OF SHUTEN-DOJI AND...
...QUIETLY BURIED HIM...
...IN HIS OWN LEFT CHEEK.
POOSH
POOSH
The End.
FATHER...
KRAK
KRAK...
I WILL CREATE YOUR RELIQUARY ON MY OWN PERSONAGE... ON MY FACE.
CRUMBLE
CRUMBLE
UNTIL THE WORLD OF DEMONS WE ENVISIONED TOGETHER HAS BEEN BUILT...
UNTIL THEN, I AM...
CRUMBLE
CRUMBLE

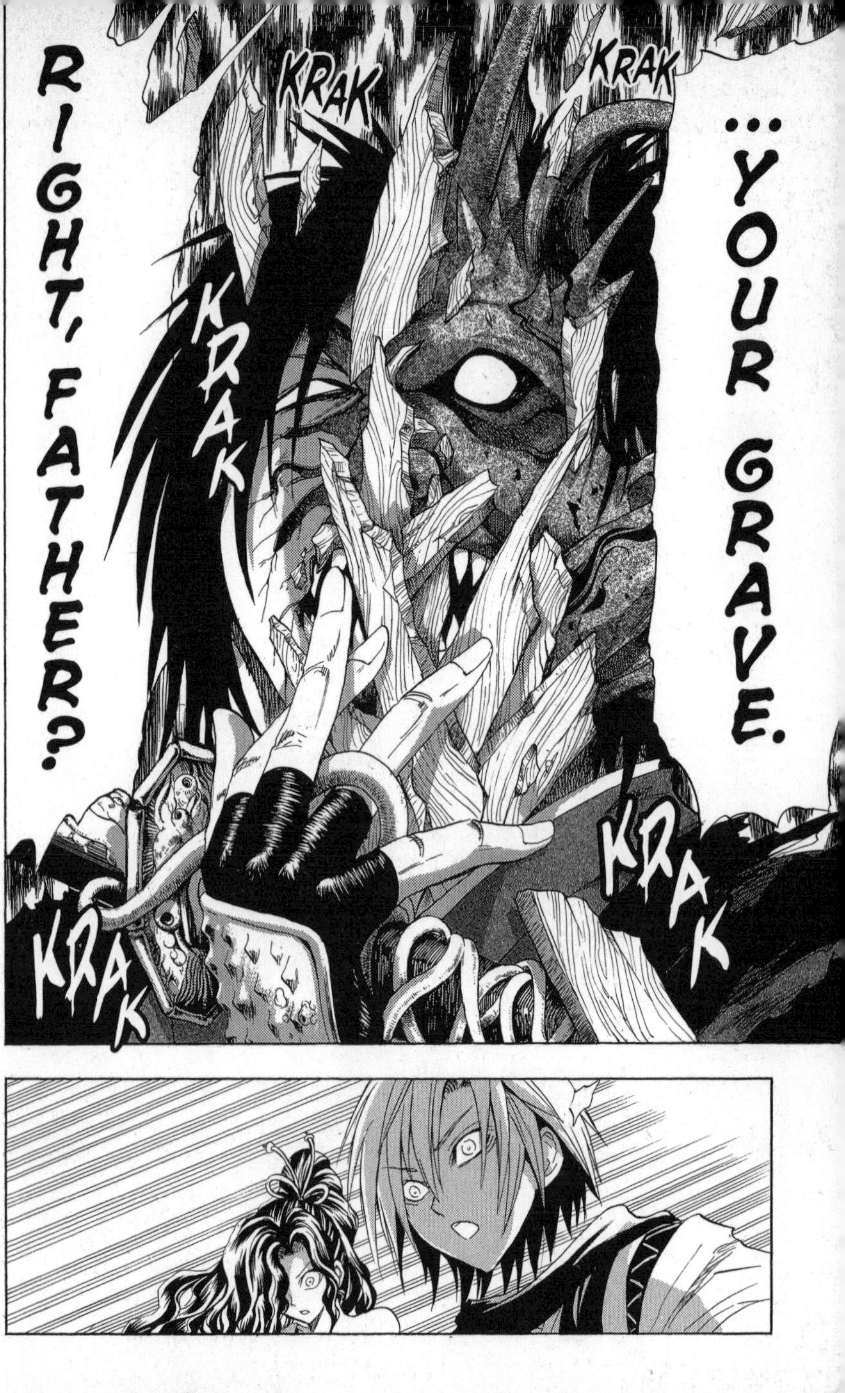
KRAK
...YOUR GRAVE.
KRAK
RIGHT, FATHER?
KRAK
KRAK
KRAK

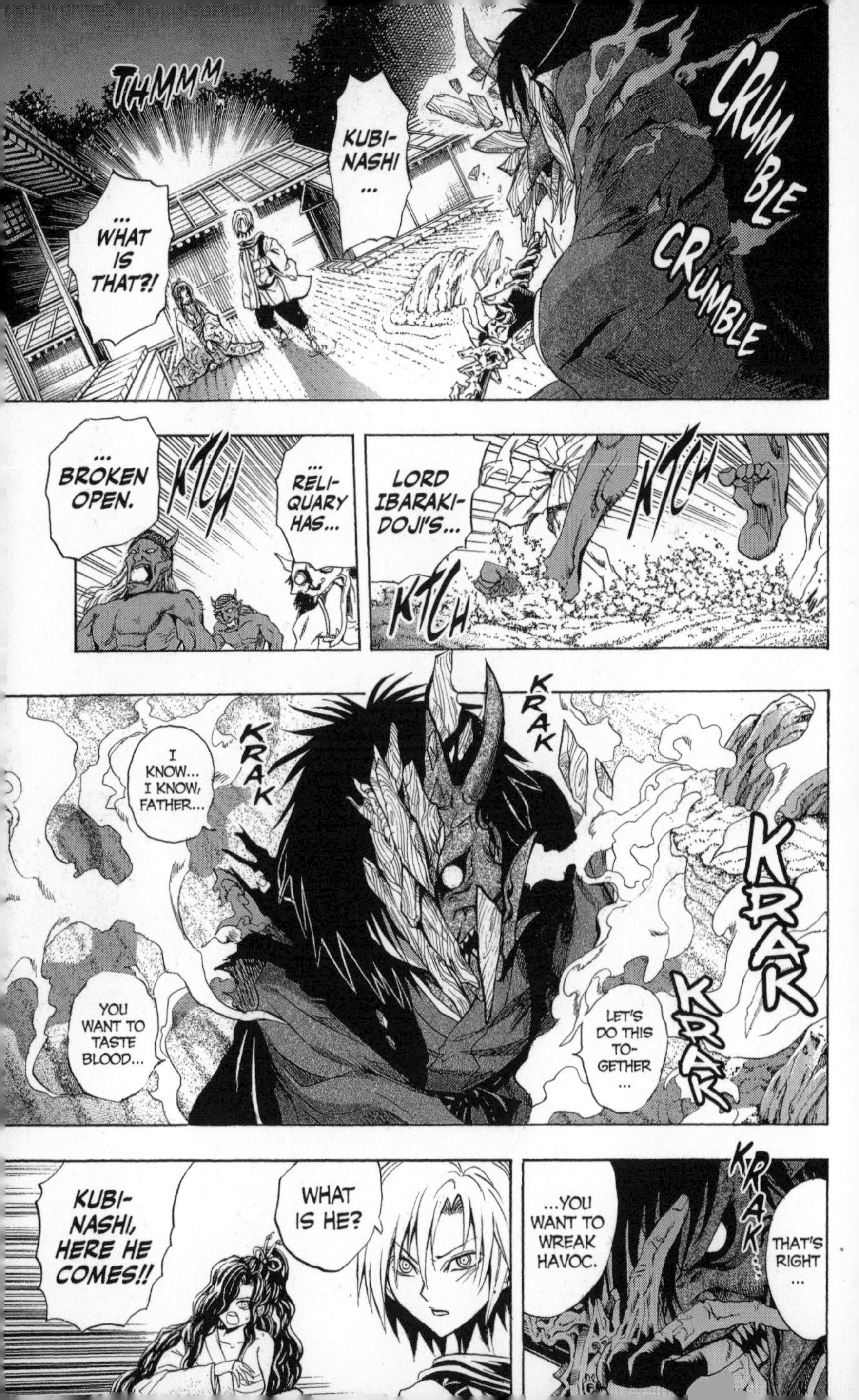
CRUMBLE
CRUMBLE
KUBI-NASHI...
THMMMM
...WHAT IS THAT?!
KTCH
LORD IBARAKI-DOJI'S...
KTCH
...RELIQUARY HAS...
KTCH
...BROKEN OPEN.
KRAK
KRAK
KRAK
I KNOW... I KNOW, FATHER...
LET'S DO THIS TO-GETHER...
YOU WANT TO TASTE BLOOD...
KRAK KRAK...
...YOU WANT TO WREAK HAVOC.
THAT'S RIGHT...
WHAT IS HE?
KUBI-NASHI, HERE HE COMES!!

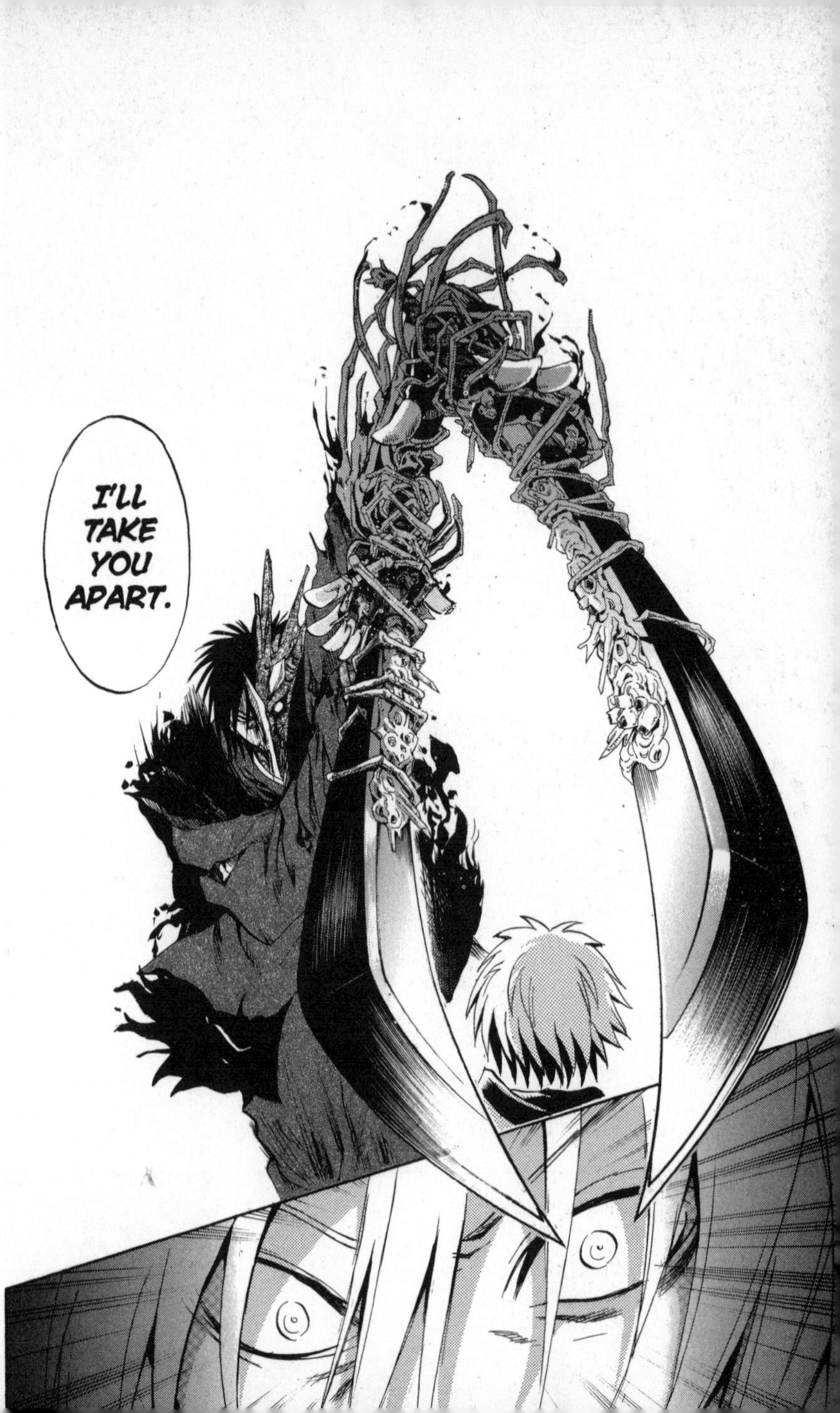
I'LL TAKE YOU APART.

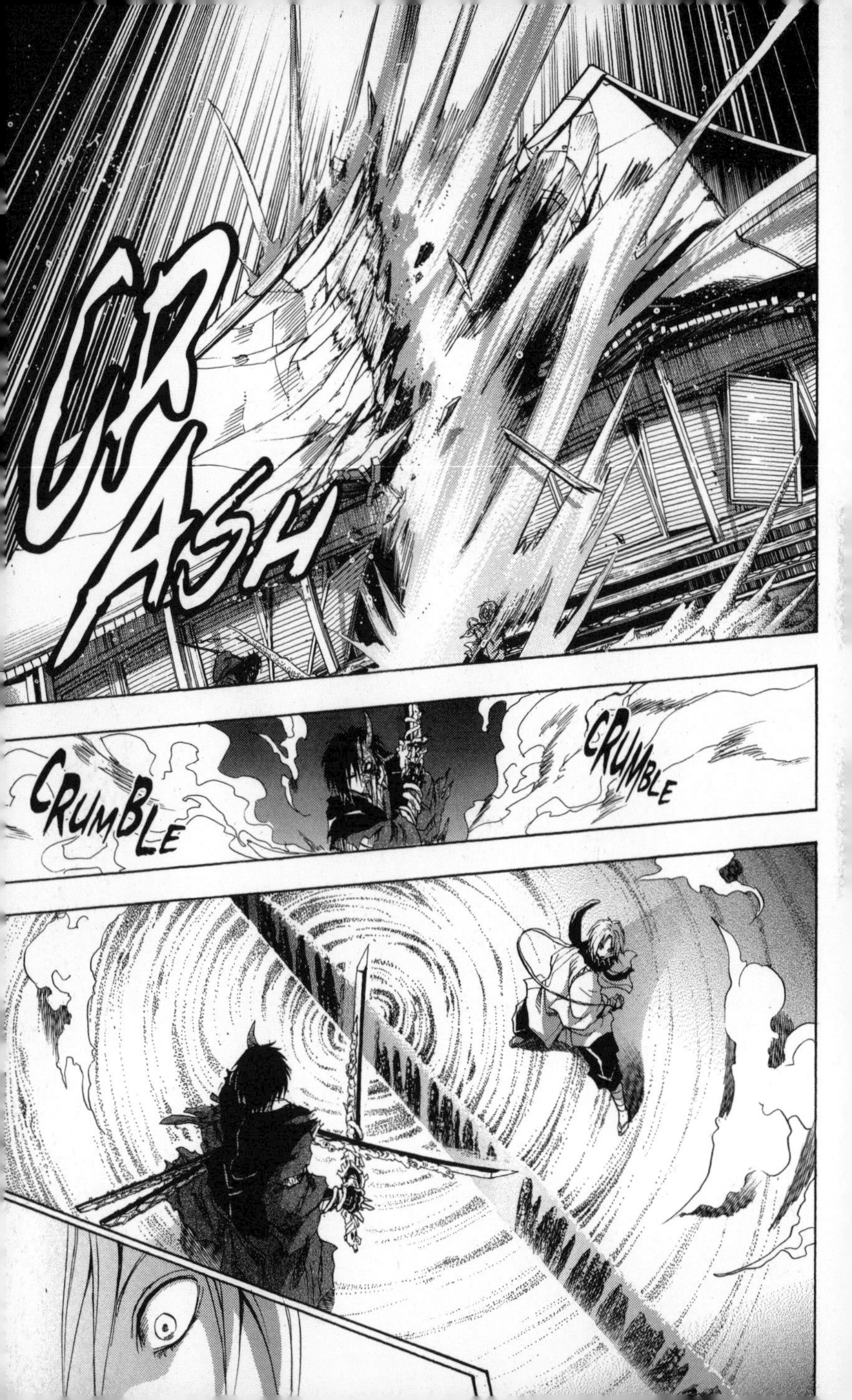
CRASH
CRUMBLE
CRUMBLE

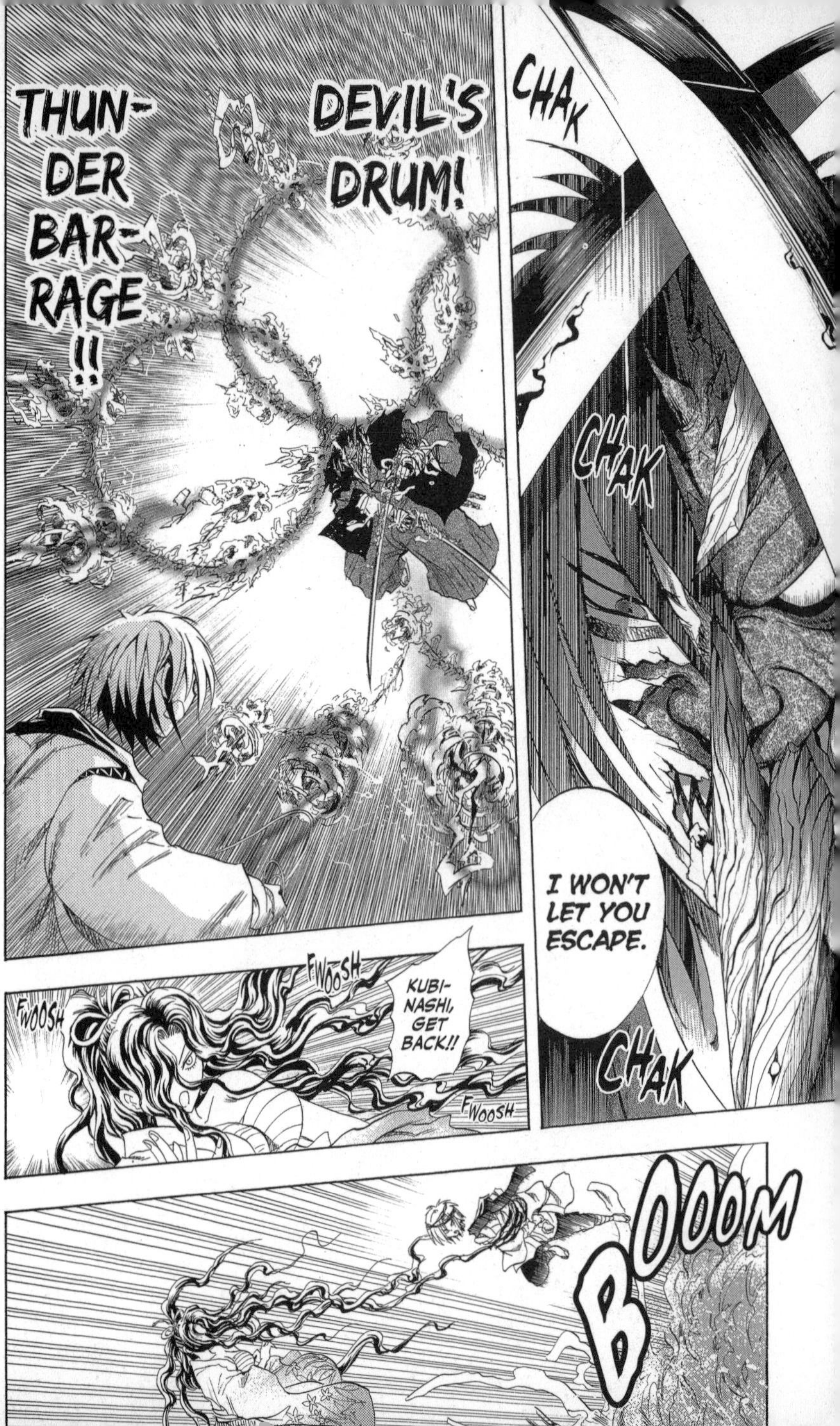
CHAK
CHAK
I WON'T LET YOU ESCAPE.
CHAK
DEVIL'S DRUM!
THUN-DER BAR-RAGE!!
FWOOSH
KUBI-NASHI, GET BACK!!
FWOOSH
FWOOSH
BOOOM

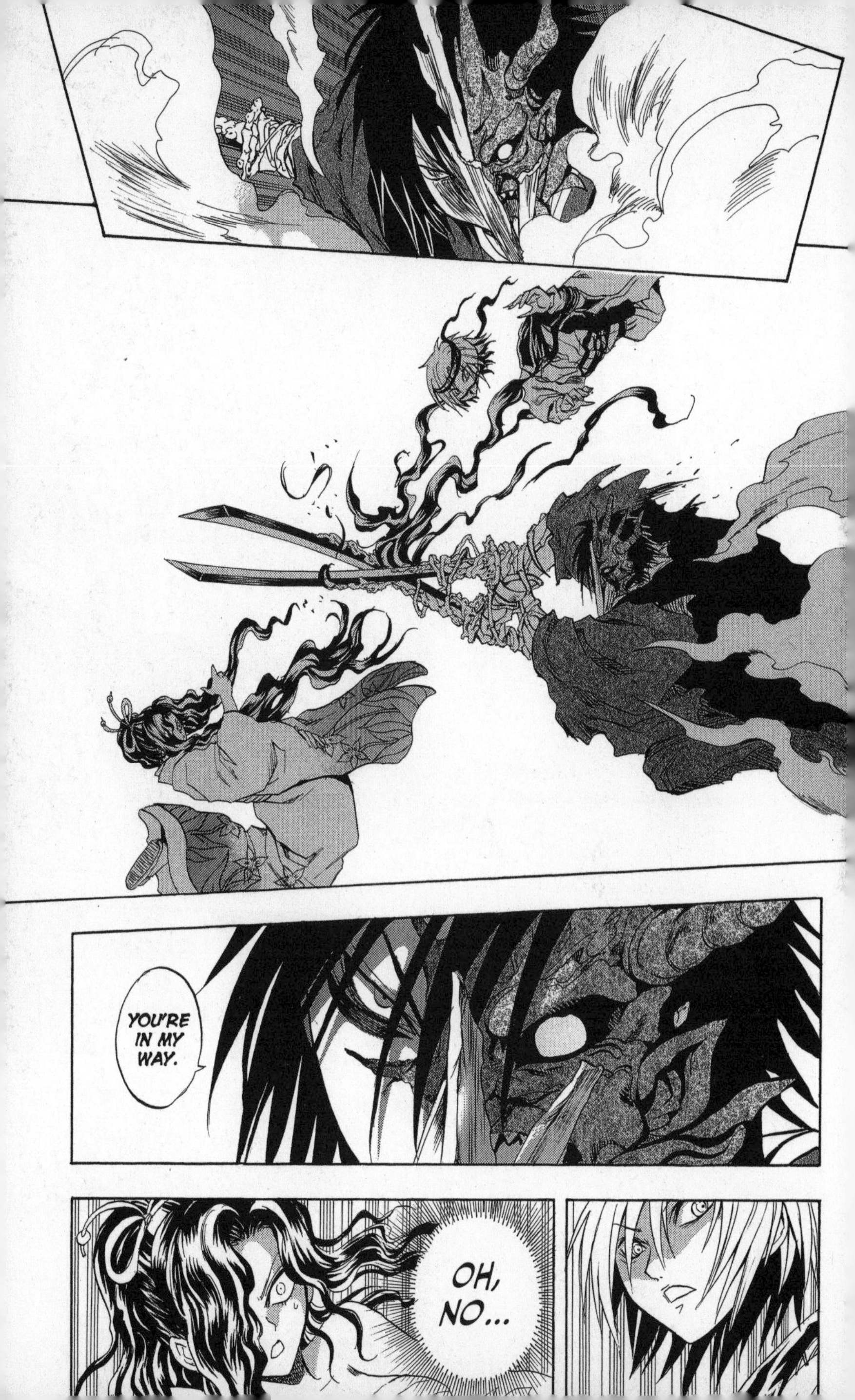
YOU'RE IN MY WAY.
OH, NO...

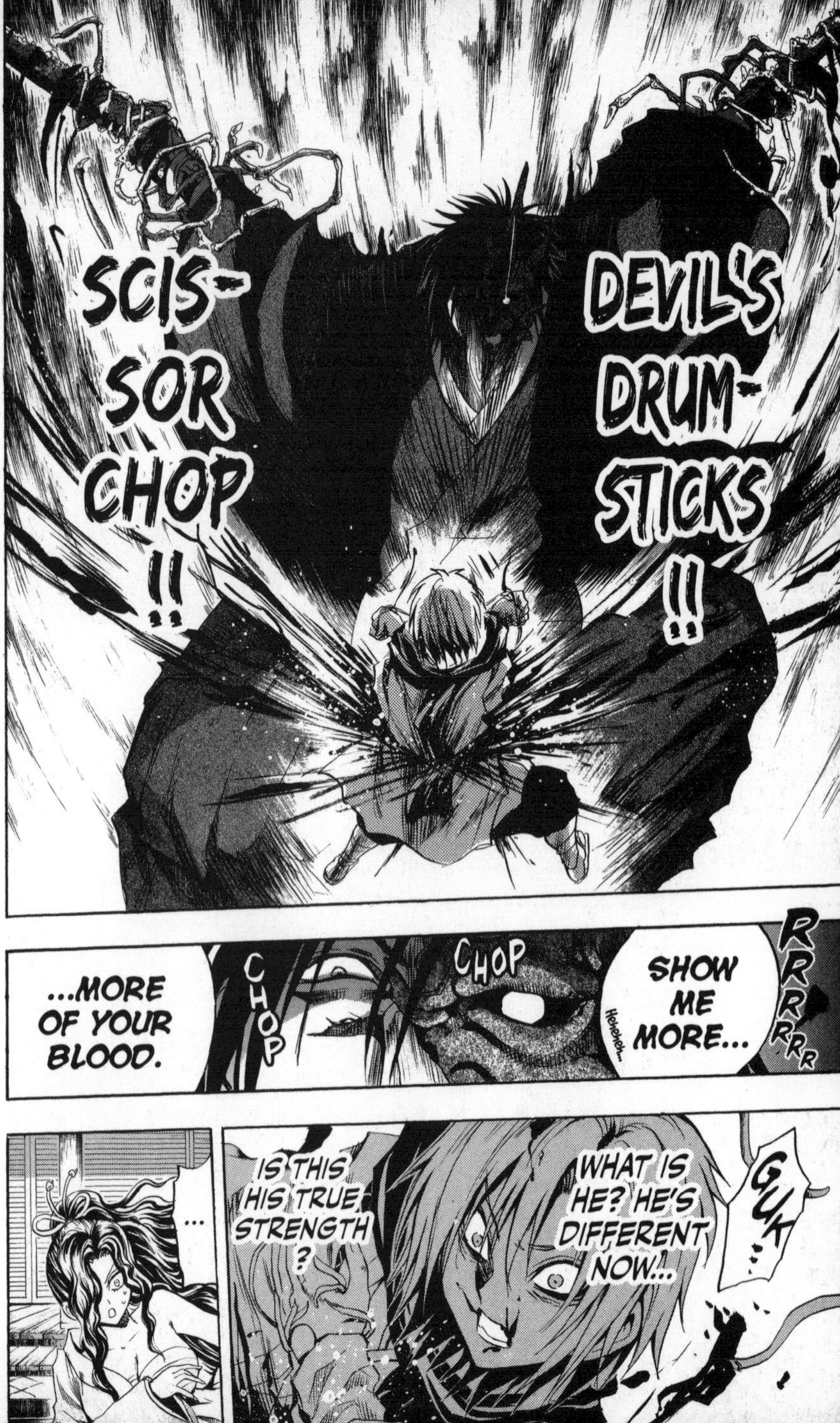
DEVIL'S DRUM-STICKS!!
SCIS-SOR CHOP!!
RRRRRR
SHOW ME MORE...
Heheheh...
CHOP
CHOP
...MORE OF YOUR BLOOD.
GUK...
WHAT IS HE? HE'S DIFFERENT NOW...
IS THIS HIS TRUE STRENGTH?
...

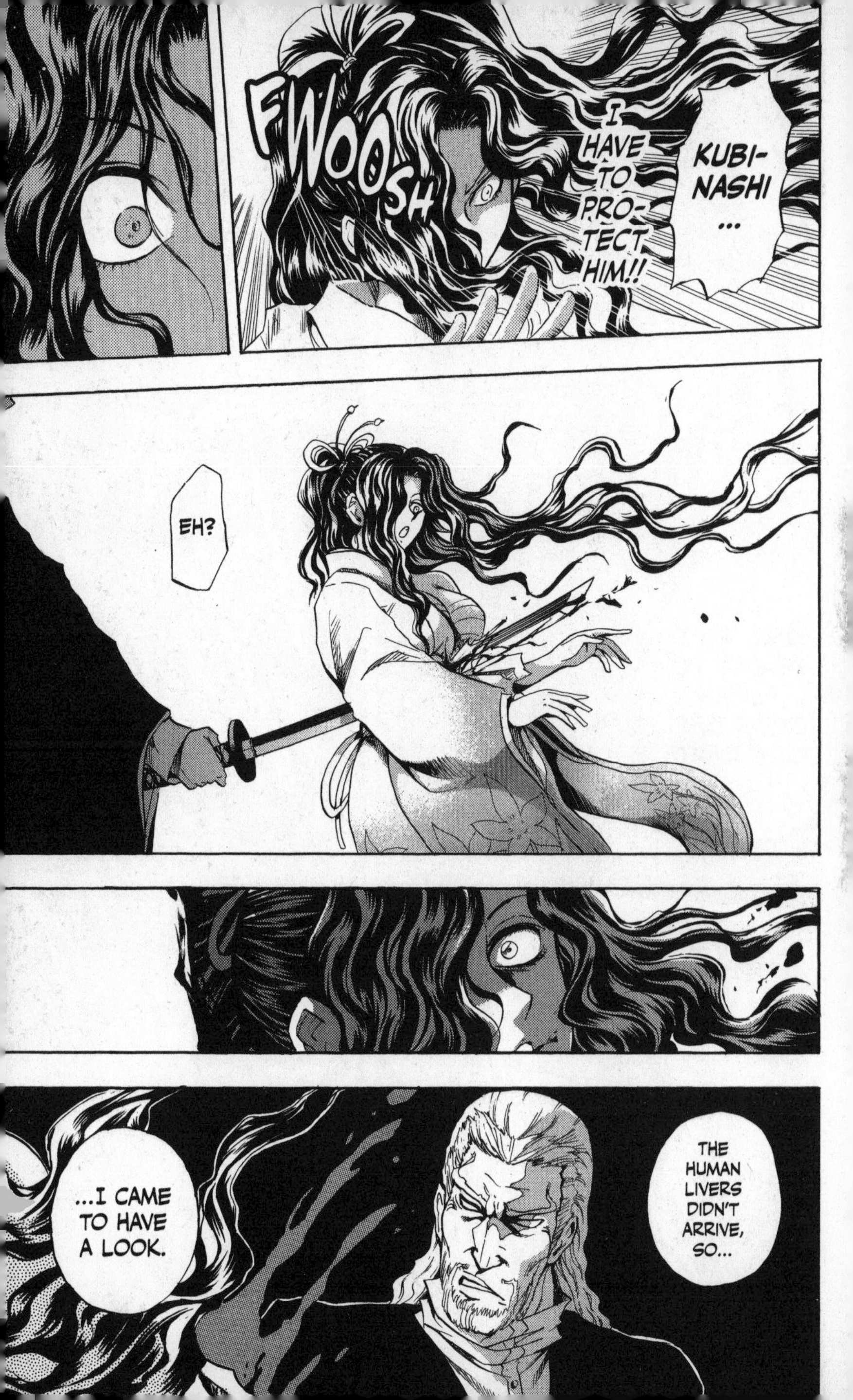
KUBI-NASHI...
I HAVE TO PRO-TECT HIM!!
FWOOSH
EH?
THE HUMAN LIVERS DIDN'T ARRIVE, SO...
...I CAME TO HAVE A LOOK.

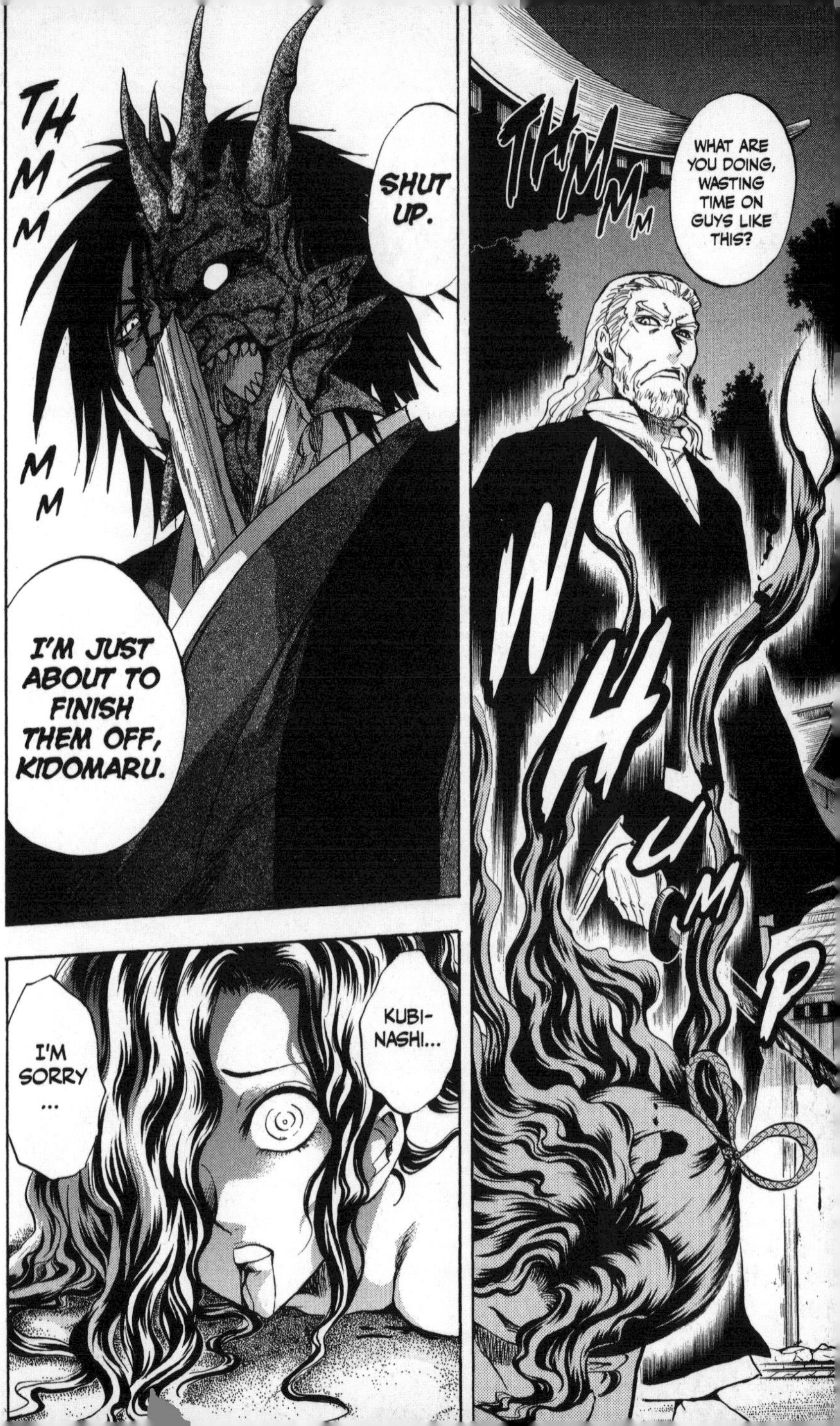
THMMMM
WHAT ARE YOU DOING, WASTING TIME ON GUYS LIKE THIS?
WHUMP
THMMMM
SHUT UP.
I'M JUST ABOUT TO FINISH THEM OFF, KIDOMARU.
KUBI-NASHI...
I'M SORRY...

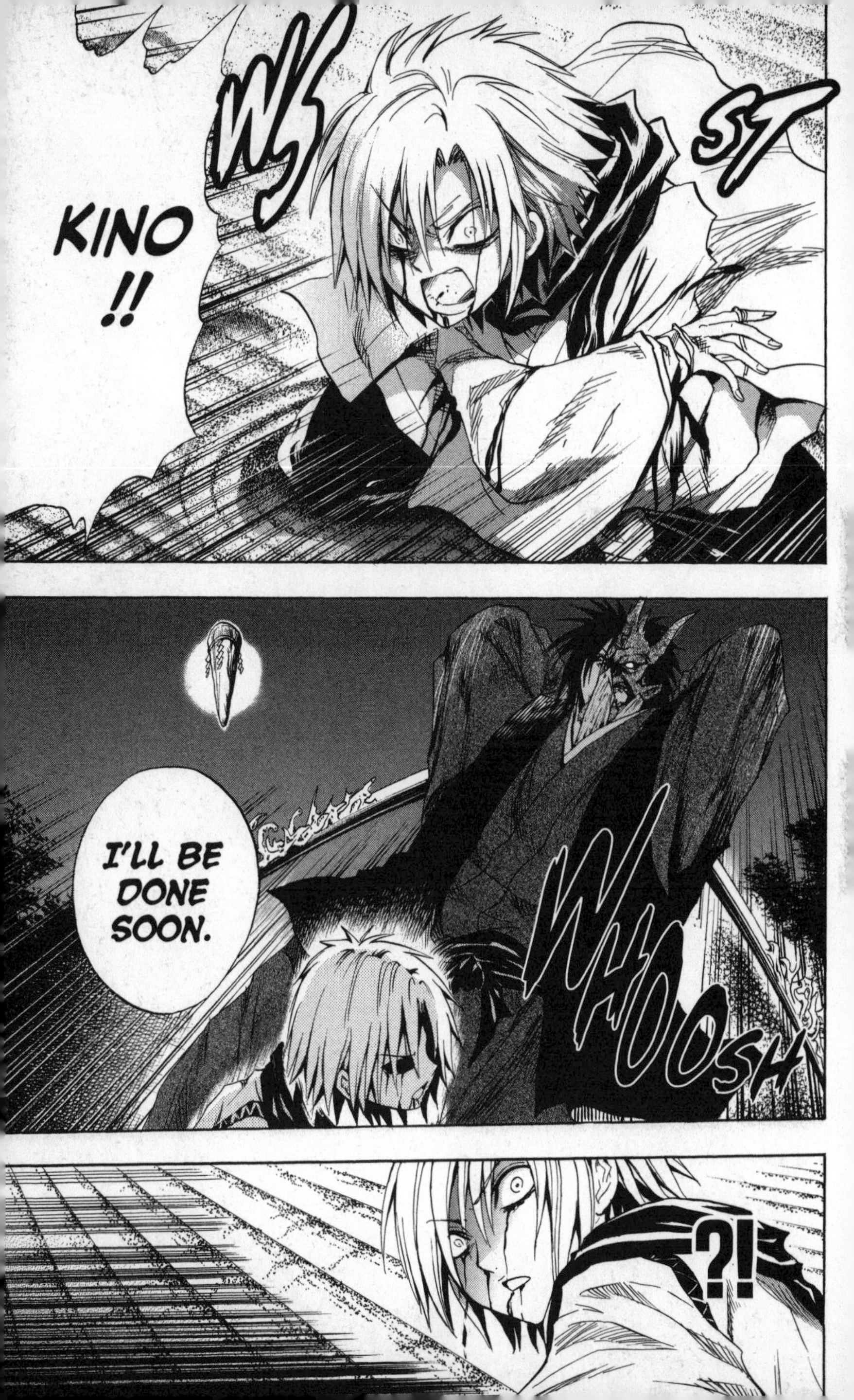
WHOOSH
KINO !!
WHOOSH
I'LL BE DONE SOON.
?!

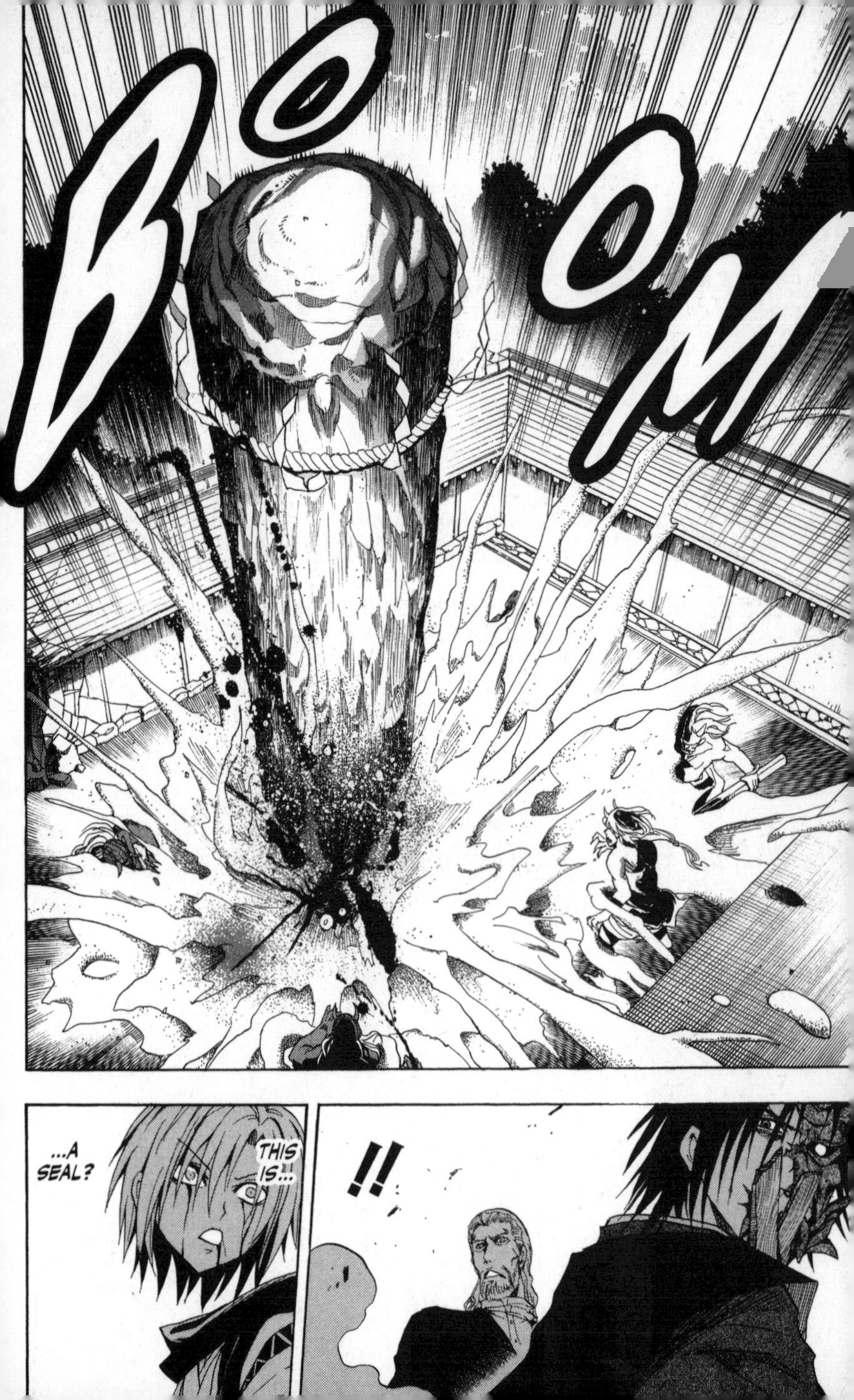
BOOM
!!
THIS IS...
...A SEAL?

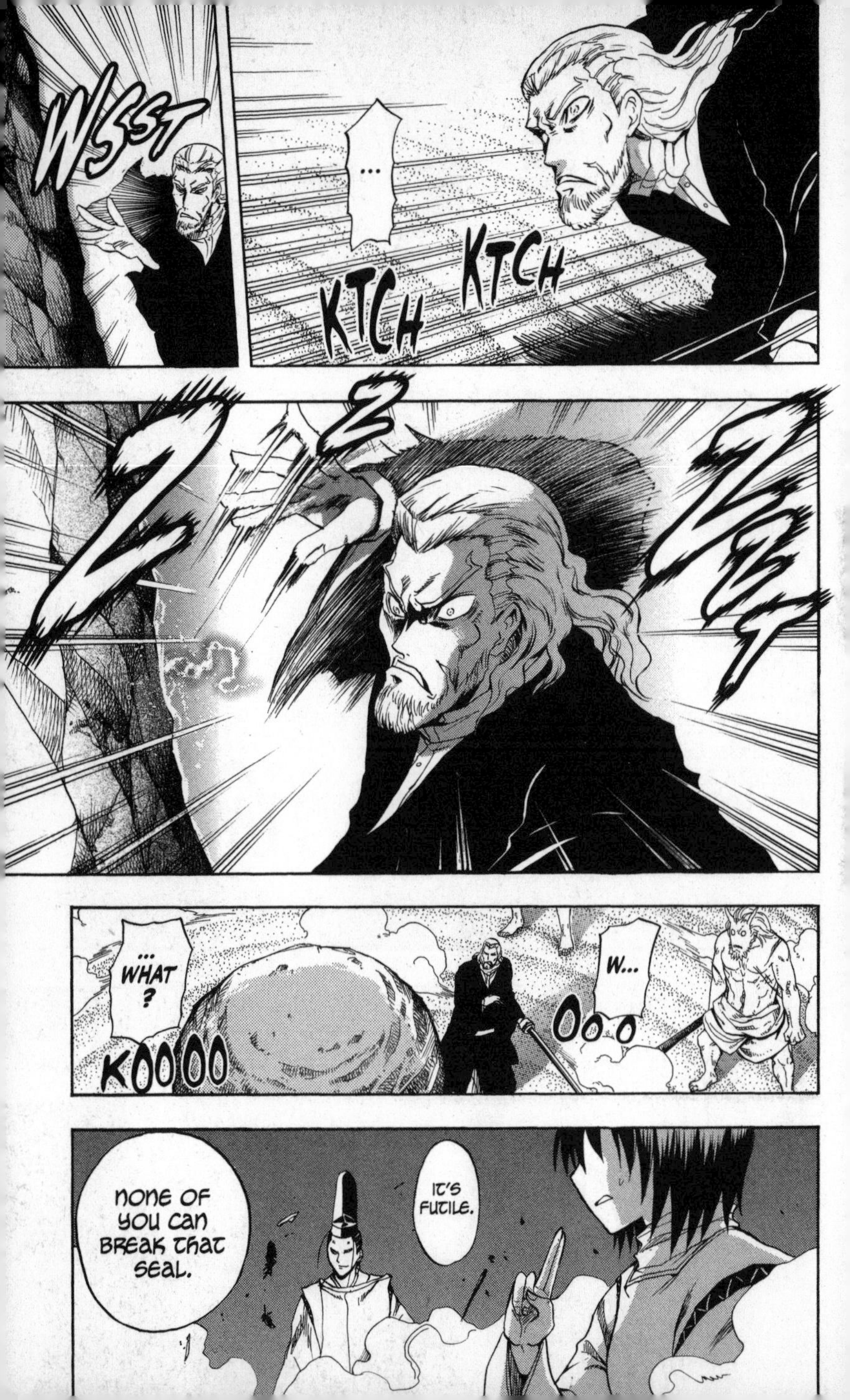
...
KTCH KTCH
WSSST
W...
OOO
... WHAT?
KOOOO
IT'S FUTILE.
NONE OF YOU CAN BREAK THAT SEAL.

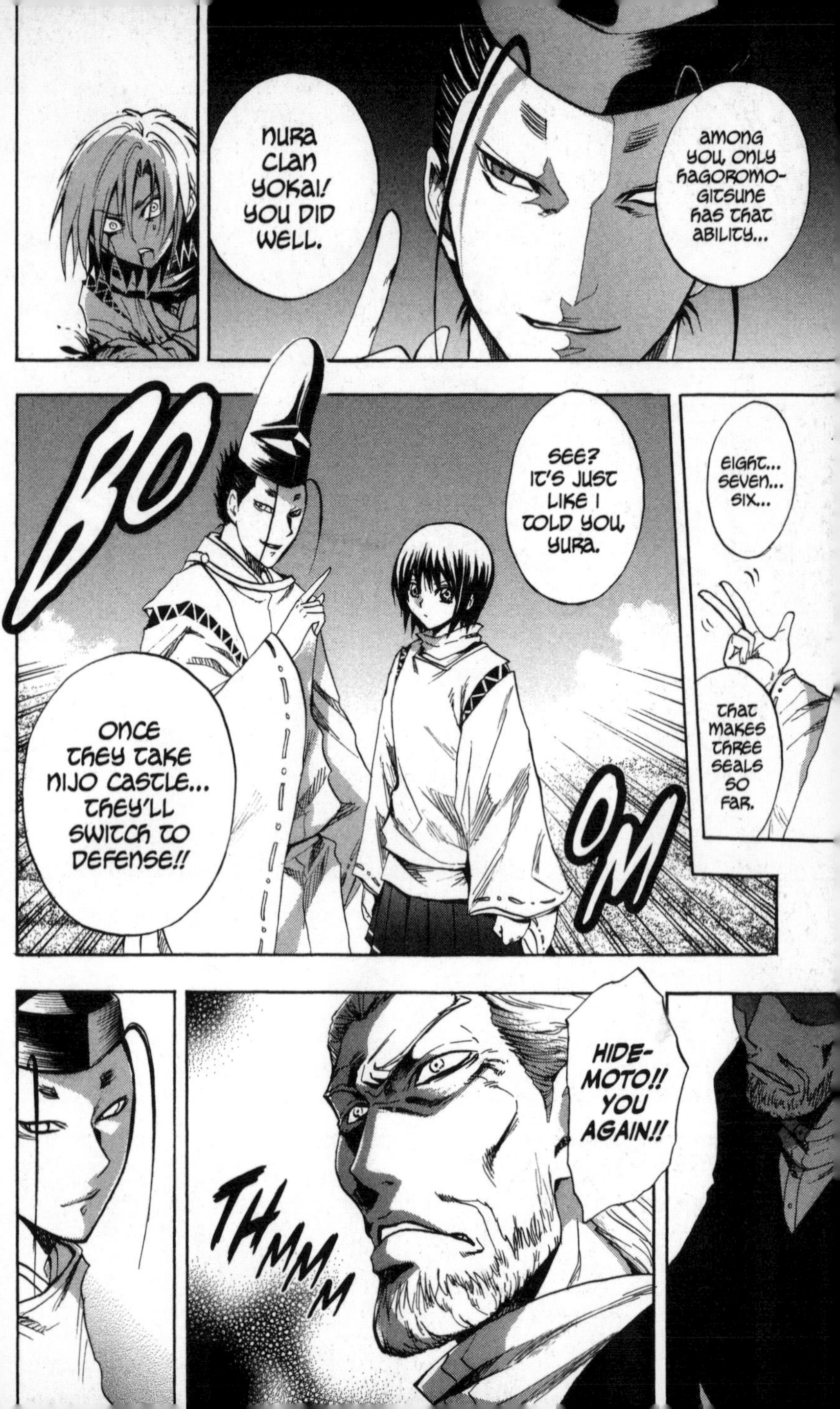
among you, only hagoromo-gitsune has that ability...
nura clan yokai! you did well.
eight... seven... six...
that makes three seals so far.
see? it's just like i told you, yura.
BO
OM
once they take nijo castle... they'll switch to defense!!
HIDE-MOTO!! YOU AGAIN!!
THMMMM

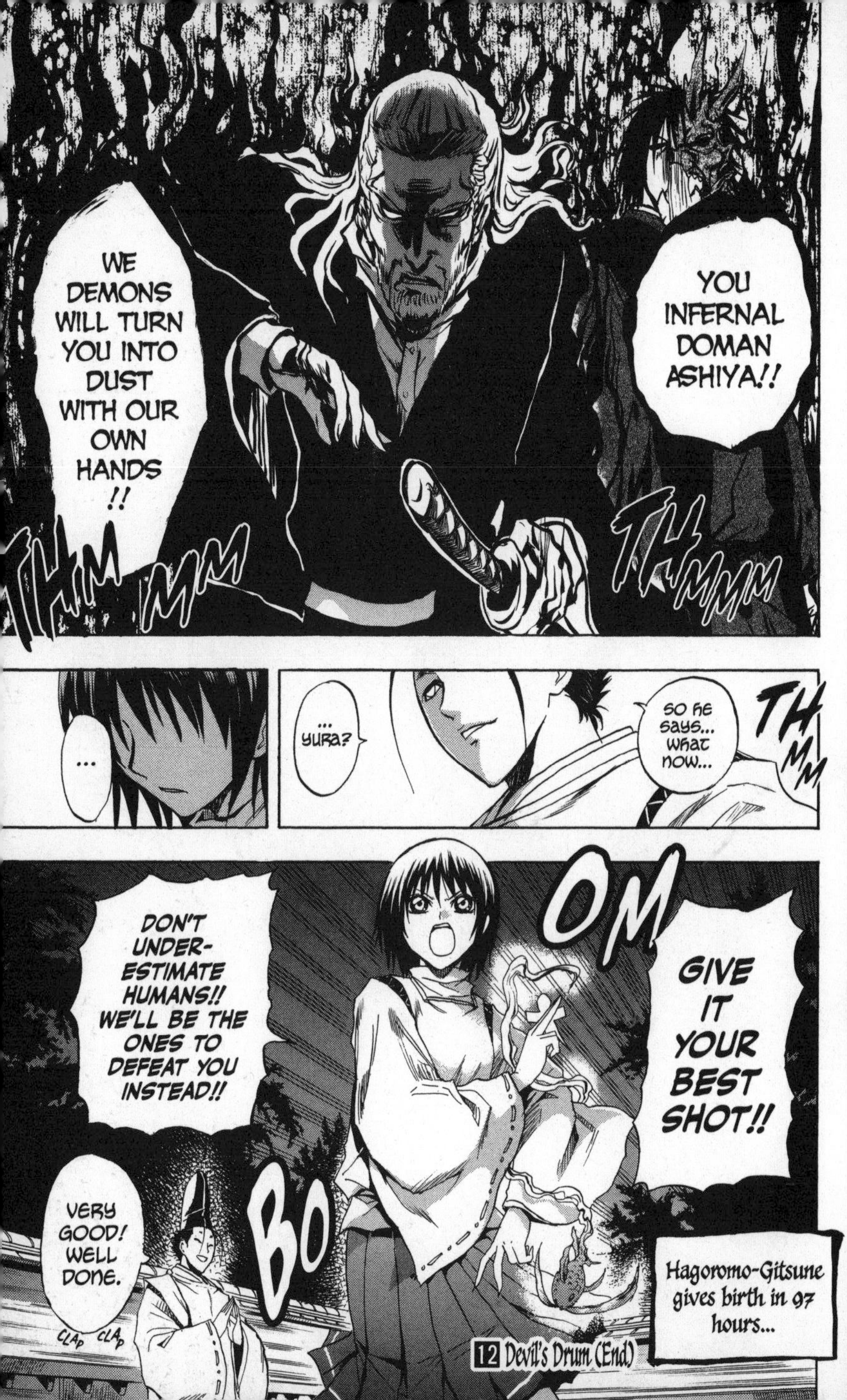
YOU INFERNAL DOMAN ASHIYA!!
THMMMM
WE DEMONS WILL TURN YOU INTO DUST WITH OUR OWN HANDS!!
THMMMM
THMM
SO HE SAYS... WHAT NOW...
...YURA?
...
GIVE IT YOUR BEST SHOT!!
OM
DON'T UNDER-ESTIMATE HUMANS!! WE'LL BE THE ONES TO DEFEAT YOU INSTEAD!!
BO
Hagoromo-Gitsune gives birth in 97 hours...
VERY GOOD! WELL DONE.
CLAP CLAP
12 Devil's Drum (End)

Bonus Story: The Nura Clan Record of Three Generations - Dawn of the Edo Period

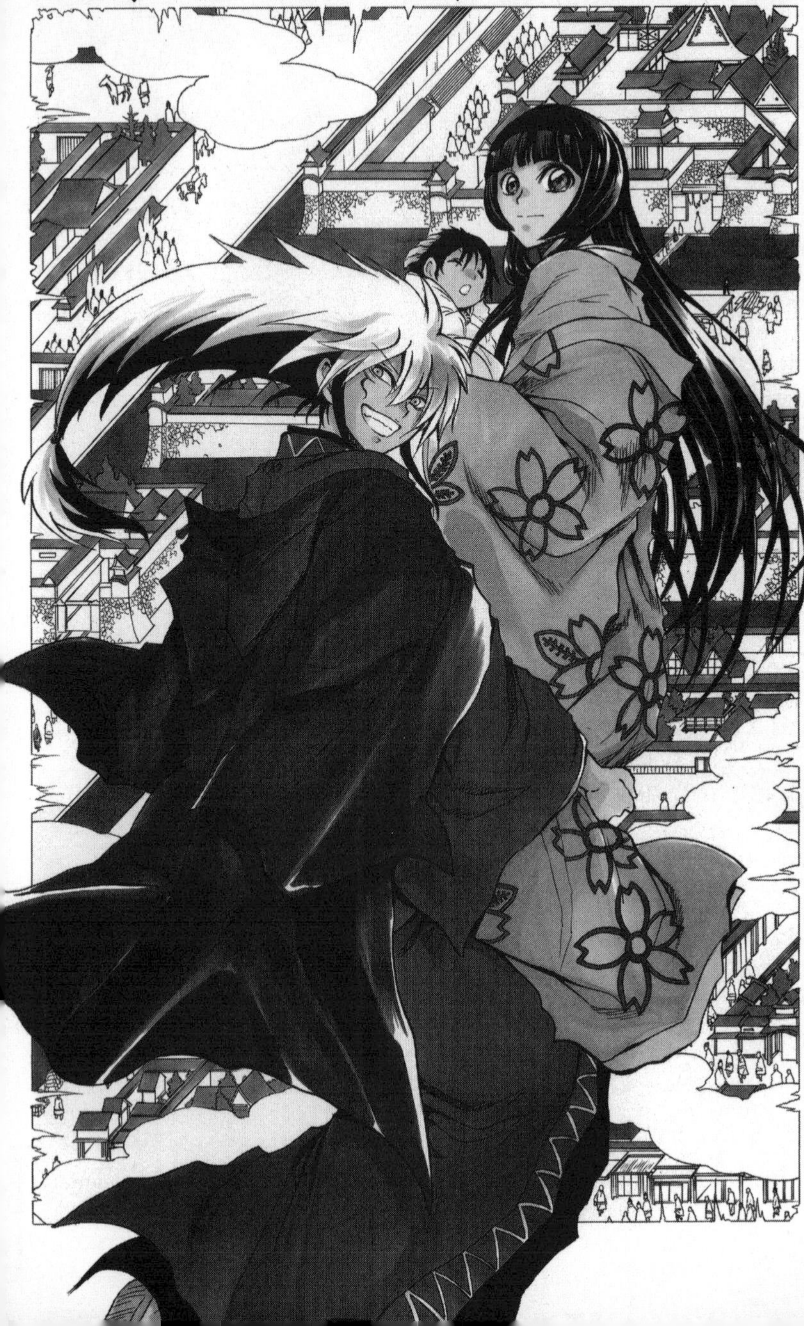

READ THIS WAY

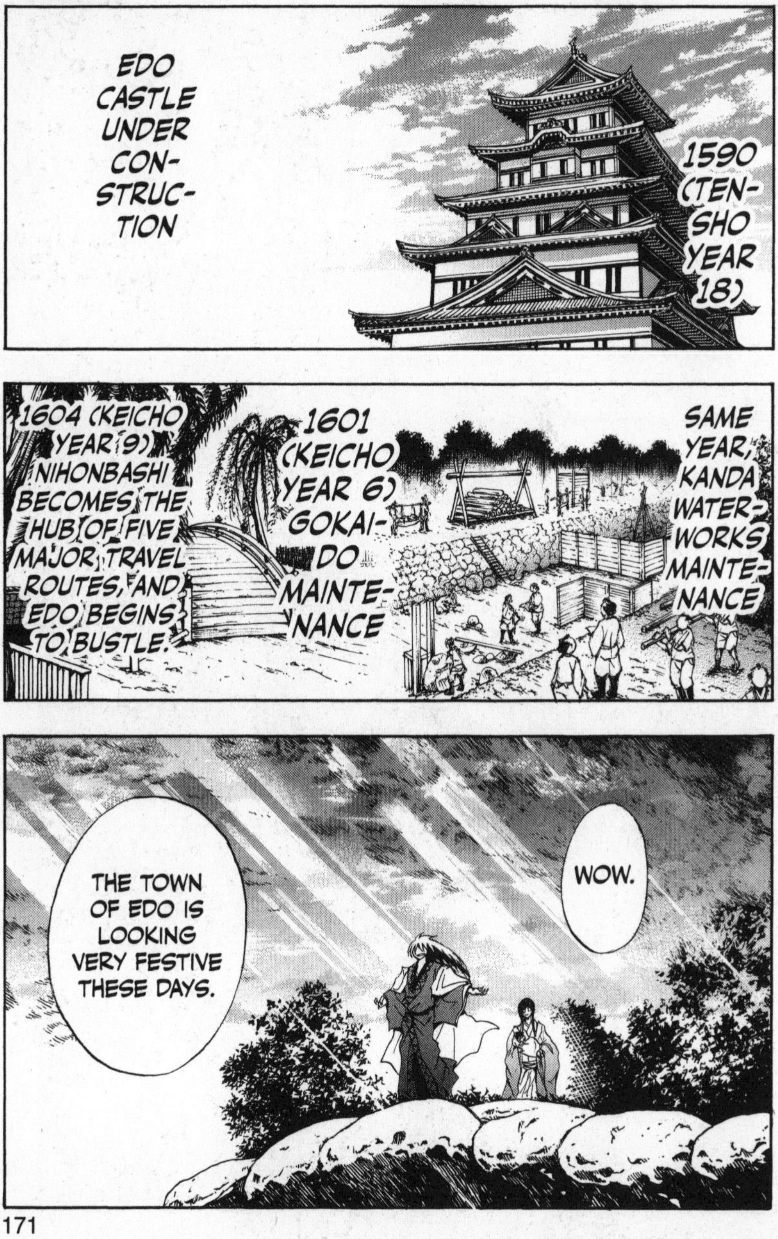
1590 (TEN-SHO YEAR 18)
EDO CASTLE UNDER CON-STRUC-TION
SAME YEAR, KANDA WATER-WORKS MAINTE-NANCE
1601 (KEICHO YEAR 6) GOKAI-DO MAINTE-NANCE
1604 (KEICHO YEAR 9) NIHONBASHI BECOMES THE HUB OF FIVE MAJOR TRAVEL ROUTES, AND EDO BEGINS TO BUSTLE.
WOW.
THE TOWN OF EDO IS LOOKING VERY FESTIVE THESE DAYS.

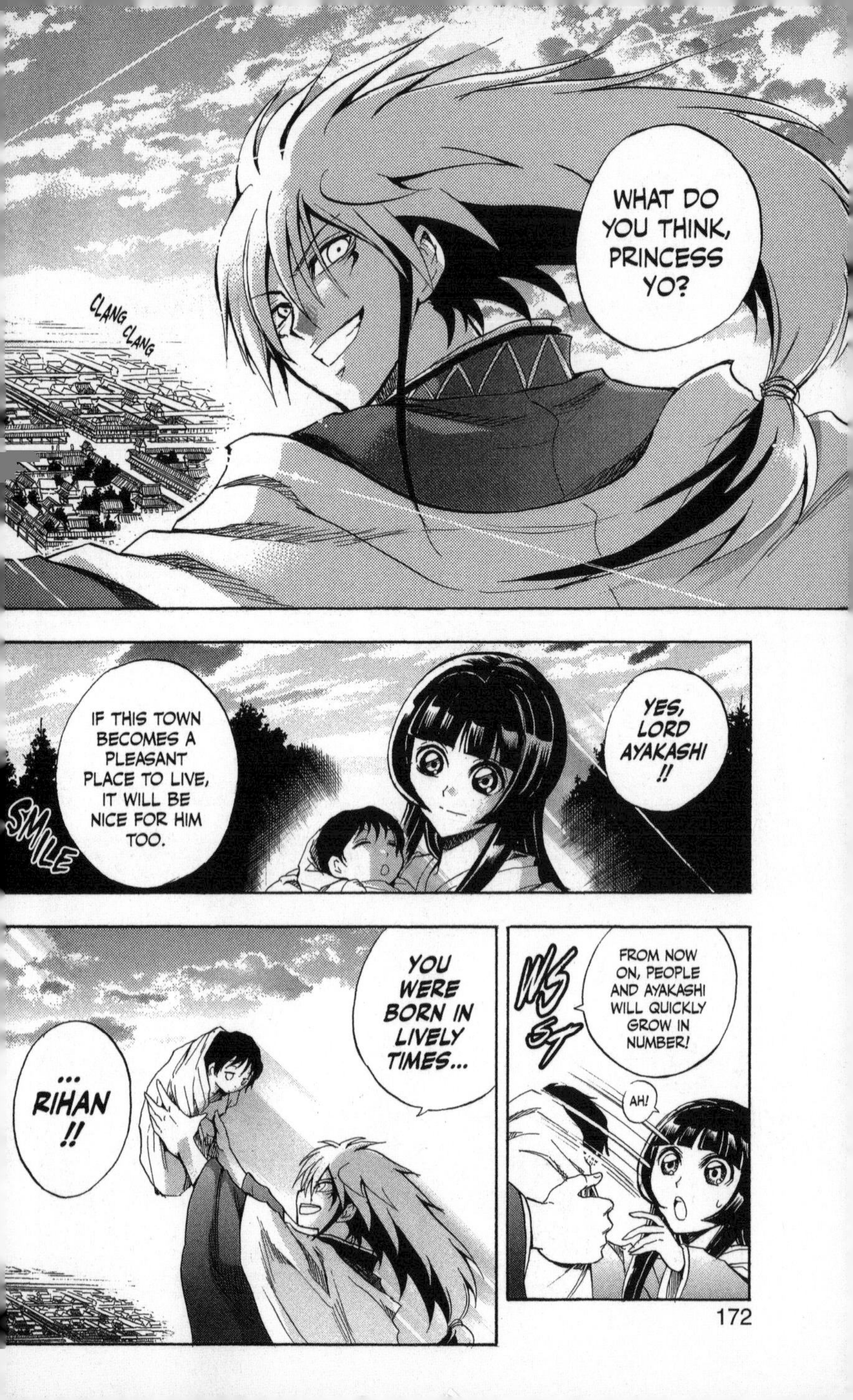

WHAT DO YOU THINK, PRINCESS YO?
CLANG CLANG
YES, LORD AYAKASHI !!
IF THIS TOWN BECOMES A PLEASANT PLACE TO LIVE, IT WILL BE NICE FOR HIM TOO.
SMILE
FROM NOW ON, PEOPLE AND AYAKASHI WILL QUICKLY GROW IN NUMBER!
AH!
YOU WERE BORN IN LIVELY TIMES...
... RIHAN !!

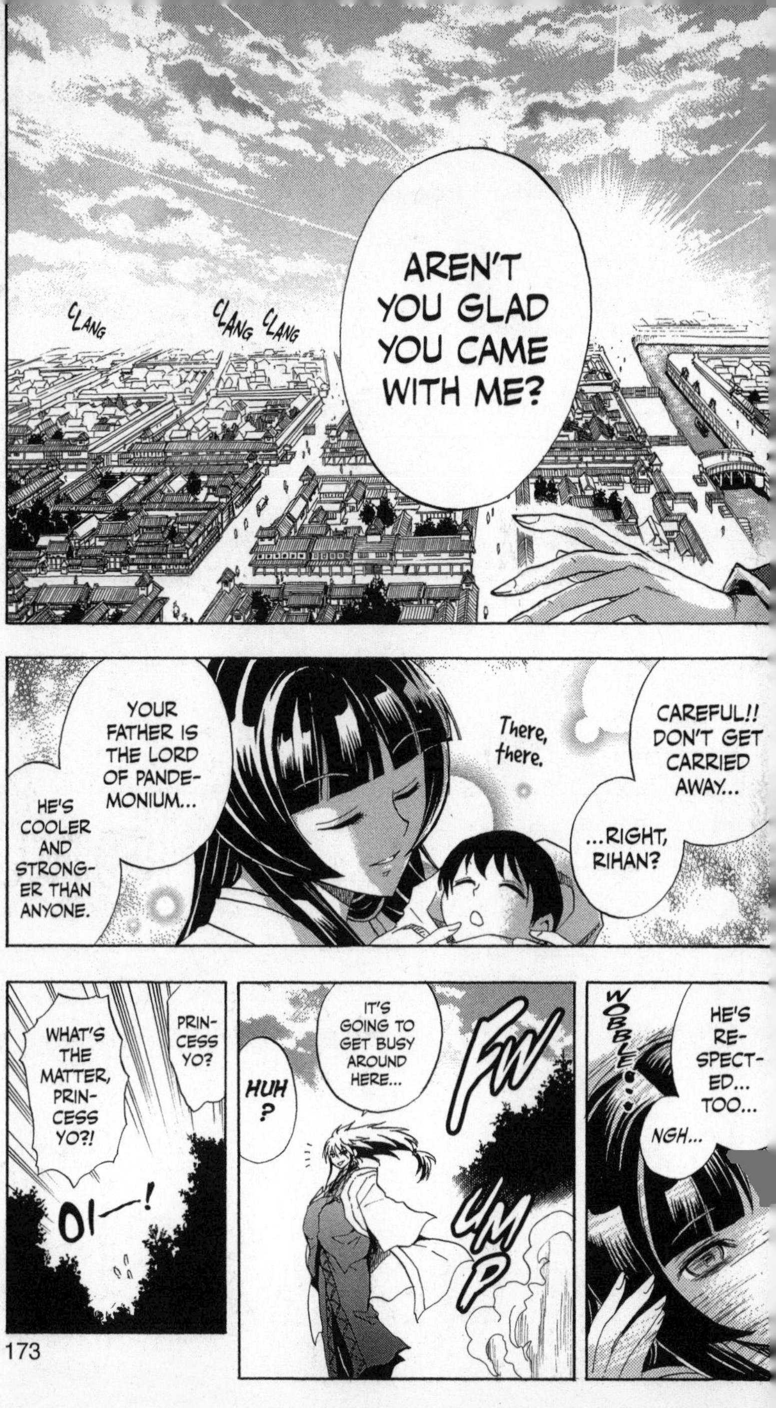
AREN'T YOU GLAD YOU CAME WITH ME?
CLANG CLANG
CLANG
CAREFUL!! DON'T GET CARRIED AWAY...
...RIGHT, RIHAN?
There, there.
YOUR FATHER IS THE LORD OF PANDE-MONIUM...
HE'S COOLER AND STRONG-ER THAN ANYONE.
WOBBLE
HE'S RE-SPECT-ED... TOO...
NGH...
FWUMP
IT'S GOING TO GET BUSY AROUND HERE...
HUH?
PRIN-CESS YO?
WHAT'S THE MATTER, PRIN-CESS YO?!
OI—!

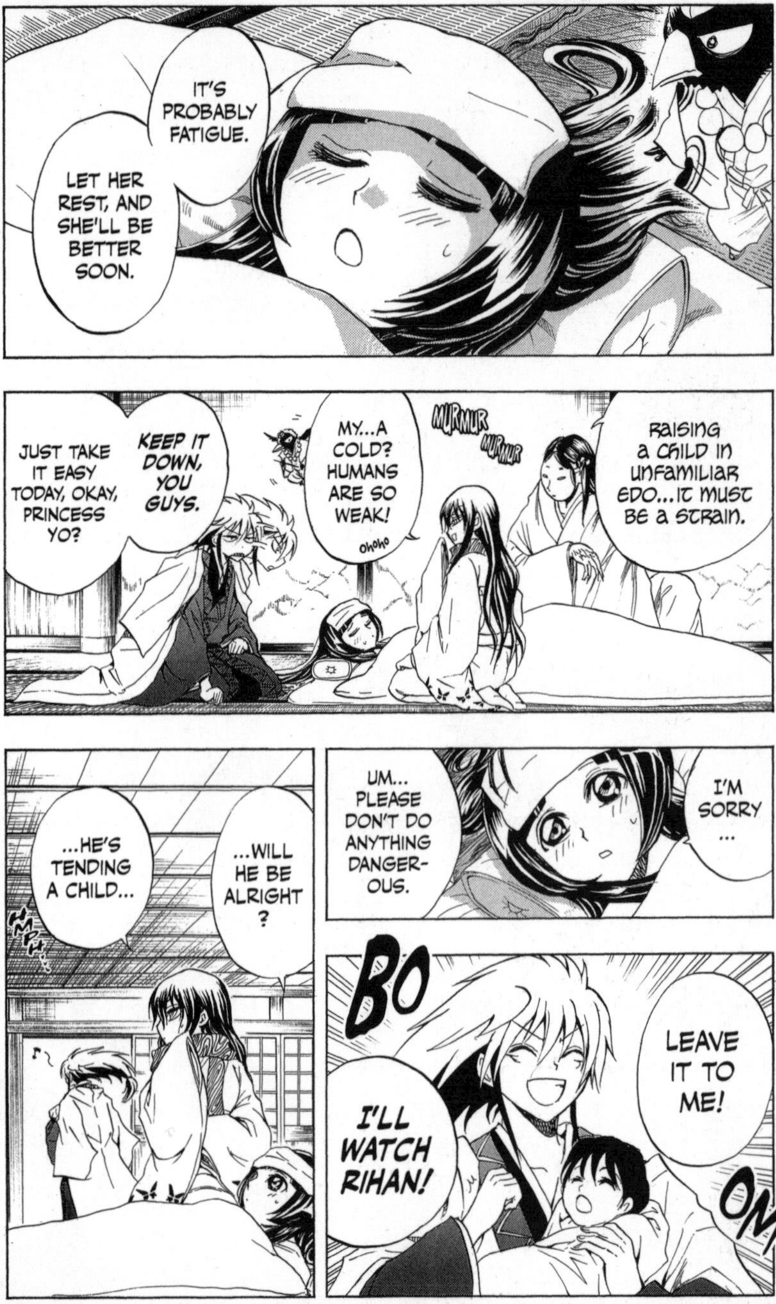
IT'S PROBABLY FATIGUE.
LET HER REST, AND SHE'LL BE BETTER SOON.
RAISING A CHILD IN UNFAMILIAR EDO...IT MUST BE A STRAIN.
MURMUR MURMUR
MY...A COLD? HUMANS ARE SO WEAK!
OHOHO
KEEP IT DOWN, YOU GUYS.
JUST TAKE IT EASY TODAY, OKAY, PRINCESS YO?
I'M SORRY...
UM... PLEASE DON'T DO ANYTHING DANGER-OUS.
BO
LEAVE IT TO ME!
I'LL WATCH RIHAN!
OM
...WILL HE BE ALRIGHT?
...HE'S TENDING A CHILD...
HMPH...

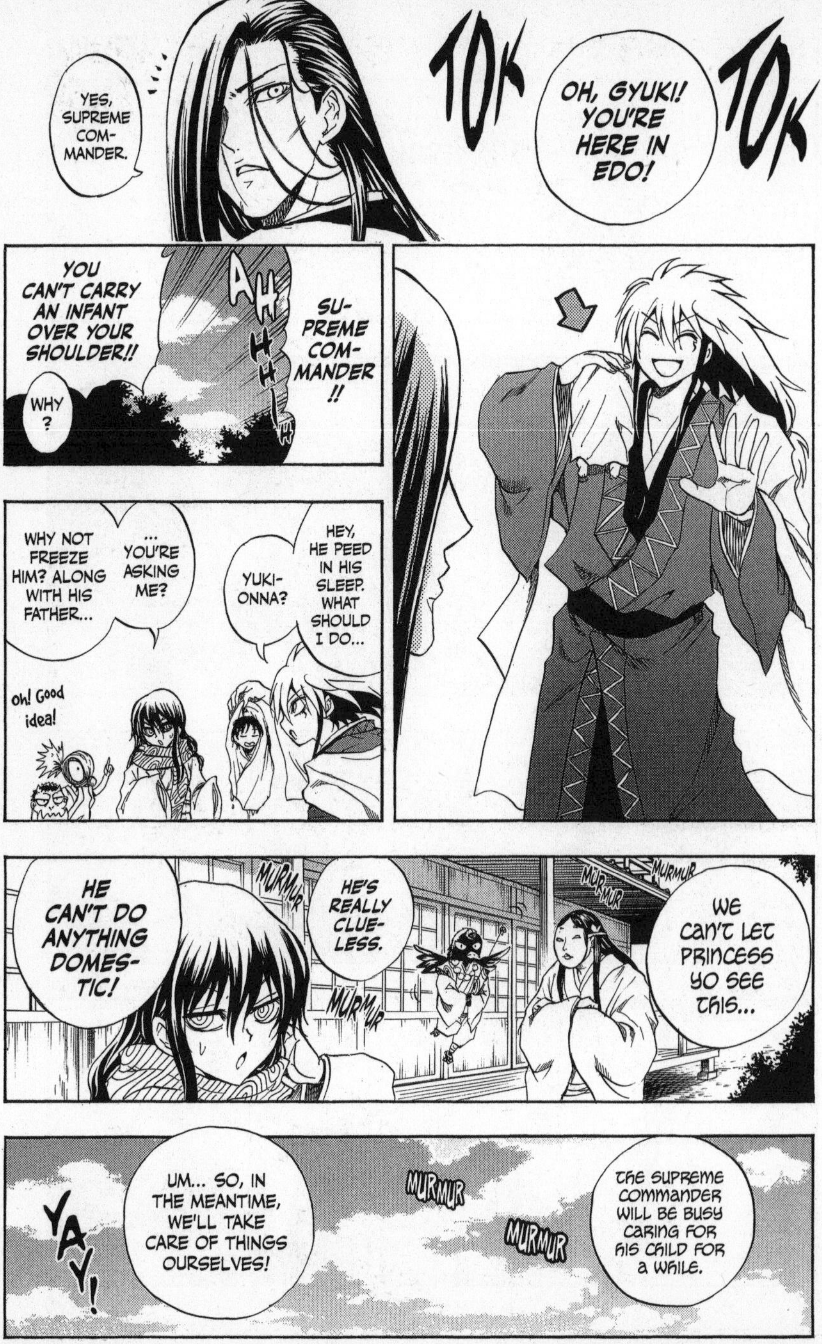
TOK
OH, GYUKI! YOU'RE HERE IN EDO!
TOK
YES, SUPREME COMMANDER.
SUPREME COMMANDER!!
AHHH-H
YOU CAN'T CARRY AN INFANT OVER YOUR SHOULDER!!
WHY?
HEY, HE PEED IN HIS SLEEP. WHAT SHOULD I DO...
YUKI-ONNA?
... YOU'RE ASKING ME?
WHY NOT FREEZE HIM? ALONG WITH HIS FATHER...
Oh! Good idea!
MURMUR
MURMUR
WE CAN'T LET PRINCESS YO SEE THIS...
HE'S REALLY CLUELESS.
MURMUR
MURMUR
HE CAN'T DO ANYTHING DOMESTIC!
THE SUPREME COMMANDER WILL BE BUSY CARING FOR HIS CHILD FOR A WHILE.
MURMUR
MURMUR
UM... SO, IN THE MEANTIME, WE'LL TAKE CARE OF THINGS OURSELVES!
YAY!

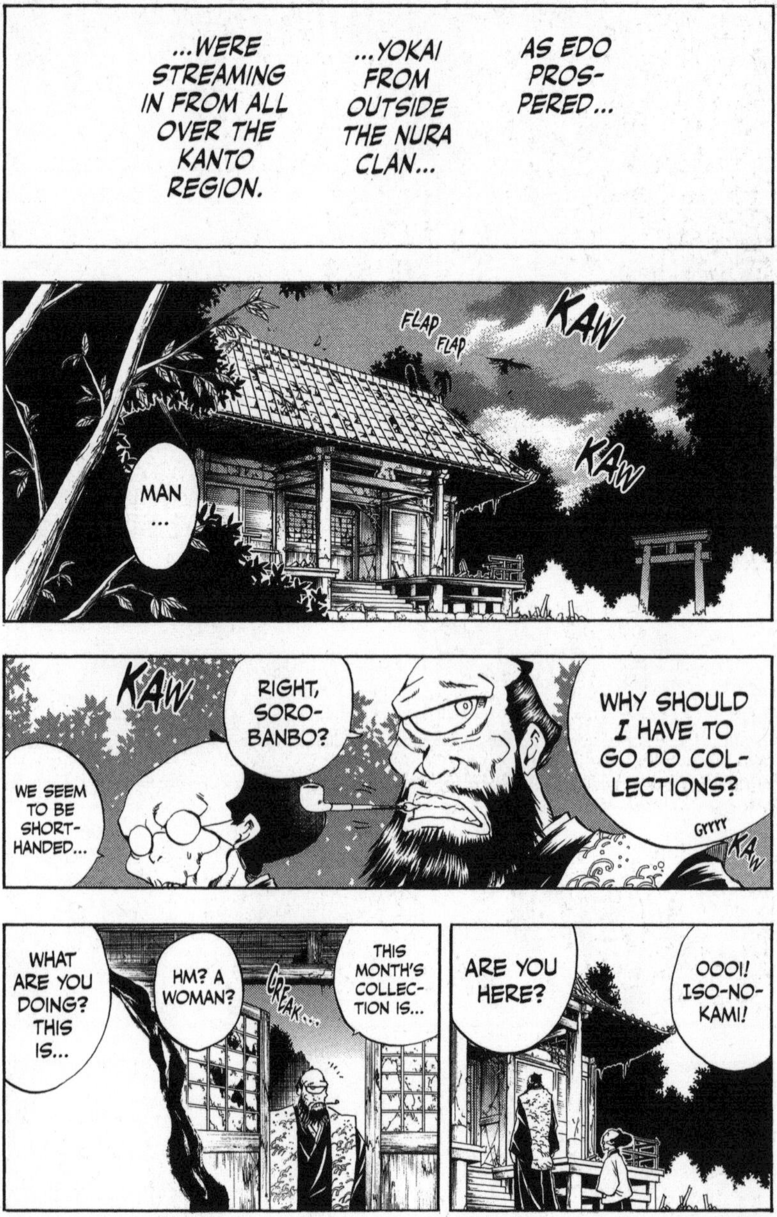
AS EDO PROSPERED...
...YOKAI FROM OUTSIDE THE NURA CLAN...
...WERE STREAMING IN FROM ALL OVER THE KANTO REGION.
KAW
FLAP FLAP
KAW
MAN...
WHY SHOULD I HAVE TO GO DO COLLECTIONS?
GYYYY
KAW
RIGHT, SOROBANBO?
KAW
WE SEEM TO BE SHORTHANDED...
OOOI! ISO-NO-KAMI!
ARE YOU HERE?
THIS MONTH'S COLLECTION IS...
CREAK...
HM? A WOMAN?
WHAT ARE YOU DOING? THIS IS...

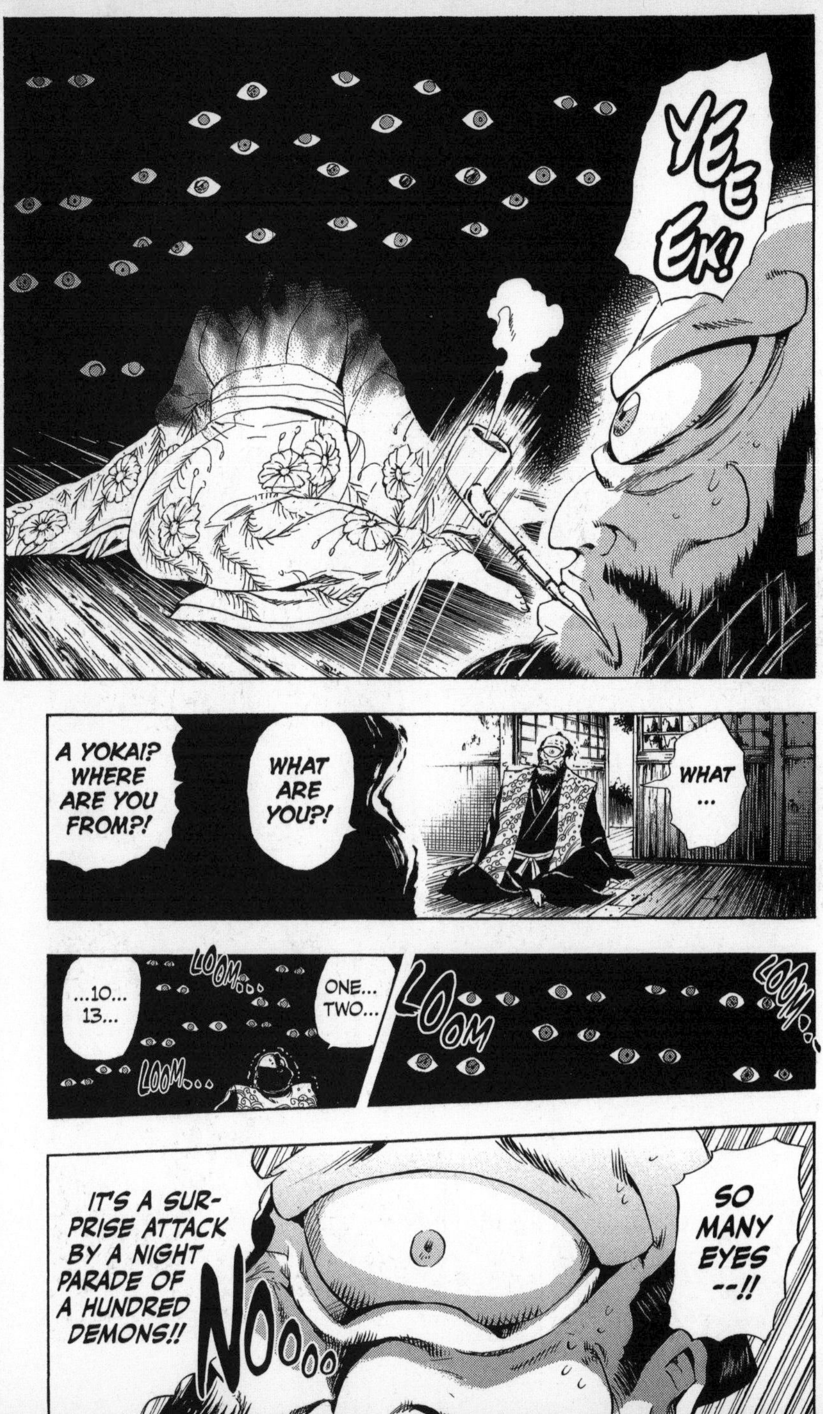
YEEEK!
WHAT ...
WHAT ARE YOU?!
A YOKAI? WHERE ARE YOU FROM?!
LOOM...
LOOM
ONE... TWO...
...10... 13...
LOOM...
LOOM...
SO MANY EYES --!!
IT'S A SURPRISE ATTACK BY A NIGHT PARADE OF A HUNDRED DEMONS!!
NOOO...

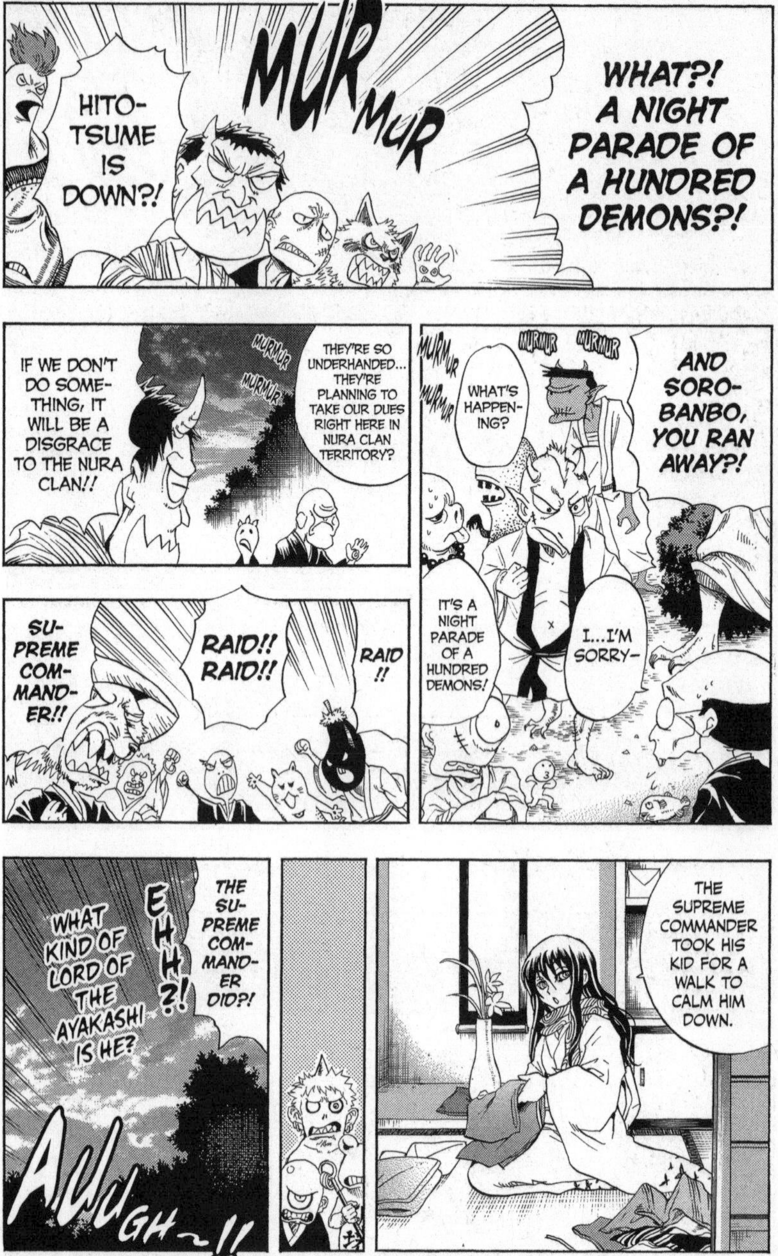
WHAT?! A NIGHT PARADE OF A HUNDRED DEMONS?!
MUR MUR
HITO-TSUME IS DOWN?!
AND SORO-BANBO, YOU RAN AWAY?!
MURMUR
MURMUR
WHAT'S HAPPEN-ING?
MURMUR
MURMUR
I...I'M SORRY-
IT'S A NIGHT PARADE OF A HUNDRED DEMONS!
THEY'RE SO UNDERHANDED... THEY'RE PLANNING TO TAKE OUR DUES RIGHT HERE IN NURA CLAN TERRITORY?
MURMUR
MURMUR
IF WE DON'T DO SOME-THING, IT WILL BE A DISGRACE TO THE NURA CLAN!!
RAID !!
RAID!! RAID!!
SU-PREME COM-MAND-ER!!
THE SUPREME COMMANDER TOOK HIS KID FOR A WALK TO CALM HIM DOWN.
THE SU-PREME COM-MAND-ER DID?!
EHHH?!
WHAT KIND OF LORD OF THE AYAKASHI IS HE?
AUUGH~!!

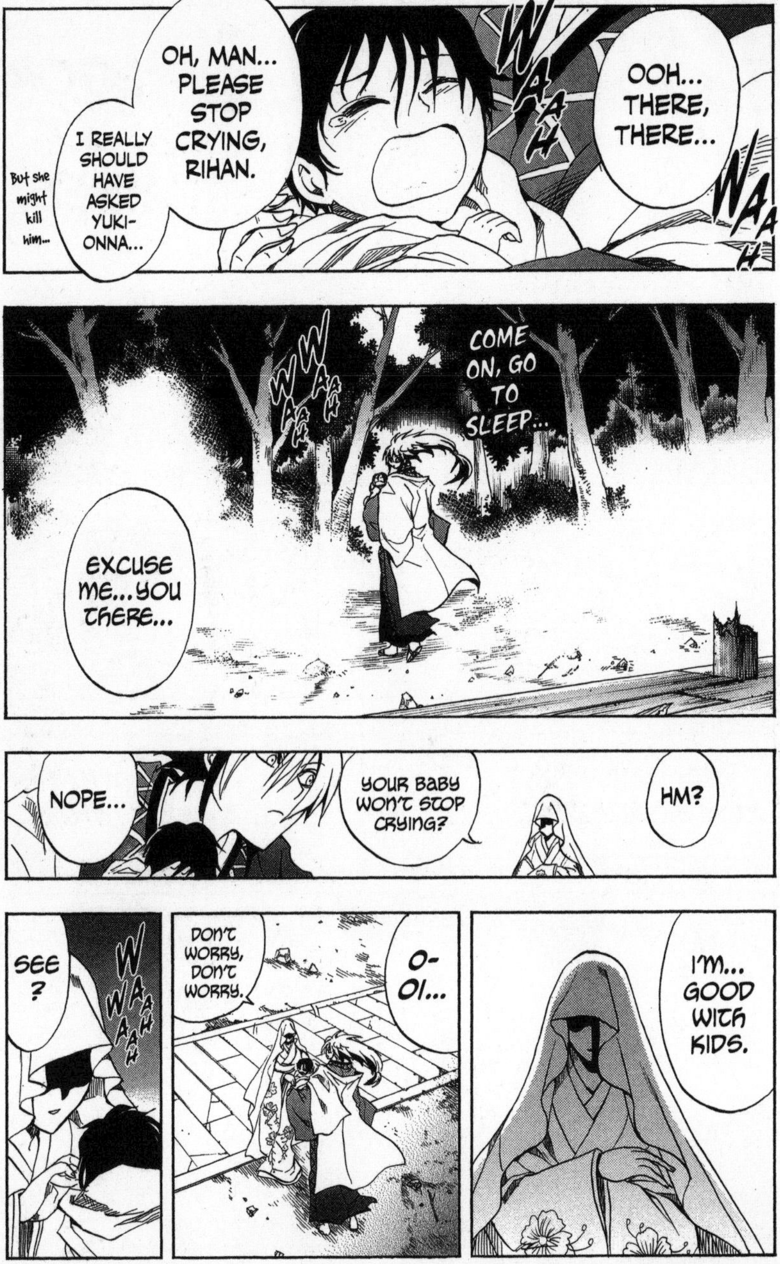
OOH... THERE, THERE...
WAAH
WAAH
OH, MAN... PLEASE STOP CRYING, RIHAN.
I REALLY SHOULD HAVE ASKED YUKI-ONNA...
But she might kill him...
COME ON, GO TO SLEEP...
WAAH
WAAH
EXCUSE ME...YOU THERE...
HM?
YOUR BABY WON'T STOP CRYING?
NOPE...
I'M... GOOD WITH KIDS.
O-OI...
DON'T WORRY, DON'T WORRY.
WAAH
WAAH
SEE?

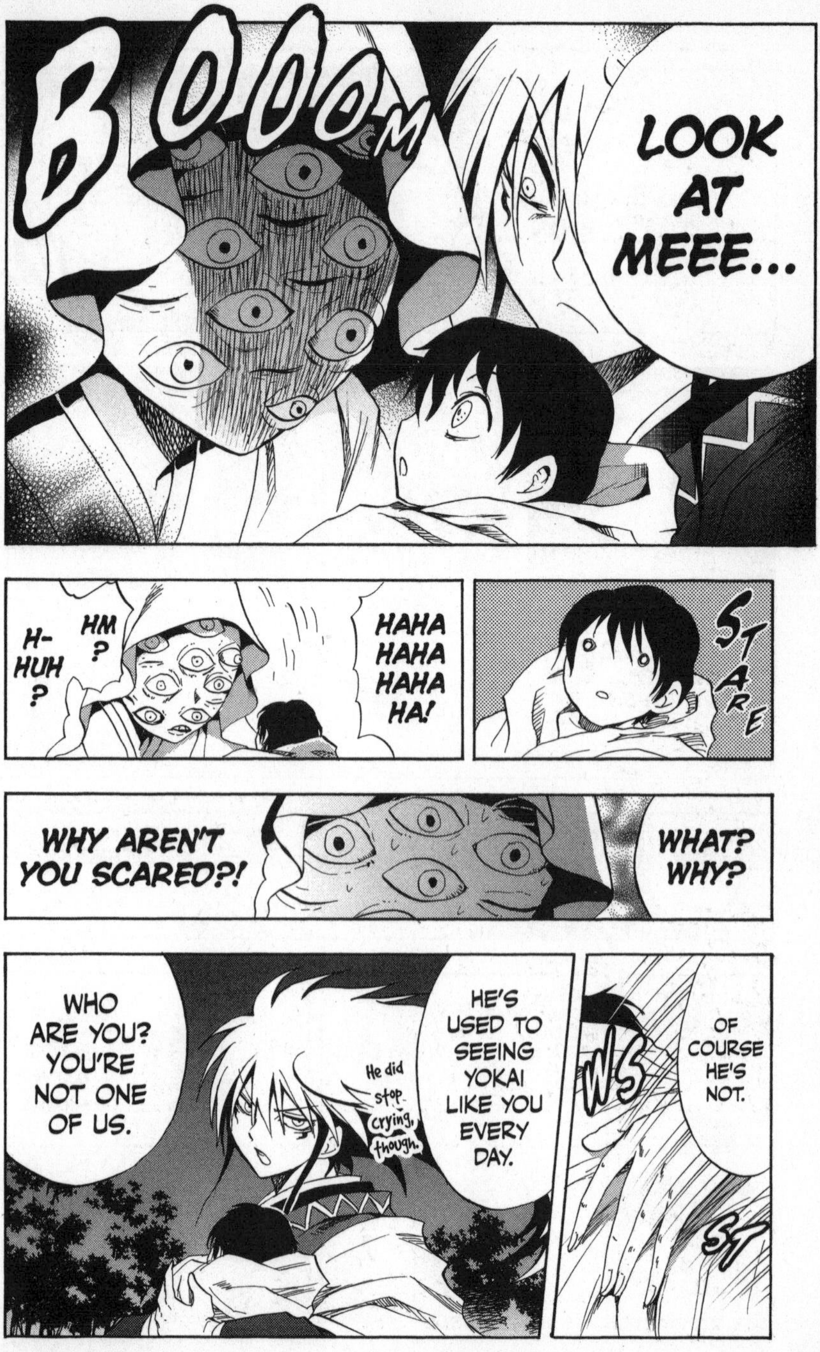
LOOK AT MEEE...
BOOOM
STARE
HAHA HAHA HAHA HA!
HM?
H-HUH?
WHAT? WHY?
WHY AREN'T YOU SCARED?!
OF COURSE HE'S NOT.
WS
ST
HE'S USED TO SEEING YOKAI LIKE YOU EVERY DAY.
He did stop crying, though.
WHO ARE YOU? YOU'RE NOT ONE OF US.

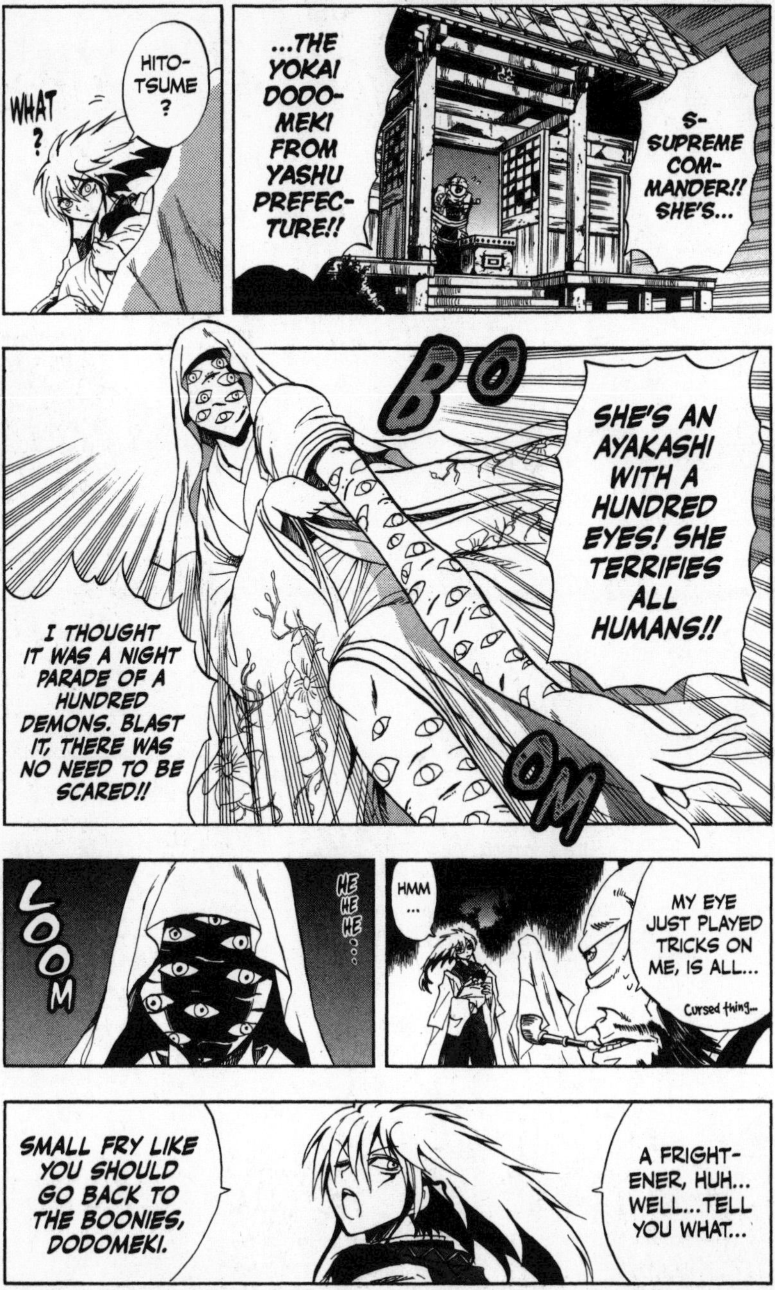
S-SUPREME COMMANDER!! SHE'S...
...THE YOKAI DODOMEKI FROM YASHU PREFECTURE!!
HITO-TSUME?
WHAT?
BOOM
SHE'S AN AYAKASHI WITH A HUNDRED EYES! SHE TERRIFIES ALL HUMANS!!
I THOUGHT IT WAS A NIGHT PARADE OF A HUNDRED DEMONS. BLAST IT, THERE WAS NO NEED TO BE SCARED!!
MY EYE JUST PLAYED TRICKS ON ME, IS ALL...
Cursed thing...
HMM...
HE HE HE...
LOOM
A FRIGHT-ENER, HUH... WELL...TELL YOU WHAT...
SMALL FRY LIKE YOU SHOULD GO BACK TO THE BOONIES, DODOMEKI.

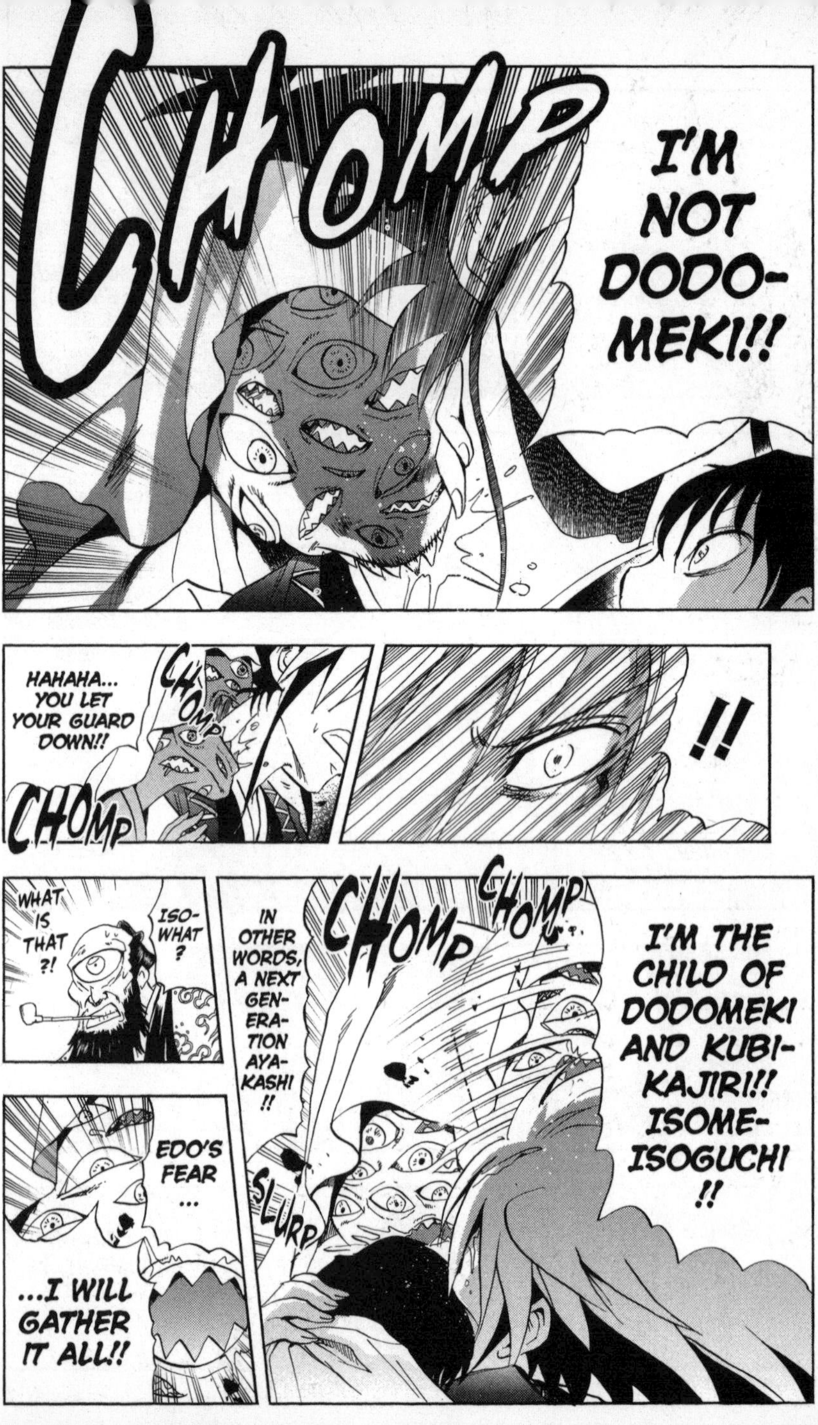
CHOMP
I'M NOT DODOMEKI!!
!!
HAHAHA... YOU LET YOUR GUARD DOWN!!
CHOMP
CHOMP
CHOMP
CHOMP
I'M THE CHILD OF DODOMEKI AND KUBI-KAJIRI!! ISOME-ISOGUCHI!!
IN OTHER WORDS, A NEXT GENERATION AYAKASHI!!
SLURP
ISO-WHAT?
WHAT IS THAT?!
EDO'S FEAR...
...I WILL GATHER IT ALL!!

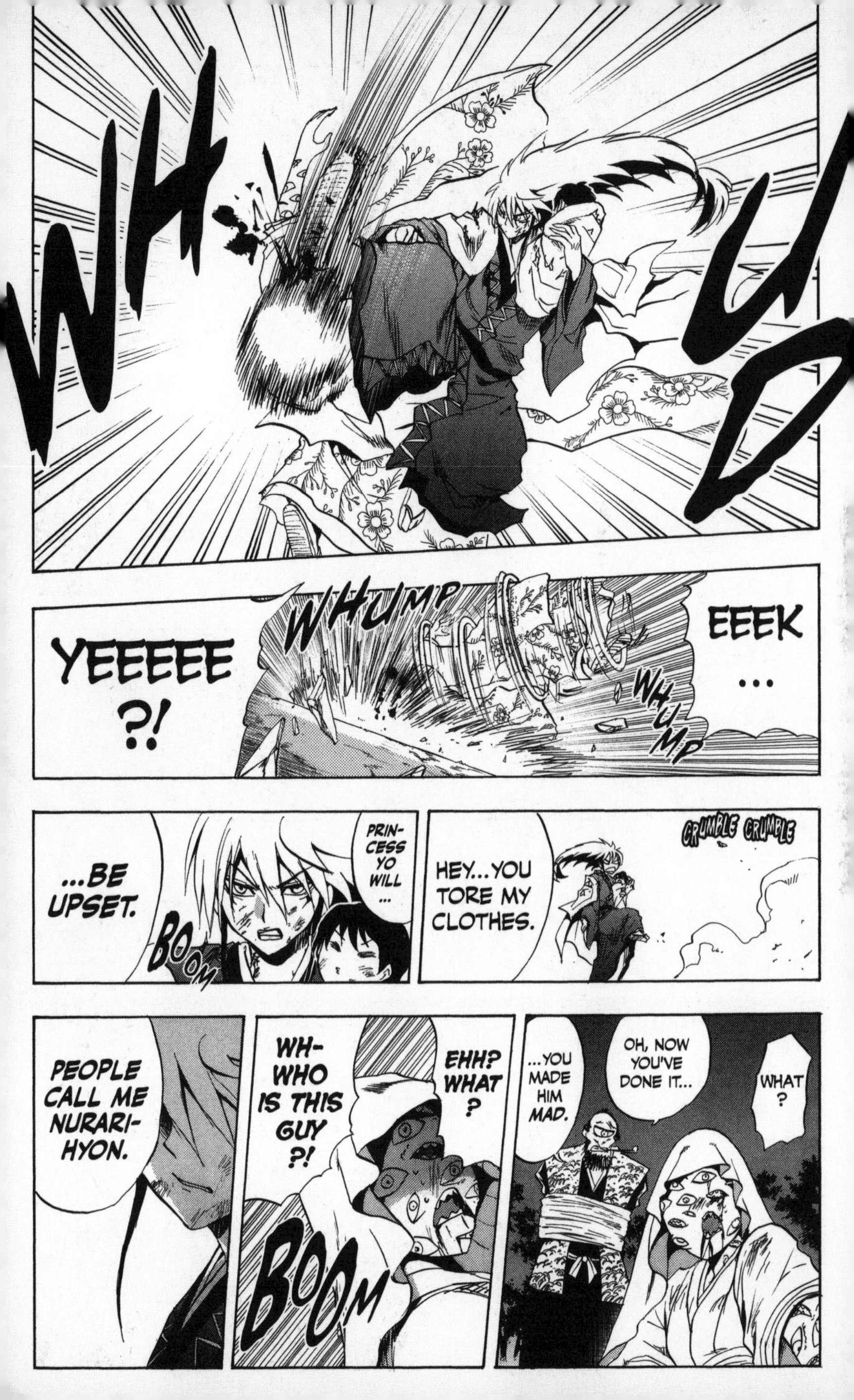
WHUD
EEEK ...
WHUMP
WHUMP
YEEEEEE ?!
CRUMBLE CRUMBLE
HEY...YOU TORE MY CLOTHES.
PRINCESS YO WILL ...
...BE UPSET.
BOOM
WHAT?
OH, NOW YOU'VE DONE IT...
...YOU MADE HIM MAD.
EHH? WHAT?
WH-WHO IS THIS GUY?!
BOOM
PEOPLE CALL ME NURARIHYON.

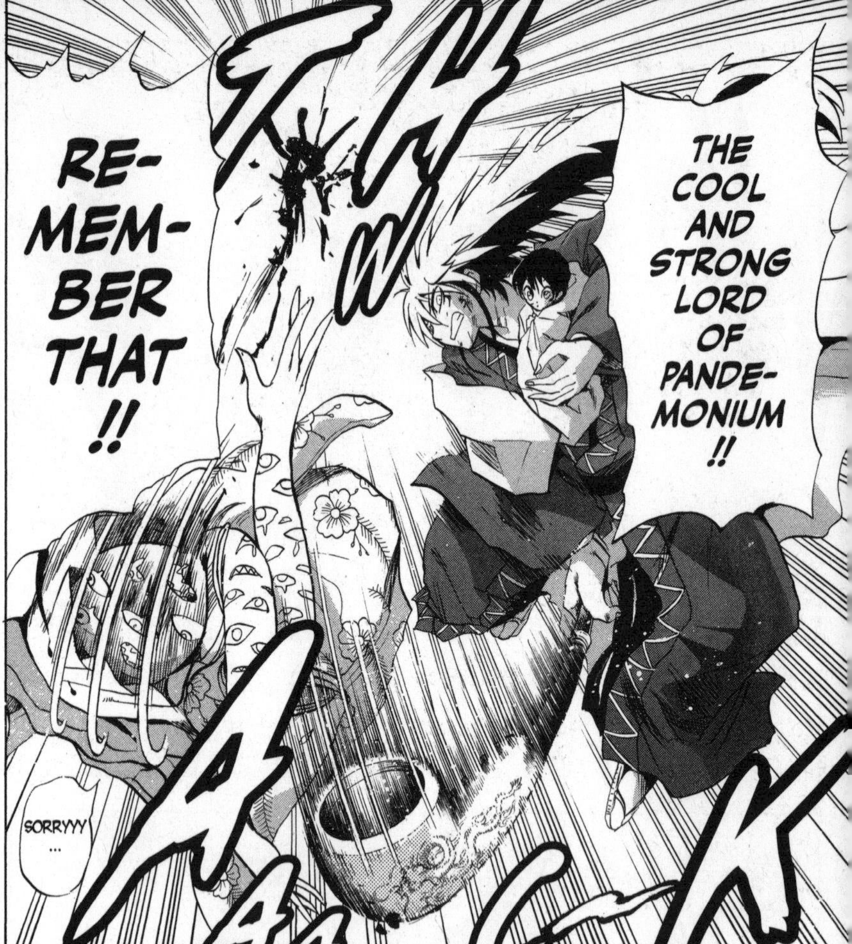
THE COOL AND STRONG LORD OF PANDE-MONIUM!!
RE-MEM-BER THAT!!
THW
SORRYYY...
AACK

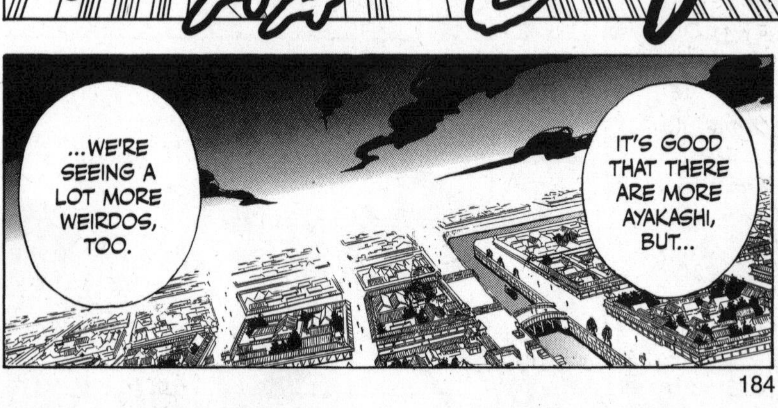
IT'S GOOD THAT THERE ARE MORE AYAKASHI, BUT...
...WE'RE SEEING A LOT MORE WEIRDOS, TOO.

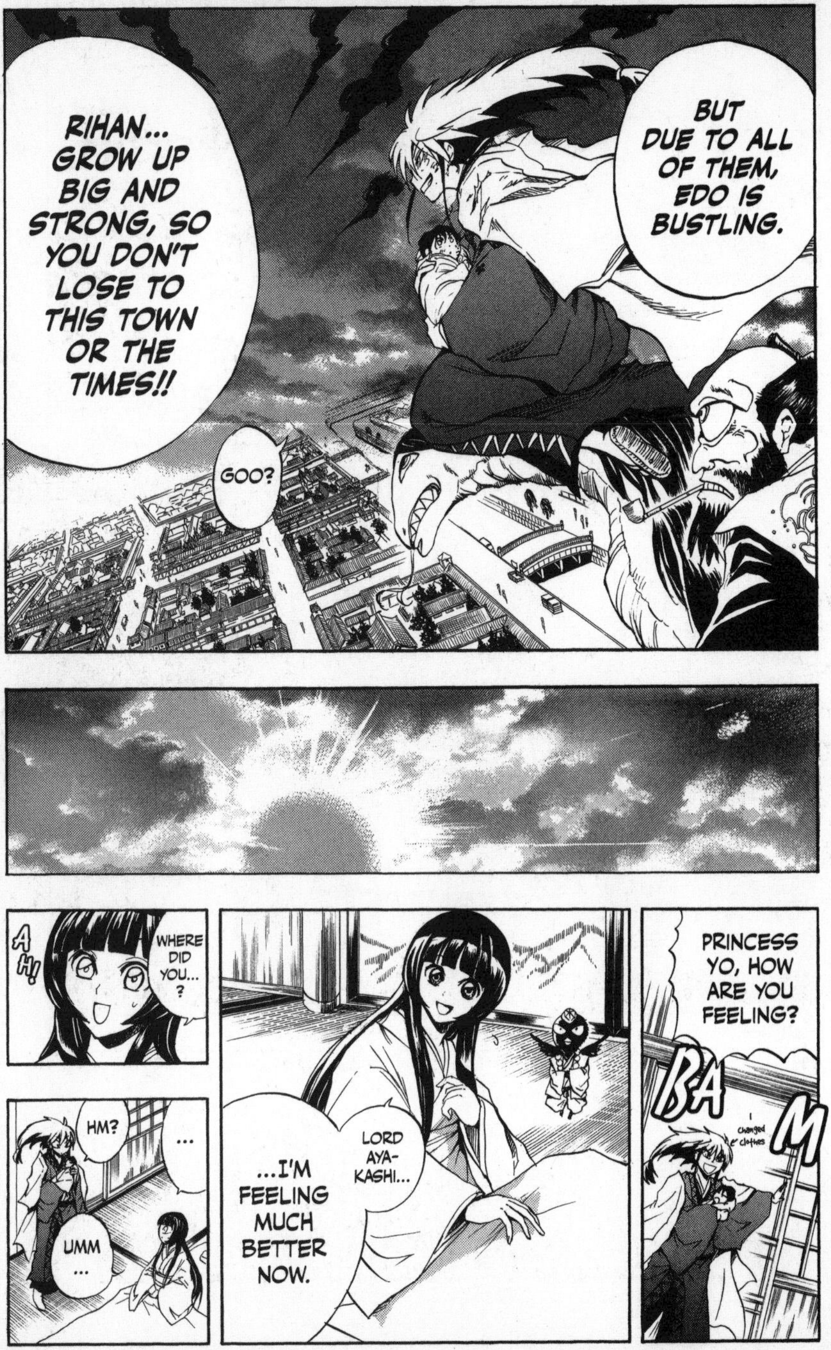
BUT DUE TO ALL OF THEM, EDO IS BUSTLING.
RIHAN... GROW UP BIG AND STRONG, SO YOU DON'T LOSE TO THIS TOWN OR THE TIMES!!
GOO?
PRINCESS YO, HOW ARE YOU FEELING?
BAM
I changed clothes
LORD AYA-KASHI...
...I'M FEELING MUCH BETTER NOW.
AH!
WHERE DID YOU...?
HM?
...
UMM ...

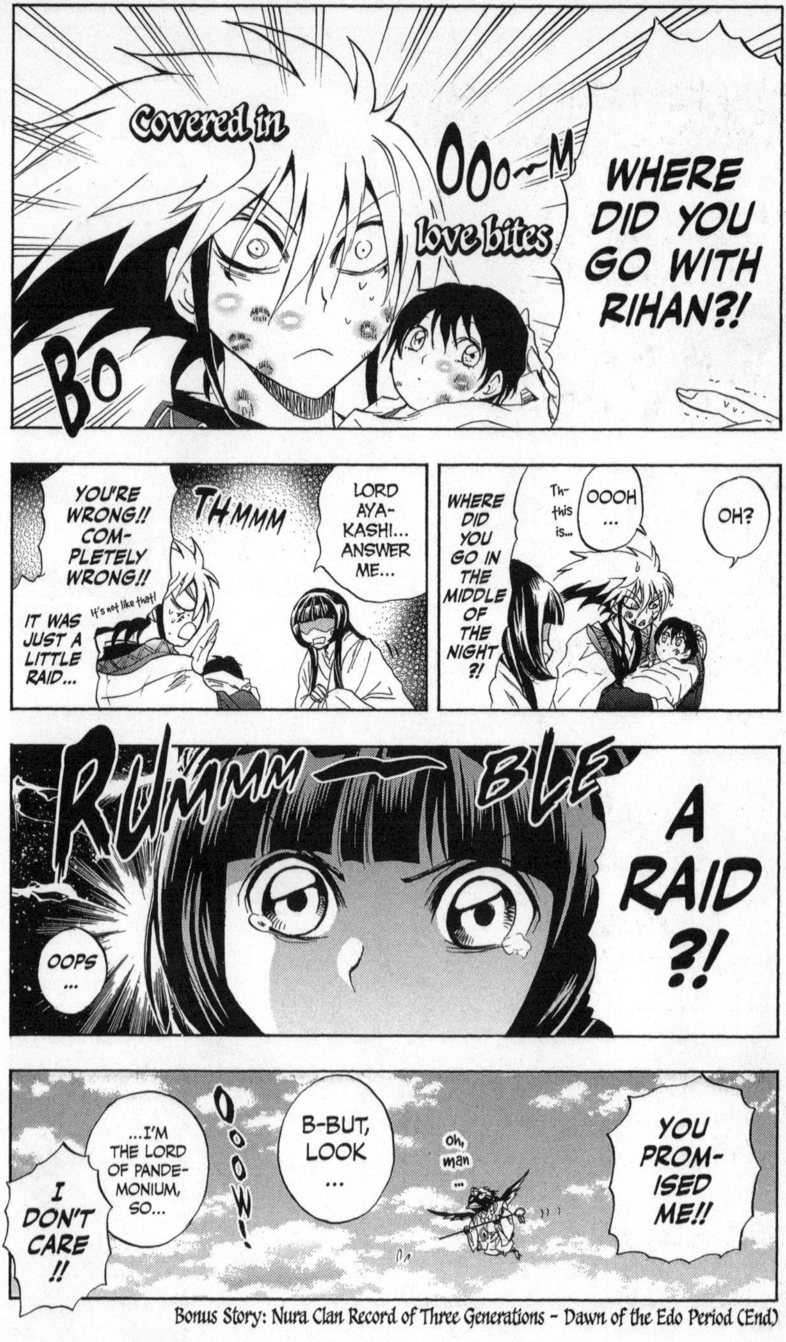
WHERE DID YOU GO WITH RIHAN?!
OOo~~M
Covered in
love bites
BO
OH?
OOOH ...
Th-this is...
WHERE DID YOU GO IN THE MIDDLE OF THE NIGHT?!
LORD AYA-KASHI... ANSWER ME...
THMMM
YOU'RE WRONG!! COM-PLETELY WRONG!!
It's not like that!
IT WAS JUST A LITTLE RAID...
RUMMM— BLE
A RAID ?!
OOPS ...
YOU PROM-ISED ME!!
oh, man ...
B-BUT, LOOK ...
O-O-OW!
...I'M THE LORD OF PANDE-MONIUM, SO...
I DON'T CARE !!
Bonus Story: Nura Clan Record of Three Generations – Dawn of the Edo Period (End)

Kurikuri

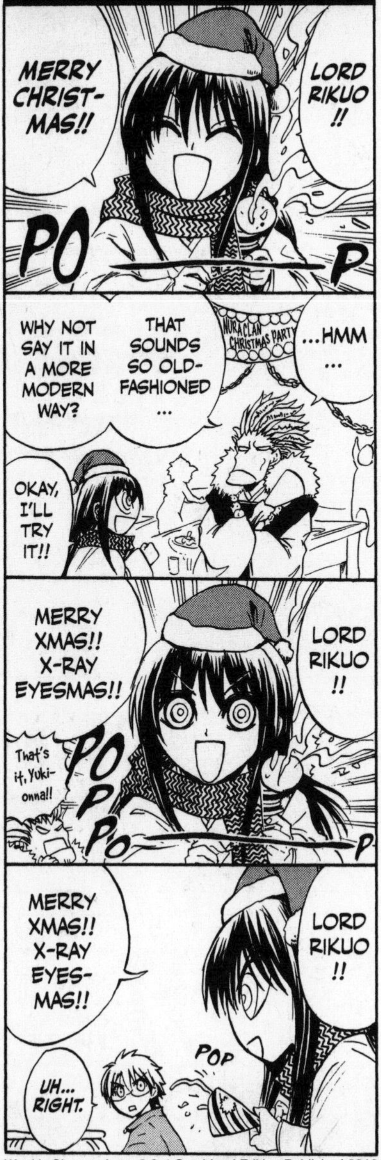
LORD RIKUO!!
MERRY CHRISTMAS!!
PO—P
...HMM...
NURA CLAN CHRISTMAS PARTY
THAT SOUNDS SO OLD-FASHIONED...
WHY NOT SAY IT IN A MORE MODERN WAY?
OKAY, I'LL TRY IT!!
LORD RIKUO!!
MERRY XMAS!! X-RAY EYESMAS!!
POPPPO—P
That's it, Yuki-onna!!
LORD RIKUO!!
MERRY XMAS!! X-RAY EYES-MAS!!
POP
UH... RIGHT.

Weekly Shonen Jump 3 & 4 Combined Edition Published 2010

Bonus Story: Yura Returns to Kyoto...Baptism by Her New Brothers

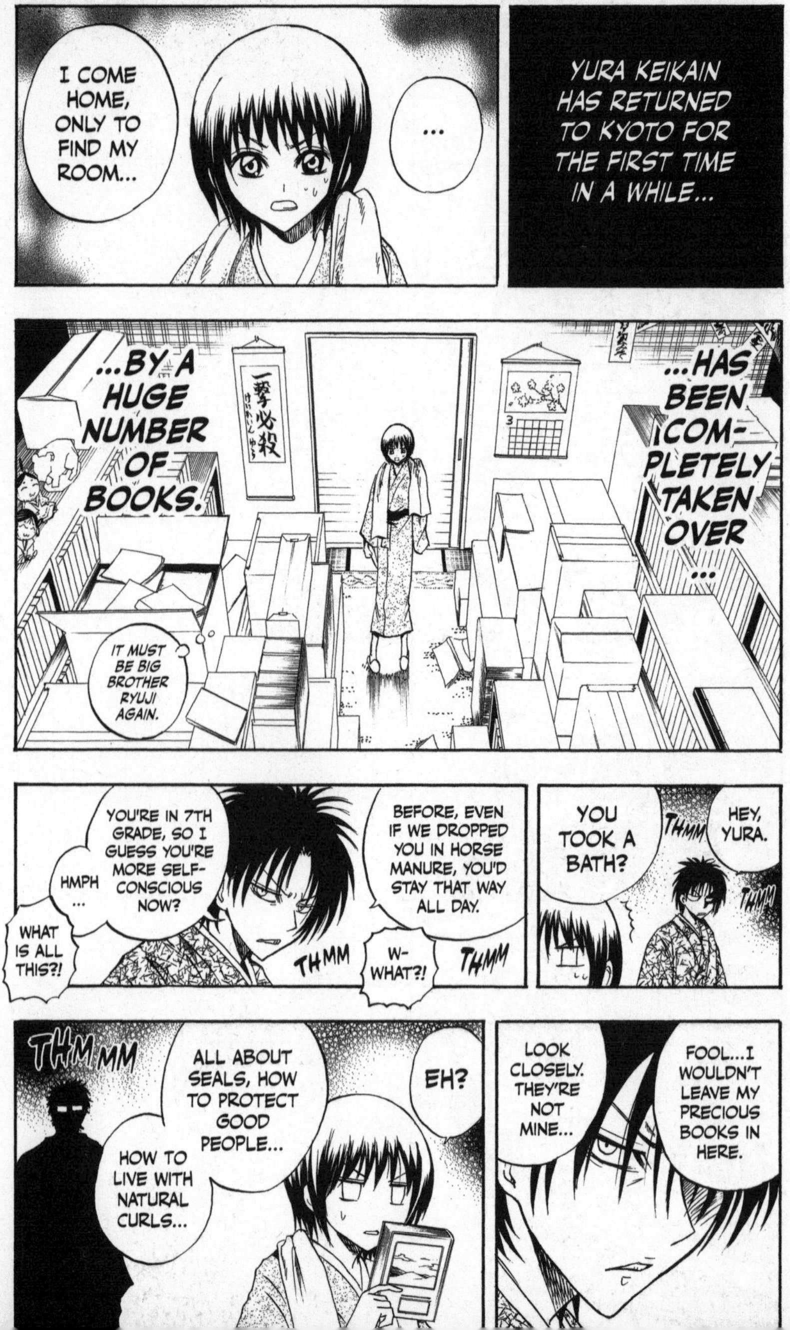
YURA KEIKAIN HAS RETURNED TO KYOTO FOR THE FIRST TIME IN A WHILE...
...
I COME HOME, ONLY TO FIND MY ROOM...
...HAS BEEN COMPLETELY TAKEN OVER...
一撃必殺
...BY A HUGE NUMBER OF BOOKS.
IT MUST BE BIG BROTHER RYUJI AGAIN.
HEY, YURA.
THMM
YOU TOOK A BATH?
THMM
BEFORE, EVEN IF WE DROPPED YOU IN HORSE MANURE, YOU'D STAY THAT WAY ALL DAY.
THMM
W-WHAT?!
YOU'RE IN 7TH GRADE, SO I GUESS YOU'RE MORE SELF-CONSCIOUS NOW?
THMM
HMPH...
WHAT IS ALL THIS?!
FOOL...I WOULDN'T LEAVE MY PRECIOUS BOOKS IN HERE.
LOOK CLOSELY. THEY'RE NOT MINE...
EH?
ALL ABOUT SEALS, HOW TO PROTECT GOOD PEOPLE...
HOW TO LIVE WITH NATURAL CURLS...
THMMMM

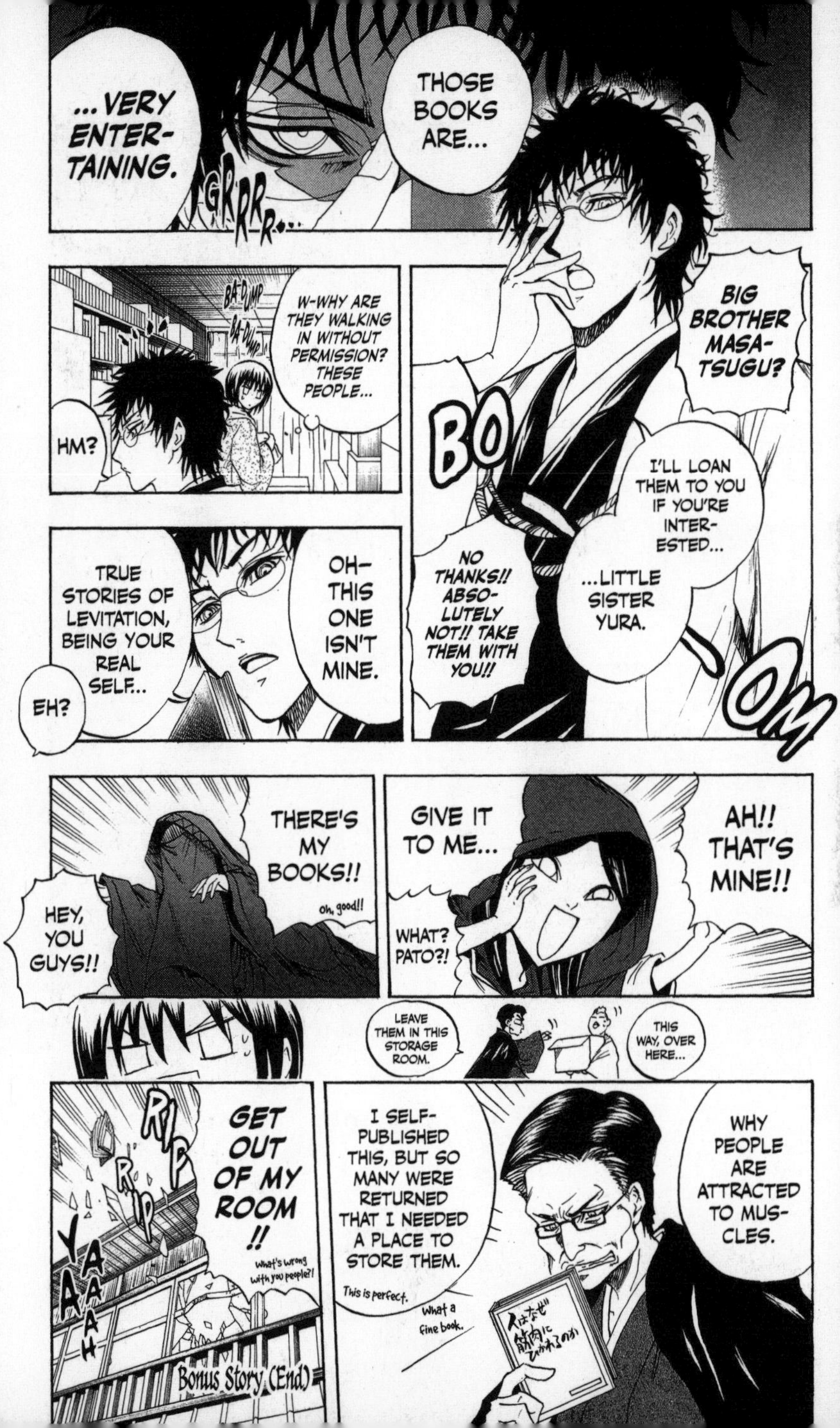
THOSE BOOKS ARE...
...VERY ENTERTAINING.
GRRRR...
BIG BROTHER MASATSUGU?
BO
I'LL LOAN THEM TO YOU IF YOU'RE INTERESTED...
...LITTLE SISTER YURA.
NO THANKS!! ABSOLUTELY NOT!! TAKE THEM WITH YOU!!
OM
W-WHY ARE THEY WALKING IN WITHOUT PERMISSION? THESE PEOPLE...
BA-DUMP BA-DUMP
HM?
OH— THIS ONE ISN'T MINE.
TRUE STORIES OF LEVITATION, BEING YOUR REAL SELF...
EH?
AH!! THAT'S MINE!!
GIVE IT TO ME...
WHAT? PATO?!
THERE'S MY BOOKS!!
oh, good!!
HEY, YOU GUYS!!
THIS WAY, OVER HERE...
LEAVE THEM IN THIS STORAGE ROOM.
WHY PEOPLE ARE ATTRACTED TO MUSCLES.
I SELF-PUBLISHED THIS, BUT SO MANY WERE RETURNED THAT I NEEDED A PLACE TO STORE THEM.
This is perfect.
What a fine book.
人はなぜ筋肉にひかれるのか
GET OUT OF MY ROOM!!
What's wrong with you people?!
RIP RIP RIP
YAAAAH
Bonus Story (End)

A Certain Bandit

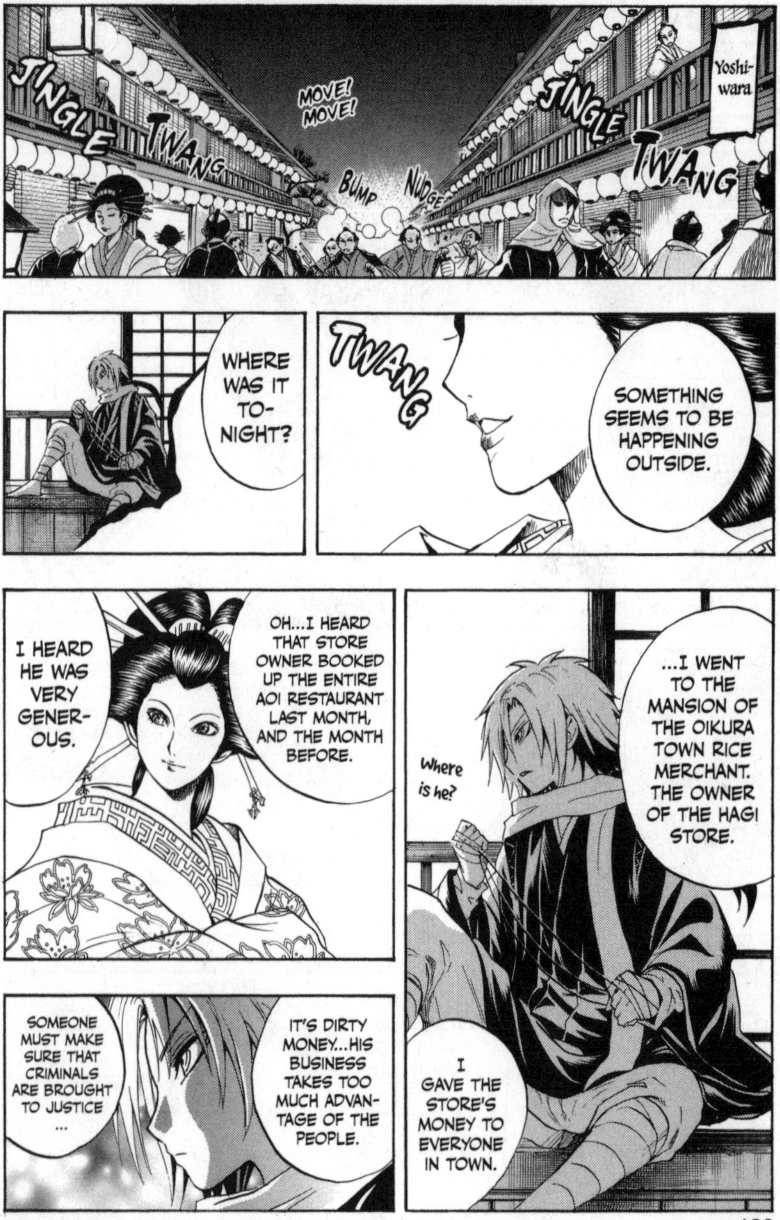
Yoshi-wara
JINGLE
TWANG
MOVE! MOVE!
NUDGE
BUMP
JINGLE
TWANG
TWANG
SOMETHING SEEMS TO BE HAPPENING OUTSIDE.
WHERE WAS IT TO-NIGHT?
...I WENT TO THE MANSION OF THE OIKURA TOWN RICE MERCHANT. THE OWNER OF THE HAGI STORE.
Where is he?
I GAVE THE STORE'S MONEY TO EVERYONE IN TOWN.
OH...I HEARD THAT STORE OWNER BOOKED UP THE ENTIRE AOI RESTAURANT LAST MONTH, AND THE MONTH BEFORE.
I HEARD HE WAS VERY GENER-OUS.
IT'S DIRTY MONEY...HIS BUSINESS TAKES TOO MUCH ADVAN-TAGE OF THE PEOPLE.
SOMEONE MUST MAKE SURE THAT CRIMINALS ARE BROUGHT TO JUSTICE ...

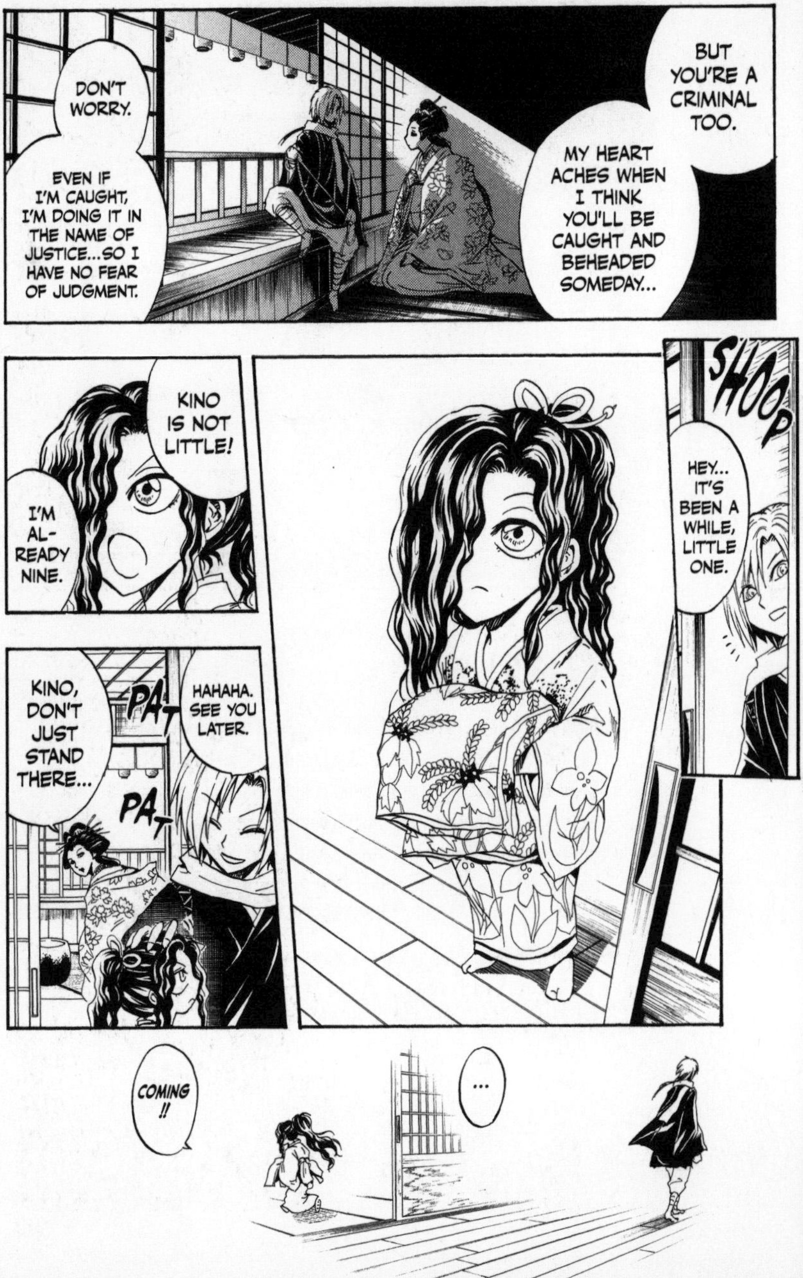

BUT YOU'RE A CRIMINAL TOO.
MY HEART ACHES WHEN I THINK YOU'LL BE CAUGHT AND BEHEADED SOMEDAY...
DON'T WORRY.
EVEN IF I'M CAUGHT, I'M DOING IT IN THE NAME OF JUSTICE...SO I HAVE NO FEAR OF JUDGMENT.
SHOOP
HEY... IT'S BEEN A WHILE, LITTLE ONE.
KINO IS NOT LITTLE!
I'M AL-READY NINE.
HAHAHA. SEE YOU LATER.
PAT
PAT
KINO, DON'T JUST STAND THERE...
...
COMING!!

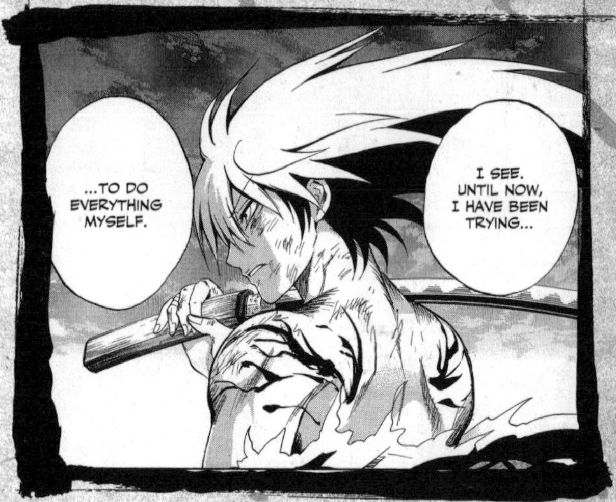
I SEE.
UNTIL NOW,
I HAVE BEEN
TRYING...
...TO DO
EVERYTHING
MYSELF.

IN THE NEXT VOLUME...

CONFLICT

Rikuo trains for a rematch against the yokai Tsuchigumo, who has his friend Yuki-Onna in his clutches. To get him up to par, Gyuki of the Nura clan has ordered Rikuo to attain a technique worthy of the Lord of a Hundred Demons in just three days. But time is running out and Rikuo hasn't gained anything but bumps and bruises. Will he be able to save Yuki-Onna?

AVAILABLE FEBRUARY 2013!